The

RESTORATIVE WAY

Cover design by Kostis Pavlou.
Copyediting by Coralie Emberson.
Interior book design and typesetting by Steve Rogers.

Library of Congress CIP is on file.
ISBNs:
979-8-9899893-0-0 (hardcover)
979-8-9899893-1-7 (paperback)
979-8-9899893-2-4 (ebook)

Restorative Way

ACKNOWLEDGMENT FOR DR. WILL BLEDSOE & RESTORATIVE WAY

"Dr. Bledsoe's approach to conflict resolution is unique in that it not only heals broken relationships (both interpersonal and institutional) but creates an enduring framework to prevent the recurrence of ongoing destructive cycles. In short, Dr. Bledsoe offers those he works with the chance to see conflicts as neither intractable nor inevitable, but rather as opportunities in which we can all see our shared humanity, find workable solutions, and grow."

—Matt Walton, CEO

"Dr. Bledsoe is the consummate professional. His insight into the human condition is deep, broad, and profoundly informed by his empathy for all. Will's love for his fellowman is palpable."

—David Bork, one of the world's leading pioneers in family business consulting since 1968

"My work in the field of conflict management was greatly influenced by his on-the-ground insights. He is a no-nonsense practitioner and scholar who provides an immediate compass for the rest of us."

—Jeannette Holtham, Founding President of Youth Transformation Center

"Dr. Bledsoe's development and delivery of Restorative Communication programming has changed individual lives, and strengthened schools, organizations, and communities."

—Bryan C. Taylor, Ph.D., Director, Peace and Conflict Studies Program, University of Colorado at Boulder

"Dr. Bledsoe researched our culture and our community. He identified what he called our 'unrealized relationship assets.' He took what was best about us as a community and accentuated it."

— Anne J. White, Founder & Principal, Pure Goodness Consulting

"I am so grateful for how you are bringing the Restorative Way forth in these times of uncertainty. I honestly don't know where I'd be had it not been for Dr. Bledsoe's sharing his experience, wisdom and guidance! I find that I am being transformed by this process. The perspective Dr. Bledsoe offered reminded me of who I am and what I am made of. He helped me shift my consciousness from 'taking the hit' to 'making a stand!'"

—Carolyn L., Parent

"The point is that Dr. Bledsoe saw me. I was 22 years old, grasping for identity. He turned my crime into an invitation: '*What do you stand for?*' No one had ever asked me that before."

—Ben E.

"I was overwhelmed with the depth and variety of Dr. Bledsoe's contributions. Will truly embodies the values and actions of an engaged citizen, whose work contributes to the vitality of the communities we serve."

—Dr. Stanley Deetz, Director, Center for the Study of Conflict,
Collaboration and Creative Governance at C.U. Boulder

"We hired Dr. Bledsoe to work with us on restorative communication in one of our schools where trust among adults had broken down, leading to less effective teamwork and lower levels of collaboration in the school. Will coached the entire staff through a series of exercises and conversations, the result of which was restored trust, increased effectiveness, and an entirely new collaborative decision-making process in the school."

—Dr. Rob Stein, Retired School Superintendent

For Jana Jo and Tayler Denae

Contents

Foreword

One of my favorite professors, decades ago, told me something that I have never forgotten and often referred to. Quoting Grossman's law, he said, "For every complex problem, there is a simple, easy to understand wrong answer." I agree. However, I am honored to be able to introduce you to Dr. Bledsoe, who has a part of the right answer to a complex problem.

What is the complex problem? Human survival. I have known Will for a number of years and believe his work and mission are of vital importance and critical to our survival as a species. That may sound hyperbolic to the reader, but I believe it is absolutely true.

"Polycrisis" is a newly coined term that describes the unrelenting news of pain, suffering, inequality, climate-related disasters, inequity, wars, mass migrations, violence, resource depletion, and pollution, all of which threaten long-term human existence at an unprecedented and alarming level. As parents, grandparents, sons, daughters, brothers, sisters, aunts, uncles, and citizens of our world today, we are facing an interlocking series of crises unprecedented in number and size. Like singular storm cells that join others and create a superstorm, there is a growing sense that each of these individual crises are reaching a state of critical mass and because of their compounding effect on each other, may very well, sooner or later, result in unimaginable catastrophe.

Unlike supercells, which we know will eventually pass, there is a sense that these crises will not be getting any better, and only worse. That awareness can create an individual and collective sense of hopelessness, powerlessness, helplessness, isolation, and overwhelm.

I am not one who is concerned about our planet's future, I am confident that it will be fine. My concern is whether or not human beings will be a part of it.

In light of all the dire news, one can be left wondering, "What in the world can I, one person, do about any of this?" If we cannot find an answer that makes sense to us, we tend to quit looking, give up, close our eyes, and just pay attention to what is in front of us. We move on with our daily lives, trying not to think too much about our children, grandchildren, and their children's future. We try to not think too hard about the legacy that our descendants and generations to follow will inherit.

The tools most dominant today involve domination and retribution, finding ways to exert power and control over others. The evidence is in, that does not work in the long run. It never has, and it never will. As Will points out, the only question is how much damage and destruction we will do to ourselves, each other, and especially our children.

The Lakota would suggest that anytime anyone senses a connection with something bigger and more beautiful than ourselves, they are in a spiritual moment. Restoration is a means to foster that sense of innate humility and connection. Will's book suggests simple steps and strategies to help us move in the direction of restoring that innate connection with tools implementable at any level of human interface.

So, what can a person do? A lot. Hope can be fueled by paying attention to the history of our species. For example, it is clear that Neanderthals, who for a while co-existed with us humanoids, were bigger, faster, and stronger than we were. Despite that, we human beings are in existence now, and they aren't. How did that happen?

Science suggests it is due to our ability to work together. To cooperate. To plan. And, to execute such plans. This book touches on some of that ancient wisdom that is pertinent to today's circumstances. The restorative process builds on that social survival instinct. The depth of connection provided by restoration, I believe, is our only hope.

Thankfully, this book offers a beautiful, simple, practical, insightful, based on best practices method to do what our ancestors did, to come together and work together. It is a book about restoration. Most of us have heard that term when it has been used to describe what we have been able to do to a wetland, for example.

This book is about human lives and relationships being restored. Not repairing, not patching, not cobbling together from spare parts a feel-good momentary solution, but full-on depth restoration.

Restoration, as Will describes and practices it, is a vastly more profound concept than repair. Restoration is not about just returning things to their original condition. It is repair plus, adding a level of quality that did not exist before, thus making the finished product far superior in quality to the original. This is especially true with our relationships, not only with ourselves and each other, but with the natural world.

This book asks us to consider using the restorative process within ourselves, on a personal level, as well as with others in our lives. These techniques are not what we DO with ourselves or to another, rather they teach us a way of BEING with ourselves and others. As Will explains and demonstrates, restoration is a way of living.

The tools found here invite us to start the restorative process where we live, and with whom we live. While restoration begins in ourselves, it then deepens and expands to our partnerships, our families, our community, our workplace, our nation, and our world.

And as Will suggests, a restoration of awe, wonder and reverence for the unfathomable mystery of the universe.

Will's approach fits within an ancient cultural wisdom, that being the ability to see the interdependence and interconnectedness with every aspect of life. This is an ancient perspective, or as Will calls it—a worldview.

This is not an "ivory tower perspective." Will has a master's theoretical grasp of the concept and philosophy of restoration, but he brings that understanding and experience to each client he works with on a practical level. He is constantly crafting, honing, testing, and creating effective best practices by working in the trenches.

While rich in documented referenced research, this work is not just a fine academic tome, but a practical "how to" guidebook. Will gives us tried and true tools and techniques with robust scholarly and practical experience. This book includes real-life case studies, simple, yet profound strategies, and Will's personal reflections on what he has experienced as he has honed and polished his craft of helping others move away from retribution.

Perhaps most importantly, Will shares his own story of personal restoration, one that involves his making peace with the various parts of himself so he can model the restorative process for others from the inside out. He understands, as do I, that restoration is a process best lived from the inside out. The degree to which we are at peace with ourselves will be what we put out into the world. The world needs us all to be at peace with ourselves, each other, and the natural world—desperately.

Welcome to this man's life work. And, by the way, he is an excellent storyteller. Enjoy.

—Ted Klontz, Ph.D.

CHAPTER ONE
The Break

It is a major crisis of meaning for the West; at the deepest level, it is a loss of hope. The anxiety and solutions to this crisis cannot be addressed at a mere surface or problem-solving level.[1]

— Richard Rohr

When our crisis is one of hatred, anxiety, and despair, don't look to politics to heal our hearts [...] To do the big thing—to heal our land—we have to do the small things.

Yet for all too many of us that feels empty, like our small actions are simply inadequate to address the giant concerns that dominate our minds. And so, we ignore or neglect the small thing we can change to focus on the big thing we barely impact.[2]

— David French

Depending on whom you ask, the world is either "going to hell in a handbasket" or, to use the title of a Tennessee Williams play, just going through a "Period of Adjustment." I tend to believe the latter, but the handbasket people have a valid point. It seems like everywhere you look, there's a crisis. As Richard Rohr observes in the above quote, it is an existential crisis of meaning, mattering, and loss of hope about the future.

To this, I suggest it is also a crisis of perception. One of the main themes of this book is about how to shift that perspective from "it's never going to change" to "we can make that change" on both a personal and collective level. Maybe we need to stop looking to the West to solve the problems the West has created. One of the arguments made in this

1

book is that we can (and must) look to Indigenous wisdoms and the natural world to reimagine the meaning and purpose of life.

This is a book about restoration, restorative justice, the restorative process, and how to apply it to many different situations and scenarios. It is my hope that by the end of this book, you will meaningfully understand the power and depth of the restorative perspective. You will also discover how you can put that perspective into action in your own day-to-day world by adopting some very simple communication practices. But before I begin to take you through the details of restoration and why restoration matters now more than ever, I want to make sure I properly set the stage.

Just before I began writing this book, I facilitated a series of online discussions over the course of three months with a small group of clients. The name of the series was "Restoration Matters" and was designed to help us "look through the lens of restoration" at both the local issues in their workplaces, families, communities, and personal frustrations, and also the global issues and crises we're all facing. This book is essentially a reconstruction of that online discussion.

The two questions we asked were, "What does restoration have to say in this particular situation?" and, "If we understand that, what can we do to make restoration happen?" Referring to the quote by David French above, in sum, we were asking, "How can we do the small things that just might facilitate a positive change on the big things?"

Our online "circle" was an eclectic group. It consisted of a lead administrator at an elementary school ("Joan"); a high school history teacher ("Devonte"); a director of a nonprofit organization providing mental health services ("Kris"); a director of a healthcare facility ("Melissa"); a former police officer who was the CEO of an addiction recovery center ("Brad"); a retired nurse ("Barb"); and a president of an environmental restoration company ("Aaron"). None knew each other prior to our meetings.

It was a difficult discussion and painful at times. We wanted to explore the connection between what was happening in the larger world and the destructive impact of those events/crises on the lives, relationships, and mental health of people with whom we live and work. More than any one issue our group pointed to as most worrisome, it is the pervasive social atmosphere of contempt, hatred, animosity, and retribution that they described as most demoralizing. As Kris, the director of the nonprofit mental health services provider, summed it up, "Our collective nervous system is shot. The atmosphere of contempt is like an existential trauma. It's a dark cloud that hides the sun."

Aaron offered, "If we don't change how we fundamentally relate to the environment, it won't matter how we relate to each other. Sorry to sound so pessimistic right from the start."

No one disagreed.

"Maybe we need to change what it means to 'be in relationship,' period," I suggested.

Including the environment, each member in our group expressed what they observed as a noticeable deterioration in how people were treating *each other*. Their observations ran the gamut from toxic micro interactions at work, to the macro level of hate speech happening in public discourse, social media, our society, and certainly in our politics. They weren't only talking about the situations in their workplaces or professions. They were also talking about the much larger social landscape we all inhabit.

Whether it was the way physicians, nurses, and techs were treating each other; the way the director of a school was treating administration and faculty; the way faculty treated each other; the way parents treated faculty and how students treated each other and teachers; the way an audience shouted down Aaron making a presentation to a community about the environment; or as Brad, the retired police officer and CEO of the recovery center, remarked, "The hate speech by elected officials, politicians, and their followers and the resulting violence."

> **All of these verbal and physical assaults signified a break in universal humanistic values of basic human dignity, mutual respect, integrity, and concern for the well-being of others.**

"Nothing is going to change," said Barb.

"I disagree," I said. "Otherwise, why are we having this discussion? Restoration is an inherently optimistic term because it implies that things can, in fact, be restored for the better. I encourage us to keep that optimism in mind as we move through our discussions."

They didn't realize it at the beginning, but their decision to participate in our group discussions and search for solutions signified an "entering into a transition," into a reflexive time of *betwixt and between*. "Things have to change, but we're not sure exactly what needs to change, or how to make that change happen."

They enrolled in our discussion to learn about restoration and, however despondent, still hopeful that developing a restorative perspective, as well as restorative communication skills, methods, and practices would equip them to make a positive difference in their immediate social environments. This small group was refusing to *"ignore or neglect the small thing we can change."* They were committed. They just needed inspiration, encouragement, support, and some craft. I needed their inspiration and encouragement. I learned as much from them as I hoped they learned from me.

Our group was diverse in profession, age, gender identity, and ethnicity, but each person was hopeful, maybe sensing that restoration and the five-step process (explained below) used in restoration held a key to shifting the way people treated each other not only in their respective immediate interpersonal and professional relationships, but perhaps in much larger contexts such as public policy, politics, education, healthcare, recovery, and most definitely, the environment.

It was these discussions, their questions, observations, insights, revelations, frustrations, humor, and inspirations, that led to finally writing a book about restoration. Friends and clients had been pushing me to write this book for years. Truth told, I needed these conversations to make this happen.

This book references not only our conversations, but also hundreds of other "restorative conversations" I've had over the course of the last 22 years. Some of these conversations happened in restorative justice circles to address criminal violations within the justice system.

Some happened with justice system officials, judges, police officers, neighborhood associations, and university officials as I undertook to build a university-based restorative justice program to process student crimes happening in the larger community and off-campus.

Some happened in conflict resolution cases I've facilitated in various workplace and institutional settings such as K–12 schools, universities, hospitals, and businesses. Many come from courses I've taught at the university level, workshops I've conducted, and seminars I've presented on restorative practices. As important, many conversations happened with families.

Restoration is much bigger, deeper, and more far-reaching than restorative justice. But restorative justice introduced me to restoration.

❖⟩⟩⟩———⟨⟨⟨❖

When our group met for the first time, I explained that my first encounter with restorative "justice" happened when I was nine years old. "My father got me a job raking leaves for a neighbor who had just lost her husband. I was going to make ten dollars, which to a nine-year-old back in the '60s was like winning the lottery. Visions of buying that new baseball bat consumed me.

"I made short work raking the leaves into a big pile," I explained, "and then I started screwing around, practicing my swing with the rake. The rake flew out of my hands and into a window. I finished bagging the leaves, made the slow, mournful walk back to my house, and waited for my father to come home. I was sure I was going to be sent to Donkey Island from the movie *Pinocchio*. I thought about hopping a train and going on the lam, a nine-year-old fugitive running from the law.

"I didn't dare tell my mother what I did. My mother and father had very different philosophies when it came to discipline. These two different approaches to human misconduct are what our group discussions will explore," I told the group.

"My father came home and as soon as he entered the house, the phone rang. It was our neighbor. Busted.

"'Hello, Kathryn. Uh-huh, okay.' My dad looked at me. 'Uh-huh. All right. Well, thanks for telling me. We'll be over in a bit,' he said.

"My dad sat down and asked, 'Did something happen?' He wasn't angry. Thinking back, he could've asked me, 'What did you do?' My mother probably would've asked, 'What the hell did you do?' I confessed. 'All right. Thanks for being honest,' he said. 'Let's go see Kathryn.'

"Sitting there in her living room, broken window in sight, I explained to Kathryn what happened. Kathryn said, 'Thank God. When I came home and saw the broken window, I panicked because I thought someone had tried to break in. Ever since Hap [her husband] passed away, I've been struggling with living alone.'

"I apologized. My dad said, 'We'll fix the window.'

"We went to the building materials store, got the glass, and then he and I replaced the broken window. He had me do it, teaching me how to remove the broken glass, install the new glass with new pins, and apply glazing. The glazing was the difficult part, so he followed my nine-year-old attempt, making sure I learned how to do it correctly. He said, 'We'll need to come back after it dries and paint it.' A few days later, we did that.

"Later in the evening, after we had completed the repair, Kathryn called and asked if we could come over. I was sure I was going to get a good lecturing. Instead, she thanked me for being honest and taking responsibility. Then she paid me. She said, 'We all make mistakes.' She also said, 'You did a good job raking the leaves, and you deserve to be paid. Probably not a good idea to swing a rake like a baseball bat.' Sheepishly, I thanked her. I had no expectation of getting paid.

"When my dad and I got home, he asked me what I had learned. 'Not to screw around with a rake,' I said. 'What else?' he asked. 'To be honest?' I asked. 'Yes. What else?' he asked. 'How to fix a broken window,' I said. 'Yes. More importantly, how to make things right again when we've made a mistake that has hurt someone.'

"Then he asked, 'What else do you think you should do?' I had no idea what he was talking about, but I was afraid it would be to tell my mother. 'Tell Mom?' I asked. 'Maybe,' he said. 'If you feel the need to, but that's not what I'm talking about. How much did Kathryn pay you?' he asked even though he knew.

" 'Ten dollars,' I said. 'The new glass cost $2.50, the glazing and pins cost $2.50,' he said. My first thought was, 'There goes the new bat.' 'Do you think it's right that I should have to pay for that?' he asked. 'No,' I said. I paid him the $5. He said, 'Now you've made things right with me.'

'What about the bat?' I asked. He didn't answer. He just looked at me with a dry grin that only a father knows how to do. Clearly, my major league baseball career would have to wait a few years."

I explained to our discussion group, "What my father essentially did was ask 5 basic questions.

1. What happened or is happening?
2. Who or what is being negatively impacted?
3. What, exactly, is that impact?

4.   Why is this happening?

5.   What needs to happen to repair the damage, and keep it from happening again?

"I shared my story of what happened and what I did. Kathryn shared her story of what happened when she came home. She shared how it had impacted her. The reason it happened was because I was screwing around with the rake. We recognized what needed to happen to make things right. We took the necessary actions to accomplish that. I learned a valuable lesson.

"These five steps, or questions, are the basic script used in restorative practices. They are going to form the foundation of our discussions, and we'll do a deep dive into how they work in specific contexts and situations throughout our discussions. I'll provide numerous examples, cases, and stories.

"But for my father, it was just a common-sense approach. He didn't know anything about restorative justice. He wasn't trained in any restorative practices or restorative parenting. The way he responded was, for him, just intuitive.

"My point is that restoration and the restorative process is just common sense.

"Since this is our first meeting, I am only briefly introducing these five steps. There are two reasons for this. First, these steps are the practical application of a method, but that method *represents a worldview* that has profound implications for the challenges we're facing currently, as a society and as a species.

"As we'll see, this simple, common-sense approach emerges from deep philosophical roots in an ancient and Indigenous wisdom that sees life, all life, as a constitution of relationships. In essence, restoration is much deeper and more expansive than restorative justice."

"Can I interrupt?" asked Barb.

"Of course," I said.

"What was your mother's approach to discipline?" she asked.

"I'll talk in more detail about that approach later in our discussions, but for now, I'll just say that she was raised in a culture that believed if you 'spare the rod, you'll spoil the child.' She disciplined the way she was disciplined," I said.

"But that's a great question to ask, Barb, because the thinking that punishment is a necessary, justifiable, or most effective retaliatory response to errant behavior or misconduct came from somewhere. It, too, represents a worldview, and if we're willing to look at that worldview, we'll see that the relational worldview of restoration stands in stark contrast to a western worldview that relies almost exclusively on force and retribution as a means of establishing control over people's thinking and behavior. And retribution is much bigger and deeper than just a punitive response to misconduct.

"As we'll discuss, retribution is a mindset. As Howard Zehr (2005) suggests, retribution is a paradigm. That paradigm is inscribed in our minds, imaginations, and relationships. Retribution is 'where we go' when someone disagrees with us. We flip the switch to judgment and contempt. Why is that? That's our biggest problem.

"These two worldviews have not only been colliding across the course of human history, but they also continue to be at war with each other in this current historical moment, and most importantly, in ourselves; in how we think.

"Though this philosophical conflict, for lack of a better term, has been going on for centuries and perhaps even further back, the consequences have never been greater for the well-being of our children, communities, governance, and the environment," I said. "In my opinion, on a social level, we're addicted to retribution. Restoration is an intervention in that addiction.

"Second, and this is how I want to begin our discussion, these five steps and the process of restoration—because it is a process—fit within an equally ancient three-stage universal pattern of how humankind has historically moved from crisis to regeneration.

"Restoration is simply a pragmatic process residing within this three-stage pattern which facilitates movement through a crisis with objectivity, into the humbling and tension-filled time of accountability, and finally a re-emergence back into our humanity. This can happen on both a personal and collective level of experience."

Barb said, "You're an idealist."

"Maybe so. But I'm also a realist. Like you, I know what we're up against. But I've seen restoration work too many times to doubt it," I replied. "Restoration pursues civility and collaboration instead of condemnation."

A Beginning Frame

I asked our group to take a step away from the barrage of specific global crises we are facing collectively, and any particular crisis they felt was happening in their respective professional and personal lives.

I asked, "Is there an initial bigger or 'macro' frame we can use to get some perspective about what's happening writ large, and that might help us make sense of 'where we're at in this historical moment'?"

"An inflection point," commented Devonte.

"Yes," I said. "Others who've come before us have been through what we're going through now. My folks went through the Great Depression, World War II, McCarthyism, the Cuban Missile Crisis, Vietnam, the assassination of John F. Kennedy, his brother, and Dr. Martin Luther King, Jr. How did they get through it? Is there a recognizable pattern they experienced that might at least provide some perspective? Can recognizing that pattern provide some *orientation* and instill some hope, or at least some perspective?"

I explained the concept of the "double consciousness of experience." [3]

> "We participate in the action but also report about it; we are part of the experience but also detached witnesses to that experience." [4]

I said, "This is the perspective we need to take throughout our discussions. Engaged, but detached and observant at the same time. Small picture/big picture. As we begin the process of learning about restoration with the goal of facilitating it, we'll need to develop this capacity for 'detached observance.' This perspective gives us the ability to meet people where they're at, engage with them, all the while conscious of the wisdom of restoration."

I offered that anthropologists and social scientists have suggested that there is an identifiable three-stage "structure" to crisis and how people over history have experienced personal, cultural, and social change.[5]

"In the simplest of descriptions, the first stage is a complete breakdown in norms ('breach'). The status quo falls apart. What we've believed was valuable and most important no longer is. Who we think we are no longer fits. The stories we tell ourselves no longer resonate. Simply put, the old ways of relating to each other and ourselves no longer work. What used to matter, doesn't matter anymore. Faith in a future starts to die."

"That sounds like Nietzsche's statement, 'God is dead,'" said Devonte.[6]

"Nietzsche was pointing to the dissolution of traditional Christian and Greek philosophical and moral foundations and principles that western civilization had relied upon for centuries to guide social behavior.

"This break is often marked by upheaval, revolution, assault, and violence. The violent assault on the Capitol and attempt to prevent the peaceful transition of power on January 6, 2021, is a stunning example of a breach of democratic norms. Every mass shooting, school shooting, synagogue or church shooting is a clarion of breaking apart. The rise in white supremacy, attacks on gender diversity, separating and caging immigrant children from their mothers at the southern border, and the assault on women's reproductive health—they are all examples of moral dissolution. Let's not forget the assault on facts and truth.

"The second stage—liminality ('betwixt and between') is a moment when we realize we're at an inflection point and we enter into a period of radical instability, disorder and chaos, and insecurity. We can no longer return to 'what was'; no longer rely on old ways of thinking; we don't know what we will become or what will matter moving forward. The future is uncertain and tenuous.

"This is a time marked by paradox, fear, anxiety, aggression and defensiveness, denial, blaming, deception, scapegoating, animosity, and contradiction. The meaning of life and what it means to be human is up for grabs. One could argue that this is the stage we're in now on a national level, but also globally," I said.

"I completely agree with this," said Brad.

"Me too," said Devonte.

I continued, "The third stage can be described as a time of renewal, reincorporation, reconstitution, reconnection, and reintegration.[7] 'At its height, it signifies complete interpenetration of self and the world […] a sense of union […] a sense of harmony with the universe is made evident and the whole planet is felt to experience communitas.'[8]

"In the culmination of this stage, a new identity has emerged (i.e., '*this* is who we are'); new values and meanings (or a recovery of timeless humanistic values and meanings) are affirmed; new norms begun; and 'new ways of being in relationship' (community) materialize," I explained.

"That's the anthropological explanation. Examples of this three-stage pattern can be seen in religious and spiritual traditions.

"In the Christian tradition, Jesus was crucified on Good Friday. The promises, hopes, wisdoms, reassurances, and securities he embodied and the sense of purpose and meaning he provided his followers was over. The time between his death and resurrection was marked by profound insecurity ('Will he return?'); fear and denial (Peter); dispersion and despair ('What is to become of us?'). On the third day, Jesus resurrected; the world was born anew with a new understanding of his teachings (reincorporation and interpenetration of meanings).

"This same three-stage structure can be applied to Buddha's experience of enlightenment. Siddhartha left the comfort and predictability of his father's palace, searched for but ultimately renounced the existing brahman asceticism, sat down under a tree, surrendered, and waited. Enlightenment emerged with the realization 'life is suffering.' His 'restorative action' was to have compassion for all living beings and the human condition. He became the Buddha.

"In Judaic, Islamic, and Catholic atonement practices, followers enter into a 'time away from time' for fasting, self-reflection, confession, and atonement, and are cleansed, 'made anew' through repair, amends-making, forgiveness, and a recommitment to making positive changes in their lives.

"In many Indigenous traditions and healing practices, the 'patient's spiritual/psychological malady' is diagnosed, and a ritual cure is prescribed. The patient prepares to enter into a liminal time through acts of cleansing. The liminal time and space is marked by participation in a ritual ceremony where origin stories and prayers are recited, and the presence of sacred beings is invoked and made present.

"The third stage of reintegration is marked by the participant's emergence from the ceremony after experiencing transformation and healing, and a restoration of relationship with themselves, the tribal community, and 'all that is.'

"Outside of a religious or spiritual context, this same pattern can be seen happening in organizations and workplaces. For example, when a school or organization (like a hospital) reaches out to me, it is because the social climate has become untenable. Their traditional ways of resolving conflict and addressing misconduct are failing. It's a type of organizational relational climate crisis. They reach a point where they say, 'How we've been addressing this is failing.'

"They then begin a search for a better way, which, I might add, is what we're doing here with our discussions. That search marks an entry into a liminal time of openness to new ideas, new policies, and new practices.

"But that time is rife with tension and insecurities because it requires reflection about why previous approaches, methods, and ways of relating are not working. It forces them to redefine their values and goals. If they choose a restorative way, that too is rife with confusion and resistance because it confronts conventional thinking and ways of responding to human imperfection as it manifests in destructive conflict.

"But once they do implement restorative policies and practices, they begin to see the workplace or school relational climate begin to shift. Incidents of destructive interaction, conflict, and upheaval begin to decrease. People are more content because *they now have a way to talk through the issues that arise* in a way that helps them reclaim dignity and civility. Each of us has come together in these discussions to explore that way. Intrinsic to that exploration is a hope and conviction that things can change for the better.

"It's the middle stage of liminality that is the most anxiety ridden because (a) we can't go back, and (b) we don't know where we're going. We're not who we thought we were, and we don't know who we will be. What do we let go of, and what do we take with us? How would we know how, or what, to choose? Metaphorically speaking, 'the world has been turned upside down. How are we going to turn it right-side up?'

> **"If a social drama runs its full course, the outcome (or 'consummation,' as Dewey might have called it) may be either the restoration of peace and 'normalcy' among the participants or social recognition of irredeemable breach or schism."** [9]

"But this middle stage is also where possibility is born; where the seeds of restoration exist; and where the potential for rehumanization and reclamation of inherent dignity lives."

> **"Liminality can perhaps be described as a fructile chaos, a storehouse of possibilities, not a random assemblage but a striving after new forms and structures, a gestation process, a fetation of modes appropriate to postliminal experience."** [10]

I asked our group if using this three-stage perspective was helpful for them. "What sticks out for you?" I asked.

Devonte, our history teacher, said, "Those boundaries are not cut-and-dry. The breaking apart seems to be continuous and increasing."

Joan, our school administrator, commented, "These stages describe what's happening in my school. Our old ways of interacting with each other that were consistent with our cultural values are being discarded by our school director." She added, "We're stuck in a time loop like the movie *Groundhog Day*. Every day is a day where our director breaks with our cultural tradition of transparency, mutual respect, and equal consideration. It feels like a violation."

"*Groundhog Day* is a perfect example," I said. "Look at what happens in the end. The character 'Phil' undergoes a tortuous liminal stage until he finally realizes it's about love for love's sake, not Phil's sake. When that *a-ha* moment happens, the liminal loop is over. Phil's life moves forward. He's a different man.

"This plot follows an ancient archetypical story. Jesus goes into the desert for forty days and nights of temptation. Siddhartha leaves the palace and enters the world of deprivation and suffering. The knight in shining armor enters the dark castle, the door slams shut, and the knight's armor is useless. He remains in the dark until the armor rusts off. It's only until the armor of ego and conquest falls away that the castle door opens, and the kingdom is revealed in all its splendor. The kingdom is not the knight's to conquer, but his to care for and serve.

"There are endless stories of women undertaking the same journey. When Harriet Tubman refused to be enslaved and escaped, she began a journey through the wilderness rife with profound anxiety and real life-and-death consequences and danger. That journey resulted in her guidance of others to freedom through the Underground Railroad.

"Rosa Parks refused to give up her seat on the bus. Her act signified a rejection of segregation. Emmett Till's mother Mamie made the courageous decision to open her son's casket and expose the cruelty and savagery of racial violence. It's the hero's/heroine's journey. Sister Souljah stood up and advocated for the teaching of African American history in schools, helped organize the National African Youth-Student Alliance, and became an outspoken voice against racially motivated violence.

"All of these stories are about people saying 'enough!' and that statement marked a transition into a time of betwixt and between. But what they are telling us is that a new way of being and relating is possible if we're willing to do the arduous work of confronting or dismantling our paradigms in this time of liminality," I said. "Each of us, I include myself, by participating in these discussions are basically saying, 'We need a paradigm shift in how we relate to each other, and how we relate to the environment.'"

Brad, the former police officer and CEO of the recovery center, said, "I can see how these stages fit with recovery. A client comes to us in crisis, and we guide them through this middle stage in hopes of stepping into a new way of living without drugs and alcohol and integrating them into a healthier life. But that middle stage of holding themselves accountable, ideally in a compassionate way, can be torturous."

Both Barb, the retired nurse, and Kris, the director of the mental health nonprofit, agreed. "Patients come to us in a health crisis and our work is to help them recover and heal."

Aaron, the CEO of the environmental restoration company, explained, "This describes the process of restoring a wetland. The wetland is in decline. We restore the ecosystem, and the wetland thrives once again. The middle stage is finding out what's causing the demise. But also trying to convince people that ecosystem restoration is the only way."

"Hang onto that observation, Aaron, because we're going to use the restoration of an ecosystem as an Indigenous wisdom that can guide the restoration of human relationships," I said.

I explained, "However useful this three-stage structure is in gaining some perspective, it's just a theory. It's a way of thinking conceptually about crisis that, ideally, can inform or lead to taking constructive action to facilitate positive change—whether it's in a workplace or on a much larger social context."

"Or personal," said Kris.

"Especially personal," I said. "Toward the end of our discussions, I'll share my own experience of this process."

I asked our group, "All of us are here because we see the need for a change. If we use this three-stage framework to get some initial perspective, what are you seeing in your workplaces that you might classify as a 'breach' or breakdown? What's the evidence?"

In general, the group reported a(n):

- Increase in the number of conflicts. Conflict happening on a daily basis.
- Increase in the toxicity of conflict. Simple disagreements escalate into shouting matches, obscenities, and bitterness.
- Increase in bullying and demeaning gossip.
- Increase in sick days and turnover.
- Decrease in morale and mental health.

Brad commented, "It's interesting that while we've identified or described this break happening in our workplaces, you could say these same things are happening societally; in our communities."

"Great point," I said.

"I think the most alarming sign that things are getting worse is the uptick in the number of people reaching out to us for mental health services," said Kris.

I asked the group, "Playing the devil's advocate, objectively speaking, do you really think these issues are getting worse, or have they always been happening and each of you, in your own way, have just reached a point of personal exhaustion?"

"Both," said Melissa. "But others in our facility are just as fatigued, and it's not just our facility. It's healthcare in general. The pandemic took us beyond the point of exhaustion. We've always had conflict, but it seems like the conflicts have become much more emotionally charged and volatile. People are quicker to anger. Disagreements escalate into shouting matches, and people say things to each other that are more hurtful and punishing. There's definitely more obscenity."

"I never used to get interrupted or shouted down in my community presentations," said Aaron. "Our approach requires thinking differently than the conventional ways of addressing environmental breakdown, but to have people attack your character is what has changed. It's gotten very personal."

"Our country has always been at war with itself over issues of race," said Devonte. "But when parents threaten teachers and school board members with violence over curriculum about gender, civil rights, and slavery, it's a sign that we're going backward. Devolution. What concerns me is that when parents lash out with threats and racist terms, it sends the message to their kids that it's okay to do that." He continued, "They think it's okay to do that to each other. I also think that as a profession, with so much pressure being put on us, we take it out on ourselves. You start to question why you ever became an educator. The stress has to come out somewhere. So, to answer your question, yeah, it's gotten way worse."

We took a moment to let this sink in. "It's depressing," said Barb.

I said, "Seeing as how these three stages are just conceptual and it's difficult to name a definitive break or breach in norms, let alone an obscure term such as liminality, I'd like to ask you to describe in one word or sentence a norm you think has been broken. It could be a value or principle, or maybe a belief. The point is, something we used to think was important or rely on to guide our behavior, no longer appears to be."

"Decency," said Barb.

Melissa commented, "Compassion. We don't seem to care much about each other like we used to. I'm not just talking about compassion between healthcare workers. I'm talking about in general as a society."

"Open-mindedness," said Kris. "Too much judgment and accusation, and zero curiosity."

"Aaron?"

"I'd say respect. Respect for ourselves and the natural world."

"Joan, what about you?" I asked.

"All of these, and empathy. We don't put ourselves in the other person's shoes or are even willing to see things from a different perspective," she said.

Devonte responded, "Honesty. Lying has become normalized."

Brad answered, "Accountability. It's the lack of accountability that troubles me the most. Maybe it's because I used to be a cop, but I see people not being held accountable for what they say and what that leads to."

Barb, whom we would come to appreciate for her levity and frankness, said, "So, doctor restorative dude, what's the answer here? How do we get to the third stage?"

I riffed with her, as dryly as I could say. "In one sentence? Go stand in a river. Do goat yoga. Meditate 'til you evaporate. Go on a pilgrimage. Ride a horse. Eat more fiber. Become a vegetarian. Embrace your inner wokeness."

"That's more than one sentence," said Barb.

After we stopped chuckling, I said, "It's just my opinion, but each of us in our own way has already personally stepped over any metaphorical threshold into the so-called space of betwixt and between. We're doing that by stopping, turning around, and asking, 'What the hell is going on?'

"You've named the break. These universal, life-affirming values and principles appear to be on the decline and replaced by their opposite, both on a public level, but also in your workplaces. Whether it's hate speech in public discourse and the media, or bullying and condescending speech where you work, it's clearly a marked departure away from the norms of civility and toward a norm of contempt. That's why it's a crisis.

"I say this because you've confronted the fact that there is a lack of accountability both on a public level and also in your workplaces. It's that lack of accountability that is most threatening. So now, we're looking for a way to take action that will 'reclaim' accountability. The question is, how do we do that? I include myself. How do we 'reclaim the value and performance of accountability'?

"I think one of the things we're seeing is that the lack of accountability happening on a public level breeds the lack of accountability on the micro level of everyday interaction. If hate speech or deceit is not being held accountable publicly, it's understandable that people wouldn't think they should be held accountable for that same behavior in our workplaces and/or communities.

"Again, it's just my opinion, but if we can find a way to implement, or practice, accountability with repair and mercy in our workplaces and communities, in other words, on the ground level of everyday interaction, maybe, just maybe that will percolate up and start to empower people to hold public figures and others accountable for their communication behavior."

"Do the small things that will affect the big things," said Aaron.

"Maybe. What you'll see in our discussions is that the five steps of the restorative process are a way to restore accountability. Whether it's in a one-on-one dialogue with someone, or in a group encounter where you're confronting an incident, a 'breach,' that has happened, the restorative process is about accounting for the negative impact of that incident or pattern; uncovering why it happened; discerning what needs to happen to repair the damage; and then putting a plan of action in place to potentially keep it from happening again.

"I'm going to sound like a professor here. The three stages were initially used, or 'discovered,' by anthropologists looking at rituals of passage enacted in various cultures throughout the world for thousands of years. They observed a universal, or common, structure to the performance of transformation.

"The question is, how do we use this 'space between' constructively? If the values and principles you've identified as missing are to be restored or reclaimed as important, and then reinstituted, how does that happen? I think one thing to keep in mind about liminality is that it's not for the faint of heart because it requires accountability, and inherent to accountability is confrontation.

> "The restorative approach to accountability—if restoration of the values-based norms you've identified is the goal—is to uncover the underlying reasons and motivations for why those values and principles have been discarded."

"What makes this liminal space of accountability contentious is that it may expose beliefs and ways of thinking that people don't want to talk about, or are in denial about," I said.

"You mean like looking at why the assault on the Capitol happened or the rise in hate speech is happening?" asked Brad.

"Yeah. Maybe there is something deeper and more pervasive in a twisted or wounded social psyche that exists under the surface of those events, as well as the more local interactions you've described happening in our workplaces and communities.

"As an initial approach to thinking about this, I suggest that those events are manifestations of a paradigm; *a particular way of looking at the world.* If we can name that paradigm, understand how paradigms work, and realize that restoration represents a different paradigm, we stand a better chance of utilizing this theoretical liminal space to initiate making a paradigm shift.

"Without putting the cart before the horse, in my experience, the way to accomplish a paradigm shift in how people treat each other is to first help them see that they're operating out of a paradigm that is not only counterproductive, but also self-defeating and dangerous."

"So, in other words, it's not 'them' or 'us' but a way of thinking we've developed that we're not even aware of," said Devonte.

"That's exactly it. If the goal is to change that paradigm, you have to give people an experience of a different paradigm. To do that, as a practitioner of restoration, which is what you all are going to be, we first have to confront the worldview that disregards those values. This is what happens in the 'middle space' of betwixt and between.

"Second, you have to show them a better way by giving them an experience of a better way. One way to accomplish that is by changing communication practices. If we implement restorative communication practices which would 'do the work' of reclaiming, or reinstituting, the values you named such as respect, dignity, integrity, accountability, civility, and empathy, people will begin to 'live into' the new paradigm. That's been my experience. But like I said, letting go of the old paradigm is not easy. It's destabilizing for most of us.

"We're essentially holding the old paradigm accountable for its negative impact, but also presenting an alternative paradigm. Getting through it successfully requires soul-searching and leadership. We have to not only believe in what is possible but also be willing to do the work of helping others see how the changes will benefit them. Am I making sense?" I asked.

Devonte asked, "I have trouble with the term 'alternative paradigm.' Why are you describing these basic values as 'alternative'? These are timeless values and principles that are found in the world's great religious traditions. It's not like they're new."

"Maybe that's part of the problem," I said. "Maybe those values have been stuck in doctrine and orthodoxy and need a new context to be expressed. When I say 'alternative,' I'm not talking about the values themselves. I'm talking about a way of reimagining their importance and reclaiming them on a secular level; in everyday interaction. The values haven't lost their meaning. They still matter. We just need to give people a new way of actualizing them in day-to-day interaction and seeing their value in their own social experience.

"The last thing I'll say is that the restorative process has a ritual structure. There's a beginning, middle, and end. People come together and confront something that has happened that has caused disharmony. They 'name' the breech. The next two steps are the middle stage where the meaning of what happened is discussed. What was the impact? Why did it happen? What does this mean? What are we going to do about it? What character of people do we choose to be in this situation?

"The third stage, the 'moving forward stage,' is where a plan of action is decided upon to 'restore good relations' or restore civility. That last step answers the question, 'this is who we are,' " I explained.

"It's like a performance," said Devonte.

"That's exactly right," I said. "It is a performance but it's a serious performance, not an aesthetic or superficial performance. It's a cultural enactment designed to accomplish something serious and resolve something that is threatening the common good. What makes it a ritual is when it's occurring consistently over time. A good ritual is transformative."

The Conversations as Chapters

The structure of the book follows the structure of our conversations. Those conversations happened in three parts. In the first part, Chapters 2 and 3, we explored the genesis, nature, and function of paradigms. We framed paradigms as "implicit meaning-making structures" emanating from more ancient worldviews.

We then looked at the nature, function, and presence of power and how paradigms ensure the sustainability of power. We then asked the question, "Where is power in your own workplace environment, and how is that being communicated?" It was my argument that the problems and crises we face locally, socially, and environmentally are largely the result of a "power-over" paradigm. We asked, "Where does this paradigm come from, and how is it continually reinforced?"

In Chapter 3, we looked at retribution and the threat of retribution as a means of creating and sustaining power paradigmatically. Scholars of restorative justice typically define restoration by contrasting it with a "retributive paradigm." Where did the retributive paradigm begin? How did it evolve and why is it so hard to break away from? How come we don't see it?

To explore this, we looked at the function of stories and more specifically, stories of origin—those original narratives that explain how human beings came to be, how we should relate to each other and the environment, and what happens to us if we don't abide by that story. Inevitably, we looked at the function of pain, punishment, and the power of threatening violence to the body as a means of securing that story's authority and more importantly, the consequences of challenging that authority.

In Part Two, which included Chapters 4–7, we focused on restoration. Chapter 4 explored what scholars call "the restorative paradigm." We recognized that paradigm as equally ancient but characterized it as a relationship-centric paradigm that confronts a western (male) "power-over" mindset which manifests in our justice system, schools, families, and workplaces.

As we discovered, the restorative paradigm invites us to recognize "the face of the other" and the inherent dignity of life which exists in all living beings, including the environment. We reviewed a case where the restorative approach directly challenged culturally inherited bigotry, and how the offender was integrated into a much larger "sense-making system."

In Chapter 5, we looked at how to put the relationship-centric paradigm into practice through restorative communication practices. Referring to the case presented in Chapter 4, we looked at how communication constitutes our experience of relationships, and how restorative communication uniquely constitutes a return to civility, ethics, and principles of "right relationship."

We then looked at a specific practice called S.H.A.R.E.™, modeled after the basic script used in restorative justice encounters but that expands and extends that conversation model into contexts outside of criminal justice such as workplaces, families, and schools. We asked the question, "How can this work in our own respective interpersonal and work environments to resolve destructive conflict?" I provided some examples. Lastly, I presented our group with "The 7 Principles of Restorative Communication™."

Following up on Kris's initial observation and comment that "our collective nervous system is shot," and our group's recognition that "we're collectively experiencing a type of existential trauma" from all the contempt and animosity happening in the public sphere and in our own workaday lives, in our sixth discussion (Chapter 6), we focused on the presence of unresolved and recurrent trauma. More importantly, we looked at how restorative communication could provide an effective way to engage with a person (maybe ourselves) who is experiencing a moment of overwhelm and nervous system dysregulation. We asked, "What does that person need in that moment from us?"

In this discussion, I presented the S.H.I.F.T.™ trauma-responsive restorative communication technique and provided examples of situations where I was able to support a person caught in the grips of trauma-based distress. Considering that unresolved trauma is consistently an underlying issue compelling destructive behavior and interaction (and our view of the world), the group found this technique to be especially relevant to their work environments and interpersonal relationships.

Our seventh discussion (Chapter 7) explored how to implement these two practices programmatically. As I argued, "Patchwork attempts at restorative communication practices just don't work." Drawing from my own professional experience building restorative programming, I explained that taking a "systems approach" is the only way to shift a culture in an organization and embed a relationship-centric worldview in practice.

I covered the 4 P's of restorative implementation: *People, Policy, Program, and Practices*. We covered each of these components and how working together, they provide a foundation and "scaffolding" for building a restorative culture. I provided a graphic of this approach, a chart of practices, and paid particular attention to bullying.

In Part Three of our discussions, we began in Chapter 8 with the question, "Why bother with restoration when nothing seems to change and so much needs restoring?" I asked our group about their original motivation for participating in these discussions and related a well-known parable of a little girl on a beach returning thousands of starfish back to the ocean one at a time. As she explained, every starfish mattered.

This took us into a discussion about moral imagination and how a decline in participation in religions and church attendance has left a gap in a collective moral consciousness. I suggested that one solution is to return to an Indigenous ecological wisdom about interdependence. I provided an example of one man who "looked to a lake" to reclaim moral responsibility for the environment, but also what it teaches us about human relationships.

In our ninth discussion (Chapter 9) I reminded our group that looking through the lens of restoration can take us as deep and far back in time as we're willing to go. As such, restoration is uniquely qualified to look at trauma, both personal and/or individual, but also intergenerational and transgenerational trauma.

I asked our group, "How does what happened back then, maybe generations ago, continue to harm us now, and continue to degrade our relationships?" I suggested that once we understand that, we're confronted with the question, "What are we going to do about it?" Where does our responsibility for what happened back then begin—and end? Are we responsible for the harm our ancestors caused? What if that harm continues across generations? Shouldn't we at least know? What does this knowledge give us? More importantly, what are the consequences of not knowing?

In this discussion, we looked at how transgenerational trauma happens on various levels of experience, both personal and social. As challenging and rife with insecurity as it was, I offered my own personal experience of childhood trauma, its lifelong impact, and how I used the restorative approach as a method of "trauma-tracking" to pursue reconciliation and re-story a past. That pursuit led me to understand how childhood trauma impacts brain function, chemistry, and both social-emotional and spiritual development—the capacity to experience a unifying presence or reality that transcends circumstantial adversity.

In our final discussion (Chapter 10), I reminded our group that "to restore is to return someone or something, like a relationship, to an original, ideal, or intended condition." I asked, "What is this condition?" We used terms such as "a feeling of belonging, inner peace, gratitude, emotional balance, psychological well-being, and maybe the sense of a presence, an awareness of an All-Encompassing Love."

I also asked, "How can a person get there when their brain won't let them? How do you restore the relationship the brain has with the mind when it comes to unresolved, and perhaps generationally transferred, trauma? If that is even possible, what is the outcome on experiential terms?"

In this final discussion, I shared my experience with Eye Movement Desensitization Reprocessing (EMDR), which I described as "radical reintegration." My experience with EMDR resulted in profound forgiveness and what I describe as "depth restoration," an experience of "right relationship with all that was and is."

Our time together as a group came to a close with a discussion guided by the question, "What is your takeaway from all that we discussed? What did you find most meaningful about restoration?" In essence, I asked, "How does restoration matter for you, and what are your concerns moving forward?"

CHAPTER TWO

Paradigm Shift

Maybe you are searching among the branches for what only appears in the roots.
—Rumi

Liminal Accountability

In our second online discussion, I explained to our group that looking for the reasons why something is happening using restoration as a lens is both microscopic and panoramic. It can expose both the underlying thinking of an individual in a specific incident, as well as deeper and more pervasive cultural forces, social norms, and entrenched beliefs and mindsets that fertilized that thinking, like a paradigm.

"One of the dilemmas that arises if we see the intersection of individual beliefs with meta-belief systems and worldviews is deciding what to do about it. If we catch a glimpse of a fundamental flaw in a belief system that promotes retaliation, do we challenge that system? What if that glimpse exposes a source of that belief system (e.g., religion), but to challenge or criticize it risks retaliation from the believers? What are the consequences if we don't?"

As I explained to our group, "Restoration doesn't discriminate what it illuminates. We may not recognize what we're seeing or choose to ignore, deny, or excuse what is shown, but that doesn't mean it's not there, doesn't exist, won't continue to harm, and doesn't need to be confronted and, ideally, corrected.

"We may also choose to emphasize or accentuate aspects or elements of what we see or prioritize certain issues and reasons over others; but that says more about the perspective, interest, or bias of the viewer than the view.

"Because restoration is reflexive, it can show us our own incongruent belief systems and ways of thinking (both individually and collectively) that no matter how destructive they are to the well-being of self and others, we refuse to challenge them. They've become 'sacred cows.'"

I warned, "Exposing these ways of thinking and believing and their sources is risky business—especially when those sources have been deemed morally unassailable, like religious fundamentalism and nationalism. That exposure and challenge can incite contempt in those who have the most to lose if those beliefs are challenged, *activate fear in those who challenge*, silence their voices, and shut down investigation."

> **"There is a principle which is a bar against all information, which cannot fail to keep a man in everlasting ignorance—that principle is contempt prior to investigation."**
>
> **—Herbert Spencer (1820–1903)**

"One glaring example is the emotionally charged debate over teaching Critical Race Theory. Another is diversity, equity, and inclusion education in schools. There are people who vehemently oppose teaching these subjects *without ever having actually investigated what they are about*, or why they are so important to developing a more humane world.

"In truth, restoration is not without its own inherent bias. It, too, is a paradigm. Looking through that lens is an intentional act. We're purposely looking for ways of thinking that signal something is not right, not what it could or should be and, therefore, causing a degradation of our personal and social relationships."

Paradigms

"The statement, 'We need a new paradigm,' usually comes when people are so frustrated by attempts to resolve an ongoing problem, situation, or issue that they're ready to just completely start over from the ground up."

As I explained to our group, "The liminal time is an opportunity for recognizing any paradigms in place and holding that paradigm accountable for how it is directing human thinking, behavior, and decision-making. Why do we think and believe the way we think and believe?

"The terms *paradigm* and *paradigm shift* have become somewhat cliché. The problem is not with the terms themselves, but with the casual way they've been used.[1] Both terms remain useful concepts for describing and understanding how entrenched collective ways of thinking develop, and how that thinking can lead to real-world consequences.

"Most of us have a general sense of what the term *paradigm* means, but it bears clarifying. In simplest terms, a paradigm is a "system of beliefs and theories (schema/model) that people accept as a 'true' (most accurate) explanation about 'the way things work' and what they mean (Kuhn 1962)."

> **Paradigms shape our approach not only to the physical but also to the social, psychological, and philosophical world. They provide the lens through which we understand phenomena. They determine how we solve problems. They shape what we "know" to be possible and impossible. Our paradigms form our common sense, and things which fall outside the paradigm seem absurd.**
> **—Zehr, 1990[2]**

I continued, "Paradigms are essentially implicit 'meaning-making structures' ('interpretive frames'). They tell us what is meaningful. They materialize in policies, organizational structures, and communication practices which direct human interaction, problem-solving, conflict resolution, and decision-making. They are implicit because they function subconsciously, in the shadows, to compel and direct social attitudes and behavior.

"Paradigms lead to the establishment and continuance of power ('prioritizing'). They 'locate' authority and reinforce the power of authority by maintaining a status quo which rejects alternative ways of thinking and acting. We see this happening in various contexts: religion; science; family systems; justice; education; workplaces; and environmental 'management.'

"I know this sounds highly conceptual or philosophical, but bear with me. One of the ways in which paradigms function is in language and narratives—the words we use, the stories we tell ourselves about ourselves, and the claims we make in those stories about the meaning of life ('the point'), what's important, and why we exist (purpose)—our *raison d'être*.

"However unseen or inconspicuous paradigms are as 'world-organizing schema,' their impact is felt in lived experience; in the way human beings treat each other (and the environment) and rationalize that treatment (through various arguments and reflexive reasoning) when responding to behavior—and opinions—that challenge or threaten the status quo, the established order.

"There are a multitude of reasons why paradigm shifts are so difficult, if not impossible, to accomplish. First, we mostly don't realize that we're operating within a particular paradigm (system of beliefs). They are much bigger and deeper than we can imagine. They have historical precedence and as such, become established as the status quo. In effect, they have become entrenched ways of thinking that have transcended time and become institutionalized. 'Why do we think the way we do and do things the way we do? Because we've always thought this way, and always done it this way and that makes it "right."'

"We unconsciously inherit them from our families, our cultural milieu, and the institutions that govern our lives. In a very real sense, we're 'born into paradigms already in progress,' like being cast in a hidden script. Because we can't see them, we don't know that we're filtering our view of reality through them. This element of obscurity endows them with extraordinary power over our perspective; our view of the world, the ways 'things work' and 'should work,' and what they mean.

"Second, they serve a purpose. Paradigms can be understood as arising out of a very basic need for human beings to make sense of their experience and order out of chaos and confusion. Paradigms are human constructs that hide the fact that they are constructs. They provide a sense of predictability, reliability, and, as Elaine Scarry (1985) might suggest, 'relieve the mind of the labor of having to figure things out anew each time.'³

"Third, people who benefit the most in terms of status and power arising out of a paradigm have a vested interest in making sure the paradigm remains in place—even if they themselves are unaware of the reality that they are operating within a paradigm, and in spite of the destructive impact on other people, or the planet, that paradigm may authorize."

I commented to our group, "I realize I'm sounding like I'm obsessed with this concept of paradigms. The deeper point I'm trying to make is that rather than focusing on what's wrong with people, it's more constructive to focus on what's wrong with the paradigms we're all subject to, and that guide how we treat each other and how we view reality. If the destructive thinking and actions are going to change on a systemic or global level, then *the paradigm has to be held accountable for its influence and impact.*

"Following the restorative process, we have to name what is happening, understand why it's happening, and face the reality of the impact. What comes up for you after hearing this?" I asked.

"It's awfully philosophical and theoretical," said Devonte. "But the example of opposition to teaching CRT (Critical Race Theory) is spot on. In this case, it's a much deeper race-based paradigm attempting to control a curriculum. Pedagogies are paradigms. In my opinion, people who oppose teaching CRT are trying to suppress critical thinking. They're acting as gatekeepers to what counts as education."

"Fear and its manipulation rhetorically is one of the issues we'll be talking about," I replied.

"What comes up for me is that I don't stop and think about paradigms," said Aaron, the CEO of the environmental restoration company. "And yet, that is exactly what I'm up against when I try to convince people to change their mindset around using pesticides and chemical fertilizers. It doesn't matter how much data you throw at them about environmental damage; their minds are impenetrable. The control part is clear when if someone in their community agrees with me, they get immediately ostracized by others. They get labeled a heretic in their own community," he said.

"You just said something really important about paradigms," I replied. "Thomas Kuhn was a philosopher of science who theorized that when people in a community don't share the same paradigm, then they struggle to communicate in any meaningful or rational way across the boundaries of those different paradigms.[4] Kuhn suggested that when this happens, when people can't even participate in a constructive debate or argument, it devolves into 'hurling abuse' at the other side."[5]

Brad, the retired police officer/CEO, responded, "This is what is happening in our political discourse."

"I agree," I said. "Democracy is about rational, constructive debate. Debate requires listening and trying to understand where the other side is coming from. But when one or both sides devolve into judgment, 'othering,' slander, character assassination, and retribution, the possibility of resolving differences and reconciliation evaporates. It shuts down engagement. Democracy disappears."

"Like a bad marriage!" said Barb. When she said this, we all had a hearty laugh.

"I'm kind of stunned," said Melissa, the director of the healthcare facility. "It's hard to hear this, but that's what's happening in our facility. It happens in gossip, and it happens in emotionally charged conflicts. I thought it was just us. Just our workplace."

Joan, the administrator of the elementary school, commented, "This is what happens with our director. If you challenge her in any way, she gets defensive, judges you, and then makes negative side comments to others about your capability. It's a type of shaming and retribution."

"I'm curious," I said. "Does she ever refer to, 'That's our policy'?"

"All the time," she said.

Power and Paradigms

I continued, "I want to shift our focus to the topic of power and the relationship between paradigms and power. Each of you, myself included, are proposing a different paradigm when it comes to how people treat each other, whether it's in a workplace, or quite frankly, on a much larger social landscape. It helps to understand people's resistance and where that comes from.

"One way to understand that resistance is to appreciate the role that power and control play in the existing paradigm we're proposing to replace. We have to know the institutional or entrenched mindset we're up against, why people resist and sometimes vehemently protest implementing restorative practices. So much of that has to do with power and status.

"I say this because restoration, restorative communication practices, represent a different paradigm when it comes to power. By 'power,' I mean status, the authority to determine an outcome, how disagreements and conflict are resolved, decision-making, and ultimately, how people treat each other, especially when we make mistakes.

"My point is that power, in itself, is not bad. It's *how it is exercised* and how it is expressed or shared that creates problems in relationships and how people interact with each other—whether that's an interpersonal relationship, group relationships, organizational or professional relationships, or on a much larger scale of social relationships.

"Before we get to the relationship between power and restoration, I want to ask each of you three questions. First, in your respective professional communities or workplaces, who has the most power? Where is power located?

"Second, how is that power communicated, or expressed?

"Third, what are the consequences, or impacts, of how that power is expressed, on people and relationships?" I asked our group.

Brad spoke first. "I can see where you're going with this. I was in the military and power resides at the top. It is a hierarchy of rank. The same is true for law enforcement. Decisions are made at the top and those below, subordinates, are expected to carry out that decision. There's no discussion. You do what you're told. If you don't, you get reprimanded, disciplined, and possibly demoted.

"This power structure is critical for accomplishing a mission. There has to be someone in charge and there have to be those below executing the orders. It's highly efficient. Without that power structure, it would be total chaos," he said.

"Anarchy," said Devonte.

"Yes. However," Brad continued, "this is where I struggle as a CEO. I'm used to people just doing what I tell them to do. When they don't, I get frustrated. I know I come across as demanding and cold. I've been told it's in my tone of voice, my impatience, and unwillingness to collaborate. When it comes to conflict between staff members, my instinct is to sit the parties down and tell them what they need to do to resolve the issue. My assistant told me I'm like the bull in the china shop. She told me people are afraid to challenge me. I have a lot to learn. Old habits are hard to break."

"I appreciate your observations and honesty," I said. "My takeaway from what you said is that vertical power structures are necessary in certain contexts, but perhaps, not so constructive in others. Is that fair to say?" I asked.

"Absolutely. The power-over organizational structure is necessary and efficient in certain contexts, but not when it comes to dealing with people's feelings, especially when working with people who are struggling with addiction and other traumas. Our clients are wounded. The last thing they need is for me, or one of my staff, to tell them to 'straighten up.'

"There's something else about this hierarchy," he continued. "So much of it depends on the quality of leadership at the top. There are people who have power because of their status or rank, that have no business having that much power. But because they do have that power, any bad decisions they make aren't challenged. It reminds me of the saying 'power corrupts.' But it's not the power that corrupts. It's the people who abuse that power that corrupt it," he finished.

I asked our group, "Does this resonate with any of you?"

"I feel relieved to hear this," said Melissa. "It helps me to understand that there is a paradigm of power that our physicians, and some nurses, are operating out of. I don't mean literally operating, but in terms of how they relate to each other to get things accomplished. The physicians are at the top. They have to be. It's their decisions that have life-and-death consequences. That's a tremendous responsibility and pressure, and I think we often don't fully consider that. I guess what I'm saying is that hearing this makes me feel compassion for our physicians in a way I don't think I ever thought of before. So, it's not 'them'—it's a hierarchy that really has to be in place.

"But I also think that what causes problems is when people get offended, or get their feelings hurt, when a physician or nurse 'unloads' on someone for making a mistake. Physicians carry such weight and responsibility that it's understandable they would get angry and vent at the person who made the mistake. The problem is that people end up feeling very disempowered and resentful. Arguments erupt into shouting matches.

"The reason I'm interested in restorative communication is to see if there's a way that we can help our physicians and nurses address those mistakes without resorting to berating and overpowering each other. The stress everyone is under on a daily basis, and especially now because of the post-pandemic trauma, is understandable, but the level of toxicity is killing morale," she finished.

Barb spoke next. "I understand that physicians, especially surgeons, are under a lot of pressure. We all are. Nurses are under pressure, too. But I also think the power they have can go to their heads. Not all, but many. Physicians have more status and sometimes that status leads them to believe they're beyond criticism. If you report a physician for being verbally abusive, there are no consequences.

"So, I agree that it's not the power, but the person who abuses that power. Listening to this discussion makes me realize that one of the main reasons I retired early is because there was never any accountability. Nothing changed, and it didn't matter what hospital I worked at."

"So, if I read what you're saying correctly, status and the power that status endows negates awareness of the necessity of fairness in relationships?" I asked.

"That's it. Power trumps consideration," said Barb.

"Is that a pun?" I asked.

"No," she said.

"This is helping me to understand what's happening in our school with our director's leadership style," said Joan. "No one questions her style. As director of the school, she has the authority to make decisions. But the way she exercises that authority is through force and intimidation. She never explains the decisions she makes and never asks for input. It's almost as if she doesn't care how her decisions will impact others. Maybe it's her own insecurity.

"Like I said, you can't challenge her because she either cuts you off and won't listen, or she takes it personally and retaliates by putting you down in front of others or behind closed doors. People are extremely resentful. They're afraid to even talk about what's happening because of that."

Aaron shared next. "I own a technology company with fewer than 10 employees, so I don't think the inner-organizational dynamic applies to us. We're very collaborative. I think that's in part because we all really care about each other. We rarely have disagreements, let alone actual conflict.

"Our biggest challenge is the bureaucratic power of decision-making that local, state, and federal agencies have over stakeholders and our ability to secure permits to implement our technologies. The frustrating part is that their process of approving a permit can take months, if not years. A lot of our work is environmental crisis response, like when an ecosystem is close to the edge of being beyond repair. It seems as if the urgency is just not important. Bureaucratic webs kill the environment.

"When you try and speed the permit process up, you always get the same answers: 'We're doing the best we can'; 'Your application is under review'; 'We'll let you know,' etc. What frustrates me is that you get passed around to various departments and no one ever seems to take personal responsibility for getting things done. It's the classic bureaucratic molasses. So, there's a power structure, or hierarchy, in place, but I think it's more about the power that an institution has over the environment. It's definitely a paradigm, but I would call it a paradigm of paralysis."

Kris, the director of the nonprofit mental health services, spoke next. "If we have power struggles it's mainly on our executive board and it usually has to do with budget. There are definitely some board members who try to exert their power based on their experience, but for the most part, it doesn't get toxic. People usually work their differences out.

"As I listen to what you're all saying, I keep thinking of the connection between power and mental health. Aaron, you mention the bureaucracy of government agencies. In our case, it's the insurance companies and Medicaid who have all the power. If a client comes to us in need of immediate help, but they don't have health insurance or their policy doesn't cover mental health benefits, that has real and often drastic consequences.

"But then there's the psychological or emotional trauma that lack of coverage causes. If you're desperate and you're told you're not covered, it's like being told 'you don't matter.' When this happens, clients often blame us. They take it out on us. We're regularly threatened.

"We're fortunate in that we have providers who basically work for free, but when you're sitting across the desk from someone who is in crisis, and you have to tell them they're not covered by their insurance or Medicaid won't cover their chosen provider, things can get scary very fast. We become the scapegoat for that rage.

"When I see school or workplace shootings, like you, I immediately think, 'Why didn't someone see that coming?' Then I get angry because mental health and unresolved trauma are still seen by those who make policy decisions, those in power, as not import-ant enough to actually make immediate and meaningful changes. I mean, what is wrong with us? I guess I just needed to vent. It's frustrating and it's heartbreaking," she said.

"You're not alone in that frustration," I said.

"This is a great discussion," I continued. "Thus far, we've been describing a verti-cal 'power-over' configuration where power existing at the top of hierarchical struc-ture is exerted over those with lesser status. Whether it's a physician over a nurse or tech; a director over a faculty or administrator; a school board over a curriculum; a government agency over permitting environmental restoration; an insurance compa-ny over a client—all of these are examples of a vertical organizational structure. It's a paradigm.

"You've also described the negative consequences, or impacts, on people, relation-ships, and even progress, when the power endowed by virtue of status is exercised in un-constructive, or unthoughtful, ways. It's inevitable that resentment, retaliation, gossip, bitterness, silencing or suppression of voice, collaboration, etc., is the outcome.

"But a paradigm goes much deeper and is much broader than just a structural, or an organizational context. I think where the concept of a paradigm becomes most useful is when we understand it as a particular way of looking at the world, a worldview.

"A paradigm is essentially a model or theory about the way things work. That theory is based on fundamental assumptions about human nature, our reason for being, our place in the cosmos, how we know what we know, etc.," I said. "We filter our view of reality through the paradigm, and we can miss the foundational assumptions that para-digm is built on."

"The big 'why,'" said Aaron.

"Exactly," I said. "I realize that, once again, I'm starting to sound way too philo-sophical here. But if we're committed to making a paradigm shift toward restoration by implementing restorative methods and communication practices, *we have to understand that restoration is first and foremost a worldview that stands in stark contrast to a western view of the world* that configures relationships along a vertical, or hierarchical, axis.

> **"The single most important question we can ask in challenging any paradigm—especially a paradigm which defines how human beings should relate to each other and the environment—is, 'Where did this thinking begin?"**

"If paradigms can be characterized as 'inscribed ways of thinking' that become insti-tutionalized over time, *where's the original inscription* (if one exists)?

"If we don't ask where this way of thinking began, we'll never fully awaken to the inherent rhetorical persuasive power of that paradigm or be given the opportunity to challenge it if it doesn't align with our values."

"You're asking us to look at the historical roots of both paradigms?" asked Devonte.

"I am," I said. "But before we dig into the 'restorative worldview,' and because we're still in this liminal stage of accounting for the existing hierarchical paradigm of power-over which is vulnerable to the abuse of power, it helps to understand the philosophical or mythological roots of that paradigm, and the assumptions being made," I explained. "What, or where, is the original hierarchy, and what are those assumptions?

"Because when you begin to propose implementing restorative methods, you're going to be coming up against this worldview and those assumptions," I added. "It's been my experience that, for the most part, people don't know that their resistance to restorative practices is coming from some very deep unconscious assumptions about humanity and our purpose—the big why," I said.

"And the environment," offered Aaron.

"Especially the environment," I added. "The power-over paradigm which authorizes not only power by virtue of status, but also how to enforce or exert that power, came from somewhere. I'm asking us to look at where."

"Are you talking about Genesis?" asked Devonte.

"That's one story of origin," I said. "But it's an important example because it is undoubtedly the 'master narrative' that has had the most influence on western civilization after the Greeks. That narrative explains among other things, how human beings came to be, what our place is, what our purpose is, how we should relate to the natural world and each other, and perhaps most important—what will happen if we 'contest the narrative'; if we challenge the author and don't follow the rules.

"We may think, 'that's an archaic story' and is only relevant to fundamentalist religious thinking, but its influence on our collective mindset about status, power, justice, and conflicted human behavior remains," I said.

"Because it established a paradigm," said Devonte.

"It gave birth to a vertical power-over way of thinking that continues to be a dominant way of thinking about what it means to be human and how we should treat each other when we disagree or act out against each other. I suggest that this vertical way of thinking is a root cause of man's inhumanity to man and our complete lack of respect for the environment," I said. "I use the term 'man' intentionally," I added.

"I'm getting ahead of myself here. Before we look at Genesis as the 'western creation story,' what it says about status, power, and justice, and how that perspective has become ingrained in a collective western mindset, we need to look at the power of storytelling. Because when we go out to implement restorative practices or programming in a workplace, school, or community, we're telling a different story—one that opposes the 'top-down' story of dominance, force, and control," I explained.

"We're instituting a new story and a new paradigm. We're participating in re-storying. We're essentially resurrecting an earlier origin story. It just wasn't written down.

"I realize that I'm taking us all into some deep and stormy water. I want to check in with you before we end this session. What comes up for you with what I've presented, and we've discussed?" I asked.

Kris spoke first. "I'm trying to filter what you're saying through the lens of mental health. It's clear to me that there is a mindset out there that thinks that if a person is struggling with a mental health issue, it means there's something wrong with them, like a weakness. It's the same paradigm, to use your term, that people with physical disabilities have had to face. The term 're-storying' is intriguing because that's what we're trying to do in our community. We're advocating for a different story about mental health, one that is calling for a change in our paradigm, our conventional way of thinking about mental health issues."

"I feel like you're asking us to jump into a big river and swim against the current," said Aaron. "But I'm used to that. Pretty much everything you've said makes sense, power, control, mindsets. I'm interested in what you have to say about Genesis and how it relates to the environment. I'm also interested in this concept of 're-storying.'"

"I'll admit I'm anxious to get to restorative practices, but I can see you're building a foundation for that. This discussion has certainly made me think about the connection between paradigms and power," said Brad. "Not that it's necessarily going to help me implement restorative practices in our recovery center, but it might help me gain some perspective on what's happening in our politics. I'm looking forward to understanding the relationship between restoration and power. I like the metaphor of swimming against the current."

"I'm looking forward to understanding restorative practices too," said Melissa. "I'm thinking about our cultural values of compassion and kindness and questioning whether this power-centric paradigm, as you call it, aligns with those values. Because we definitely have a vertical organizational structure, so I'm wondering how we can address the power imbalance between our physicians and staff in a way that expresses those values."

"I love this kind of stuff, but then, I'm an armchair philosopher," said Devonte. "I'm looking forward to seeing how you think Genesis figures into our current paradigm of justice. My gut tells me you're going to talk about retribution."

"I am," I said.

"I'll admit to feeling overwhelmed by all of this and find it a bit depressing," said Joan. "It's awfully intellectual and theoretical. I just want to find a way to reclaim our old culture. We used to be so supportive of each other. It was a happy place to work. It was our spirit, our culture, that made us who we are. That's why parents wanted their kids there.

"My sense is that the power-over paradigm is what's killing our culture and I don't know what to do about that. I feel powerless to do anything. Our director 'talks the talk' and boasts about our values to parents, but it's not sincere. The way she treats faculty and staff is the exact opposite of what she tells parents. Maybe that's what I'm depressed about. It's crazy-making. Sorry to sound so negative."

"You're not being negative," I replied. "You're speaking your truth about your experience and what you're seeing. That's not being negative. It's being honest, and it's the first step in the restorative process. My sense is that what you're observing—and feeling—is how the abuse of power leads to the suppression of voice. What you're describing is a punitive style of leadership. Does that sound accurate?" I asked.

"That's it. She punishes people," she replied.

"Hang in there with me," I said. "Because that punitive mindset is what we're going to be talking about next."

To the group I explained, "I know it may seem like we're way off the topic of restoration and restorative communication practices. My objective in talking about paradigms and power is to take advantage of this 'liminal period' where we take the time to question the status quo.

"Each of us, in our own way, is sensing that relationships have deteriorated both on a public level and in our workplaces. I don't think we're being overly sensitive about that, especially when you meaningfully consider some of the crises we're facing.

"It's my argument that any crisis we face, whether it's in politics, education, healthcare, the environment, etc., points to a crisis of perception. It's our perception, our view of the world, and our role in it that has created the crisis.

"Changing our perception is about changing paradigms. From a restorative perspective, this requires changing our foundational view of the world and our place in it. We have to ask ourselves, 'Why are we here? What's the point?'

"I'm reminded of the famous Albert Einstein quote: 'We cannot solve our problems with the same thinking we used when we created them.' I take this to mean we can't make a paradigm shift unless we step outside of the paradigm that we're in, name it, and hold it accountable for the cultural and social norms it has produced and continues to authorize either explicitly or implicitly regardless of the consequences.

"There are other paradigms, other stories of origin, and other ways of interacting when we're in conflict or disagree, that I believe, and I think you sense, are available. But these stories and ways are not the dominant paradigm. Before we get to this 'other restorative paradigm,' a different story of origin, and pursue different practices, we have to hold the existing paradigm accountable. This is what we've been doing thus far, but we have a bit more to go.

"What I hope you'll see is that the impulse to judge, blame, punish, and resort to violence as a method of reclaiming or maintaining power comes from somewhere. I seriously don't think it is our species' first, or original, or even instinctive response. We've been conditioned."

Reflection

I began this talk with a discussion about liminality because I wanted to emphasize that by entering into this "dialogic space of betwixt and between," we were giving ourselves the freedom to step back and look objectively and critically at systems of beliefs (paradigms) that unconsciously guide people's thinking and actions. In essence, what I was saying was that paradigms carry assumptions about what it means to be human, the nature and function of relationships, status, power, and justice.

Strategically, I was initiating one of the precepts of restoration and restorative practices, which is to try and "separate the inherent value of a human life from the behavior." My implicit argument was that behavior is what people do, not who they are, and that behavior is often guided by assumptions and historical ways of thinking embedded in paradigms.

My point was that paradigms have tremendous power because we don't recognize that we're operating within a paradigm. Paradigms embody subconscious blueprints, cognitive schema that may or may not be life-affirming or pro-relationship.

To ground this perspective about paradigms, I asked our group to look at their own workplace and professional experience, identify paradigms, and talk about the impact of a "power-over paradigm." I offered that each of them, in their own way, was asking for a paradigm shift, both locally in their respective environments, and based on their observations of an existential crisis on a much larger social landscape.

I explained that we can't make a paradigm shift unless we step outside of the paradigm that we're in, name it, and hold it accountable for the cultural and social norms it has produced and continues to authorize either explicitly or implicitly regardless of the consequences.

I suggested that one of the ways in which paradigms are established and maintained is through stories. To make a paradigm shift, we need to ask, "Where did this paradigm begin? Was there an 'origin story' that gave birth to this paradigm?"

This question set the stage for our next discussion, which would look at the function of a story of origin in establishing a master narrative which authorizes the axiom "justice demands retribution and retribution demands punishment." How is the unquestionable authority of that narrative established and maintained? Some scholars suggest it is through weaponizing the threat of pain and violence to the body.

CHAPTER THREE
Retribution and the Conversion of Pain into Power

We refuse to acknowledge important information when it's given to us because it rattles how we are used to thinking. It makes us have to reconsider the conventional wisdom we have clung to. It makes us have to wonder if we're wrong about one thing, what other fundamental beliefs might we be wrong about?

—Kareem Abdul-Jabbar (2022)

When our discussion group assembled for our third conversation, I explained that before we could begin to understand restoration as an approach to human misconduct, we would first need to "wrestle" with its opposite—retribution.

"Restoration challenges retribution on numerous levels. We'll talk about what those levels are," I said.

"When scholars of restorative justice and restorative school discipline practices explain the restorative approach, they often do so by distinguishing it from a retributive approach," I said. "We'll do the same, and I'll reference some of the distinctions early scholars of restorative justice have made, but I intend to go deeper and farther back into the mythological origins that equate 'justice' with 'doing violence to the body' in response to infraction, transgression, and what we define as 'crime.' What we'll see is that retribution has 'sacred' origins. That designation as 'sacred' is what makes retribution an unassailable philosophy; divinely authorized or justified.

"Some of the arguments that advocates and proponents of a restorative approach make begin with a criticism of, or opposition to, retribution. For example, 'retribution and punishment only continues the cycle of violence.' This is what I call the pragmatic cause-and-effect 'Ghandian' argument that 'an eye for an eye makes the whole world blind.'

"This is backed by a second argument, which is what I would call the 'criminologist argument,' that retribution and retributive correctional responses are not cost-effective and don't lower recidivism rates (prevent reoffending). In this argument, retributive justice doesn't address the underlying mental-health or social-structural issues that compel criminal behavior like racism and economic depravity—and in fact, only exacerbate them. One of the criteria restorative justice scholars point out is the high recidivism rate of conventional retributive justice.

"A third argument is what I would call 'the postmodern, poststructuralist, Derridean deconstructive' approach which says that the language of retribution is, in itself, a type of retribution and continuously reauthorizes its own power by inference. The 'fact' of the existence of retribution is carried forth, and it becomes self-substantiating in language and symbols. The existence of prisons and punishment, and the threat of doing violence to the body, is in itself an authorization for the validity and necessity of retribution," I said.

"Wait. Stop," said Barb. "What the fuck did you just say? I have no idea what you just said."

"Neither do I," said Aaron.

"Me neither," said Brad.

"Me neither," I said. And then I started laughing at myself. It was my intention in our discussions that we inject some humor.

"Will, that sounds like a really bad academic cocktail party discussion," said Devonte.

I had to take a moment to regain my composure. It was that funny, to me anyway. It was that true.

"You're insane," said Barb.

"Thank you. I agree," I said. "I'm glad we got that out of the way. That's what a Ph.D. does to you. You learn how to talk about things in a way that nobody understands, including yourself!"

After I collected myself, I said, "Bear with me because as mind-scrambling as what I just said sounds, it's actually extremely important when talking about retribution. Because it says that the very notion of retribution, the 'story' of retribution as a response to injustice, its history, carries within it a 'memorialized' threat of pain and violence that extends way beyond criminal justice and into a trans-historical mindset about human behavior and especially conflict. It's a cognitive blueprint."

"I'm sorry, but I still don't know what the hell you're talking about," said Barb.

"What you're saying is that the philosophy of retribution and its history runs so deep in the human psyche that we instinctively and unconsciously reject any alternative out of fear of retribution. It has become our reference point," said Devonte.

"Yes!" I said. "It's a paradigm."

"Why didn't you just say that?" asked Barb.

"Because my brain makes things as complicated as they can be," I said.

"You should get some help with that," said Barb.

Laughter.

Devonte spoke. "So, every time we're presented with an alternative, such as restorative justice, our defense of retribution gets stronger and more cemented in our psyche," he said.

"That's exactly it," I replied. "The notion of restoration threatens our belief system. We're afraid to let go of it. It's the threat of punishment that controls people. You explained it better than me."

"Where's my Ph.D.?" asked Devonte.

"I'll give you mine," I said. "But you have to assume the student loan debt."

"No thanks," said Devonte.

I continued. "We are so conditioned to think that justice demands a violent response against 'the offender' that when we hear an alternative, like restoration, we vehemently defend retribution as the only 'appropriate,' 'natural,' or 'moral' response to human error that results in transgression." I added, "And we don't realize it. Why is that?"

"That's what Kareem Abdul-Jabbar was saying in the quote," said Devonte.

"I think so. My point is that since we're all in this liminal space, it is worth asking, 'why is it that retribution has such a strong grip on our "justice imagination"?' Why do we almost never stop and question its validity or effectiveness?

"One answer is that retribution is a type of 'cognitive schema.' It's a historical way of knowing, an original way of knowing, at least in western terms, about justice that when confronted with an alternative like restoration, it disrupts our 'blueprint' for what justice is, and how justice should be conducted. And it's not just justice. It influences how we treat each other when we believe we are offended or feel threatened.

"Second, and this is probably the most important point that I believe Derrida was making, because we so ardently hold onto the notion that justice requires retribution and the infliction of retaliatory pain and punishment, it makes us vulnerable to being manipulated."

"So, it's cultural conditioning," said Devonte.

"Yes. It's a moral conditioning even though retribution may/may not be 'moral' even if it contradicts what we might instinctively sense is 'moral,' " I said.

"Like imposing the death penalty because murder is immoral," said Devonte.

"That's a great example. If we're advocating for a different way, a restorative way, we have to recognize that retributive conditioning runs so deep we need to ask, 'Where did it begin, how did it develop, why did it develop, and why is it so hard to break away from?' " I said. "Let me give you an example."

"Thank God," said Barb.

"Hold on," said Brad. "This is starting to make some sense. Especially the manipulative part. When politicians are running for office, they inevitably use a 'get tough on crime' and 'lock them up' message or platform," he said.

"You nailed it. In that context of persuasion, retribution is what's called a 'trope.' In addition to being a very real action of applying punishment, it is also a metaphor that symbolizes safety and protection from 'the bad guys' through enforcement, retaliation, and punitive power. That metaphor can be used to manipulate people's fears. It gets twisted.

"It's the oldest dirty rhetorical trick in the book and it goes like this. A politician says, 'Those people over there are dangerous and threatening. They're out to get you. They will commit crimes because "that's who they are." They are evil and you are not safe.'"

"Thugs, rapists, super predators and drug dealers," said Devonte.

"Exactly. The message is, 'If you vote for me, I will make sure you are protected. I will make sure they are apprehended and thrown in jail or cages. I am your only hope.

"'I am your retribution,'" I said.

Brad said, "Activate their fears, point to a scapegoat, and then make the claim that 'you're the only one who can protect them.'"

"That's it," I said. "It's manufactured fear for the purpose of diversion. It's the worst kind of rhetorical persuasion because it not only suppresses logic, but it completely ignores a quest for civility. Let me ask you a question. How were you disciplined when you were a kid and you 'misbehaved'?"

"I got whacked," said Barb.

"So, physical punishment?" I asked.

"That was just the beginning," she said. "Then came the grounding, the 'I'm disappointed in you,' 'You're letting us down,' statements and the real zinger—'I'm doing this for your own good.'"

"That last statement is what I call displacement, or 'the inversion,'" I said. "It's the ultimate gaslighting, and it has mythic/sacred origins. That's what we're going to talk about when we look at Genesis. Threat overrides rationale. Threat of violence is a logic-blocker. It takes our consciousness hostage. But first, a story."

Confronting the Retributive Mindset "In the Moment"

"When I first started to present restorative practices to schools, workplaces, and communities, I didn't fully appreciate just how deep the resistance runs to a nonretributive way of addressing violations or transgressions, infractions, or antisocial behavior in general.

"No matter how much evidence I would provide that 'proved' the effectiveness of restorative methods in reducing incidents, how many young people it kept out of the criminal justice system, how satisfying people reported it to be, or how it could transform a workplace social climate, there were always people who were vehemently opposed to pursuing it without even understanding what it entails. It was contempt prior to investigation. 'It's too soft,' they would say. 'People need to be punished when they break the rules. It's the only way they'll learn. It's the only way they'll stop doing what they're doing.'

"When you seek to implement restorative practices in your workplaces or communities, you're going to be faced with this same entrenched resistance, either aggressively and vocally, or passively and silently. It's helpful to understand where this resistance comes from; how deep and far back it goes.

"At first, I thought I just wasn't explaining restoration very effectively or wasn't convincing enough. Then I thought, 'Who am I to challenge retribution or the use of punishment?' Isn't retribution necessary in certain contexts when a person, group, or even nation refuses or is incapable of stopping what they're doing? Isn't punishment or retaliatory violence warranted in those situations? It's not an either/or answer.

"Nobody that I know of would argue against waging war against Hitler and the Nazis, or the Japanese after bombing Pearl Harbor. There was no other option. Neither Hitler nor Japan were interested in rational discourse. War was necessary—to protect and prevent and preserve. So, retribution has its value and place. But it's about the motivation, the reason.

"These questions forced me to get as clear as I could about these terms: retaliation, retribution, punishment, and eventually, the function and power of the retaliatory infliction of pain. When it comes to addressing less catastrophic violations, I asked, 'Why is retribution so cemented in human psychology, both individual and social? Is there a middle ground?'

"I came to realize that the objections to restoration were not about the people who voiced their objections, but about a way of thinking, a mindset. The objection to the restorative approach was less about restoration *per se*, and more about the power that retribution and its justification for the use of punishment has over people's thinking—including my own.

"The most challenging part of advocating for restoration and restorative practices in communities is engaging with mindsets about what constitutes accountability, and what is the 'correct way' to respond to harmful behavior. In our first discussion, I mentioned that pursuing restoration requires 'standing in the middle of tension.' In this case, it means standing in the middle of differing opinions (often emotionally charged) about accountability.

"On one hand, there is the sentiment that the most effective way to change or prevent destructive behavior from happening is through coercion and the threat of punishment. This is essentially a 'force and control' approach.[1]

"On the other hand, there is what I call the 'minimizing' or 'non-consequence' response. This sentiment, however well-intentioned, is overly lenient, permissive, accepts excuses as reasons, and takes promises as commitments to change. Typical statements include, 'They didn't mean it,' 'It's not that bad,' or 'It is what it is; let's just move on.' In essence, this is the 'pat on the wrist' response.

"As we'll see later in our discussions, from a restorative perspective, accountability transcends both of these sentimentalities in the pursuit of deeper answers for why something happened, which can lead to authentic change and sustainable solutions. Accountability means the *ability to account* for these deeper reasons in order to effect transformation. Bear with me on this.

"Let me give an example. When I was proposing a new university-based restorative justice program to a neighborhood association, there was one particularly vocal resident who interrupted me about five minutes into my presentation with, 'This is bullshit!' He went on to declare, 'These kids are offenders and need to be thrown in jail and immediately kicked out of the university with no questions asked. It's the only way they'll learn. And their parents should be heavily fined. What you're proposing is just another lame oatmeal attempt to minimize selfish behavior. It won't work. Nothing will change. They'll just continue to wreak havoc in our neighborhood.' Clearly, he was operating out of a 'retributive paradigm' about accountability.[2]

"But I understood why he felt that way. He was beyond frustrated. He felt violated and angry for a very good reason. Rather than contest his position (which would result in a power struggle), I chose to go deeper with him. I asked him, 'What is the worst part of living in this neighborhood with so many college students?'

"He didn't hesitate. 'It's their drunken disregard for property, the blow-out parties and garbage, pissing in the streets and on our lawns, and screaming and yelling every night and into the morning.'

"I asked him, 'How long has this been going on?' He replied, 'Ever since I've lived here but it's gotten worse.' I asked, 'Why do you think it's gotten worse?' He replied, 'Because they just don't give a damn and their parents don't teach them about respecting others. They have no consequences. And most of us are afraid of retaliation if they know we've called the police.'

"I validated his anger. I said, 'I can't fully understand your experience because I don't live in your neighborhood, but I can understand how having to experience this kind of behavior would be maddening. If I had to endure this every day and night, I'd feel frustrated and angry too.'

"I asked others attending the meeting, 'How many of you feel the same?' Just about everyone either nodded or raised their hand. One woman spoke up. 'I'm exhausted by this behavior too, but I don't think throwing them in jail or kicking them out of school is the answer. That seems a bit harsh and let's face it, most of these kids have no idea what it means to be a responsible neighbor. This is the first time most of them have lived away from their parents. And when you throw hormones, alcohol, and parties into the mix, they have no awareness of others. But I do agree that something needs to change.'

"I searched for a middle ground. I said, 'It sounds like what's missing, and what you're all asking for, is accountability. On the one hand, you want students to be held personally accountable for the damage they cause, and on the other hand, you want them to learn about what it takes to live respectfully in your community. Is that right?'

"Another member spoke up. 'The other problem is that every year brings a wave of new students, and the cycle continues.' I said, 'Okay. So, what I hear is that any effort that is effective in addressing this problem needs to be sustainable. It needs to consistently deliver the accountability over time. Is that right?' One resident added, 'Yes, because in all honesty, I've lived here for almost twenty years and as much as I love my neighbors, if this doesn't improve, I'm going to have to move.'

" 'Got it,' I said. 'So, there's an urgency to this.' 'Yes,' he replied. I then explained the components and procedures of the new program, which, I proposed, would deliver both the immediate and the sustainable accountability they were seeking."

I asked our discussion group, "Can you see what I mean by the challenge of confronting a retributive mindset?" Everyone affirmed it was clear.

I continued, "To challenge the use of punishment is to challenge history, and the power that punishment and the threat of punishment enables, protects, and sustains. To challenge that mindset is to challenge an ancient paradigm that equates punishment with justice or discipline, and this can be disorienting and destabilizing when punishment is all we know or have experienced. It can also be threatening to people who benefit from the power that punishment and the threat of punishment provides and sustains."

"The desire for retribution comes from anger," said Brad.

"It can. But it's not the anger that is bad. It's understandable. It's the conversion of that anger into a demand for retribution that makes us vulnerable politically," I said.

Distinction

"Thirty years ago, when restorative justice was just beginning to emerge as an alternative to conventional punitive-based justice responses to crime, like I said, criminologists introduced the concept of a restorative approach by distinguishing it from a retributive approach. Howard Zehr's seminal book, *Changing Lenses* (1990), described retributive justice as an institutional paradigm."

Retributive Justice

> **Crime is a violation of the state, defined by lawbreaking and guilt. Justice determines blame and administers pain in a contest between the offender and the state directed by systematic rules.**[3]

"From a retributive perspective, accountability is satisfied when the law is upheld and the person(s) who committed the offense 'held accountable' by being punished.

"The *communication process* of achieving accountability involves collecting and presenting evidence, determining what laws were violated/broken, charging and prosecution, determination of guilt/innocence (judgment), sentencing, and the application of an appropriate punishment. The pursuit of accountability, as both a process and an outcome, resides as an institutional responsibility and is executed by legal professionals who are third parties to the incident.

"The rationale for retributive justice rests on the belief (and historical tradition) that punishment will (a) satisfy the victim's need and right for 'just deserts' (*lex talionis*), (b) serve as a deterrent for future violations/crime, and (c) maintain and ensure social order.

"Retired Navajo Supreme Court Justice Hon. Robert Yazzie (2005) describes the western institutional retributive approach as a *vertical system*: [4]

A 'vertical' system of justice relies upon hierarchies and power (Barton, 1968). That is, judges sit above the parties, lawyers, jurors, and other participants in court proceedings. The Anglo-European justice system uses rank, and the coercive power that goes with that rank, to address conflicts [...] The goal of the vertical system, or adversarial law, is to punish wrongdoers and teach them a lesson [...]

Adjudication makes one party the 'bad guy' and the other the 'he good guy'; one of them is 'wrong' and the other is 'right.' The vertical system is so concerned with winning and losing that when parties come to the end of the case, little or nothing is done to solve the underlying problems that cause the dispute in the first place. [5]

> **Vertical adversarial adjudication relies upon power, force, and coercion. When powerful figures abuse their authority, there is authoritarianism and tyranny. (Sagan 1985) [6]**

I asked our discussion group, "What came up for you when you read this?"

"I'll go first," said Brad. "A lot came up for me. The 'abuse of authority and authoritarianism' piece speaks to me. As you all know, I was a cop for thirty years. Cops are the enforcement part of the justice system. I was the 'good guy' who caught the 'bad guys.' It was a profound responsibility for public safety. There *are* 'bad guys' and there *are* 'good guys.'

"But for some, the power that responsibility carries with it can be intoxicating. Some cops get 'power drunk' and when that happens, abuse happens. I've seen officers who were remarkably good people, totally committed to public service, become hyper-aggressive. Maybe it's the survival part of our brain that gets activated. When you're facing someone who's pointing a gun at you, it's no different than being in a war. That adrenaline can be addictive to some. In others, it shows up as depression and PTSD.

"But it's the deeper and larger cultural mindset, paradigm as you call it, that startles me the most about this piece. It's not just the justice system or enforcement that subscribes to this power-over mindset. It's all of us. I really like what you said about politicians using retribution as a rhetorical strategy.

"It's the same dualistic good/bad, right/wrong, us/them, win/lose thinking that has created such a toxic social climate. And I'm just as vulnerable as anyone when it comes to judging someone as 'good or bad,'" he said. "I understand what you said earlier about the threat of retribution creating opposition, which then gives it an opportunity for 're-inforcing' itself. That makes sense now."

"Can I interject?" asked Devonte.

"Of course. I could go on about this for hours," Brad said. "I just need to add that this is why I wanted to participate in these discussions. There has to be a better way than win/lose," he finished.

"Your comment about this being a much deeper and broader cultural mindset rings true for me," said Devonte. "It's not just the justice system. It's history. The Anglo-European justice system is just one example. This top-down view of the world fueled conquest, colonialism, slavery, and the justification of eradicating people of color, like Native Americans. It's the same sick rationale Hitler used to justify the Holocaust. Apartheid in South Africa is another example. So, it's not just the justice system. It's the system of justification, and that goes far deeper and further than law. It is a paradigm that came from somewhere.

"As a political paradigm, it continues to hypnotize people, not just white people, into thinking that discrimination, racism, classism, genderism, and 'othering' is justifiable and normal. I like what you said about power, Brad. It's all about power-over," said Devonte. "And that usually means putting people down in order to have power over people who have no voice or representation," he added.

"And the environment," said Aaron. "The environment has no political voice."

"Amen," said Brad.

"Hang on to your observations about the connection between retribution and power because that theme will continue throughout our discussions. What we'll see is that restoration has a different conception of power," I said. "Does anyone else want to comment on this part of the reading?" I asked.

Kris shared, "What stuck out for me was the underlying problems piece. A lot of our clients have had substantial interaction with the courts. Though the courts are getting much better at actually being compassionate with offenders, like drug courts, if those underlying problems in a client's life are not dealt with, they'll be back in front of the judge.

"Yazzie's vertical paradigm of 'guilty/not guilty' is not designed to work with mental health issues. It just isn't. There's no gray area. The system, the paradigm, is bigger and more powerful than the people. Whether or not a client gets the help they need is too often dependent on the sensitivity and wisdom of a particular judge. Mental health shouldn't be a reason to punish someone. Homelessness shouldn't be a crime. That's just my opinion," said Kris.

I continued, "One of the things we'll see when we start to talk about restorative justice is that it can provide that middle ground of working with underlying issues that the courts most often can't," I suggested. "Anyone else before we move on?" I asked. "We have a lot to cover, and I want to keep us moving."

Melissa spoke. "I just want to say quickly that the win/lose approach to conflict is the paradigm we're stuck in at the hospital. People are quick to blame the other and then ask the executive team or human resources to punish the other. So, this makes sense," she said.

I offered, "I think what we're seeing is that even though this reading is about the Anglo-European vertical system of justice, that hierarchical paradigm which generates dualistic thinking of good/bad, either/or isn't limited to justice systems. What you're essentially asking is, 'Where else do we see this structure?' and, 'How is the power inherent to this structure maintained in those sites?'

"The obvious examples beyond the justice system are schools and workplaces. Those residing at the top of the organizational structure (e.g., the vice principal or supervisor) have the power and authority, by nature of their assigned status in the hierarchy, to enforce conduct policies. Implicit are the dualistic judgments of good/bad, proper/improper, right/wrong, guilty/not guilty, acceptable/not acceptable, etc."

It Wasn't Always This Way …

"It wasn't always this way," I continued. "Scholars of restorative justice suggest that prior to the Old Testament, earlier legal systems which also informed the foundation of western criminal and civil law advocated for nonviolent restitution—paid not to the state, but directly to the victims and the families of victims. If I understand this right, 'retribution' was not synonymous with violence, but reparation.

> Early legal systems emphasized the need for offenders and their families to settle with victims and their families […] Crime was viewed principally as an offense against the victim and the victim's family.[7]
>
> This was true in small non-state societies, with their kin-based ties, but continued to be the case after the advent of states with formalized legal codes.[8]

"Restorative Justice scholars Van Ness and Strong (2002) provide reference to pre-Biblical legal codes such as the Code of Hammurabi (c. 1700 B.C.E.) and Code of Lipit-Ishtar (c. 1875 B.C.E.), which both emphasized direct restitution to victims and victims' families. The Sumerian Code of Ur-Nammu (c. 2050 B.C.E.) and the Code of Eshnunna (c. 1700 B.C.E.) both required restitution directly to the victims 'even in the case of violent offenses.' The earliest collection of Germanic tribal laws, the Lex-Salica (c. 496 B.C.E.), required restitution for crimes 'ranging from theft to homicide.'"[9]

"Wait," said Brad. "I thought the Code of Hammurabi is where we get the concept of 'an eye for an eye.'"

"It is, and more than likely before that according to other scholars. There is continuing debate around whether that phrase meant literally removing the offender's eye, or whether it meant the principle of proportionality and reciprocity. The point being made here is that the goal of these early justice processes was to restore equality and balance between the parties involved. It was about the relationship between the parties involved.

"The use of violence as vindication for an offense wasn't always the norm or precedent; there were ancient pre-western civilization justice customs and practices that defined retribution primarily as restitution, repair, and as a type of reconciliation not only of the event or incident, but of the relationships between parties.

"In explaining the language of Ancient Hebrew Scriptures, it was/is the concept of *shalom*, which describes 'the ideal state in which the community should function [...] In short, the purpose of the justice process was, through restitution and reparation, to restore a community that had been sundered by crime. 'Vindication was about reparation.' [10]

"Van Ness and Strong (2002) explain that a 'new model of crime emerged' with *The Leges Henrici Primi* written in the twelfth century whereby 'the king became the paramount crime victim sustaining legally acknowledged (although symbolic) injuries.' "

> **The actual victim was ousted from any meaningful place in the justice process, illustrated by the redirection of reparation from the victim in the form of restitution to the king in the form of fines.** [11]
>
> **Restitution, which is both past-oriented and victim-centered, was eventually abandoned, with fines, corporal punishment, and the death sentence taking its place as the central responses to wrongdoing. Whipping, using stocks, branding, and other forms of public retribution not only inflicted physical pain on offenders but served to humiliate them as well.** [12]

"Both scholars explain that prior to *The Leges Henrici Primi*, 'William the Conqueror and his successors found the legal process an effective tool for establishing the preeminence of the king over the Church in secular matters, and in replacing local systems of dispute resolution.' [13] Hang onto that statement," I said.

"In this pivotal historical 'moment,' we see three things happening. First, local dispute resolution customs that were focused on reconciliation, and the legal processes designed to facilitate that, were appropriated by the king/state. The state took ownership of the process.

"Second, 'justice' becomes not a tool for nonviolent resolution (local customs), but as a weapon wielded in service of establishing and maintaining political power.

"Third, and this is a key point we'll focus on later in our discussion, what we now call retributive justice is accomplished by imposing fines and doing violence to the body.

With state-sponsored public performances of physical violence, the human body has now become an artifact for propaganda. The political power of retributive justice lies in its capacity to use fear and the body in pain, and its memorialization of pain, against itself. I'll explain what I mean by this in greater detail below.

"It's not unreasonable to think, 'Well, that was the Middle Ages,' but the retributive paradigm—the establishment of authority and power by the imposition of punishment and sanctioning—is still the guiding template; not only for our justice system, but in how schools respond to student misconduct; HR departments respond to employee misconduct in the workplace; and parenting discipline practices. The rationale for the infliction of pain, however subtle, remains.

"For example, in a majority of schools, student misconduct is deemed a violation of the student code of conduct. It is the schools' responsibility (right) to *enforce* the code by sanctioning the student. The same is true in the workplace when employees violate the company's code of conduct.

"In parenting, the thinking 'spare the rod, spoil the child' is an axiom of the retributive tradition that transcends generations in families. Why apply physical punishment as a method of discipline? Because …

- That's the way I was disciplined by my parents and teachers.
- The threat and/or application of corporal punishment will serve as a deterrence and prevention of further misbehavior.
- Punishment effectively controls that behavior.
- That's what the experts are telling us we should do.
- It's for your own good."

"That's the way I was disciplined," said Aaron.

"Me too," said Brad. "My old man smacked me."

"Me three," said Barb.

"Me too, but it was my mother," said Devonte.

"It wasn't until we were presented with the evidence of long-term psychological harm resulting from corporal punishment that we began to question its validity."

> **"Nearly one-third of parents in the United States report spanking their children every week, often to detrimental effects and implications.**
>
> **Preschool and school age children—and even adults—[who have been] spanked are more likely to develop anxiety and depression disorders or have more difficulties engaging positively in schools and skills of regulation, which we know are necessary to be successful in educational settings."** [14]
>
> **—Jorge Cuartas**

"However, the punitive paradigm *by virtue of its institutionalization* remains intact," I said.

"It's certainly in our politics," said Brad.

I continued, "Before we dig deeper into the paradigmatic roots of retribution as a justification for violence, I want to restate that hierarchical paradigms are not inherently bad. They are simply an organizational method to enable a collective to accomplish a shared goal and important tasks."

"Like the military," said Brad.

"Exactly," I said.

"It helps to think of a paradigm as an 'organizational tool' that can serve a progressive life-affirming and relationship-centric function, or an 'organizational weapon,' which can be manipulated as a mechanism for ensuring power remains in the hands of a few at the expense of others. When that happens, subordinates within that paradigm avoid challenging those in power because to do so would challenge the legitimacy of the paradigm and their own status within it.

"I want to share a case that I worked on in order to contextualize what I've been saying about power-centrism."

Not Just Theory: A Case of Institutional Centrism

> **Our prayers and support are offered for the victims of sexual abuse and for those whose faith is shaken based upon these actions. [...] The safety and well-being of our students, faculty and staff is paramount as we educate the leaders of our faith and humanity. [...]** [15]

"I want to remind us that at the beginning of our discussion I suggested that as a lens, restoration is both microscopic and panoramic. It can expose the intersection, or convergence, of both an individual's beliefs and thinking, and a larger belief system such as an institutional paradigm.

"I also suggested that exposing the source of these ways of thinking and believing on both a personal and paradigmatic level is risky business—especially when those sources have been deemed morally unassailable.

"There is one case in particular I want to share that demonstrates how 'institutional-centrism' works. I became aware of the case when I was fourteen years old and a sophomore at a Catholic boarding school for boys in the 1970s.

"My older friend (junior) confided in me that he 'had sex' with one of the priests. Both of us were in a 'priesthood-brotherhood program' that was designed to help students who sense they might have 'a spiritual calling' explore what being a priest or brother might look like.

"As my friend explained, it wasn't just one time.

"This priest was in charge of running the campus store which sold soft drinks, candy, and school supplies to students. I remember him showing me and some other boys some pornographic material one time. When I got older, I realized that showing us that material was designed to 'test the waters' to see if any of us was vulnerable. I wasn't. In fact, I left the priesthood/brotherhood program almost immediately.

"I told my friend to report it and he did. He reported it to two other priests who were the administrative heads of the school. Both were prefects.

"In addition to reporting the incidents, my friend explained to both of these priests that he was concerned that the offending priest would also target younger students at the school. Their response was to move my friend out of the offending priest's English class to another. My friend's parents were not informed. According to my friend, no subsequent action or discussions occurred about the sexual abuse while he was a student. It's important to recognize that what classifies this as 'abuse' is because it was initiated and enacted by a person in a position of power and influence. My friend was 16 when it happened. The offending priest took advantage of this young man's developing sexuality.

"The priest remained at the school. I kept my friend's secret for the remainder of my time at the school. After I graduated, I left the Church. I never went back.

"Years later, my friend attended a wedding. The offending priest also attended this wedding. After the ceremony, the priest called my friend and asked him to come to his hotel room. Apparently, the priest was still acting out and no intervention had occurred. My friend hung up on him.

"My friend spoke again with one of the former prefects at the school. This was the same priest to whom he had reported the initial incidents. The former prefect offered my friend 'any assistance he might need' such as therapy or counseling. My friend declined."

Barb interjected. "What the prefect was saying was that the problem is not our failure to address it, but your inability to heal from it."

"I think so," I said. "Whether it was intentional or not, it was a subtle type of gaslighting.

"We would eventually learn that there were several priests at this school who had been accused of sexual abuse over the years. Upon investigation, the allegations were deemed credible. One was the school counselor. Another was in charge of recruiting new students (including me). Both of these priests were at the school when my friend and I were students. Some incidents had occurred long before my friend and I were there. Clearly, this was a pattern.

"In 2000 a priest was 'arrested and charged with 14 counts of indecent solicitation of a child and other crimes, including sodomy, of a 14-year-old boy' over the course of 14 months in 1993–94.[16] This was right around twenty years later than when my friend reported his own abuse.

The parents were lured by the promise the school would provide an 'ideal Christian environment,' a nurturing family atmosphere and "teachers who were willing to go the extra mile" […]

'Father Gilardi enticed [the boy] with tobacco and alcohol and invited him into faculty areas that were ostensibly off-limits to students,' the suit says. 'Making use of empty classrooms and school videotape equipment, Father Gilardi began exposing [the boy] to pornographic materials. Shortly thereafter, Father Gilardi began sexually abusing [the boy].'[17]

"Over the course of forty years, I kept in close contact with my friend and witnessed the residual impact of what had happened to him. It was always on his mind. Always on my mind. Unresolved. There were moments of rage, disgust, shame, and resignation. There was alcohol abuse and depression.

"In 2015, I decided to do something to help my friend. I reached out to the former prefect who offered 'any assistance' to my friend, as well as another priest who was also at the school during the time the abuse happened. This second priest had become the Minister of the Province overseeing the Capuchin Franciscans assigned to the school. One of his responsibilities was to investigate allegations and incidents of sexual abuse by priests. Though he was at the school when the abuse happened, as he explained to me, he was unaware it had occurred.

"Upon deeper investigation, the Minister found no official documentation or report of the molestations committed on my friend in Provincial records. Neither of the two prefects had documented what happened to my friend. The incident was subsumed and suppressed.

"I proposed facilitating a series of discussions between both priests and my friend. The other prefect of the school was in failing health and too incapacitated to participate. The offending priest was deceased. I explained to the former prefect that 'more than anything, Matt wants answers about why the offending priest was not immediately removed from the school, and why he was allowed to continue as a pastor at another local parish. Why was it suppressed?'

"We scheduled a time to meet in person, and I laid out the protocol and agenda for the discussions. I explained that the process would involve a 'Pre-Conference Preparation Interview' conducted individually by me to prepare participants for the group discussion (conference).

"I explained that during the group encounter, we would discuss the incident, why the offending priest wasn't immediately removed, and corrective actions taken by the school, and what the impact had been on Matt. I explained that the outcome of this group discussion would be a 'Reparative Agreement' that would stipulate actions the former prefect and the Province will take to repair harms identified and/or any additional professional support deemed necessary for the continued restoration of Matt.

"I also explained that I would prepare a final report for the participants and the province which would include: (a) chronology of the completed Restorative Process, (b) brief and general review of the issues discussed during the conference, (c) details of the Reparative Agreement, and (d) review of participants' reflections of the entire process and stated satisfaction or dissatisfaction both with the process and its outcomes.

"I had great hope for Matt that, finally, he would get answers to the questions he had been carrying for over four decades. More than anything, I wanted him to be able to speak his truth about what was done to him and how it had impacted his entire life. I earnestly wanted him to find some sense of closure by holding the former prefect directly accountable for his inaction and suppression of the abuse. But I also thought about the potential unburdening and healing that might occur for the former prefect.

"As we got closer to the meeting, Matt backed out. I was disappointed, but I understood why. 'What's going to make anything happen now? Fr. "Gary" is dead,' he said. 'All I wanted was answers and for them to apologize. None of them ever apologized. Now it wouldn't make any difference if they did,' he added. I silently disagreed about the 'not making any difference' statement, but respected his wishes and cancelled the process. I also reminded him that the fact that both priests were willing to meet with him and discuss what happened demonstrated their commitment to helping Matt find healing and closure.

"It is my belief that had we been able to have this discussion, the suppression would've been held accountable, or at least there would have been an understanding of how it happened and why. The prefect's thinking and reasons would've been accounted for. Most importantly, Matt might've experienced a depth of justice he had been longing for his entire life. He didn't want to punish the prefect. He just wanted answers."

Turning back to our discussion group, I said, "Looking through the restorative lens of accountability to better understand why this happened—both the abuse and the lack of immediate response—foregrounds the manner in which an institution's interests can take precedence over people's well-being.

"It would be convenient to just blame the two school leaders who failed to report it and/or address it by removing the perpetrator from the school. Certainly, they should have been held accountable for their decisions. But I think it's more constructive to ask, 'why didn't they act?' Why didn't these two school leaders (or other individual priests who might've known it was happening) make it *immediately* known to the community that it had happened or was happening? What were the pressures or anxieties they had to deal with?

"Though Matt and I will never know for certain because we never got the chance to ask, I think one answer lies in the potential damage it would've done to the reputation of both the school and the local Franciscan prelate had 'the story' gotten out. Another possible reason might've been that they were simply ill-prepared to respond to such a severe violation. Keep in mind this was the seventies.

"But maybe there was a deeper reason. Maybe this type of behavior was endemic. Eventually, twelve friars with connections to local churches in the surrounding area would be found to have 'credible allegations' of sexual misconduct.[18]

"Their response (lack of) when it happened was what we've been describing as *institutional-centrism*. The reputation, interests, and protection of the institution and its leaders and members took priority over the well-being of an individual. That centrism can lead to suppression of a survivor's voice for fear of being shamed or excluded and potentially victim-blamed. As well, any status of 'sacred trust' ascribed to friars and priests might've been compromised. The opposite of faith is suspicion.

"The result was not only a traumatized young man who spent the next forty-plus years of his life trying to find resolution on his own, but also a failure to implement measures that might have prevented other students from abuse.

I asked our discussion group, "What comes up for you after hearing about this case?"

"Anger," said Barb. "This is just one more example of how the Catholic Church protects sexual predators. How many more of these stories do we have to hear about? If ever there was a valid reason for retribution and punishment, it is this," she added.

"In this case, I suggest that 'retribution' would've been motivated by the need for transparency and to protect the students by removing the priests and ensure they wouldn't do it again. So, however much anger was felt by those who were impacted, the necessity for retribution was driven by the need to know the truth and protect rather than revenge.

"My question is, 'Why didn't the prefects expose this immediately and take the necessary actions to remove any of the priests who were committing the violations?' I also think that had word 'gotten out' that it happened, enrollment in the school might have decreased. So maybe there was a financial reason for suppressing it.

"The point I'm trying to make is that this is an example of how an institution's reputation, its centrism, its self-identity, guarded by its members can take priority over the well-being of some of its members who would not have been victims if it weren't for their membership in that institution; in this case, a parochial institution. Reputation took precedence over accountability leading to restoration.

"I've often thought about how other priests who were at the school might've been impacted by what these offending priests did. Or, how they might've felt if they knew it was happening and felt pressured to keep it a secret. There were some remarkable priests, brothers, and teachers at this school. The academic aspect to this school was exceptional. I'm sure the abuse hurt them as well. Think about the violation of trust they must have felt. And let's not forget the community. Think about how their trust was violated.

"This is just depressing," said Aaron. "I can see how had that discussion between your friend and the priests happened, it could've brought some closure to your friend. And you," he added.

"And opened a few closets," added Barb.

"What comes up for me is how powerful shame is," said Brad. "Shame motivates protection and suppression. The irony here is ugly. Men responsible for teaching young men about God or becoming leaders, instead, commit one of the most heinous crimes and 'in shame,' suppress it," he said.

"My question is 'what is their conception of God?' I asked."

"It's not just Christians," said Melissa. "Shaming is human," she added.

"On an institutional level, shaming is a rhetorical strategy," I said. "This seems like a good transition into talking about a master narrative of original retribution and shaming," I suggested. "We've looked at the justice system as being a vertical paradigm with power at the top, but what happens when a story of origin establishes a blueprint or model for that hierarchy, and the persona of God is one of both creator and shamer?" I asked. "Because it's not just a religious blueprint, it's also a social blueprint."

Stories of Origin

I reminded our group of the questions in the five-step restorative process:

1. What happened?
2. Who was impacted, and what was that impact?
3. What are any underlying motivations, reasons, or issues we can identify that explain why it happened?
4. What do people need?
5. How can we meet those needs—what's our plan?

"I want to shift our focus from the justice system and institutionalized paradigm of retribution to *stories of origin*—those stories that serve as a foundational master explanation for how human beings came to exist, why we exist, and establish expectations for how human beings should relate not only to authority and each other, but ourselves, the natural world, and the cosmos; the unexplainable 'great beyond.'"

"This sounds like Joseph Campbell," said Brad. "Mythology," he added.

"Campbell looked at stories of origin and their ritual reenactments that explain 'how we got here' and what that means. He was concerned with myths, but also the actions or behaviors those myths directed. He also looked at how those stories became internalized both on an individual level, and in a larger cultural or social consciousness over time," I said.

"Like archetypes," added Brad.

"Yes. That 'collective subconsciousness,' as Carl Jung might describe, and those beliefs provide a blueprint, an orientation so to speak, for how people treat each other. But we're going to use a slightly different frame to interpret a story of origin. We're going to be doing a bit of rhetorical analysis, looking at how pain, punishment, and the threat of both function rhetorically to establish a persona of unquestionable power, dominance, and control," I said.

"Sacred punishment," said Devonte.

"Sacred violence," added Brad.

"Yes. The instant we designate something as 'sacred,' we've given it extraordinary power over our imagination. The reason that we're looking at a story of origin is because even though we may think that this story is archaic and solely 'religious in context,' the fact is it is still relevant by nature of the paradigm, the worldview it established and the social institutions we've built based on that 'top-down' worldview."

"Like justice," said Barb.

"Yeah. Religion, justice, family, education, politics, etc. Most important, it's a blueprint or 'cognitive schema' for how human beings should relate to each other and the environment. It is *the* master script that has directed Anglo-European thinking for centuries. My point is that even though we may not think the story is believable anymore, it's relevant because of how profoundly entrenched it is in cultural memory and how it has influenced our subconscious collective view of reality," I explained.

"So, in other words, a person doesn't have to believe the story for the story to have an effect?" asked Aaron.

"Exactly," I said.

"But before we look at Genesis, we need to know a bit about how stories work. This understanding will help us when we get to talking about restoration, restorative practices, and restorative communication. For now, I'll just say that restoration uses storytelling much differently than how it is used in western retributive justice and misconduct practices like in schools and workplaces. Retributive justice uses stories to determine guilt or innocence. Restorative justice uses stories to discover what needs to be repaired or healed."

Storytelling Beings

"Human beings are storytelling beings. We think in terms of language and narrative (story).[19] This means that we rely on symbols, stories, and personal narratives to 'literally make sense' of any event, experience, or situation. When we tell a story about something that happened, might have happened, or is happening, we're constructing a view of reality, a 'schema,' or a 'type of theory for what happened' (Sunwolf & Frey 2001).[20]

"At the same time, the stories we tell function psychologically to construct both personal and social identity. As Hauser (2002) explained, the stories we tell ourselves and others about ourselves and others define who we think we are and 'are developed in the context of communities to which we belong: family, religion, locale, nation, profession, ethnicity, language, education, sexual orientation, gender, organization, and so forth.'[21] What this means is that the stories we construct about our experience embody paradigms, worldviews, cultural values, and foundational beliefs.

"Because human beings are so dependent on language and story to make sense of our experience, we are vulnerable to the persuasive (rhetorical) power that language and narrative have on our imagination. Our ability to use language and story to interpret and construct a 'reality' and our identity distinguishes us as a species but gets us into trouble. Our words can build bridges or start wars.

"Literary theorist and philosopher Kenneth Burke (1897–1993) remarked that humans are 'symbol-using, symbol-misusing animals.' [22] Our ability to use language and story often keeps us from becoming what we're fully capable of as *human* beings as Abrahams (1986) suggests.

> **"We now acknowledge that all life involves the construction of agreed-upon fictions and that the least harmful, the least hegemonic, are those that assert self-worth. All terms connected with institutional practice become a little suspect because of the power distribution and systems of control they have carried with them."** [23] **(Abrahams 1986)**

"Our words and stories can liberate us or punish us. We can see this happening throughout history, and currently as our nation (and world) struggles (often violently) to define a future and an identity as a species. The use of language and narratives as either tools and/or weapons is as old as storytelling itself.

"But stories and narratives are also 'symbolic spaces' of contestation. This means that we can challenge that story, that version, what it means, and the logic it attempts to argue. We'll see this demonstrated in a restorative justice case I'll share with you later in our discussion.

"Langellier (1999) emphasized that narratives are 'sites of struggle' where those cultural and social relationships that both sustain and constitute narrators' identities *materialize and become contestable*. In this vulnerable, potentially *performative* moment, 'the forces of discourse, the institutionalized networks of power relations,' all of which constitute the subjectivity of both narrator and audience, materialize and become apparent. Langellier suggested that in this liminal space, negotiation of personal, cultural, and social identities occurs." [24]

I said to our group, "In simpler terms, it means that when a story is told, it reveals more than just an account of what happened or is happening. It represents and reveals something about ourselves. It reveals who we think we are in the telling, and what we believe about ourselves not only personally, but also as a community or nation with a history.

"Take the myth of 'The Lost Cause' and how some tell the story of the Civil War as being not about slavery and emancipation, but about suppression and a violation of states' rights, 'white culture,' supremacy, and white values in the South. That story/myth interprets the Civil War as a war of oppression which 'casts white people' as victims of Northern aggression," I said.

"It's a false narrative," said Devonte.

"It is to us, but for those that believe it it's not. When we hold that story accountable for being false, we're not only contesting the veracity, but also the thinking that continues it. What Langellier is saying is that when that story is told, the story is functioning as a performative act of personal and collective identity construction—'by telling this story in this way I'm not only constructing a view of reality, but I'm constructing who I think I am, who we think "we" are, and who we think "you" are.' I have a social-psychologist friend who interprets the myth of the 'Lost Cause' as a strategy to deflect or avoid feelings of 'organic shame' inherent to slave ownership. Believing you're the victim is a way to circumvent or avoid the truth that you were, in fact, the offender."

Devonte added, "That victim narrative fueled and justified retaliation against Black people."

"Yes. It did and it still does. That story served as a tool for preserving the myth of white supremacy, but also a weapon as it scapegoated Black people and attempted to justify racism and violence against them. At the same time, that narrative fueled the construction of the institution of Jim Crow laws. Think about those who tell the story that the assault on the U.S. Capitol on January 6th was a 'peaceful protest.' My point, and I believe what Langellier's observations show us, is that stories and narratives are extremely powerful agents in establishing, justifying, or furthering the hatred and dehumanization of others," I said. "What we'll see happen in restorative practices is that storytelling is used to liberate and rehumanize."

"Wow," said Kris.

"Yeah. But here's the thing. And this will become clear when I share about a particular case later in our discussion. What Langellier means by 'sites of struggle and contestation' is that when that story is told, it creates the opportunity for us to say, 'Wait a minute, that doesn't ring true for me. I am not who you portray me as, and neither are we as a community. And by the way ... we don't believe that is who you are either.'"

"That's dangerous," said Devonte.

"It is. But what's more dangerous is not contesting it," I said.

"In this particular case that I'll share, we were able to identify and confront 'the forces and underlying reasons' that led to an offender committing an act of violence. We were able to show this offender that while they are responsible for what they did, 'it wasn't them, but what was told to them and done to them' that motivated their thinking and behavior. We pointed out how they were acting out of that story and that it was not only false, but also self-destructive. But I'm getting ahead of myself.

"The obvious point I'm trying to make here is that stories are not be taken for granted. Whether true, accurate, or not, they have the power—especially when they are continued through history—to establish worldviews, paradigms, and institutions. They have the power to justify behavior and in the context of our discussion here, the justification for retribution.

"With stories of origin, those first narratives that serve as *foundational 'sacred' explanations* of how and why life began, and what relationship human beings have within the cosmos, what happens when that story carries within it the implicit threat of divinely ordained retributive violence? Like I asked a moment ago, what happens when 'the Creator' is also 'the Punisher'? What happens when the master narrative carries within it a warning to never contest the story, challenge the Narrator, or attempt to negotiate power relations established in that story? How does this impact our beliefs about justice?" I asked.

"Fascism and dictatorships," said Devonte.

"Brainwashing," said Barb.

"Trauma," added Kris.

"Hang onto that, Kris," I said. "Because I think you're onto something about how stories of threat can activate our survival instincts and overwhelm our perception or imagination, and suppress critical thinking," I added. "This is a good segue into talking about the relationship between pain and punishment, and how language and story can exploit that relationship to establish uncontestable authority.

"However, before I move us into the rhetorical power of pain and its conversion into the political power of retribution, I want to provide a bit of backstory. Because we're going to be looking at how Genesis 'sanctified retribution,' I want to explain what motivated my search for this understanding and how I was introduced to the work of Elaine Scarry (1985)."

Body of Christ/Body of Man

"I have a great-grandfather on my mother's side of the family who was a member of a Hispanic Catholic Brotherhood (Los Hermanos de Nuestro Padre Jesus, Nazareno) in New Mexico in the mid to late 1800s. The Brotherhood practiced ritual penitential self-mortification. They made the story of Jesus, his persecution, physically evident in their rituals of devotion.

"To the outsider, flagellation and self-inflicted punishment as a performance of penance may seem archaic. In fact, the practice existed in Europe long before the Spanish came into New Mexico," I said. "It's still an expression of religious fervor today in many parts of the world during Holy Week."

"It's not just Catholics," added Devonte. "Some fundamentalist Shia Muslims practice this too."

"Right, and in both traditions it's about using the body, and more specifically, the infliction of pain, to legitimize a religious text. And in both traditions it has often been condemned as an aberration by religious leaders.

"In my own extended family (especially my grandfather), many disparaged 'Los Penitentes' as a cult. Even the Church in the late 1700s attempted to prohibit penitential acts and distance itself from an expression they considered to be archaic zealotry.

"But my thinking was that the extreme physical penance my great-grandfather practiced had to have some profound religious creative significance because the Brotherhood was unwilling to abandon their practices when the Church became more 'institutionally established in New Mexico.' Penance, and more precisely, physical pain through whipping, was providing an intimate encounter with the figure of Jesus that had enabled Hispanic Catholics to spiritually negotiate tremendous hardships, and without the presence of clergy.

"In many of the small villages in northern New Mexico and southern Colorado during this time, the Catholic Church's ecclesiastical presence (priests and friars) was almost nonexistent, sporadic at best.

> **Persons in peripheral communities, as well as many inhabitants, especially the poorer ones, of core settlements were thus left largely to their own devices in religious matters.**[25]

"In local civil matters, the Spanish government in Santa Fe was equally absent. Consequently, villagers established their own communal authority and provided for their own welfare. The hardship was great. In 1780 a devastating smallpox epidemic hit New Mexico. Albuquerque, San Felipe, Cubero (which was my great-grandfather's village), Santa Cruz, Pecos, Santa Fe, Chimayo ... all the towns and pueblos along the Rio Grande suffered immensely.[26]

"Considering the lack of any adequate means to combat such an unexplainable and deadly foe, the Brotherhood, in whatever semi-formal administrative structure it may have resembled, either began or became more organized in an attempt to provide what the Church and State could not—faith, religion, governance, welfare and charity, and perhaps most importantly a sense of security and stability in the face of a debilitating adversity."

"So, they took matters into their own hands," said Brad.

"Literally," I said. "What better way to establish or 'anchor' the authenticity of the story of Jesus than through a physical reenactment of his suffering, persecution, crucifixion, sacrifice, and ultimate resurrection? The Brotherhood inscribed this narrative on their own bodies not only for themselves, but for others in the village to experience visually and sensorially. Jesus' suffering was not a concept but an embodied reality.

> **They embodied in their own bodies His agony, His scourging, His crowning with thorns, His carrying of the cross to Calvario, His being fastened to it and raised from the earth.**[27]
>
> **The body is not simply an element in a scene of confirmation; it is the confirmation.**[28]

"So, off of the text and onto the body," commented Devonte.

"That's a great way to put it. The body became the text, but it was the sensation of pain and the reason for the infliction of that pain that legitimized that story for the believers. The dynamics of pain, the ways in which the sensation of pain removes any doubt in the believer's mind about the experience ('factualness') of Christ's suffering, reveals why pain is such a powerful persuasive source for establishing the unquestionable authority of a narrative.

"What we'll see in our next discussion is that the human body in its most vulnerably embodied state of pain becomes at once the most verifiably nonnegotiable justification of divine retribution."

Pain, Punishment, Power, the Body, and Imagination

"As a matter of definition, the word *pain* has its roots in the Latin word *poena,* which translates literally as 'punishment.'[29] Etymologically, the two terms are indistinguishable. While revenge and/or retaliation may be the motive, and retribution the justification, fundamentally, punishment is about the infliction of pain on another human being(s) (or ourselves).

"As Elaine Scarry (1985) suggests, one of the reasons why punishment and the threat of punishment is so powerful is because rhetorically, it uses our own private and interior factual experience of pain, our memory of it, and our own vulnerability and fear of pain, against us. What Scarry is suggesting is that retribution and the threat of punishment uses the vulnerable body, its sentience, and our attempt to comprehend it (imagination of it) as a rhetorical weapon against itself."[30]

Kris spoke up. "So, in other words, if a parent hits a child, they're using the child's experience of pain to establish their unquestionable authority and rationale. Or in the case of domestic violence, the abuser is using the victim's memory of their experience of pain to threaten and retraumatize them. The abuser doesn't necessarily have to commit another act of violence. It's the victim's memory that continues to empower the abuser. Is that right?" she asked.

"Exactly. If I understand Scarry correctly, it is our interior experience of pain, its 'all-consuming reality,' and our mind's struggle to comprehend it that authorizes or empowers 'the punisher' to provide the rationale. Statements such as, 'You deserve this,' 'It's your fault,' 'You caused it,' 'This wouldn't be happening to you if you hadn't done what you did,' are emblematic. In essence, the 'meaning' of the pain, the reason or justification for the pain is determined not by the person experiencing it, but by the person/entity causing it. It is, perhaps, the ultimate gaslighting or 'victim blaming.'

"As Scarry suggests, it is the projection of the interior of the human body, its sentience, its vulnerability to pain, its experience of physical pain, onto an object/artifact (or persona) that then endows that artifact with meaning or significance, and consequently, the power of that artifact (e.g., a symbol or a narrative) to reciprocate a projection back to the body, affecting the body's experience of itself.[31]

"I know that sounds really esoteric and conceptual, but what she's saying is that artifacts are endowed with the extraordinary power to alter the body's experience of itself. It's a transaction. We project our pain, and an artifact provides the reason for it. We need to remember that stories are artifacts.

"One example Scarry (1985) uses is a bandage. In the attempt to solve the problem of torn skin, a bandage is created to perform the work of the skin. When placed over the wound, the bandage effectively *relieves the sentient problem* and thus alters the body's experience of itself. A bandage, as an artifact, is essentially a tool.

"The same could be said of a chair, made or created to perform the labor of the spine and legs in supporting the body. Even the earliest of human inventions, tools, were created to perform the work of the hands and fingers in the production of food or clothing. They were extensions of the human body in a positive way. Bandages, chairs, and clothing are good. They 'reflexively point to' a resolution of a need.

"In Scarry's terms, the meaning of these artifacts is based on both our historical physical and imaginative relationship with them; our sentient memory of them. Think about how the sight of a chair feels, however subtly, after we've been standing for too long.

"However, and this is important to understanding how the language of violence and wounding attain so much power, when this dynamic of sentient endowment involves the projection of pain, the process of signifying an object/artifact, interpreting what it means, is unique. The sensation of pain and its memorialization within the body is capable of resignifying already created objects/artifacts in ways that *rather than point to resolution or relief*, instead, point to the power to destroy; to 'unmake the world of the person threatened or punished.'"

> **"What is quite literally at stake in the body in pain is the making and unmaking of the world."**
> **—Elaine Scarry** [32]

"The example Scarry provides is a hammer. A hammer was originally intended (created) to perform the work of the hands. It's a tool. But when the hammer is instead turned against the surface of the skin, against the body, it becomes a weapon in our imagination. It is the fact of pain, its undeniability, that determines and verifies its meaning and identity of that artifact. Our vulnerability to pain can serve to reinterpret a tool as a weapon.

> **The hammer that hammers a man to a cross is a weapon and the hammer used to construct the cross itself is a tool.** [33]

"Another example is a belt. A belt is created to hold pants up. But when a child is whipped by a belt, the belt becomes a weapon. I'll explain more about an example of this when I get into talking about my own story, but to this day, when I see a skinny leather belt, I have a sense memory of being whipped. In this way, the identity of that belt shifted from tool to weapon and remained in memory. The rationale for using the belt as a weapon is provided by the person/parent doing the whipping," I explained.

"Like when a parent says, 'You brought this on yourself,'" said Barb.

"That's it," I replied.

"What Scarry is saying is that what signifies, or determines, the artifact's different identities is the different relationship it has, the projection it receives from the human body. The tool is one of creation. Conversely, the recognizable intentional action behind the weapon is the exact opposite, unmaking or wounding," I said.

"This is really trippy stuff," said Aaron.

"Scarry makes two additional points about artifacts that can help us understand why punishment and punitive thinking have become so entrenched, and thus, so difficult (if not impossible) to relinquish.

"First, artifacts are shareable. As such, the relationship the body has with that artifact is communicable socially. Second, because of this sentient memorialization, the power of the artifact as a weapon is able to maintain its signification, or 'identity of authority,' in a self-substantiating way *across history, long after any specific instance of body alteration occurs.*"

"This is what Derrida was saying," said Devonte.

"I think so. The logic is straightforward. The 'fact' of pain, its undeniability, is a deeply personal and private experience that Scarry suggests 'obliterates' the conscious contents of our imagination. It is a consuming experience.

"But when the experience of pain is projected onto an artifact to be shared, like a story, that artifact is endowed with profound social and political power to establish an authority-by-threat over the collective human imagination.

"Think about how the symbol of a swastika continues to harm with the acts of violence it represents, literally "re-presents" and has memorialized. It's the sign of a weapon representing the most inhumane destruction of life. That memorialization remains (and should remain) in our cultural psyche as a threat," I said.

"Think about all the statues of historical figures who committed atrocities. These are socially memorialized symbols that continue to threaten the body. Think about mascots in sports that confiscate Native American identities. They are socially shared symbols but invoke a deeply personal and historical cultural experience of violence, injustice, pain, and suffering. Think about the former president holding a Bible up. In that moment, with that gesture, was the Bible a tool, or a weapon?"

"An upside-down weapon," said Barb.

"The fact that it was upside-down is prophetic," said Devonte.

"This process of resignification is happening with the America flag," said Brad. "The flag has always symbolized unity, 'these United States.' But when I see the ultra-right or

Trump supporters waving the flag like they did during the assault on the Capitol, they're weaponizing it to further dissension and violence."

"The identity of the flag has been converted to mean its exact opposite. Disunion.

"I realize this explanation is complex and perhaps better suited for the fields of cultural studies, linguistics, philosophy, and maybe politics. But from a rhetorical perspective, Scarry's exploration of pain and its sentient endowment of artifacts points to the power of language and narrative, both of which are artifacts. Like I said, stories are artifacts. We created them.

"Just as a hammer, flag, or mascot can carry within it the memorialization of both tool and weapon depending on its relationship with the human body, so too can a narrative carry within it this ambiguity. Hang on to that term 'ambiguity.'

"This is what Scarry suggests is happening in the story of Genesis, which she is identifying as a narrative artifact."

> **Divine power has a visible substantiation in the alterations in body tissue it is able to bring about. Man can only be created once, but once created he can be endlessly modified; wounding re-enacts the creation because it re-enacts the power of alteration that has its first profound occurrence in creation.**[34]

"Employing the dynamics of projection/appropriation/reciprocation and signification, it becomes possible to distinguish the role of the body's vulnerability to alteration in both establishing and substantiating the narrative authority of God in the Old Testament," I said.

"The omnipotent judge," said Aaron.

"The 'original author' who we never see but can only believe uncontestably exists," I added.

"We need to remember that the Old Testament can be appreciated as a *foundational narrative* that has profoundly influenced the evolution of western justice thinking and codes of discipline.

"According to Scarry, the disembodied Voice of God only becomes apprehensible to the human mind and imagination in the changes 'God' is able to author in the human body through scenes of reproduction and wounding:

God's invisible presence is asserted, made visible, in the perceivable alterations He brings about in the human body: in the necessity of human labor and the pains of childbirth, in a flood that drowns, in a plague that descends on a house, in the brimstone and fire falling down on a city, in the transformation of a woman into a pillar of salt, in the leprous sores and rows of boils that alter the surface of the skin, in an invasion of insects and reptiles into the homes of a population, in a massacre of babies, in a ghastly hunger that causes a people to so glut themselves on quail that the meat comes out of their nostrils, in a mauling by bears, in an agonizing disease of the bowels, and so on, on and on.[35]

"Scarry explains that in scenes of multiplication, it is God's voice which pre-empts human reproduction:

Genesis is filled not only with the emphatic material reality of the forever multiplying human body, but with God's voice which takes two different forms, a command ('Be fruitful and multiply') and a promise ('You will be fruitful and multiply'"(13:16) ... 'Look toward heaven, and number the stars, if you are able to number them ... so shall your descendants be' (15:5) ... 'Behold ... you shall be the father of a multitude of nations ... I have made you the father of a multitude of nations.' (17:4, 5)[36]

"It is through the promise or command of God's voice that the multiplication of humanity becomes understood as a 're-enactment of the original creation.'[37] Perhaps the most evident scene of body tissue alteration is the 'making' of Eve from Adam.

"The persona of God's presence within the narrative of human multiplication and reproduction is verbal and consequently, *outside the realm of matter.* In other words, God's disembodied voice accompanies human events but never materially or physically enters them. To put it bluntly, God doesn't have a body. As such, the narrative voice functions as an artifact, not 'of the human body,' but endowed with the ultimate power to affect the experience of the body.

> **The literal event of procreation and multiplication is never simply an event in and of itself but becomes in the first form an obedient acting out of the thing that had come before, and in the second form a divine fulfillment of the thing that had come before ... in both instances an alteration in the sheer quantity of human matter is given a referent that is profoundly immaterial.**[38]

"What is important to recognize here is that the human body is able not only to substantiate itself materially, through its own feeling, through its own sentience, but that *it is also capable of substantiating something beyond itself,* mainly the immaterial Voice of God.

"The magnification of humanity which occurs through the scenes of reproduction benefits both human beings and God. Yet, in the scenes of wounding, the exact opposite occurs. Although in both instances, it is the human body which verifies and validates the 'reality of God,' in the act of wounding, it is the contraction of people which substantiates the authority of the Narrative Voice—and *establishes the uncontestable divine justification of retribution and punishment:*

'Their flesh shall rot while they are still on their feet, their eyes shall rot in their sockets, and their tongues shall rot in their mouths. And on that day a great panic

from the Lord shall fall on them, so that each will lay hold on the hand of his fellow, and the hand of the one will be raised against the hand of the other.' (Zechariah 14:12–14) [39]

"The relationship between God and the human body in scenes of multiplication is, as was mentioned earlier, mediated only by the body's physical alteration. In scenes of wounding, however, this relationship of power-over is *mediated by a separate third sign*, a weapon.

"In this instance, the sign of the weapon becomes the material sign of God's power, whether actually present or verbally implied, whether it is an actual weapon or it is the appearance of a now malevolent occurrence of nature.

> **"I will spend my arrows upon them; / they shall be wasted with hunger and devoured with burning heat; / and poisonous pestilence ... If I whet my glittering sword ... I will make my arrows drunk with blood."** **(Deuteronomy 32)** [40]

"Scarry states that though the occasion for wounding is often described as a result of disobedience, it can also be understood as *a scene of doubt*, a failure to accurately imagine God's existence.

Unable to apprehend God with conviction, they will—after the arrival of the plague or the disease-laden quail or the fire or the sword or the storm—apprehend him in the intensity of the pain in their own bodies, or in the visible alteration in the bodies of their fellows or in the bodies of their enemies. [41]

The infliction of hurt is explicitly presented as a 'sign' of God's realness and therefore a solution to the problem of his unreality, his fictiveness." [42]

"Can I interrupt?" asked Devonte.

"Always," I replied.

"So, a lack of faith is a reason for retribution?" he asked.

"Yes. Justifiable divine punishment," I said.

"Wait," said Brad. "This is exactly what is happening with Trump. A lack of 'faith' in him is his justifiable reason for revenge and retribution," he said.

"A lack of faith implies a failure of the human imagination to remake one's interior in the image of God," I said. "In this instance, it's the image of Trump. That dynamic of how the imagination is manipulated into 'endowing' unquestionable authority is, well, Biblical."

> **They refused to hearken, and turned a stubborn shoulder ... they made their hearts like adamant lest they should hear the law and the words.** **(Zechariah 7:11, 12)**

> They refused to take correction. They have made their faces harder than rock. (Jeremiah 5:3)
>
> He who hardens his heart will fall into calamity. (Proverbs 28:14)
>
> He who is often reproved yet stiffens his neck will suddenly be broken beyond healing. (Proverbs 29:1)

"Wounding, punishment, and the sign of a weapon become a means by which God perceptually overwhelms human resistance (doubt) through threat of violence, enforcing 'his' identity through the very real factualness of human sentience and even more potently, pain. Remember, this is all happening in a story, a created narrative artifact."

"Men wrote the Bible," said Barb. "And the idea of 'God' was used as a weapon for social control?" she asked.

"Interesting observation," I said. "Though it may appear that belief simply accompanies an absolute surrender of the interior of the human body or that surrender is required of belief, Scarry says it is instead *the dynamics of belief* itself, an extension or projection of the most 'concrete and intimate parts of oneself with an objectified referent.'[43] The act of believing, faith itself, has become a mandate by the threat of violence and the factual reality of our vulnerability to pain."

Brad interjected, "So in essence, faith is enforced through fear of violence."

"Yes. I think so," I said.

> Belief is the act of imagining. It is what the act of imagining is called when the object created is credited with more reality than oneself. It is when the object created is in fact described as though it instead created you. It ceases to be the 'offspring' of the human being and becomes the thing from which the human being himself sprung forth ... it is not simply the willingness to give one's interior to something outside oneself but the willingness to become the created offspring of the thing in whose presence one now stands.[44]

"Let me try to summarize this extremely complex and mind-bending rhetorical analysis. Beginning with pain's certainty, its totality, or potential for consuming the contents of consciousness and our imagination, and then continuing with pain's 'non-directional' projection or its 'objectless-ness,' its appropriation or capture of meaning by an artifact existing outside the boundaries of the body becomes the method by which the identity of power/authority is formed.

"The human embodiment of that artifact (God's Voice) requires the projection of the facts of sentience into it which establishes and substantiates its power over sentience.

Inherent to this capture or appropriation is the obscuring of the site of origin, *the human body*. It overwhelms our ability to recognize it as a created artifact, a story, a fiction.

"It is within this dynamic of appropriation that awareness of the cause of the pain or body alteration is transformed as *human belief*, and further permits the conflation of the former identity of a tool into a weapon."

> **The Lord saw how great the wickedness of the human race had become on the earth, and that every inclination of the thoughts of the human heart was only evil all the time. The Lord regretted that he had made human beings on the earth, and his heart was deeply troubled. So the Lord said, "I will wipe from the face of the earth the human race I have created— and with them the animals, the birds and the creatures that move along the ground—for I regret that I have made them." (Genesis 6:5–7 NIV)** [45]

"I want to reframe this rhetorical analysis within our evolving understanding of neuropsychology. Kris, I think this might be what you were referring to. We know that humans have a 'primal survival brain' which reacts to threat in three ways: fight, flight, or freeze. In the case of this story, if we fight, we will be overpowered and annihilated. If we flee, we will be caught—there is nowhere to hide from an 'all knowing and all-seeing God.' This is the story of Adam and Eve after biting the apple of knowledge. They had nowhere to hide. If we freeze, we will be blamed and shamed for not having enough faith."

"So, if I understand this, pain and the threat of pain makes us vulnerable to any rationale being provided by the punisher," said Devonte.

"That's exactly it," I replied. "We never challenge it, for to do so would lead to punishment. The threat of violence, retribution, and pain keeps us from voicing our doubts. Is it any wonder why politicians use this same rhetorical strategy to 'scare people' into voting for them?"

"Hitler. Mussolini. Trump," said Brad.

Silence.

A Brief Summary

"Stories of origin are foundational explanations which *literally* establish a worldview; an original paradigm for how we got here and how we should relate to the cosmos and each other. This particular story of origin is arguably "the master narrative" or sponsoring cultural artifact that has been central to western Judeo-Christian civilization, relationships, and thinking about justice as retribution.

"As I said earlier, we may think 'we don't believe this anymore' or 'this story is archaic,' but the power of origin stories we consider to be 'sacred' lies in their ability to establish an unassailable reality, a version of history, and transcend that history while simultaneously directing or influencing a future history.

"As Scarry implies, we may or may not recognize the source of that influence. That is the nature of created artifacts. Once created, they can obscure the fact that they are, in fact, human creations or constructs.

"One could argue that this obscurity is what keeps them from being challenged, and thus, ensures the continuation of their power over human imagination and social experience across time. The justification for retribution and the legitimacy of violence as a component of retribution is inscribed in 'social consciousness.'

"In essence, the story doesn't have to be 'believed in' anymore for the residual social influence of the paradigm/worldview it established to continue to direct thinking," I said.

Devonte said, "Now, your earlier comment about how retribution creates its own opportunity for opposition and then overpowering that objection through threat of violence makes sense."

"I hope so because my point is that retribution and its conflation as justifiable, divinely justifiable violent retaliation is so interwoven into western human consciousness that restoration is literally 'fighting a fight that was created by the philosophy of retribution itself,'" I said.

"So, what role does Jesus play?" asked Melissa.

"I'd like to suggest that Jesus, the story of Jesus, the New Testament, is the reconciliation of that original wounding," said Devonte.

"What do you mean?" I asked.

"The story of Jesus converts or reverts faith back into a tool," he said. "If the Old Testament used faith as a weapon of submission to a wrathful God, the story of Jesus resignifies or reinterprets the identity of God as a loving father."

"What happened in the end?" I asked.

"The sign of the weapon reasserted itself in the image of the cross. It's what you were saying about Derrida's claim that retribution sets up an opportunity for its own reestablishment," he said. "In the end, it's the power of retribution executed by the Pharisees that won."

"I agree that the sign of the weapon reasserted itself, but I'm not so sure it won. Because what did Jesus's surrender represent?" I asked.

"The ultimate nonviolent response to violence," said Melissa.

"I think so. His act of surrender signified nonnegotiable compassion at all costs. He forgave the people consumed with retribution. He demonstrated compassion for his persecutors. As an 'artifact,' the New Testament re-storied what human beings are capable of by demonstrating our own vulnerability to pain but showed us that the restorative justice answer might be unconditional forgiveness. The justification for retribution and the legitimacy of violence as a component of retribution is inscribed in 'social consciousness,'" I said. "Forgive them, for they know not what they do."

"But what about accountability?" asked Aaron.

"Good question. I think that by demonstrating compassion, he was also demonstrating an understanding of the political forces, the cultural mindsets, the underlying issues and paradigms that his persecutors were operating out of. So, in effect, he realized that it 'wasn't them' but a story they were acting out. But in the end, what did his forgiveness provide?" I asked.

"Resurrection," said Devonte.

"And restoration. Restoration of a relationship with something far deeper and beyond human imperfection. A restoration of inherent human dignity as a possibility," I said. "In the end, 'it is the peacemakers who shall inherit the earth,' it says in the Beatitudes. Restoration is a way to make peace for sure, but the story of Jesus is telling us it isn't easy. Restoration requires sacrifice. We have to sacrifice, or surrender, our own penchant for judgment and retribution. We have to 'let go' of our retributive thinking.

"I want to summarize what we've discussed before we reflect on what I've said.

"The evidence that the paradigm established in Genesis (and the Old Testament in general) continues to influence us can be found in current ways of thinking about justice, gender, and the relationship that human beings have with nature. Archaic or not, the relevance and influence of this particular 'master' story of origin remains. It is a subconscious template:

- Relationships are configured along a vertical axis of descending power with an uncontestable dominant but disembodied male God at the top, man-as-created by God in his image just below, woman as subservient to both, the natural world subordinate to, and exploitable by, both God and the human being.
- The manner/agency in which this axis of subordination is 'kept in line' is through justifiable retribution, violence, punishment, pain, and the threat of both.

"If we look at this story of origin as a paradigmatic 'first' narrative, which for thousands of years has served as a master monologue/metaphor for how human beings should relate to the cosmos, each other, and the environment, we can see how punishment and the infliction of pain as an agency of authority and overpowering are deemed necessary and *justifiable* as responses to disbelief, human misconduct, antisocial behavior, and resistance. 'If God does it and we're made in "His" image, it must be okay for us to do it too, and to each other.'

"This highlights your quoting of the former president, 'I am your retribution,'" said Aaron.

"Yes. In that statement the man has become an artifact of retribution. Not a human being, but a symbol of a weapon. His scowling mugshot is the symbol of a weapon that embodies the threat of hateful revenge. But we can also see how this artifact of retribution has justified the confiscation of women's bodies (and reproduction itself). Look at how the former president has treated women.

"In this narrative context, it becomes 'justifiable' that women's bodies are property to be possessed and legislated over. Perhaps the sign of the serpent is an attempt at symbolic justification for condemning and/or shaming women? Perhaps it is the categorization of 'male/female' that informs current exclusions of gender fluidity? That myth has political ramifications.

"We can also see how perceiving of the natural world as an endowment has led to treating it as a domain to be possessed, an entitled property, a commodity to be consumed, or a reminder of God's wrath when storms, fires, quakes, and floods occur," I said.

"Divinely justified apocalypse," said Devonte.

Closing Discussion

"All of this is so highly academic and complex," I said. "What is your takeaway from this?"

"What you're saying, if I comprehend, is that first, retribution didn't always mean retributive violence. It used to mean restitution to those whom an offender had harmed. So, retribution was initially a 'non-violent tool,' or social justice artifact, a way to restore balance or harmony in social or communal relationships. Is that right?" asked Brad.

"Yes," I said.

"Okay. Second, that tool—which I would call the promise of reconciliation, became a weapon when reconciliation demanded submission to 'a retributive authority.' Seems to me that this is what Scarry was saying. Reconciliation, or submission, was forced through threat of violence," said Brad.

"That's a great way to put it," I said. "The idea and meaning of reconciliation was captured and reframed as 'forced reconciliation with an authority' rather than reconciliation with our neighbor to maintain civility in the community. Reconciliation as a tool for human responsibility for relationships became a weapon when it was appropriated by the state."

"Lastly, and I think this is your main point about Genesis, retribution is a divinely endowed form of justice. So, 'justice and retribution' were forever married in meaning. If justice was a tool, retribution made it a weapon," he said. "Do I have that right?"

"Yes," I said. "We conflate the meaning of justice as retribution and that 'original conflation' happened in an original narrative, a story of origin, that is deemed 'uncontestable.'"

"But Jesus was contesting this," said Aaron.

"In the story, Jesus was demonstrating an alternative approach to justice. He was showing us how accountability, empathy and forgiveness could happen in the same breath," I said. "Literally, in his last breath."

"He was restoring the meaning of reconciliation. Converting back to a tool," said Devonte.

"I think so. I would argue that he was restoring an original justice instinct that relied on empathy. But that realization of an empathic approach to accountability was and is an Indigenous wisdom," I said. "It existed long before Jesus.

"We'll explore that in our next discussion. If there is one takeaway from this heady discussion it is this—restoration holds power-over thinking accountable and in doing so, exposes and destabilizes long-held assumptions, initiated in a myth, about what it means to be human.

"It holds power-centric thinking accountable by holding the language and narratives that use the threat of retributive violence accountable for their negative impact on people and relationships. From a restorative perspective, words, stories, and symbols matter. When those words promote violence, they are, in themselves, a violation of civility and human dignity.

"If you'll remember, at the beginning of our discussions I suggested that 'restoration' is an inherently optimistic term. It implies that something can, in fact, be restored. But as we'll see as we move through our next series of discussions, that optimism is grounded in pragmatism because restoration gives us the language and communication practices to enact and achieve restoration. In my mind, restoration restores the purpose and function of language, stories, and communication back into a tool for connection, healing, and relationship rebuilding," I finished.

"Can I respond?" asked Devonte.

"Of course, always," I said.

"This discussion exposes the fallacy of the phrase 'sticks and stones will break our bones, but words will never hurt us.' Bones heal. If I understand what Scarry is saying, when words become weapons, the harm they cause continues to harm because they are now 'inside of us,' in both our individual and collective, or social, imagination. Once spoken, they transcend generations because they are now a 'shared artifact,'" he said.

"I couldn't have said that any better," I replied. "It helps me to think of retributive language as a weaponized vernacular, a normative way of communicating about what we consider anti-social behavior and conflict. We don't stop and ask, 'How are the language we're using and the stories we're telling impacting our experience of each other and directing the future of our relationships?'"

CHAPTER FOUR
A Restorative Worldview— It's About Relationship

Worldviews largely determine people's opinions on matters of ethics and politics. What you think about abortion, euthanasia, same-sex relationships, public education, economic policy, foreign aid, the use of military force, environmentalism, animal rights, genetic enhancement, and almost any other major issue of the day depends on your underlying worldview more than anything else …

They shape what we believe and what we're willing to believe, how we interpret our experiences, how we behave in response to those experiences, and how we relate to others.

—James M. Anderson (2014) [1]

In this fourth discussion, I wanted our group to see that restoration is more than just a process or an outcome, more than just an "alternative" conflict resolution method or a range of restorative justice practices.

I explained, "Restoration is a way of looking at the world through the lens of relationship. In contrast to a 'top-down,' power-centric view of the world, restoration is a relationship-centric worldview that emphasizes interaction and distribution. Interaction invites inclusion. Distribution enacts equality.

"As a worldview, it lends itself to contemplating some timeless and weighty philosophical questions. In the whole infinite expanse of the universe, why do human beings exist? Is there a purpose or some grand design? What's the point? Is there really a point, or is it all just meaningless coincidence?

"Who hasn't looked up into a cloudless, starlit night sky, awestruck by its vastness or witnessed a shooting star, and wondered about 'the big Why'? In these moments, the *mysterium tremendum* pierces the mundane and bewilders the mind.

"I remember sitting on the edge of the north rim of the Grand Canyon one night, hypnotized by the Milky Way and thinking, 'Who do we think we are?' We're so in-

71

consequential except to ourselves. We're so infatuated with ourselves. What's the point beyond ourselves if there is one? The next morning when I unzipped the flap of my tent and peered outside, I was surrounded by wild turkeys. Maybe they knew the answer.

"Human beings have looked inward, outward, above, below, and beyond in an attempt to answer those questions. We've created astronomy, astrology, mythology, religion and/or theology, philosophy, history, science, culture, art, and even politics looking for answers.

"Each of these methods of inquiry has its own particular perspective, interest, language, and ways of reasoning, defining, and concluding. As Thomas Kuhn (1962) explained, each mode of inquiry creates its own paradigm, its own way of looking at things, its own way of asking about those things, its own way of interpreting meaning and arriving at conclusions, and assembled 'communities of agreement, beliefs, and thought.'[2]

"Restoration is no different in this regard," I said. "It too is a paradigm with its own particular goals, interests, ways of questioning and reasoning, and logic.

"Restoration's answer to 'the big Why' is pretty simple and straightforward—*to be in relationship.*

"Here are a few expensive words. This claim is *teleological* (i.e., 'relationship is its own purpose'); *existential* (i.e., 'reality exists as, or manifests as relationship'); *ontological* (i.e., 'the nature of Being is relationship' or 'relationship is *a priori* to Being'); and *epistemological* (i.e., 'the way we know about Being/existence is through relationship and interaction').

"If we accept restoration's claim to be accurate, that 'to be in relationship' is our *raison d'être* (reason for being), then recognition of that truth can liberate us from the isolating existential angst of not knowing what our purpose is as a species and invites us into conscious awareness (ideally) of the *reflexive* nature of relationships. As our relationships with each other and the natural world go, we go," I said.

"As our relationship with the environment goes, so goes the environment (and us with it). As our relationship with the past goes, so goes our relationship with the present and future. As our relationships with others go, so goes the health of our communities and society. As our relationship with ourselves goes, so goes our physical, emotional, mental, and spiritual health and well-being. Accepting this enables us to prioritize our experience of relationships to either evolve us or prevent us from evolving. It's all about relationship," I said.

I asked the group, "What comes up for you after hearing this?"

Kris spoke first. "This is something that is so obvious it's not obvious."

"Why do you suppose it's not obvious?" I asked.

"Because we're complacent. We take relationships for granted," she said.

"Why is that?" I asked.

Devonte answered, "Because we're taught from an early age that the meaning of life is to get our own needs met and accomplish things or accumulate things."

"I like that," said Brad. "If we're so focused on meeting our own individual needs, we'll use our relationships and other people. A relationship becomes a means to an end rather than an end in itself. Relationships become transactional. After our last discussion about the Biblical roots of a retributive worldview, it struck me that we've been brainwashed into a desperate seeking of personal salvation, rather than responsibility for reconciliation and shared healing, right here and right now."

Devonte added, "We desperately need to teach the power of reconciliation to kids."

"I agree, but reconciliation with what?" I asked.

"With each other," he said. "In schools, reconciliation means reconciliation with the rules."

"Amen. Let's keep going," I said. "There is a moral imperative that *emerges* from the recognition that 'to be in relationship' is the fundamental reason for why human beings exist. This imperative begins in the recognition of the inescapable fact of interdependence, cohabitation with and *within* the planet, and the necessity for *embracing* 'the other,'"

Brad interjected, "What do you mean by 'moral imperative?'"

"If we accept that the meaning and purpose of life is to learn how to be in relationship, then we must also accept that there are ways of thinking and acting that recognize the inherent value of those relationships," I replied.

"And reject those beliefs or actions that dishonor or devalue relationships," added Aaron.

"Exactly. A moral imperative is a principle that we feel conscientiously compelled to abide by. If we agree that our reason for being is to be in relationship, then we are compelled to accept certain nonnegotiable responsibilities for participating in—and I would argue, 'behold or respect' those relationships," I said.

"And restoring those relationships when they are broken," added Aaron.

"Yes," I said. "That's the restorative imperative. But here's the thing, and it's important to understand this nuance or subtlety. That moral imperative may be a principle that we adopt in policies or practices, but it originates in our most basic human need to connect with others. It's organic. It's not a law but a recognition of the need for mutual consideration and respect.

"The recognition of *responsibility* for respecting our relationships materializes from our capacity for empathy—which is a recognition of the other person's experience. Empathy activates the moral imperative to care for each other. And empathy only comes when we recognize the suffering of others, when we see 'them' as 'us.'

"Philosopher Emmanuel Lévinas (1906–1995) theorized that the only act that really changes a person's perspective about the meaning of life and our purpose is an encounter with 'the face of the Other.'[3] In that instant of encounter, who we think we are—our 'self-made self'—is called into question. We are confronted with the inescapable 'fact' of relationship, and a potential liberation from 'our own subjectivity and bondage of self-interest.' It's risky. Who we think we are—what we profess that we stand for—might change.

"If I read Lévinas accurately, he suggests that it is in this moment of face-to-face encounter that a type of *organic morality* of responsibility emerges. Richard Rohr (2019) writes that encountering the face of the Other 'leads to transformation of our whole being. It creates a moral demand on our heart that is far more compelling' than any religious doctrine or commandment.[4] I read this to mean that authentic morality can't be mandated, but only experienced. On the deepest level of experience, we can't command or force people to 'be moral.' We can't dictate morality. We can only bring ourselves to a moment of encounter where we realize that there is more that we have in common than we were previously aware."

Brad asked, "So what you're saying is that 'morality' is not a set of laws but an experience?"

"Yes. I think this is what Lévinas is suggesting. Morality is an experience, holistic, and a very human phenomenon that emerges—and can only materialize—through encounter. If in that encounter we're able to recognize the other person's suffering as our own, put ourselves in their shoes, we have a better chance of actually taking action to help that person and in doing so, unlock our own shackles of self-absorption.

"Put another way, Lévinas seems to be saying that morality is an instinctive *human potential* that presents itself the instant that you and I encounter each other face-to-face. I want to emphasize 'potential':
- I cannot not acknowledge you ... denial leads to angst.
- If I listen to your story ... I might hear my own.
- If I understand your experience ... I can better understand my own.
- If I realize our shared human condition ... I am changed.

"If we don't look into the face of the Other, it does not deny the Other's existence. Quite the opposite. It denies our own. To not look into the face of the Other—not be moved by the face and story of the Other—to attempt to deny the face of the Other—activates our own existential angst and feeling of separation and isolation," I said. "Denial leads to objectification, and that objectification 'justifies' treating others as less than human."

"It's about connection," commented Melissa.

"Yes. Connection is what it's all about. What we'll see as we move into a discussion about how the restorative encounter actually works, is that the restorative process relies upon a face-to-face meeting and discussion. That face-to-face interaction creates the conditions for reconnection, for us to recognize the face of the other, see their suffering, and be sufficiently morally moved to actually do something about it.

"Joan, I'm wondering how this is impacting you. You look like something's coming up for you," I asked.

"I just felt this overwhelming feeling of sadness. I think of the people and families trying to get into our country on the southern border. They look desperate and terrified."

"Yeah, and then we separate them and throw them in cages," said Barb. "And then politicians weaponize their faces by calling them thugs, thieves, rapists, and drug dealers."

Devonte added, "We did the same thing with Native Americans. We called them savages. We stole their kids and put them in Indian schools. We've never asked, 'how have we made you suffer?'"

"Religious internment camps," said Aaron.

The group was silent for a moment. It felt like shared reverence.

I asked, "What is the missed moral potential here?"

Devonte shared, "That experience of empathy would guide our immigration policy and motivate reparations to Native Americans and African Americans."

"Compassion and empathy would keep us from treating them as enemies and others," said Melissa.

"Or problems," said Aaron. "It's a weaponization of ethnicity."

"I want to share this explanation of Navajo Peacemaking and justice by Hon. Robert Yazzie, Navajo Supreme Court Justice. Yazzie writes:

> *Distributive justice is concerned with the well-being of everyone in the community. For instance, if I see a hungry person, it does not matter whether I am responsible for the hunger. If someone is injured, it is irrelevant that I did not hurt the person. I have a responsibility as a Navajo, to treat everyone as if he or she were my relative and therefore to help that hungry or hurt person. I am responsible for all my relatives. This value, which translates itself into law under the Navajo system of justice, is that everyone is a part of a community, and the resources of the community must be shared with all [...] This affects the legal norms surrounding wrongdoing and elevates restoration over punishment.*[5]

"I am my brother's keeper. That requires humility," said Aaron.

"I want to keep us moving," I said. "We have a lot to cover. The point is that when relationship becomes an ethic that guides our behavior, we don't get to pick the face of the Other. We don't get to play 'God.' We don't get to pick the colors of the rainbow.

"If we fail to realize, allow, and accept this, we remain unchanged and unevolved. Our personhood, cultures, and communities remain stuck in a transactional universe. As Scarry might say, 'without recognizing the other' we are literally 'unmaking' the world. We make ourselves small. We revert or devolve into primal retributive thinking.

"I think what Lévinas is telling us is that when we encounter the face of the Other, we're faced with a moral dilemma. We can either ignore it and not be moved—which I would argue makes us spiritually sick, or we can be vulnerable and allow that face to move us—which continually heals our spirit. If we open our hearts to the face of the Other, our comfortable (complacent) identity as an individual existing separate from, different from, and therefore not responsible for another is disassembled by the simple and unavoidable fact of 'us,' and this impacts our own psychological, emotional, and spiritual well-being.

"This relationship-centric worldview is the philosophical foundation for the restorative paradigm, restorative justice, and restorative communication practices. Bear with me as I provide a bit of the backstory of how restoration as an approach to justice evolved."

> **Crime is a violation of people and relationships. It creates obligations to make things right. Justice involves the victim, the offender, and the community in a search for solutions which promote repair, reconciliation, and reassurance.**[6]
> —**Howard Zehr (2005)**
>
> **The circle is the symbol of Navajo justice because it is perfect, unbroken, and a metaphor of unity and oneness. It conveys the image of people gathering together for discussion.**[7]
> —**Robert Yazzie (2005)**

Restorative Justice

"The majority of people have never heard of restorative justice. This is changing, but 'RJ' is still considered new and different. It's only in the last thirty years that the criminal justice system has begun to develop and implement restorative justice as an alternative to conventional prosecution, sentencing, and punishment. But a restorative approach to justice is not new. In fact, it's ancient.

"Although some scholars have suggested that the conceptual origins of restorative justice emerged from Judeo–Christian spiritual traditions because of its emphasis on reconciliation and forgiveness, the practice of restoration within the peacemaking traditions of tribal communities was sustaining Indigenous peoples as Western societies passed through the rise and fall of Greece, Rome, the Christian Middle Ages, the Renaissance, the advent of monarchies, the development of capitalism, and the establishment of a modern democracy.[8]

"In truth, a restorative approach to human violation existed thousands of years before the historical figure of Jesus when human beings lived primarily in small tribes and/or clan units. Perhaps restoration was our species' original justice instinct before retribution and the institutionalization of punishment became our collective official state-sponsored justice response.

"We know for sure that current western restorative justice practices have emerged from the peacemaking traditions and practices of tribal peoples such as the Diné, Cree-Ojibwa, First Nations People of Canada, the Māori, and others. So restorative justice is not a new approach but rather a return to an ancient non-punitive and Indigenous wisdom about how to respond to human wrongdoing, and what justice means and should accomplish.[9]

"From a sociological perspective, there's a logical reason why early tribal communities pursued restoration as a response to wrongdoing: the survival of the tribe depended on *harmonious relationships* between members. When the survival of the whole depended upon the continual health and contribution of each of its members, it was paramount that good relations existed and be restored between members.

"If one person did something that harmed another, good relations were broken between the victim and the offender and other members of the tribe. The constructive/rational response was for the offender to be held responsible for *repairing the harm* they caused. If the offender did not make things right, they risked exclusion and the loss of community resources, and the community lost a valuable contribution.

"It was therefore equally critical that not only harm to the victim be repaired by the offender, but *the underlying reasons why the offender committed the violation in the first place be addressed and corrected.* The health of the whole depended on the health of the individual and vice versa.

"Retribution, retaliation, and/or vengeance and punishment, on the other hand, did not facilitate relational harmony. Retribution did not resolve, repair, or restore the relationship between the survivor and offender and/or the offender's relationship with the larger community. The satisfaction of vengeance through violence was deemed counterproductive to fostering interdependence and ensuring continued cohesiveness between members. Restoration was a pragmatic approach.

> ... (retributive) methods do not repair damaged relationships, families, communities, and society; instead, this process promotes further conflict and disharmony.[10] (parentheses added)

"Punishment was ineffective in producing a necessary and fundamental change in the offender's thinking, attitude, and behavior in order that they would not offend again. Exclusion and the feeling of separation was more potent as a deterrent.

"This may seem idealistic, but when you think about it, punishment diverts an offender's attention away from the real issue, which was the pain and suffering the offender had caused another member (and the tribe). What was most effective/pragmatic was when the offender accepted responsibility for violating, felt remorse for what they had done, and *sincerely* wanted to make amends and repair the harm they had caused. *Remorse and a desire for reconnection was the sought-after motivating change mechanism* and not fear and/or the pain of reprisal punishment.

"In addition, punishment did not address any underlying material, physical, emotional and/or psychological issues in the offender's life that may have compelled them to violate in the first place. The surest guarantee that an offender would not reoffend was the healing/correction of those issues. In this regard, we can see a more complete understanding of the word *accountability*.

"As I said earlier, from a community justice perspective, accountability means not only taking responsibility for repair, but also 'the ability to account' for any and every underlying reason that led to the harmful act.

"To discover why a person did something harmful to another is to create the opportunity to *address and correct the root cause* and not just treat the symptom (the resulting violation behavior) with retaliation and/or punishment. If the ultimate goal is to prevent further violations, accounting for and repairing the broken psychological or emotional parts of the offending individual offers the best chance. Rather than condemn, punish, and banish the individual, the restorative solution was to heal the individual and reintegrate them back into the community as a contributing member. The guiding principle is inclusion, rather than exclusion.

"The same is true of the person who was harmed by the offender. One of the primary western legal arguments for punishment is the proposition that if an offender is punished, the survivor will be vindicated or satisfied. While there's no arguing that an offender needs to be held accountable for what they did, and that this will ensure that the injustice experienced by a survivor is recognized and addressed by the community, the pursuit of punishment often diverts attention from the survivor's primary need—the repair and healing of any physical/material, emotional, and/or psychological damage in order to restore the survivor back to a place of well-being.

"Tribal communities understand this, which is why in addition to holding the offender accountable for the harm they caused and subsequent reparation, ritual ceremonies of healing are prescribed and performed for both survivor and offender; and in which the entire tribal community participates.

> The word *guilt* implies a moral fault that commands retribution. It is a nonsense word in Navajo law due to the focus on healing, reintegration within the group, and the end goal of nourishing ongoing relationships with the immediate and extended family, relatives, neighbors, and community. [11]

"A 'violation' is fundamentally perceived as a 'break in right relationship' and justice a matter of physical, mental, emotional, and even spiritual health and restoration. The individual life is an integral part of a larger, sacred web of relationships. Every attempt should be made to address, heal, and correct the underlying issues.

Western Adoption

"In the early 1990s, juvenile justice systems began to learn from and utilize tribal ways of dealing with crime. The search for a better way was motivated by a sincere desire to keep youthful offenders from entering the system and becoming just another statistic. It was clear that conventional prosecution and sentencing or incarceration was fostering the potential for reoffending instead of reversing it.

"With the intention of keeping youths out of the system and creating a more effective (satisfying) response that would produce an authentic change in the offender, thereby decreasing the chances of reoffending, progressive-thinking criminologists and justice system professionals started asking native communities how they approached justice.[12]

How It Works

"As restorative justice continues to evolve, a range of models and practices have been developed to address various and diverse violation and/or conflict circumstances. In fact, a restorative approach to resolving destructive conflict and/or violation continues to expand into schools, workplaces, families, civil disputes, divorce, churches, and prisons.

"However, regardless of the specific model used, *the core practice involves bringing together those who have been both directly and indirectly impacted by a violation into a face-to-face encounter* to discuss what happened and why, recognize who was harmed, discover how they were harmed, and create a plan of repair. Those impacted 'take ownership' of the resolution.

"Though it's not necessary to go into the specifics of how cases get administratively processed, in a typical justice system scenario the courts offer restorative justice to offenders and survivors under certain conditions. Generally speaking, the offender has to admit they have committed the offense, be willing to meet with those they have impacted, and accept responsibility for repairing the harm. Second, the survivor has to be willing to meet with the offender.

"In those circumstances where the actual offender/survivor are not willing to meet, restorative justice programs sometimes rely on the use of surrogate offenders and/or survivors who 'play the part' respectively. Though not ideal, the process gives those participating an opportunity to discuss the event in an organized and thorough way with others, uncover and validate the harm, and create the plan for repair.

"Even with a surrogate survivor, offenders can still be held accountable for what they did, how they hurt others, and what they need to do to repair the harm. Similarly, survivors are able to tell their story, decipher how it impacted them, and receive the support they need from other participants to recover.

"There are numerous nuances and details to how restorative justice cases are administered and coordinated by courts (and in schools) that don't need to be explained here.

The purpose of this basic explanation is to provide a beginning picture of how restorative justice works and indicate that the process itself is a powerful tool in helping survivors organize and address a violation in a constructive way, which leads to restoration and potential closure.

"Whether the process is applied during a conventional restorative justice conference encounter involving numerous participants or used as a method of interpersonal relationship restoration, the process provides a *conversational structure* that facilitates an encounter where there is a comprehensive discussion of what happened, the identification of exactly what needs to be repaired, and then the creation of a plan to make those repairs.

"Today, a restorative approach to human violation and conflict continues to expand beyond the boundaries of criminal justice and into contexts of non-criminal conflict too numerous to cover here. While restoration may be identified with restorative justice, in fact, it's an approach and process that has a much broader and useful application in other environments such as schools, workplaces, families, the environment, etc."

As I explained to our group, "It is exploring this broader application that brought us together.

> **"Fundamentally, however, the ongoing evolution (revolution, perhaps) of restoration as a way to reconcile human relationships damaged by violation represents a return to an ancient practical wisdom about justice."**

"Regardless of where restoration is pursued (i.e., schools, workplaces, etc.), it involves people coming together to address something harmful that has happened. An important point I want to make is that this 'coming together,' this encounter, foregrounds the role of language, communication, and interaction in the restorative process which we will explore in a later discussion about restorative communication and restorative practices."

A Case

Turning back to our group, I reminded them once again that using restoration as a lens can expose the intersection of personal beliefs and perspectives with culturally inherited beliefs and norms. "The question is how do we identify that intersection, and what do we do about it when we see it within a context of a violation such as a crime, destructive or dehumanizing interaction, or even in hate speech?"

Brad asked, "What you're saying is that culturally inherited beliefs can be underlying issues?"

"Yes. In addition to mental health or behavioral issues which are underlying issues that may have compelled the individual to commit a violation, culturally inherited beliefs about other people can also be seen as motivating factors. If you don't address those beliefs when you see them, the opportunity to confront them and change them is lost," I said.

"Like racism and discrimination," said Kris.

"Racism, discrimination, genderism, etc. The core belief that if someone doesn't look like us, think like us, or talk like us, making them less human and less worthy of respect, is a culturally inherited belief, a deep-seated worldview that is generationally transferred, but individually expressed. This much seems obvious. We inherit our family's or cultural group's biases.

"What restoration says is that a violation where these factors are in play is an opportune moment for accountability, which leads to possibility of changing those beliefs. Inasmuch as we looked at retribution as a paradigm, that paradigm can get activated in how we evaluate, judge, condemn, and retaliate against diversity," I said.

"So, not recognizing diversity is a violation of relationships," said Devonte.

"Yes. One case that I think exemplifies how the restorative encounter can be used to identify and address underlying beliefs and guide someone to getting help in changing those beliefs involved an incident of felony menacing with a weapon.

"In this case, a white male ('Rick') in his mid-20s was convinced a Latino male (in his 30s) was following him in traffic. Rick slammed on his brakes, got out of his pick-up truck, walked back to the other man's car holding a handgun, and yelled, 'Why the fuck are you following me, you *****?!' The stunned driver ('Leo') put his hands up and yelled, 'Easy, easy! I'm not following you! I'm just going home from work!'

"Rick got back in his truck and drove away. Leo got Rick's license plate number and called the police. Within an hour, the police arrested Rick. He was charged with felony menacing with a weapon and if convicted, was facing one to three years in prison, and/or a fine of anywhere from $1,000 to $100,000.

"When Rick went before the judge, he admitted to what he had done, and that he had 'pulled a gun,' but explained that he was convinced the other man was following him. He told the judge that his father 'is a building contractor who hired some Mexicans to do some work for him and when he didn't pay them because they didn't do a good job, they started calling him and harassing him for the money.'

"The judge decided to refer Rick's case to restorative justice. She told him, 'You need to take a serious look at why you think you were justified in threatening this man. You may have a license to carry a firearm for self-defense, but that doesn't give you the right to threaten someone who you thought was following you in traffic. That man has a right to confront you with what you did to him. If you complete the restorative justice program, I will take your participation into consideration before I pass sentence.'

"When I spoke with the judge, she said, 'There's something deeper going on here and I'm hoping you can find out what that is.' I understood what she meant. This was more than just a road-rage incident.

"Following protocol, I met with both men individually at their homes. These preliminary individual interviews help facilitators explain the restorative process, how the group discussion will go, and what a typical outcome of that discussion will be (a 'restorative contract' that details reparative actions the person who offended can take to make things right).

"The interviews also give the facilitator a chance to gauge the demeanor of the person who committed the offense, and the person who was harmed. It is the responsibility of the facilitator to ensure revictimization or retraumatization doesn't occur in any restorative encounter. Just because a person admits to committing an offense doesn't mean they are willing and/or capable of realizing or accepting responsibility for how their actions negatively impacted the other person.

"In addition to these goals, probably the most important aspect of these preliminary interviews is to gain the trust of participants. When someone has experienced a violation, the facilitator needs to create an interactional space of emotional safety. This means 'holding' that person and their experience with sincere understanding, profound empathy, and most of all, advocacy.

"When engaging with someone who has committed a violation, this means being able to work through any defensiveness, denial, and/or shame. Later in our discussions, I'll present a technique called S.H.I.F.T. that can help you create that 'space of safety.'

Leo

I met with Leo first. After I introduced myself and explained why I was meeting with him, I said, "I'm really sorry this happened to you, Leo. I can only imagine how terrifying it must have been."

Leo was visibly shaken. He explained, "I thought he was going to kill me. The first thing that went through my mind was my kids would be without their father and my wife would be without me. My parents flashed through my mind, too. Afterwards, I got really pissed off. I'm still pissed off. Who does this guy think he is? My friends wanted to find him and beat the hell out of him. Do I have to start carrying a gun now?"

After a moment, Leo asked me, "Have you ever had someone point a gun at you?" I took a breath. I had a decision to make. Do I share my own personal experience?

"Yes, I have," I said. "I know what it feels like. Your entire life flashes before you in an instant. It's traumatizing. And I wish I would've had the opportunity to confront him in a discussion like this."

Leo said, "I know you're here to explain what that discussion would look like, but why the fuck would I want to meet with this guy? This dude is sick. Guys like this shouldn't be allowed to carry guns. He's going to end up killing someone."

"I agree," I replied. "I felt the same way when it happened to me. I was 18, and an off-duty police officer thought I cut him off in traffic and followed me to my apartment, got out of his car, ran over to me before I had a chance to get out of the car, pointed a gun at me, and started raging at me. I was terrified. For months, I tried to understand why he thought I had cut him off. I never had the chance to ask him, 'Why were you so pissed off at me?' I carried that question inside of me for years. It was never resolved. I never got the answer."

I asked Leo, "I'm wondering what questions have been going through your mind. What questions would you ask him?"

Leo replied, "What the fuck is wrong with you? Why did you do this to me? Is it because I'm Latino? I'm a teacher, for Christ's sake! I have a master's degree!"

I told Leo that Rick was being charged with a felony, but because he had admitted to committing the crime, the judge wanted to give Leo the opportunity to ask him any questions and tell him how he was impacted by what he did before she sentenced him. She also wanted to give him an opportunity to take responsibility for the harm he caused by hearing from Leo and others in the community.

"Who are the others?" he asked.

I replied, "Well, for one, anyone you want to be there to speak their truth about how this impacted them. Maybe your wife, or a family member, or a friend. The officer who arrested him will be there, as well as a couple of others who live in the community and want to hold him accountable for how this impacted the larger community."

I said, "When he pointed a gun at you, he pointed a gun at everyone. Does that make sense?" I could tell this statement made an impact on Leo because he seemed to relax a bit. I took a chance and added, "This kind of behavior endangers the whole community, Leo. You're not alone in feeling outraged."

He asked, "What happens if I don't want to meet with him?"

I was very matter of fact. "I'm not an attorney," I said, "so I don't know what will happen. What I can say is that right now, he's facing one to three years in jail and a substantial fine of up to $100,000. He's already pled guilty. But the judge referred his case to us before she decides what his sentence will be."

Leo asked, "So if I decide to meet with him, it'll look good for him, and the judge will go easier on him?"

I said, "Not necessarily. The outcome of this discussion will be what's called a 'reparative contract.' This contract will stipulate actions that he will need to take to repair the damage he caused to you, your family, and the larger community. If he doesn't agree to the contract, or if he fails to complete that contract within a specified time, the judge will take that into consideration before she sentences him."

He asked, "Who decides what's in that contract?"

I said, "We all do. You, your wife, if she participates, the other members from the community who will participate in this discussion. The purpose of the contract is to lay out concrete actions he'll need to take to repair the harm he caused you."

Leo said, "This dude needs some serious therapy and anger management. He shouldn't be carrying a gun."

I continued, "This is not a 'get out of jail free card.' The judge is simply giving you and others in our community the opportunity to confront him, and him the opportunity to understand why and how what he did was unacceptable. It's a chance for him to take responsibility for the damage he caused before she makes her final decision about what his sentence should be."

Leo asked, "So this is like a chance for him to wake the fuck up?"

I answered, "Well, in a manner of speaking, yes."

Leo asked, "So even if we meet with him, there's still a good chance he'll go to jail?"

I was honest, "I can't answer that. What I can tell you is that this doesn't replace the court's responsibility to uphold the law and what he did was a felony."

Leo restated, "This guy should never be allowed to carry a gun—ever."

I said, "Well, that's something the judge will have to decide. Again, I'm not a lawyer, but as I understand it, if someone is convicted of a felony weapon charge and is sentenced to jail, they lose their right to own a firearm. In this case, he'll probably not only lose his job, but he'll also have to mark that little box on any future job application that asks, 'Have you ever been convicted of a felony?' So, in all likelihood, he'll have to explain what he did to any potential employer."

"Who is this guy? Has he done this before?" Leo asked.

I said, "I haven't talked to him yet. I wanted to talk to you first. Though I don't know if he has a criminal record, my guess is that he's never been charged or convicted of something this serious. The judge wouldn't have referred his case to us if he did. She would've just sentenced him."

"Is he married? Does he have any kids?" he asked.

"He's divorced and he has a son. I don't know how old his son is," I said.

"Pretty shitty example to set for your kid," he commented.

"I agree," I said. "If his son knows his dad could go to jail, it's probably scary for him."

"I don't know. It seems that by meeting with him, I'd be doing him a favor. My wife is terrified that this guy will find out where we live. The last thing we want is contact with him," he said.

"I get it," I said. "It's completely understandable that you and your wife would feel that way. This is completely up to you. I'm not here to try and convince you to do this."

I continued, "What I can tell you, after having done quite a few of these, is that being able to directly confront someone who threatened us or violated us and speak our truth about it in the presence of others who were also impacted can be transformative. Demanding that they tell us why they did it keeps us from always wondering about it. Let me ask you, have you been trying to figure out why he did this to you?"

"Nonstop," said Leo. "Who did he think I was? It keeps me up at night," he added.

I said, "This is an opportunity for you to ask him. In fact, everyone wants to know why he did this."

He thought for a moment. "Let me talk to my wife," he said. "I would like to confront him."

"Why don't we do this?" I asked. "I still need to talk to him. Once I do, I'll have a better understanding of his demeanor. I'm going to ask him why he did this and if he has any understanding about the damage he caused. I'll circle back to you and share what I learned. My number one responsibility to you and the others is keeping you safe. If I sense, in any way, that he isn't willing or capable of grasping the seriousness of this, I won't move forward. His case will go back to the judge. I'm sorry this happened to you, Leo."

Leo said, "Okay. I'll have to think about this. Right now, my answer is no."

> **There is some good in the worst of us and some evil in the best of us. When we discover this, we are less prone to hate our enemies.**
> **—Martin Luther King, Jr.**

Rick

I met with Rick at his house and the first thing I noticed was an old Western-style saddle rifle hanging on the wall. I saw a chance to "bridge" with him.

"Winchester lever action 30-30 scabbard rifle. I'm guessing from about 1940-ish. Where'd you get it?" I asked.

"My dad gave it to me," he said.

"This is the same rifle my dad taught me how to shoot with when I was 16," I said. "My shoulder was bruised for weeks," I added.

"You like guns?" he asked.

"Depends on the gun and what it's used for," I said.

Rick jumped right in. "So, you're gonna ask me about what happened, right?" he asked.

"Yeah," I said. "And explain how this process works, ask some other questions, answer any questions you might have," I added. "I'm not here to judge you. That's the judge's job. Because you pled guilty, the judge is giving you the chance to take responsibility for what you did before she sentences you."

"You mean meet with him, right?" he asked.

"Maybe," I said. "My job is to see if that's a good idea. Whether or not we move forward with this depends on your willingness to take responsibility, and his willingness to meet with you."

"I did take responsibility. I admitted I did it," Rick said.

"You did, and that's a really important first step. Like I said, that's why the judge is giving you this opportunity, and that's why I'm here. But taking responsibility means more than just admitting we did it. It means taking responsibility for how it impacted other people. Does this make sense?" I asked.

"I guess," he replied.

"How do you think the man you threatened felt?" I asked.

"I'm sure he was scared," he said.

"He was more than scared, Rick. He was terrified. He thought you were going to kill him," I said.

"I wasn't going to shoot him. I just wanted to scare him," he objected.

"How would he know that? All he saw was some guy, jumping out of his truck with a gun in his hand and screaming, 'You fucking ******!' Put yourself in his shoes. What would you think if someone did that to you?" I asked.

I could tell he was annoyed with me. He didn't respond, so I asked again. "What would you think if someone did that exact same thing to you and called you some derogatory racist name?"

He thought for a moment. "I'd think, 'What the fuck is this guy's problem?'" he said.

"Fair enough. How would you feel?" I pressed.

"What do you mean?" he asked.

"Would it scare you?" I asked.

"No. I'd be pissed off," he said.

"Okay. What would you have done?" I asked.

"I would've protected myself," he said.

"How? How would you have protected yourself?" I pressed.

"You mean, would I have shot him?" he asked.

"I don't know. Would you have?" I asked.

"If I did, I would've had every right to," he said. "Self-defense," he added.

"I don't think anybody would question one's right to defend themselves, Rick," I said, "but this man was simply driving home from work. He wasn't threatening you. He had no idea who you were or why you did what you did."

I kept pushing. "Let's turn it around. What if the man you threatened also had a gun and felt the same way you do? What do you think would've happened then?" I asked.

"There would've been a gunfight," he said.

"Yeah. And either both or one of you would probably have been killed. And maybe a bystander. This happened on a crowded street," I said. "I mean, play it out. Do you see how serious this is?" I asked.

Rick was silent. After a moment, I added, "I need to understand why you did this. What were you thinking?"

"I thought he was following me," Rick said.

"Okay," I said. "Why did you think he was following you?"

"Because some Mexicans have been after my father, and we drive the same truck," he explained.

"What do you mean by 'after your father'?" I asked.

"He hired some Mexicans to do some work for him and because they did a shitty job, he refused to pay them. So, they started hassling him," he explained.

"How were they hassling him?" I asked.

"They kept calling him and started cruising by his house," he said. This explanation was consistent with what he told the police and the judge.

"Did you ever see them?" I asked.

"No," he said. "My dad told me what kind of car they were driving," he added.

"So, based on the kind of car your dad described and the fact that they were Latinos, you just assumed the man you thought was following you was one of them?" I asked.

"Yeah," he said.

"Why didn't your father just call the police and report it? Why didn't you call the police?" I asked.

"They wouldn't have done anything about it," he said.

"That's what they're there for, Rick. That's their job," I said. "It sounds like you decided that you were gonna do something about it. Take matters into your own hands, so to speak. Is that right?" I asked. My statement triggered his anger.

He blurted, "These fucking people shouldn't even be here. They should go back where they came from!"

"You mean the men your father hired, or all Latinos?" I asked.

"All of them!" he said.

"Wow." I took a deep breath. My first thought was, *There's no way I can move forward with arranging a meeting between Rick and Leo.* I needed a moment to figure out how I was going to navigate this.

"Can I have a glass of water?" I asked. He went to the kitchen. I could've ended the conversation right then and explained that I didn't think moving forward was possible, and I was going to return his case to the judge. The other option was to go deeper with him; find out where his animosity began and maybe connect the dots for him.

I fundamentally don't believe that people are born with hatred (or racism). We inherit it. We learn it. Like freshwater lakes, we get polluted. If racism is the weed, hatred is the cultural fertilizer. Left unexplored or unchecked, the social ecosystem, the community, becomes toxic. Somewhere under the harm is a deeper harm.

When he returned, he said, "Bet you think I'm a racist."

"I'm more interested in seeing if there's a connection between what you just said, what you believe, and how you reacted that day," I said. "But it does lead me to wonder, what if this guy was white? Would you have reacted the same way?" I asked.

"I don't know. Probably not," he said.

"Probably, or not?" I pushed.

"No," he responded. But then he added, "Because it wasn't a bunch of white guys that were hassling my dad. It was a bunch of Mexicans."

"Okay," I said. "I'm trying to track with you here. What you're saying is that if it was a bunch of white guys harassing your dad, and you thought one of them was following you in a car that was similar to the one they were driving, you wouldn't have confronted him by getting out of your truck and threatening him with a gun? Is that what you're saying?"

Rick got up. He was obviously upset. I tried a different tack. "Rick," I said, "you're in some pretty deep shit here. I'm trying to help you. But I need to know if your resentment against Latinos caused you to assault this particular driver."

"I thought he was one of the Mexicans harassing my dad!" he demanded.

I held my ground. "That sounds like a justification, Rick. To be blunt, I don't believe that. I don't think the judge believes that either, which is why I'm here. Because the animosity you just expressed about Latinos leads me to believe that that's why you felt justified threatening this man. You just told me if the guy was white, you wouldn't have reacted the same way."

He tried again, "I'm telling you the truth. I thought he was one of the guys harassing my dad." His statement lacked conviction.

"Do you remember what he was wearing?" I asked.

"What? No," he replied.

"He was wearing a shirt and tie," I said. "He's not even a construction worker. He has no idea who you are or why you assaulted him. He was just a guy going home to his family."

[I explained to our group, "This was a critical moment in our conversation. I had contested his story and confronted his defensiveness, but now I needed a way to gain his trust in me as his potential advocate."]

I said to Rick, "Look, I know I'm holding your feet to the fire here, but I really want to see you turn this thing around. I know you have a son. How old is he?"

"Nine," he replied.

"Does he know?" I asked.

"Yeah. My ex told him," he replied.

"Have you talked to your ex about what happened?" I asked.

"Yeah," he said.

"How did that go?" I asked.

"She hates my guts," he said.

"That must be tough on your son," I commented. "What did she say to you?"

"You really want to know?" he asked.

"Yeah, I do," I said.

"She told me I deserve to go to jail. Told me she was gonna sue for full custody," he said. "She'd love nothing better than to see me in jail."

"Ouch," I offered. "Have you talked to your son?"

"Yeah," he replied.

"How does he feel about this?" I asked.

"He's scared I'm gonna go to jail," he said.

"What did you tell him?" I asked.

"I told him I may have to," he said.

"How did he respond?" I asked.

"He cried," said Rick.

I waited a moment and added, "I'm really sorry to hear that. Sounds like you're really important to him."

We sat quietly for a moment. "Do you think I'm gonna go to jail?" he asked.

"I can't answer that, Rick. That's for the judge to decide," I said. "I don't want to see you go to jail, and my hunch is neither does the judge. That's why she's giving you this chance to take responsibility.

"This doesn't mean you won't go to jail because she has to uphold the law. What you did classifies as a felony. But clearly, she saw something in you when you pled guilty that led her to believe you could learn from this in a way that you wouldn't by going straight to jail. I'm sure she's aware that you have a son," I said.

His next statement indicated he grasped the seriousness of what he had done. "If I go to jail, I'll lose my son. I'll lose my job. My life is fucked," he said.

After a moment, I said, "Well, that's one way to look at it. It's not the way I see it."

"What do you mean?" he asked.

"Well, like I said, the judge is giving you a chance to turn this thing around. She's giving you the opportunity to make things right here. You're not powerless," I told him. "You can use this as an opportunity to step up and take responsibility for what you did. Whether or not you go to jail doesn't have anything to do with doing the right thing. Making things right. You see the difference?"

"What does that mean? Apologize to him?" he asked.

"Well, that's a start. Do you know what making amends means?" I asked.

"Yeah, it means paying someone back," he answered.

I replied, "If we stole something, or caused financial harm, then yeah, restitution would be part of an amends. But an amends is much more than that.

"An amends is demonstrating that we're sincerely sorry for what we did to them. It's not feeling sorry for what we did because of the consequences we're facing, like going to jail. It's feeling sincere remorse for what we did because of the harm we caused the other person or persons. In this case, it isn't only the harm you caused this other man and his family. It's also the harm you caused your son. He's afraid he's going to lose his dad. Are you tracking with me?" I asked.

Barely audible, he said, "Yeah."

"One of the ways we can demonstrate true remorse is to give the person we've hurt the opportunity to tell us how we've hurt them. The only way to do that in this situation is to give this man you threatened the opportunity to tell you how you impacted him and his family—if he's even willing to tell you. That takes a lot of courage on your part because it means not making any excuses for why we did what we did. We're basically saying, 'What I did was wrong and there is no excuse for what I did to you.' "

"What if he doesn't want to meet with me?" Rick asked.

"That's a great question. Why do you think he wouldn't want to meet with you?" I asked.

"Because he's afraid of me," he answered.

"Maybe. What else?" I asked.

"That he's so fucking pissed off at me that he wants nothing to do with me," he said.

"Maybe. What else?" I pushed.

"That he wouldn't accept my apology. He wouldn't believe me if I told him I was sorry," he said.

"What you just did is look at all of this from his perspective," I added.

"What can I do if he doesn't want to meet?" he asked.

"What do you think you could do?" I asked.

He thought for a minute. "I don't know. Maybe write him a letter?" he asked.

"That's one option," I said. "But there's something even more fundamental that you could do," I added. "You could change. Making amends means making a change, and that's what the judge is giving you the chance to do."

[I explained to our group that at this point in our conversation, it was clear that a subtle shift had happened in Rick's demeanor. I said, "I think he realized the seriousness of what he did. Whether this shift was because he realized the very real possibility that he would go to jail and how that would affect his son, or whether he understood how what he did impacted the man he threatened, was hard to gauge. What was encouraging to me was his apparent openness to making amends."]

I asked Rick, "Assuming you'd be interested in making a change, what would that look like?"

He thought for a minute. "Control my anger?" he asked.

"Do you think you have a problem with anger?" I asked.

"Do you?" he asked.

"I'm not a therapist, but I think it's pretty clear that you were more than just angry. You were in a rage when you threatened this man. There's a big difference between anger and rage," I said. "Rage goes much deeper than anger. It's anger on a whole other level. It's *extreme* anger. That's why it's so dangerous. It's uncontrollable anger, and it can lead to violence. If anger is a flame, rage is a wildfire. You see the difference?"

"Yeah," he said.

"Let me ask you, were you just angry, or were you enraged that day?"

"Both," he admitted.

"Thanks for your honesty," I said. "So, what would need to change?"

"Control my anger," he said.

"What else?" I asked.

"Maybe not carry a gun," he said.

"Well, let's set the whole gun issue aside for now because if you get convicted of a felony, that decision will be made for you," I said.

"Yeah, I know," he said.

"If you ask me, I think you need to look at where this rage at Latinos comes from," I said.

"You think I'm a racist," he stated.

"I don't think that's the right question to ask. I think you should ask yourself, 'Why am I so enraged at Latinos?' Where does that come from?" I asked.

I took a chance. "I'm wondering if somebody, or some group of people, maybe Latinos, did something to you that threatened you or seriously hurt you and they were never held accountable for what they did. I'm not talking about these guys that your dad or you think were harassing him. I'm talking about way before that.

"Where does your animosity come from? Did something happen to you? Because if it did, and it was never resolved, it would make more sense that you would carry such a deep animosity," I said. "It would explain why you were so enraged that day. It might also explain why you feel the need to carry a gun. What happened?"

[I explained to our group, "This is when Rick started to open up. He explained that his dad had lost his contracting business in the town where Rick was from because 'Mexicans did the work for cheaper.' His dad had to claim bankruptcy, they lost their house, and they had to move." His father blamed all of this on Latinos.]

Rick explained, "My dad hates Mexicans. He started a fight with a Mexican at Home Depot and a bunch of Mexicans jumped in and beat the shit out of him. He got charged with assault. The Mexican claimed self-defense and got off with nothing."

"Did this happen before you moved?" I asked.

"Yeah," he said.

"How old were you when this happened?" I asked.

"I was in middle school," he said.

I responded, "I'm sorry that happened, Rick. That must have been really hard for you and your dad."

He replied, "Yeah. It was fucked up. But he started the fight. But then a bunch of Mexicans started hassling me at school."

"What do you mean, hassling you?" I asked.

"They said shit like, 'Your dad's a pussy,' and, 'You better watch out, white boy. You're next,' and all kinds of shit," Rick said.

"So, they knew what happened?" I asked.

"There's only one middle school," he added.

"Did you or your dad tell the school what was happening?" I asked.

"Yeah," he said.

"Did it stop?" I asked.

"No. They started hanging out after school and yelling shit at me and laughing," he said. "You see why I hate Mexicans?"

[I told our discussion group, "I had to bite my tongue. I wanted to ask him, 'How do you know they were Mexican? They might have been from another Central American country.' And truth be told, I felt offended because of my own Latino heritage."]

Instead, I said, "I can understand why you felt angry toward those boys. They were never held accountable. I think what's more important here is if you see the connection. Because the guy you threatened wasn't those guys. He was just a guy on his way home from work. It's just my opinion, but I think what you did was take your rage of those boys and the men who beat your father up out on him. Do you see that?" I asked.

Rick didn't answer.

I decided to share a bit of my own experience with bullying. I wanted to destigmatize bullying and nudge him to a place where he'd be open to getting some professional help.

"You were bullied, Rick," I said. "I know what that feels like," I shared. I focused on the impact. "It was humiliating. It never got addressed. I was always on the lookout. I thought the world was a dangerous place. I got into fights. I carried a deep resentment and rage well into my thirties, so I understand where your rage at being bullied comes from," I said.

"But here's the thing. If we don't heal from the humiliation we felt, and take ownership of our rage, then we'll continue to feel like a victim. Those bullies will continue to bully us if only in our head, and we'll take it out on others. It sounds to me like that's what you did in this case when you raged at this man," I said.

"The real question here is, do you want to carry this shit around inside of you for the rest of your life? Because if you do, you're going to do this again." I continued, "Think of your son. Do you want to pass this resentment on to him?"

He was quiet. I let what I said just rest with him.

After a long moment, he said, "I don't want my son to go through what I did."

"He won't if you step up and take ownership for what happened to you and make amends to the other man for what you did to him," I said. "That's how you can make amends."

"Do you think this man will meet with me?" he asked.

"I don't know, Rick," I said. "I'm going to talk to him again. But regardless of whether or not he agrees to meet, or even if the judge decides to sentence you to some jail time, you can still make things right with yourself for your son's sake. You can confront what happened to you as a kid and what your dad told you about Latinos. If you don't, nothing will change."

Quick Reflection

I turned back to our group. "What do you think about this case so far?" I asked.

Joan spoke. "I'm having trouble seeing how this case relates to restorative practices in a school or workplace. This is a criminal justice case. We'll never have to address something so serious in our school."

"I thought the same thing too at first," said Melissa. "But we do have people in our facility who might be classified as racist. They may not verbalize it unless they're around others who think the same, but it's there. Same with gender intolerance. My takeaway thus far is that you can address that in a restorative conversation. Is that the point, Will?" she asked.

"Yes," I said. "You can use this conversation to expose and confront underlying beliefs that motivated an incident, whether it's something as serious as what Rick did or a conflict where someone said something hateful about another. Since you're all going to be facilitating these conversations, my point is that you have to ask, 'What is the thinking that led to this?' and, ideally, point that out to the person. This interaction, the process, is designed to ask that question; especially in your initial interview."

"But that takes a lot of skill because in this case you're also dealing with trauma," said Kris. "You've been doing this for years."

"It does take training and practice, which leads to confidence," I said. "But when you build your own team of facilitators, which we'll cover in a later discussion, it's been my experience that this expertise, trauma literacy, and the skills to engage develops pretty quickly."

I met with Leo a second time and shared about my conversation with Rick. I explained that I believed Rick realized the seriousness of what he did, that it was wrong, and that there was no excuse. I shared Rick's desire to apologize to Leo and that he accepted he needed to get some help.

"Is he sincere or is he just saying this to avoid going to jail?" he asked.

I said, "My sense is that he is sincere, but like I said, whether we meet or not, he may still go to jail. That's up to the judge."

Leo thought for a moment and said, "It wasn't just the gun. He called me a ***** ****. Doesn't that classify this as a hate crime?"

I replied, "I don't know if legally this would register as a hate crime. But clearly, what he yelled at you was hateful and it was racist. I confronted him about that. I asked him if he would've done the same thing to a white guy. He said, 'Probably not.'"

"So, he's a racist," said Leo.

"What he said was racist, and it's more complicated than that," I said. "But before I explain what I mean, I want to know how you're doing. How has this impacted you and your wife?"

"I'm still really angry. I know this guy didn't know me or thought I was someone else, but he blocked me with his truck and threatened me with a gun. There's a part of me that just wants to beat the shit out of him," he said. "I know this is irrational, wouldn't solve anything and I'd never do it, but I fantasize about it. I said this to my wife, and it scared her," he added.

"I don't think it's irrational to have those thoughts. I think it's understandable that you would feel that way. You experienced a violent assault, and you were defenseless. It's just my opinion, but I think thoughts of retaliation are not only an expression of our outrage at having been violated but also an attempt to reclaim our dignity.

"It's like saying, 'Fuck you, you can't do this to me!' I think your anger and sense of outrage is completely understandable. You're standing up for yourself after the fact. Does that make sense? I guess what I'm saying is, don't condemn yourself for having thoughts of retaliation," I added.

When I said, "You're standing up for yourself," Leo put his face in his hands and exclaimed, "This is fucked up! I keep playing what happened over and over again in my head. I can't sleep. My wife tells me I'm checked out. I can't concentrate. Every time I see a white truck, I look to see if it's him."

As gently as I could, I said, "Leo, what you experienced was a trauma. A trauma is an experience that completely overwhelms us. What you're describing is a type of post-trauma stress. We keep playing what happened over and over again trying to make sense of what happened and achieve some type of resolution and closure. Have you ever heard the phrase, 'It's not you, it's what happened to you'?"

"You think I'm experiencing PTSD?" he asked.

"I'm not a psychiatrist, so I can't speak to the 'disorder' part of PTSD, but what you're describing is a type of post-traumatic stress experience," I said. "Let me explain why I think this. When we experience a life-threatening situation, our primal survival instinct kicks in and reacts in three ways. We either fight back; flee and try to escape; or freeze. In this case, you were trapped. You couldn't fight back because he had a gun. You couldn't flee because he had you blocked with his truck. All you could do was freeze. I would've done the same thing, Leo.

"On top of that, he attacked you verbally with racist language. So, there were really two violations that happened. All of that shock and adrenaline takes our nervous system hostage. If we have the ability to fight back or escape, that adrenaline is put to good use. It gives us the energy to repel the attack or flee.

"But if we're trapped and can only freeze, that adrenaline gets locked in our body and then afterward, every time we think about what happened, it's as if we're reliving it. That's why you can't sleep and why you keep playing it over and over in your head. Every time you think about it, you experience a jolt of adrenaline. So, it's not you. It's what happened to you. It's what he did to you," I said. When I said this, Leo's eyes watered.

I added, "It's understandable that you would have thoughts of retaliation. Like I said the first time we met, I had someone point a gun at me. If someone had explained trauma to me, it would've saved me years of replaying retaliation scenarios in my head. My hope for you is that we can give you the opportunity to speak your truth about how you were impacted and ask him why he did what he did. Am I making any sense here?"

"People tell me I was at the wrong place at the wrong time. I was on my way home from work," he said.

"What's it like when people say that to you?" I asked.

"It pisses me off because they're saying I shouldn't have been there," he replied.

"People say that because they're trying to make sense of what happened, too," I said. "But the truth is that what this person did had absolutely nothing to do with you, Leo, and everything to do with him. It happened to you, but not because of you. You didn't deserve this. It was a senseless and brutal assault."

"What the hell is wrong with this guy?" he asked. "Does he realize how fucked up what he did is? Why did he do this? Was it just because I'm Latino?"

"Those three questions, 'Why did he do this? Does he realize the seriousness of what he did? And did he do it because of race?' are questions that the restorative justice program wants answered, too. You're not alone in needing answers to those questions. When we ask those questions as part of this process, we're not only representing you, but also the larger community," I explained.

"Are you up for hearing what I learned after talking to him?" I asked.

"Yes. I need to know why he did this," he said.

"Okay. Keep in mind that regardless of why he did this, there is no excuse for what he did. He needs to be held accountable not only for the harm he caused you, and really, all of us, but also the fact that he committed a felony. The courts are going to decide what to do about the felony. He pled guilty, so he's not denying that he did what he did. He's not trying to get out of it. That's important. That's why this case was referred to restorative justice."

"Why did he do this? What was he thinking?" asked Leo.

"He wasn't. He was playing out a scenario in his head. Are you interested in hearing what I learned about his backstory? Because I think it'll help you detach a bit by seeing that what he did had absolutely *nothing* to do with you, and *everything* to do with what was done to him. This doesn't excuse what he did to you, but at least, provides some potential answers to his mindset," I said.

"I understand. I'm interested in knowing," Leo said.

"Okay. When he was in middle school, his dad lost his contracting business and had to claim bankruptcy. They lost their house, and they had to move here. His father blamed it on Latino construction workers who were charging less. His father started a fight with some Latinos at a Home Depot and apparently, he got beat up. He was charged with the assault because he started it.

"Some of the boys whose fathers were involved in the fight went to the same middle school as Rick. [This is the first time I used Rick's name.] They bullied him. They threatened to beat him up and they made fun of him and his father."

"That's where his hatred for Latinos comes from?" asked Leo.

"I'm not a psychologist, but I think so," I said. "I would imagine his father constantly referred to Latinos in racist terms. When his father told him that some Latinos were harassing him and driving by his house because he refused to pay them, in Rick's mind he was back in middle school. Only this time, he was going to do something about it."

"Like carry a gun," Leo said.

"Yeah. Apparently, your car was similar to a car these workers were driving," I added. "He was acting out a story that he had in his head.

"What do you think about this?" I asked.

Leo thought for a moment. "This is fucked up. I *was* in the wrong place at the wrong time," he said.

"No, you weren't. You were on your way home from work. What he did was a result of being raised by a father who probably consistently told him Latinos were out to get them. That's the racist part. Why do you suppose he would feel the need to carry a gun?" I asked.

"Because he's afraid of Latinos," he said.

"I think it's even deeper than that, Leo. I realize I'm sounding like an armchair psychologist here, but I think in his mind carrying a gun is his way of making up for how defenseless and humiliated he felt in middle school. Carrying a gun is his way of preventing that from happening again. It doesn't excuse what he did. It explains a distorted view of reality," I said.

I asked Leo, "What do you think about what I'm telling you?"

"Did you tell him this?" he asked.

"Yes," I said. "I made the connection between what happened to him in middle school and his father's blaming of Latinos with what he did to you that day."

"Does he get it?" Leo asked.

"He gets it enough to know that he needs help, and he's willing to do that. I confronted him with the harm he caused you by asking him to put himself in your shoes. I also confronted him with the potential damage this is going to do to his son. I asked him point blank, 'Do you want your son to go through the same thing you did growing up?' He answered, 'No.'

"I believe he realizes how serious this is, that there is no excuse for what he did, and that he has some substantial repair to do. I want to turn the focus back to you. What would help you move through this? What do you need?" I asked.

Leo took a deep breath and said, "I don't know, man. I just want to be done with this. Guys like this shouldn't be allowed to carry guns. I mean, would he have done this if he didn't have a gun?"

"I want this to be over for you, too," I said. "That's a great question about the gun. I didn't ask him, but I'd like to know that as well.

"What do you think about meeting with him?" I asked.

"Part of me wants to tell him how pissed off I am and how he made me feel and what he did to my family. The other part just wants to move on and not think about this anymore. A part of me wants to see him go to jail. Another part of me doesn't want his kid to see his dad go to jail. I'm torn about whether to meet with him or not," he said.

"It sounds like you're torn between wanting Rick to be held accountable for what he did, and not wanting him to go to jail because of his son. Is that fair to say?" I asked.

"Yeah. That's it," he said.

"You're feeling empathy for his kid, but you also need what he did to you to have consequences. Yes?" I asked.

"That's exactly it. That's my conflict," he said. "I'm angry as hell. But his kid shouldn't have to pay for what he did. It's not fair to me that I should have to have that on my shoulders," he said.

"No, it's not fair," I said. "This is an opportunity for you to tell him that, but also for him to hear that from others. Are you interested in hearing what I think about how meeting with him will benefit you?"

"Yes," he replied.

"It's not an easy decision. Like I said, what you're experiencing is a post-traumatic byproduct of experiencing an assault. We just keep working on it over and over and over in our minds trying to rationalize what happened. So, in a sense, we're stuck in a loop, constantly searching for 'the answer' that will help us move on. It's like a cloud hanging over our head. We can't let it go because it won't let us go. Does this make sense?" I asked.

"Yeah. I keep playing what happened over and over. I'm really tired of this," he said.

"When we've experienced an injustice, we need others in the community to be our advocate, hear us and take what happened to us seriously, represent us, and acknowledge that what was done to us was unacceptable. We need others to validate our sense of injustice, and we need them to say that to the person who committed the offense. You mentioned shouldering the load of this decision. This is a way for others to shoulder that emotional load with you.

"In this case, it's not only about the gun. It's also about the racial epithets he screamed at you. There were essentially three violations you experienced. He blocked you with this truck. He threatened you with a gun. And he assaulted you verbally with racist terms. Are you tracking with me?" I asked.

"Yeah," he replied.

"The other people in this meeting will represent you by holding him accountable for how each of these injustices impacted you as well as the community. They'll ask him, 'Why did you do what you did?'; 'Why did you say what you did?'; and 'Do you realize how destructive this was to our community?'" I explained.

"Even though you were the one that was directly impacted, what he did impacted the entire community. This group meeting is an opportunity for you to feel supported by others," I added.

"You said the cop who arrested him is going to be there. Who else will be there?" he asked.

"In addition to myself and another facilitator ('Lois'), I'm going to ask three other members from our community. One person is a father ('Tim') whose teenage son was shot and killed at a party by another teenager. The second person is a Latino community activist who specializes in diversity ('John'), and the third is a trauma specialist and victim advocate ('Pat'). All three of these people have substantial experience with our program. And of course, if you'd like your wife or a friend to be there, I can talk with them and explain how this meeting will go. I can also put you in touch with the victim advocate before we meet," I explained.

"Let me talk to my wife," he said. "I do want to confront him, and I want to be done with this."

"I understand," I said. "I want it to be done for you too."

Preparing for the Encounter

Leo and his wife decided to move forward. In Leo's words, "I can see how this will help both of us."

When I spoke individually with the others who would be attending, I explained the incident and shared what I had learned in my conversations with both Leo and Rick. I asked each of them to think about what outcome they would like to see happen.

I explained to John, the diversity activist, that my sense was that Rick had inherited his father's attitudes and resentments. John commented, "That's how it starts, doesn't it?" I offered that I believed this was an ideal opportunity for Rick to question, if not confront, his father's attitudes and resentments toward Latinos.

John said something powerful: "Racism morphs into extremism when people search for confirmation of their feelings of powerlessness through alliance with others who feel the same way."

I spoke again with Rick on the phone and let him know we were moving forward. I explained who would be there and asked him if he wanted a support person, such as a friend, to attend. He declined. I reviewed how the conversation would go.

I explained, "We're going to talk about what happened and give people a chance to talk about how they were impacted. We're also going to explore why this happened and what can be done to repair the harm and ensure that this never happens again."

I said to Rick, "It's been two weeks since you and I met. What have you been thinking about? Are you still willing to do this?"

He replied, "My kid. I fucked up. I have to take my licks."

I was struck by his comment about "taking licks." "You acted out a story you had in your head. By taking responsibility, you're showing your kid what integrity and real courage looks like, Rick," I said.

I explained to our discussion group, "The first few moments before the group conversation starts can be thick with tension for participants who've never attended a restorative justice conference. First, there's the embodied experience of vulnerability and exposure induced by the physical space of the circle itself. People are facing each other in relatively close proximity. In discussions such as these, the circle isn't just a metaphor. It is an operational symbol that doesn't just communicate the idea of community but makes it a felt reality, an artifact of encounter. Whatever 'the community' is, it's not 'out there' but 'right here' in this circle.

"Second, there's the seriousness of, and insecurity about, the impending conversation about to happen. Whatever feelings and fears people have about what happened and anxiety about how it is going to be discussed is palpable. Third, it's the first time that the person who committed the violation and those that were harmed have met since the incident."

I added, "A good facilitator will manage this tension constructively before the discussion begins (while waiting for others to arrive). Some facilitators try to reduce this tension by making small talk, use self-deprecating humor, or instructing participants to 'breathe and feel their seat.'

"One facilitator brought a rock into the circle and asked each person to hold it and state what they felt. People sitting in that circle looked at me (as the co-facilitator) with a look of 'what the hell is this?' I wanted to take the rock and bolt. A bag of granola would've been more... Never mind.

"A good facilitator will allow this tension to simply 'be as it is' but also read it and use it to gauge, or sense, people's energy and demeanor. In addition, a veteran facilitator will 'hold a space of stability' with their own calm and assured demeanor, posture, kind face, and steady breathing. I'll explain more about this in the next chapter on restorative communication and using the body as an instrument of grounding," I said.

The Encounter

When everyone had assembled in Leo and Rick's circle, I thanked everyone for coming and explained, "We're here to discuss something serious that happened in our community, hear from those who were negatively impacted, try to understand why this happened, and put a plan in place to repair the harm." I asked each person to identify themselves and make a statement about what they hoped our discussion would accomplish.

I started with Leo. He thought for a moment. "I want to understand why you did this because I don't want this to ever happen again to someone else."

I moved to Leo's wife ("Maria"). She spoke directly to Rick. "I want you to realize the terror you caused to my husband and family." Rick appeared to take this in. He didn't look away or shift in his seat.

I asked the police officer. "I want to emphasize how this impacts public safety and what could've happened."

The father ("Tim") who had lost his son spoke next. "Rick, my hope is that you realize how precious a life is and how a moment of rage can take that life away from people."

"John," the community activist, spoke next. "I need us to understand the role that ethnicity played in this incident. My hope is that Rick can see the humanity under the skin."

"Pat," the victim advocate and trauma specialist, stated, "I'd like us to come away with a strategy and plan for getting Leo and Maria any support they need. Rick, my hope for you is that you take a look at where this rage comes from and get some help to do that."

Finally, I turned to Rick. "Rick, what do you hope to accomplish?"

Looking at Leo and Maria, he said, "I'm here to apologize for what I did. I'm not a bad man. I don't want to lose my son." Rick's statement appeared to lessen some of the tension in the circle. Leo sat back in his chair.

Quick Group Reflection

I explained to our discussion group, "Each of these opening statements were/are critical for several reasons. First, they establish aspirations and goals, and envision potential positive outcomes. They are value-based statements of possibility. Second, they are statements of both individual and group commitment and ownership of the issues. As such, they imply that this is a shared undertaking.

"In this case, Leo and Maria are no longer isolated in the pursuit of accountability and resolution. The group is now representing them as part of a community and, as such, Leo's and Maria's experience becomes part of a larger narrative.

"Concurrently, the implicit message to Rick is twofold—'This affected all of us and our community' and, as such, 'we have a vested interest in understanding why this happened and ensuring that it doesn't happen again.' This incorporates Rick's story into what Langellier (1985) suggested about personal narratives becoming part of a larger sense-making structure.[13] Both Leo's and Rick's stories were about to become a community's story as well.

"Third, there is a rebalancing, or redistribution of power happening. The overpowering and disempowerment that occurred as a result of the offense is effectively dismantled or 'leveled.' It is now the group—which includes both Leo and Rick, that has the power of decision-making.

"Importantly, and what distinguishes restorative justice from conventional retributive approaches, that power is not based on coercion or the threat of punishment by the group. Rather, it is a type of collective authority founded upon engagement and discovery, and a sincere desire and commitment to reparation and recovery," I explained. "Back to the encounter," I added.

Back to the Encounter

I thanked everyone for their statements and said, "Let's get started. We're going to talk first about exactly what happened. We're just trying to get the details and sequence of events straight. The best way to do this is to treat this as a type of report, or as if you were standing behind a camera recording it. What would that movie show us?

"Leo, would you like to start with explaining what happened to you, or would you like us to start with Rick?" Some facilitators begin with the survivor. Others begin with the offender. I think it is more constructive (and empowering) to start by giving the survivor that decision, rather than mandating or directing.

"I'd like to hear from Rick first," said Leo. I thought Leo's use of Rick's name instead of "you" was an encouraging sign. However subtle, my sense was that something had shifted in Leo's demeanor. His tone was less confrontational than before.

Rick explained that he was on his way home from his father's house. His father told him some Latino (not the term his father used) workers were "out to get him" because he didn't pay them. Those workers kept "calling him and threatening him and cruising" by his father's house in a green Cherokee.

About two blocks from his father's house, he saw a green Cherokee in his rearview mirror. He turned onto Main Street. The Cherokee followed. He drove for about four blocks. The Cherokee was still following him. At the next stop sign, the Cherokee was right behind him. He got out of his truck, walked back to the Cherokee, and "confronted the driver."

"What do you mean by 'confronted'?" I asked.

"I asked him why he was following me," said Rick.

"With a gun in your hand," I said.

"Yes. I had a firearm," said Rick.

"A gun," I said.

"Yes," said Rick.

"What kind of gun?" I asked.

"A Beretta M9," he said.

"Did you point it at Leo?" I asked. I used Leo's name on purpose.

"No," he said.

"Where was it pointed?" I asked.

"I had it pointed down," he replied.

"How far away from Leo's face was your gun?" I pressed.

"Three feet," interjected Leo.

"Is that accurate?" I asked Rick.

"Yeah, I was probably that close," he said.

"Was Leo's window down?" I asked.

"I don't remember," he replied.

"Yes," interjected Leo.

"What exactly did you say to Leo?" I asked.

"I said, 'Why are you following me?'" said Rick.

"Did you curse?" I asked.

"Yeah. I said, 'Why the fuck are you following me?'" replied Rick.

"Did you call him any names?" I asked.

Rick looked down. After a moment he said, "I don't really want to repeat what I said." I thought it was encouraging that Rick didn't want to repeat it. It signified for the group, especially Leo, that Rick knew that the names he called Leo were unacceptable. I let the discomfort in the circle sit for a moment.

"It's important that we know what you said, Rick," I pressed. "We need to know exactly what happened."

"I called him a 'd**** b*****'," he said.

"What else?" I asked.

"A f****** s***," he replied. Rick never looked up.

"Thank you for your honesty, Rick. I want to clarify something. You said you asked Leo why he was following you; did you scream these words at him?" I asked.

"Yeah," he said.

"Okay. Thanks again for being honest," I replied.

"I'm sorry I did this," said Rick.

I replied, "Hold onto that. Right now, we're just trying to get the story straight."

Quick Group Reflection

I took a moment to let the weight of Rick's account settle with the group. "Moments like these, when an offender explains what happened in graphic detail, serve several purposes in the process. First, it's the first time the survivor has had the opportunity to hear directly from the offender what they did. The more detailed, factual, and unflinching the offender's account is, the more it can function to validate the reality of what the survivor experienced.

"Second, those details help others in the circle begin to comprehend what it must have been like for the person who experienced the violation. The offender's account serves to 'enroll' others in the circle on an emotional level as 'once-removed participants' in what happened. The details make it real. Third, it signifies the profound seriousness and/or traumatic experience of the violation.

"Lastly, it presents the opportunity for that account to be challenged by the survivor, any discrepancies to be resolved, or any questions to be asked which would clarify details, which is what I did with my questions."

Back to the Encounter

I turned next to Leo. Looking directly at Rick, Leo said, "I want to know why you did this and if you've ever had someone threaten your life with a gun. I don't buy the 'I thought you were following me' bit, but I'll follow the rules."

I assured everyone, "We'll get to the deeper reasons for why this happened in a bit."

Leo explained, "I was on my way home from work. I came to a stop sign behind a white truck and I saw this guy jump out of the truck and start walking toward me with a gun in his hand screaming at the top of his lungs, 'Why are you following me?!' He came right up to my window and screamed at me again, 'Why the fuck are you following me?!' I put my hands up in the air and yelled, 'Easy! Easy! I'm not following you! I don't even know who you are! I'm just going home from work!'"

"What names did he call you?" I asked.

"He called me a f****** s*** and a d**** b*****."

Maria's eyes watered. Leo put his arm around her. I passed a box of tissues to her. There was a tangible heaviness in the circle. Facilitators are supposed to be neutral (whatever that means), but hearing Leo state what Rick called him, I felt sad. Rick sat motionless and stared at the floor.

Leo continued, "Then he just walked away, got back in his truck, and drove off. I got his license plate number and called 911. Then I called my wife."

"Thank you, Leo," I said. "I think this is the right moment to shift into talking about impact," I said to the circle. "Leo, can you describe your experience when this happened?"

Leo replied, "I can't really explain how I felt when I saw him walking back to my car with a gun in his hand other than I felt completely helpless. I felt trapped. Like a wounded deer waiting for the hunter to come over and shoot it in the head. It was an out-of-body experience. All I could do was put my hands up in the air. I thought my life was over, that I'd never see my wife or kids again.

"After he drove off, I pulled into the parking lot of a coffee shop and called 911. I was shaking. I could barely hold my phone or talk to the operator. The whole time I was thinking, 'What if this guy comes back?' The operator told me to go inside the coffee shop and wait for an officer to come.

"The police came almost immediately. I explained what happened. They told me to stay put. One officer went outside. The other officer took my statement. About five minutes later, the other officer came back inside and said they arrested the guy who did it."

"What did you feel when the officer told you they caught Rick?" I asked.

"I felt like I was going to throw up. I just wanted to go home," Leo said.

"Maria, can you describe what happened when Leo got home?" I asked.

"I knew something happened. He was shaking. We went and sat on the couch, and he told me what happened. He said, 'This guy got pissed off and cut me off and pulled a gun on me.' He said, 'They arrested him.' Then he just doubled over and started crying really hard. All I could do was just hold him.

"The kids came in from school, and they wanted to know what happened. I had to lie and tell them their dad saw a bad accident. We just all sat there on the couch. Our youngest, who's nine, started crying. We just sat there," she said.

"Do you have *any* fucking idea what you did to my family?" she said to Rick. "You threatened my entire family! You should be ashamed of yourself!" She started to cry. Leo kept his arm around Maria.

I asked, "Maria, can you talk about how this has impacted your family since it happened? How has it impacted your children?"

Maria replied, "What are we supposed to tell them? That some guy threatened their father with a gun because he was Latino? Leo wouldn't let us go out unless he drove. They know something really bad happened. They know that we're scared."

She turned to Rick. "Excuse my language, but what the fuck is wrong with you?" At this point, Pat, who was the victim advocate and was sitting on the other side of Maria, put her arm around Maria.

After a moment, I said gently, "Maria, thank you for having the courage to come here tonight, and speak your truth about what happened and how it has impacted you and your family. I want you to know that you're not alone in needing to know why this happened. It's something we all need to know and we're going to talk about that. Before we move forward, is there anything else you'd like to say to Rick?"

She finished, "I just don't understand how anyone could do something like this. Is it just because we're brown?" she asked.

Leo spoke to Rick: "This is what you did to us." Rick was motionless.

After a moment, I suggested a five-minute break. As everyone stood and started to leave the circle, Rick remained seated. I went over to him and suggested we step outside for a few minutes. I needed to gauge how he felt and what he was thinking before moving forward. Once outside I asked him, "I want to check in with you. How are you doing with hearing this?"

"I don't know what to say. I wish I could take it back. I fucked up. I *am* ashamed of what I did to these people. To Leo and his wife and their kids," he said.

"Rick, everything you just said to me is what you can say to them," I said.

"I'm not a racist, Mr. Bledsoe," he said.

"Like I said, you're the only one who knows. But what you called Leo, the names you called him, are racist names, Rick. They're hateful, violent words. From their perspective, what you did was because of the color of their skin. Because they are Latino. Can you see that?" I asked.

"Yeah," he said.

"They need to know why you did this. We all do. When we come back together, I'm going to push you to open up about what happened to you. Not to excuse you, but to possibly help Maria and Leo see why you did what you did. It's not about sympathy for you. It's about helping them, Rick. Am I making sense?" I asked. "

"Yeah. How can I fix this?" he asked.

"You can be honest with everyone. You have no defense. Let them know how you feel about what you did to them," I said.

"Will they accept my apology?" he asked. "Will it even do any good?"

"I don't know. But that's a risk you have to take if you're sincere. An apology isn't about making us feel better. It's about accepting responsibility for how we hurt the other person. It's saying, 'There is no excuse for what I did to you,' and letting them know how deeply sorry we are for the suffering we caused them. Are you willing to continue?" I asked.

"Yeah," he said.

"I know this is not easy, Rick. It takes courage. In my opinion, you're doing the right thing," I said.

Quick Group Reflection

I explained to our discussion group that after speaking with Rick, I took a few moments to strategize how to proceed in the discussion.

I said, "If I were to just 'follow the script,' the conversation would shift toward exploring why Rick did what he did. Both Maria and Leo needed some answers. I also needed to engage the participation of others in the circle. This shift is essentially a shift in focus, away from the survivor's emotional and psychological traumatic experience of the incident, and toward a more objective or analytical exploration and discussion of the reasons why an offender did what they did.

"In my experience, this shift should not happen abruptly. When a survivor lays bare their pain, that suffering needs to be recognized, acknowledged, validated, and embraced with *reverence* by others. That reverence *dignifies* the humanity of the survivors," I explained.

I continued to the discussion group, "Facilitation is an imperfect art. It's about letting the process unfold. When facilitators focus too heavily on progressing linearly through the sequence of the script, they can miss the potential that this moment has, not only for the survivors, but also for the offender and the rest of the circle.

"It is a transformational moment in the conversation that needs to be handled with extreme care. It's also about having faith in the goodness of others and trusting that they want reconciliation and healing as much as you do.

"It's important for facilitators and practitioners to realize that restoration can happen during the discussion as much as produce an outcome called 'restoration' (the reparative contract). Though I'll explain in more detail in our next discussion on restorative communication, restorative communication and interaction is a type of *performative discourse*. It 'performs,' or enacts, what it denotes or describes. If I were to just 'follow the script' and launch into a discussion about why Rick did what he did, our circle would miss the opportunity for Maria and Leo to experience a moment of support and solidarity.

"For that reason, I decided to allow Rick to express his remorse and apologize to Maria and Leo when we reconvened, rather than wait until the end of the conversation when the group discusses what needs to happen to repair the harm. My sense was that doing so would both dignify their experience, but also 'clear a space' for making a graceful transition into a discussion which required more objectivity. Maria and Leo needed to hear how Rick felt about what he did to them before they could hear about the reasons why he did what he did."

Back to the Encounter

When we reconvened, I thanked everyone for their willingness to keep going. I thanked Maria and Leo for their courage and willingness to participate and share how this impacted their whole family.

"Before we move into a discussion about how this incident impacted the larger community and explore why it happened, I'd like to give Rick the opportunity to express how he feels about what he did."

Rick's eyes were watery. He sat up, took a deep breath, looked straight at both Maria and Leo, and began.

"I don't know what to say other than I'm so sorry for what I did to you. I know my apology probably doesn't mean anything, but I'm sorry for all of it. I did something terrible to you. I was out of control. I'm sorry," he said. "I know you think I'm a racist and that I hate Mexicans. I don't. I know you don't believe me. All I can say is I'm sorry."

Quick Reflection

I explained to our discussion group, "This was the transition moment I was hoping for. Rick's statements functioned to validate both Maria's and Leo's experience, but also humanize, or at least, demythologize Rick as an offender.

"It also served to reverse the power-over dynamic that happens when someone violates another. Rick's statement, 'I'm willing to do whatever I need to do,' signified an act of submission. It is now the survivor who has the power of decision-making with regard to moving forward.

"The choice to accept/not accept Rick's apology was in Maria's and Leo's hands, not as an obligation, but as a possibility. That power redistribution would emerge again when it came time for the circle to discuss what needed to be repaired."

Back to the Encounter

I thanked Rick for his offering, and then turned back to Maria and Leo. "Is there anything you'd like to say?"

Maria was silent. Leo spoke. "I don't know what to think about this. Part of me wants to believe you're sincere, but the other part of me just doesn't believe you. And it doesn't erase what you did. I don't know you, so I don't know why you carry a gun, where your rage comes from, or why you called me such disgusting things.

"I get that it could've been any Latino driving a green Cherokee. So even though you did this to me and my family, it had nothing to do with me personally. But it did have everything to do with the color of my skin. It wouldn't have happened if I wasn't Latino. I don't trust that you won't do this again. If you want your apology to mean something, you need to get some serious help. I hope to God you don't pass this onto your own kid. And you should never be allowed to carry a gun again."

I waited a moment to let Leo's words sink in, and then asked Maria if she wanted to add anything. She declined. I thanked Leo.

"Before we explore why this happened, I suggest we discuss how this impacted the larger community," I said. "Once we have an understanding of that impact, we'll have a better picture of what needs to be repaired. The way I'd like us to move through this is to talk about the menacing with a gun violation first, and then the hate speech that Rick used."

Officer Jones spoke first. "The first thing I want to say is how much I respect both of you (Maria and Leo) for being willing to come here tonight and talk about what happened to you. Most people who experience something like this don't ever want to see the perpetrator again, let alone sit across from them in a circle like this. I want to acknowledge your courage.

"The second thing I want to say is how lucky you are, Rick, that it was Leo in the other car. If the other driver also had a gun and saw you approaching him with a gun in your hand, there would've been a shootout. Either you or the other driver would've been killed. Bystanders, other drivers, could very easily have been killed. If you weren't killed, you would be facing a murder charge and potentially life in prison.

"If another officer or I happened to be there and saw you get out of your truck with a gun in your hand, told you to drop it and you didn't, you could've very easily been shot and killed. Do you understand what I'm saying? Do you understand what very likely could've happened? Do you understand the seriousness of what you did?" he asked.

"Yes," said Rick.

"I really hope you do. This is not about your right to carry a gun. You abused that right. Consciously or not, when you got out of your truck with a gun in your hand and threatened Leo, you threatened the safety of our entire community. You threatened the safety of my fellow police officers. Do you understand what I'm saying?" he asked.

"Yes," said Rick.

"What scares me about this incident is that it could happen again. I don't know what's going to happen with your case. I don't know what it's going to take for you to never do this again. What I can tell you is that this should be a wakeup call. This can never happen again. Do you understand me?" he finished.

"Yes, I do," said Rick.

I thanked Officer Jones for his contribution and then turned to Tim (the father who lost his son). He spoke to Leo and Maria first. "Like Officer Jones, I want to express my sorrow that this happened to you and my respect for your courage and willingness to be here."

Tim reached into his shirt pocket and retrieved a photo of his son. He looked at it for a moment, and then passed it around until it came to Rick.

"You have a son, right?" he asked Rick.

"Yes," said Rick.

"How old is your son?" Tim asked.

"Nine," replied Rick.

"I want you to look at this picture. That's my son. His name is Bobby. He was in the back seat of a car with some friends. They were driving home from a party. Another car pulled up beside them and started shooting at them. They thought one of my son's friends was a member of a rival gang. He wasn't.

"My son was shot in the head and died instantly. He was 17. Two of his friends were also shot. One of them, the young man who this other car thought was a gang member, was paralyzed for life." Tim waited a moment to let the story sink in.

"Let me tell you about my son. He was kind. He was funny. He had a lot of friends. He had a girlfriend. He liked to work with his hands, build things. He was about to go to college. He was the love of our lives. He was murdered because someone thought one of his friends, who was Latino, was somebody else. The other boys in that car were also remarkable young men with bright futures. My son's best friend was the boy who is now paralyzed for the rest of his life.

"The young man who killed my son was white. He got the gun from his father. This young man will be in prison for the rest of his life. Why? I'll tell you why. Because this boy belonged to a gang of white kids who hated Latinos.

"I want to ask you, what if this was your son? Either my son, or the young man who got a gun from his father and committed a murder. My wife, the other families, and I will be grieving our loss for the rest of our lives. I don't wish that on anyone," Tim finished.

I let the weight of Tim's story sit with the group. After this truly heavy moment, I thanked him for sharing his story. I said this not only to validate his sorrow but to send the message to Rick that Tim's loss affected all of us in that circle, both personally and as an extension of the community.

Leo and Maria both responded the same way: "We're sorry this happened to your son, Tim." Tim thanked them.

Quick Group Reflection

I explained to our discussion group, "This expression of empathy and compassion for Tim was an important demonstration of people, who had only met in this circle, caring for each other. Strategically, I wanted Rick to experience not only the story of what happened to Tim and its undeniable relevance to what he did, but what a moment of shared empathy, tenderness, open-heartedness, sadness, and humanity felt like.

"I also wanted to transition into a discussion about racism and, hopefully, create a space for Rick to open up about where his own racist beliefs (however unconscious) toward Latinos came from. I instinctively felt that if Rick could open up about what his father modeled for him, it might help Maria and Leo further depersonalize what Rick did.

"In effect, what I was trying to do was put Rick's motivations and behavior into a larger context. Maria and Leo were not only survivors of what Rick did, but also survivors of a deeper and more pervasive social violation of racism. I wanted them to experience representatives from the community confront and condemn the issue of racism in the community," I explained to our discussion group.

"This seemed like an opportune moment to enroll John into the discussion. The day before our circle, I spoke with John and shared what I had learned about Rick's history. I suggested that Rick might also be a victim/survivor of racist conditioning by his father. Like I said when I talked to John on the phone before the encounter, he said, 'That's one of the ways it starts, doesn't it?' "

In that phone call, I also shared my insecurity with John about going that deep into Rick's story in the circle. I admitted that even though it makes sense to us that what Rick did was act out a belief system he got from his father, my concern was that talking about that in the circle might appear to Maria and Leo that I was justifying or excusing what he did.

John offered me support. "I don't think you're justifying what he did. You're looking for the deeper reasons why he did what he did. From what you told me about his story, on some level he was afraid of Latinos. I think if you explain that to Maria and Leo, they'll understand why you're doing it. I think it might actually help them let go of any resentment or bitterness," he said.

John continued, "Racism is a problem in our community. Bigger than most people know or care to admit. Chances are they've experienced it many times before Rick. This would give them the chance to talk about that. Besides, it might help Rick, too. It'll force him to make a decision. What's he going to say to his father? What's he going to tell his kid?" Great questions.

Back to the Encounter

After Maria and Leo expressed their sympathy to Tim, I moved us forward. "I'd like us to take a deeper look into the role that ethnicity played in what happened," I said.

Before I could continue, however, Rick interjected. "I want to say something, if that's all right," he said.

"Of course," I replied.

Speaking to Tim, Rick said, "I'm really sorry about your son and the other boy. I don't know what I'd do if someone did that to my kid. I'd probably want to get even. But I'm not that guy, that other driver who did that. I was never in a gang and I'm not a racist."

Speaking to the circle, he continued, I don't hate Mexican-Americans. I know you don't believe me, and I'm not making an excuse, but I really thought I was being followed by some Mexican workers who were out to get my dad. I did the wrong thing and I'm sorry for that.

"Leo, I'm sorry I did what I did to you, and your wife, and your family. I was out of line. I never should've done this. I never should've gotten out of my truck. If I could take it back, I would," he finished.

Officer Jones responded, "Rick, why didn't you or your dad just call the police and tell us you thought your dad was being harassed? We would have checked that out."

Rick replied, "Because we did that before where we moved from. My dad got beat up by a bunch of Mexican construction workers and he ended up being arrested for assault."

"Rick, I'm confused. You told me your dad started that fight at a building supply store," I said.

"He did. And they beat the shit out of him. They broke his jaw and kicked him when he was on the ground. They broke one of his ribs. Nothing happened to those guys. They got away with it. And then their kids started making fun of me at school, calling my dad a p**** and coward," he said.

"And you and your dad reported that to the school, right?" I asked.

"Yeah. And they didn't do a f***** thing. Sorry for my language. It just got worse," he replied. "So, you can see why we didn't call the cops about this."

Officer Jones asked, "Why did your dad start the fight?"

"Because he was really pissed off and blamed them for him losing his business. One of those guys said something smart-ass to him at the store and he lost his temper," Rick answered.

"My dad lost his business. We lost our house and had to move here," he said. "And my dad hired these other workers here because he can't do the work anymore. But they did a shitty job and so he didn't pay them."

Officer Jones asked, "Does your dad carry a firearm?"

"Yeah," Rick replied.

"And you do too," Officer Jones said.

"Yes," said Rick.

Officer Jones continued, "Because you were afraid?"

"Because we have a right to protect ourselves," Rick answered.

"I understand that. But you both started carrying firearms because you're afraid that this would happen again?" Officer Jones asked.

"Yes," admitted Rick.

At this moment in the circle, I was worried that Rick's story was taking precedence over Maria's and Leo's experience of what happened to them.

"Leo, I want to check in with you and Maria. We're starting to focus on Rick's story here. and I'd like to know how you are with this?" I asked.

Maria spoke, "Rick, we're not those people."

Rick replied, "I know that now. I made a huge mistake. I'm sorry."

"Leo?" I asked.

"This explains a lot," he said. "It's starting to make sense."

Pat, the trauma specialist and victim's advocate, spoke next. "Rick, I have a question for you. When you left your dad's house, were you upset?"

"What do you mean?" Rick asked.

"Because you seem like a reasonable person who did an irrational thing. I'm wondering if you were angry when you left your father's house, before you ever saw Leo. Did your father say something to you? I'm trying to piece this together," she said.

"I went over there because he was afraid these guys were going to do something," he said.

"Like what? What did he think they were going to do?" asked Pat.

"Like do a drive-by and shoot at his house or shoot at his truck," said Rick.

"Is that when he told you about a green Cherokee?" asked Pat.

"Yeah," said Rick.

"So, when you left his house, is it safe to say that you were on edge? You were on the lookout for those guys? And especially a green Cherokee?" she asked.

"Yeah," he replied.

"Does the word 'paranoid' fit?" she asked.

Rick thought for a moment. "I guess so."

Leo asked, "Where is your dad's house?"

"On Mesa," he replied.

"My work is on Mesa. When did you first see my car?" Leo asked.

"When we turned onto Main," Rick said.

"So, you first saw me when we were on Mesa?" Leo asked.

"Yeah. When you turned onto Main, I thought you were following me," said Rick.

"And you were already pissed off because of what your dad told you," Leo said.

"I guess so," Rick said.

"Rick, do you see the connection here between your father getting beat up when you were in middle school, what your father told you was happening here with these men, and then what you ended up doing to Leo?" Pat asked. "I don't want to turn this into a therapy session, but do you see the connection?"

Pat's question hit home with Rick because his eyes started to water. Maria slid the box of Kleenex over to Rick. We all just sat there for a few moments. This was a powerful moment in the circle. Pat had made the connection I was trying to get Rick to see when I first interviewed him.

Finally, I said, "I think this is a good time to move into talking about repair."

After Rick regained his composure, I asked, "Rick what do you think needs to be repaired here?"

In an almost childlike voice, he said, "I don't know. I just don't want to go to jail. I don't want to lose my son."

Leo responded, "I don't think you should go to jail either, Rick. At first, I did because I was angry and wanted you to be punished. I wanted you to suffer because you made me suffer. But now I see it wouldn't serve any purpose. It'd only hurt your kid."

Maria followed: "Rick, I accept your apology. I accept your apology not to let you off the hook but because I don't want to carry any more anger and bitterness in my heart."

Quick Group Reflection

Turning back to our discussion group, I explained, "In my experience, the discussion about repair is where the community, represented by a circle of engaged and concerned citizens, puts their relationship- and heart-centric minds together in a pragmatic, solution-oriented way.

"This discussion embodies what Plato and Aristotle referred to as *phronēsis*, 'practical wisdom' or 'practical virtue.' After fully exploring what happened, what the harm was, discovering the underlying reasons for the violation, the circle then collaborated to determine a 'best possible way forward' that leads to resolution, repair, and potential healing—not only for those directly involved, but potentially for the extended community as a 'social body.'

"The practical wisdom enacted in this discussion is in its recognition that repairing harm requires meeting needs. There are essentially two categories of needs. The first are those needs that were created as a result of the violation itself.

"For example, in this case, what do Maria and Leo need to move forward; feel satisfied that what happened to them has been meaningfully and sufficiently addressed? What might they need in order to experience resolution and, ideally, some healing and closure? What do they need to feel safe? What do they need from Rick and the community? What would 'repair' look like for them?

"What does the larger community need to have happen? Most obvious, or explicit, is that Rick's violation threatened public safety. Law enforcement and the criminal justice system exist to ensure that the safety of its citizens is maintained. But there are other implicit needs that reflect social norms of civility such as, at the very least, nonviolent conflict resolution and respect for diversity. In this case, the respect for diversity was violated. What does the community need from Rick to restore that respect? What would nonviolent resolution to the incident look like moving forward? What would restoring civility look like in this situation?

"What does Rick need? To be understood? To be believed? To be trusted? To be given a second chance? To be permitted to make amends for his offenses? To be pardoned, forgiven, redeemed, and reintegrated back into the community? What would that look like?

"The second category of needs are those unmet needs that, if met, might have prevented the violation from happening in the first place. This discovery is where I think the restorative process/dialogue can facilitate what I would call 'retroactive restoration.' It can serve to reach back into an offender's life and identify the historical unmet needs arising out of issues, conditions, and historical experiences (like trauma) that an offender endured and that provoked or motivated the violation.

"The logic of this practical wisdom is pretty straightforward. If those unmet needs are identified and sufficiently addressed, there's a better chance of preventing the violation from happening again.

"In Rick's case, it was apparent that his experiences with bullying, his father's assault and subsequent beating, paranoia, and bigotry had all contributed to Rick's mindset and core beliefs about safety and security. In a sense, Rick's worldview was a product of his father's making. Though it wasn't mentioned in our discussions, Rick's mother had left them and essentially abandoned Rick when he was ten years old."

Back to the Encounter: Reparation

I explained to the circle that we needed to determine a series of measurable actions that Rick could take to repair the harm he had caused. I explained that these actions would constitute an informal contract (reparative agreement) between Rick and the restorative justice program representing the community, and that if completed within a time specified by the group, a letter of completion would be submitted to the courts on his behalf before sentencing.

As we went around the circle, each member made suggestions. Maria and Leo wanted Rick to get some therapy/counseling. Pat suggested that the therapy should focus on healing the trauma that he had experienced in middle school and in his relationship with his father.

Speaking to Rick, she said, "It would be most effective if at some point, you and your father could both participate so that you can explain how his own trauma has impacted you. I know that we can't include that as a requirement in your contract, but I think it would help you as well as him."

John spoke next. "Our community has an ongoing problem with race relations in general. Gangs are an increasingly serious issue as is race-motivated hate and violence. I work with a group that conducts neighborhood discussions about diversity and inclusion. Tim is part of that group. Rick, I'd like to suggest that you come to some of these meetings and share your story, talk about what you've learned from our discussions here. I think your story is valuable, and others can benefit from hearing you. I think this would also help you develop some communication skills to confront your father's attitudes when you interact with him."

Tim spoke. "I can take you, Rick. These are really powerful discussions. They've helped me a lot."

"I'd like to do this, too," offered Leo. Everyone was somewhat stunned when he said this. "My story is the other half of what happened," he said. "People need to hear that. I think what we did here is something people need to know about."

John asked, "Can we consider this as part of Rick's community service?"

"Yes," I said.

Lois, our co-facilitator, drafted the agreement, and everyone signed it. The contract stipulated that Rick would attend weekly therapy sessions for three months and participate in six neighborhood meetings.

In closing our discussion, I asked Maria if there was anything she, in particular, needed to add. She said to Rick, "I needed to know why you did this. Now I understand."

Reconnecting with Rick

Rick fulfilled his agreement and went before the judge for sentencing. John, Tim, and Leo accompanied him and spoke on his behalf. They asked the judge not to sentence Rick to jail. The judge suspended Rick's sentence for three years, essentially placing him on probation. She told Rick that if he did not commit another offense for those three years, she would reduce his charge to a misdemeanor. She also suspended his concealed weapon permit for those three years.

> **Our media, institutions and public leadership have failed to address this crisis, framing boys and men as the problem themselves rather than as people requiring help.**[14]

I explained to the discussion group that about a year after this case, I bumped into Rick, ironically enough, in the parking lot of a Home Depot. "He and I talked for a few moments by his truck, and I asked him how he was doing."

He was articulate. He said, "I'm doing okay. This forced me to look at myself and where I came from. The therapy has been really helpful. It's helped me to find out who I am and what I stand for. I still can't believe that Leo, Tim, and John came to court with me. Especially Leo after what I did to him. That's why the judge went easy on me. I wish my dad could see that."

I asked him, "Do you still carry a gun?"

"No," he said.

"How did the diversity meetings go?" I asked.

"I'm still going. I've made friends. I took my kid to a couple," he said. "Can I ask you a personal question?"

"Sure," I said.

"Why do you do this?" he asked.

I took a moment. "Because just like you, I care. I care about people like Leo and his wife. I care about people like you, people who've made mistakes. I've been in Leo's shoes, and I've been in your shoes too with regard to being bullied. To be perfectly honest, this process helps me heal my own biases and resentments.

"Your situation is what happens when people come together in this type of process. That restores my faith in people. And what you did, how you showed up, and what Leo and the rest of our group did to support you is inspiring to me. They gave to me as much as they gave to you."

Closing Reflection

I explained to the group, "We'll debrief Rick's case in more detail in our next discussion, but I want to leave you with a few observations to think about.

"First, it would have been convenient to just label Rick as a racist, end the conversation, and send the case back to the courts. But what would that have accomplished? Maybe the better question is, what would that *not* have accomplished?

"It's reasonable to assume that had this group conversation with Rick not occurred, the connection between what happened to his father, the bullying he experienced in middle school, his fear, and his assault of Leo would not have been made. Leo and Maria wouldn't have had the chance to directly confront Rick, understand why he did what he did, nor participate in deciding what to do moving forward. All of this required a face-to-face encounter.

"Second, it would be a mistake to view this case as an exceptional incident or situation; that it was about one remorseful guy afraid of going to jail. It would also be shortsighted to assign any one reason for why this particular incident happened. I think it's more constructive to see how this deeper process of accountability revealed the intersection of an individual's beliefs with the larger culturally inherited beliefs.

"Those beliefs were underlying issues. It wasn't any one thing that led to what Rick did. It was a convergence of a multitude of factors (childhood trauma, mental health, social structures, cultural norms, and institutional policies) that otherwise, might not have been exposed.

"If there is anything remarkable about this case, it is that we were able to catch someone from falling farther. We caught Rick before it was too late. What would've happened if we hadn't?

"Third, what we see in this case is how the restorative approach is about increasing the ability to account. This accountability can constructively lead to finding those toxic sources and connect them to the destructive consequences. This connection is a function of the pragmatism of a restorative process. Once detected, solutions emerge and we are confronted with a choice/decision about what to do—both on a micro level of interaction (like the case with Rick), and also on a macro-social level.

"At the beginning of our discussion, I suggested that restoration is a paradigm that embodies a relationship-centric worldview. Restoration is essentially a technique that puts this worldview into action. It is both a philosophy and a practice. It's interesting that one of the root meanings of 'technique' (*tékhnē*) is 'to weave.' We could say that restoration is a technique which seeks to mend a tear in a community's social fabric.

"The elements of this technique are encounter, engagement, participation, inclusivity, discovery, truth-telling, accountability, acknowledgment of suffering and injury, self-determination, repair, and the recognition and meeting of needs. Referring back to Lévinas' observation that morality is experientially born in the moment we come face-to-face with 'the Other,' the restorative encounter and process provides the potential for our recognition of 'the Other-as-Us' to happen.

"I also suggested that this encounter foregrounds the role that communication and interaction plays in facilitating a recognition of the face of the Other. These elements, inclusivity, accountability, etc., are what characterize restorative communication as a type of civil discourse founded upon moral principles such as respect for the experience of 'the Other,' nonviolent resolution, empathy, and the community's responsibility for the well-being of its members.

"I don't think it's a stretch to characterize what happened in the case of Leo and Rick as a performance of rehumanization and, perhaps, a restoration of the inherent dignity of the individual and the larger community.

"A restoration of dignity occurred as a result of the convergence of accountability and empathy. Leo's and Maria's experience of harm was embraced and validated with empathy and compassion. Rick was held accountable for the harm he caused and repairing that harm. The underlying reasons and issues (Rick's history) were also accounted for, but in this accounting, empathy emerged from a recognition of his suffering as well.

"Finally, in our first discussion, I mentioned a three-stage ritual structure of social change: break/breach, liminality, and reformulation/reincorporation. In this case, Rick's assault of Leo not only classified as a criminal violation in legal terms (felony menacing with a weapon) but also signified a violation/breach of social norms of acceptable, 'moral' behavior within a community. Identifying the norms that were violated would require a book in itself, but at the very least, the assault violated standards of public safety, civility, and respect for diversity.

"Following the three stages, when a breach happens and those norms or expectations are challenged, an opportunity arises for members in a community to come together and decide whether those norms and the values inherent to those norms are still important, still valid, and, if so, determine how best to reassert or rearticulate and reestablish them. This represents the liminal stage of 'betwixt and between.'

"Though this observation may seem inordinately theoretical, the racial overtone of Rick's assault of Leo created the opportunity for a subgroup of the community to come together and determine how acceptable/unacceptable racist conduct is in the community.

"What we'll see happening with restorative communication, the restorative process (in this case, a restorative justice case) facilitates a transition through these stages by confronting what happened (the breach), ascertaining the meaning of what happened by recognizing the negative impact to people and relationships (liminal stage), and rearticulating or reasserting the values implicit in the violated social norms through the creation of a plan of concrete actions designed to enact and demonstrate those values and norms being reincorporated back into 'the community.'

"What the restorative process does is take the humanistic values and ideals of civility, rearticulate them within a specific context (incident), and put them into action."

CHAPTER FIVE
Restorative Communication

When our discussion group reconvened for our fifth conversation, we reviewed Rick and Leo's case. I explained, "When you move forward with integrating the restorative method and its various practices (applications) in your workplaces, one of the first things you'll need to do is build a core team of facilitators who meet on a consistent basis.

"The goal of your team meetings is to connect with each other and help each other develop the method and practice.

"Let's turn to the Rick and Leo case. I'd like to begin with your general observations. What struck you about what happened in this case? Was there anything that surprised you, or moved you?" I asked.

Joan spoke first. "I was stunned when Leo offered to speak on Rick's behalf at his sentencing. I don't know how to really describe it but the shift, or change of heart, that happened for Maria and Leo was ... what's the word ... radical. They went from feeling violated and angry to not only accepting his apology, but actually being concerned for him and his son. That blew me away. I didn't see that coming. How did that happen? Is this typical?"

I replied, "I don't want to get into citing a bunch of studies because there are so many variables that researchers have to consider when measuring success or defining what is 'typical.' I'll just say that for the most part, meta-analyses of numerous studies indicate that victims/survivors who participate in restorative justice processes report high satisfaction with the process.[1]

"Satisfaction is usually measured in terms of participants feeling like they were heard, understanding why the offender did what they did, believing that the offender was remorseful, apologies were sincere, restitution was made, a sense of emotional restoration occurred, and even a reduction in their post-traumatic stress symptoms.[2]

"I can say that in my experience, what happened in this case is not atypical. Leo's offer was remarkable, no doubt. But that 'change' or 'shift' that happens is one of the main reasons why I'm so invested in this process. To me, that 'shift' signifies an attainable transformative and healing experience.

"Your question, 'How did that happen?' is a great question for the group. What do you all think?" I asked.

Kris spoke first. "I think they saw how wounded he was."

"What do you mean by 'wounded'?" I asked.

"He was a victim too. I think they saw his trauma from his dad. His father basically brainwashed him. Especially when he was a kid. I think they felt sorry for him," Kris said.

"Empathy?" I asked.

"Yeah. And even compassion," said Kris.

"What's the difference?" I asked.

"Empathy is a feeling. Compassion is the action we take because of that feeling," Kris replied.

Melissa spoke next. "I agree with Kris, but I think it also had to do with Rick's remorse. He apologized numerous times, and he appeared very sincere. I think that opened the possibility for them to forgive him."

"Do you think his remorse was about what he did to them, or how it was going to impact his son if he went to jail?" I asked.

"I'm sure it was both. But I think what's most important is that Maria and Leo must've believed he was sincerely remorseful for what he did to them," said Kris.

Barb added, "I think it was also because he was held accountable. They got the chance to confront him with how much he traumatized them. They got to express their anger. They got to speak their truth. I think they needed to get that off their chest. I don't think they would've had any compassion for him if he would've tried to make excuses. I also think they got to experience the group holding him accountable. I don't know. Maybe they are just remarkably forgiving people."

Devonte commented next. "I agree about the accountability. Now I get what you were saying about accountability being 'the ability to account.' I don't think the change in Maria's and Leo's perspective would've happened if the underlying reasons, Rick's background, hadn't been fully exposed. What he did, his fear and the gun, his rage, the bigotry—all of it made sense given his history.

"They weren't excuses. They were reasons. I'm not a psychologist, but I see the connection. He was paranoid so he carried a gun. He was humiliated so he was full of rage. His fear and prejudice of Latinos came from his father. Even his state of mind when he left his father's house that day was revealed. All of that got exposed. I think they saw that what he did happened *to* them, but not because of them."

"That's a *very* important point," I said. "Because if that happens, if survivors realize that on a certain level that what the offender did, their motivation, had nothing to do with who the survivor is, it can liberate them from the psychological attachment to why the offender did what they did. Instead of thinking, 'Why did you do this to me?', it becomes, 'Why did you do this?'

"I want to shift our discussion to talking about the other members in the circle. What role do you think they played in this?" I asked.

"I'd like to weigh in," said Brad. "I was surprised, too, when Leo, along with Tim and John, all went with Rick to his sentencing. At the same time, it was familiar. It reminded me of what we often do in recovery when someone, like a patient, has to go before a judge because they've committed a DUI or some other drug or alcohol offense. We speak on behalf of the addict or alcoholic, but we only do that if that person is in recovery and appears humbled, remorseful, and sincere in their efforts to get clean and sober. We ask for recovery instead of incarceration.

"I also think the officer played a vitally important role. He confronted Rick, and really, the entire group, with the scary and very concrete reality of not only what could've happened but does happen. I think he provided a sobering life-and-death context, a deadly serious situation.

"I'm biased because I was a cop, but I thought the officer did an exceptional job of representing enforcement, but also the humanity of police officers. We call it 'putting a face on the blue,' letting people see our humanness under the uniform, that we actually do care. I mean, why did that officer choose to participate? Did he volunteer?" Brad asked.

"Yes," I said. "Granted, he was on duty, so he could've been called away at any point. But some officers attend these conferences even on their days off. I like what you said about 'putting a face on the blue' because when officers participate in conferences, it destigmatizes police. They become members of the community and not just people hired to catch the bad guys."

Brad continued, "I may be off-base here, but I think the officer also functioned as a type of social-parent."

"What do you mean?" I asked.

"He disciplined Rick by confronting him with the consequences of his actions, and he was very frank. Like what a good father would've done with his son. Like what Rick's father should have done," said Brad.

"You mean like tough love?" I asked.

"I don't know that I would call it love. It was more about saying what needed to be said. Reality-checking. There's something else about this group representing the community and I can't really put my head around it yet, but it reminds me of a recovery group. In fact, the whole process reminds me of recovery," he said.

"Can you explain?" I asked.

"Sure," Brad replied. "I wrote down a few notes. First, this was a kind of intervention. What the group was doing was essentially intervening in an obvious destructive path Rick was on. They pointed out the destructive consequences, the harm he was causing others, including himself, with this thinking and behavior. That's what we do when we conduct an intervention with an addict or an alcoholic.

"But rather than family members being involved, except for reference to his son, it was the community, the circle. What's remarkable is that the circle was able to express an earnest concern for his welfare as much as Maria's and Leo's. I guess maybe that is a type of love. *Agape* comes to mind.

"Second, we look at the addictive behavior as a symptom of underlying issues. In a manner of speaking, that underlying issue is the 'disease.' We frame the addiction as a type of destructive coping strategy, or behavioral symptom, that has become an obsession or habit. We ask, 'What's driving that destructive thinking and behavior? What are they trying to medicate or escape from?' "

Brad continued, "One of the steps in recovery is taking an inventory of fears and resentments. Really what we're doing is making the connection between a client's history, the things they've done that have hurt people, and people who've done things to them, and their addiction, their compulsion. It seems to me that this is what happened in this circle. The connection between what Rick did to Leo, his thinking he needed to carry a gun, his profiling, and his relationship with his father—all of that was made by the group. It was definitely an accounting, almost like an inventory.

"The third similarity is the amends-making part. We say in recovery that making an amends is what separates those that relapse from those that recover and stay clean and sober. An amends is not just apologizing. It's basically saying, 'Look, I have no excuses or defenses for what I did.' An amends is not just a one-time act. It's ongoing. It means, literally, changing the kind of person you are because you've finally accepted that your problems are of your own making. It means changing your belief system. That takes humility, and it doesn't happen without ongoing support. That support is not just about continuous accountability, but also healing," said Brad.

"It sounds like you're saying that 'healing' is learning to have a different relationship with yourself," I added.

Brad responded, "With everyone. With life itself. I like the term 'relationship-centric' because making a meaningful change, one that lasts, means relating to yourself and others in an entirely new way, one that is guided by a principle of being of maximum service to others.

"You focus on building relationships, but you start with repairing the relationships you've broken. You shift from being self-centered to other-centered. Like recovery, who knows whether someone, in this case Rick, will make that change? It has to happen at such a deep level.

"I have a question. Did you personally, or purposely, choose the other members of the circle based on this particular case? You mentioned that these encounters are like a performance. Did you 'cast' the participants based on their experience?" he asked.

"That's a great question," I replied. "Yes. Each of the participants had a specific role to play, an area of expertise and perspective that was relevant to the circumstances. I typically choose those participants after I've spoken to both the offender and the survivor. Those initial conversations tell me what the real issues are. I then ask people from the community who we've trained in the process to participate based on their unique knowledge and experience with those issues.

"John was invited because of his background in diversity and inclusion, and specifically, with Latinos. Pat was a trauma specialist. Tim's experience, story, and sobering perspective was invaluable. And like you said, the officer was the reality check about what could've happened," I added.

"This brings me to my last point about similarities with recovery," said Brad. "There's a comment in *The Big Book of Alcoholics Anonymous* that says, 'We are people who would not normally mix' but because we've 'survived a shipwreck,' we share an extraordinary experience and, therefore, an extraordinary connection. It's the wreck that brings us together," he said.

"Like shared suffering," I commented.

"Yeah. But also shared recovery and healing. We call it 'fellowship.' It's like an intentional community that forms spontaneously because of the shared circumstances, experiences, and interests. The last thing I'll add is that this social connection is vitally important to recovery. Addiction is an isolating and lonely experience. The antidote is connection. Recovery is like 'coming in from the cold.'

"This circle of people you assembled, who would not normally meet, was like a situational community, a community that materialized as a result of what happened. It seems to me that if it wasn't for this encounter, Maria's, Leo's, and even Rick's experiences, their traumas, would've kept them feeling isolated. I like what you said about the community 'shouldering the load' of the impact of Rick's violation on Maria and Leo, but also taking ownership of a solution."

Brad continued, "This is one of the reasons why I want to implement this process, this practice, into our recovery center. If fits with what we're trying to accomplish in recovery. I'm thinking about how to use this to guide discussions about the damage addicts and alcoholics have caused their families as a result of their addiction. Recovery is a type of restoration. I'm seeing that they're almost identical, and the principles are the same."

Kris spoke next. "Brad, you mentioned loneliness and a light bulb went off for me. I realize this was a criminal justice case and Rick was the offender, and maybe I'm just overly empathic and making a huge assumption, but I couldn't help thinking about, or really, feeling, that Rick was suffering from loneliness.

"I mean, as much as he was responsible for his assault of Leo, the crime, Leo and Maria had each other and probably numerous friends and family to rally around them. Though we don't know what Rick's social network might've been because it wasn't mentioned, I wonder if loneliness played a part in what he did. I don't know.

"He struck me as a tragically lonely figure. The reason I bring this up is because of an article I read a few years ago where the former U.S. Surgeon General Dr. Vivek H. Murthy said there was an 'epidemic of loneliness' in society," said Kris.

I asked Kris, "That's an interesting point. Assuming that loneliness played a part in what Rick did, how did this process address that? What function did this circle, this process, serve with regard to loneliness?"

"Like Brad said, it's about the connection that happened," said Kris. "This is what stunned me about this case. I mean, here's a guy who was a single dad, threatened someone with a gun, screamed incredibly racist names, and yet the people in that circle ended up embracing him.

"You mentioned that the third stage of change is reincorporation, or reintegration. I don't think Rick was ever incorporated or integrated within a community to begin with. At least not any community that actually cared about him," she added. "Maybe what he did was a kind of unconscious cry for connection?"

"I want to put up on our screens a section from a recent article in *Harvard Magazine* about loneliness that I think Kris is referring to," I said:

> **According to the research of Julianne Holt-Lunstad, professor of psychology and neuroscience at Brigham Young University, and colleagues, the heightened risk of mortality from loneliness equals that of smoking 15 cigarettes a day or being an alcoholic and exceeds the health risks associated with obesity. Researchers are now actively studying the mechanisms by which loneliness affects health, including its relationship with inflammation and harmful changes in DNA expression.[3]**

"That's exactly my point," said Kris. "Loneliness is a real malady. Every time there's a mass shooting, the shooter is inevitably characterized as a loner," she said.

Devonte spoke next. "One question I had was, who were Rick's friends? I'm not saying it was the case here, but this is how people gravitate toward gangs and white supremacy groups. It's their longing for acceptance. I thought about what would happen to Rick if he went to jail. Would he have been recruited by a racist group in prison? Because I would imagine that if there was a group of Latinos that found out about what he did, he might've become a target and aligned himself with white supremacists for protection.

"I like what Brad said about intervention. If that indoctrination was a real possibility, seems to me that this process was not only interventive, but preventative," Devonte said. "And it wasn't just the conversation that happened. It was what happened after.

What surprised me was that John invited Rick to attend those community forums on race relations. Was that predetermined by you and John?"

"We did talk about it before the meeting. We decided that it could be part of his reparative contract. But it all hinged on how he responded to the race component," I clarified.

"Even so, there's no way that would've even been a possibility if it wasn't for that circle. That's pretty radical. Almost Ghandi-ish," he concluded. "I'm wondering how I can use this format, this process in my classes to teach about history."

"I'm so glad you see that!" I exclaimed (way too exuberantly). "You can absolutely use this process to guide classroom discussions. It's simply a way to break down a big issue or topic into manageable, bite-size chunks of discussion. The key, I've found, to making past events meaningful for students is to focus on the impact on people's experience, asking them if they can identify, but also looking at the underlying reasons for why something happened. I've been using it for years.

"Before we move into talking about the actual method and how it was applied, I want to ask you: How would you describe what happened in this circle as 'restorative'? What do you think was being 'restored' here, if anything? Maybe just one word or a sentence," I asked.

"Accountability," said Barb. "I really felt like Rick was held accountable."

"I would say civility," said Devonte. "What they did was take an incident of extreme incivility and process it with civility, decency, and respect. It was a process of rehumanizing."

"Maria's and Leo's dignity," said Joan. "I think the way their experience was validated by the others was an example of re-dignifying them. What Rick did was such an assault on their dignity. But I think the way the group responded to what he did helped restore a sense of dignity. The circle embraced them. They mattered."

"I like what Joan said about dignity and mattering. To that, I would add empathy and compassion," said Melissa. "If Maria and Leo had declined to participate, if Rick would've just been sent to jail, there would've been no opportunity for empathy or compassion to be expressed or felt."

"With all of these, I would add connection," said Brad. "I don't know if we can say connection was restored because it didn't exist before Rick did what he did. Maybe it's better to say that a connection was made."

"I'd say it was trust," said Aaron.

"You mean like trust in the process?" I asked.

"Certainly that," Aaron replied. "The others that you invited to attend trusted the process because they had done these before. But I think it's more than that. I think there's something in us that wants to trust that people know the difference between right and wrong and are basically good and really do care about each other.

"Conscious or not, wasn't this essentially a leap of faith for Maria and Leo? Seems to me that on some level they trusted that they would be heard, and their experience would be taken seriously by others in that group. Otherwise, they wouldn't have been willing to participate.

"I think even for Rick, someone who obviously viewed the world as a dangerous and threatening place, might've been trusting that he would be able to not only apologize, but also express sincere remorse. I think he trusted you. I think you built his trust that if he did this, if he participated in this, he would be able to do what the judge was offering him—a chance to take responsibility. So maybe that's a kind of blind trust in a process that he didn't know anything about. If that's the case, isn't that a kind of basic trust in the goodness, or at least fairness, of people?"

Aaron continued. "You told us that to restore is to return someone or something to an original, ideal, or intended condition. Seems to me that trust, as a type of social capital, was restored, and that people will do the right thing if they're given the chance. I think it was John F. Kennedy that once said, 'Evil prevails when good people fail to act.' This was an opportunity for good people to act to rebuild trust."

"It's interesting that you describe trust as social capital. What do you mean by that?" I asked.

Aaron replied, "Just that for society to work, for an organization or community to function, it requires a baseline of trust. The more we trust our institutions, leaders, and citizens, the more content we'll be, the safer we'll feel. I think in this case we see how trust goes hand-in-hand with accountability. If there's no accountability, what's there to trust?"

I returned to Joan's earlier comment that "we'll never deal with something so serious as this in our school." I clarified that even though Rick and Leo's case was an example of restorative justice happening in a criminal justice setting, the step-by-step restorative *method* and the communication *practice* of people coming together to apply that method in a discussion is not limited to a criminal violation.

I said, "In general, the method is simply a structured or organized conversation that can be facilitated in any number of situations, contexts, or settings.

"For example, families can use it to work through disagreements, conflicts, or issues they're dealing with. Teachers can use it in the classroom to address classroom disturbances or disagreements. Schools and workplaces use it to address conflicts between staff or faculty and student or employee misconduct.

"It can be used in a one-on-one dialogue between two people to resolve an interpersonal conflict, as well as a group conversation where something has happened or is happening that is impacting the group. I've used it as a method of collaborative decision-making as well," I said.

"It helps to distinguish between the method and the practice. The method is the step-by-step structure or sequence, and the practice is the *artful application*, enactment, or 'performance' of that method.

"Does this make sense?" I asked the group.

"So, the method is the technique, and the practice is the conversation?" asked Aaron.

"Yes," I said. "The method is the tool. The practice is how you use that tool, how you apply it. Like any practice, the more you use it, the more skilled you'll become and the more effective the tool will be. Because the practice of restoration as a method requires communication and interaction, it foregrounds or emphasizes a range of communication skills that can be developed and mastered like active listening, reframing, paraphrasing, repeating back, etc. I like to use the metaphor of a musical instrument. The more adept the player, the more resonant the sound of the instrument."

"The metaphor of retribution and punishment is a hammer," suggested Aaron.

"For sure," I said. "But even that takes practice."

"And a lot of smashed thumbs," joked Aaron. "No matter how good you get at swinging a hammer, it always sounds like a hammer. It never sounds any different when it hits the nail," concluded Aaron.

"I'm sure there's a deeper symbolism to that. Here's the thing about the restorative method and its practice. The more a person uses it, or experiences it, the more they begin to think in terms of restoration. It has become second nature. We instinctively approach and process things that are happening, issues, or situations through the lens of restoring relationship. Who or what is being impacted? What is that impact? What are the underlying issues or motivations? What are the needs and what would satisfy those needs? What actions can we take?"

"Like conditioning," commented Barb.

"That's a great way to describe it. It's a way of communicating that emphasizes relationships. It's a discipline. To use the musical instrument metaphor again, after you've played a musical piece for a long enough time, you no longer need the sheet music. You know the arrangement and chords by heart. We practice, practice, practice, until it becomes our practice," I explained.

"The sheet music is the script," said Aaron.

"Exactly," I said. "Like we discussed earlier, restoration is both a panoramic and microscopic lens. The more you look through it, the more you'll begin to see the emergence of both the deeper individual reasons for why something happened, and also the larger sociocultural influences or tensions in play.

"This is what happened with Rick. Additionally, you're working to both heal the individual and ideally reconcile the relationship, but in doing so, heal the larger social or 'communal' body. Make sense?"

"The circle," commented Kris.

"Glad you pointed that out. Think about a pebble being dropped into a still pond. Imagine a conflict or destructive interaction as the pebble. It breaks the still or 'balanced surface' of the pond. The impact of that incident ripples out. The concentric rings, the ripples, are the impacted relationships.

"The first ripple represents the intrapersonal relationship. The relationship a person has with themselves. The second ripple represents the interpersonal, or 'one-on-one' relationships. The third ripple is the group relationships, like a family, a team, or group of friends. The fourth ripple represents the social relationships that constitute a workplace, organization, or community. When something happens, it's not just the two people who are impacted. That impact ripples out through other relationships. It may be indirect, but it's still an impact.

"When those ripples reach the edge of the pond or container, they begin to ripple back toward the center. In my mind, this represents the community facing what happened and taking ownership of resolution. As a facilitator, or practitioner, your job is to guide that ripple or reverberation back to its source using the method.

"Each one of those ripples represents an opportunity to more deeply understand the incident that broke the balance, and ideally, ensure that those rings of relationships are respected and repaired," I said. "How does your community or organization respond?

"Think about what the impact would be if every member of that community was thinking in restorative terms and had the experience and communication skills to process incidents and conflicts that happen every day using the method. What might the outcome be?" I asked.

"It would prevent an emotional tsunami," said Aaron.

"That's actually not a bad metaphor," I said. "Let me give you an example. Say you have two employees or staff members who have a disagreement that escalates into an argument and then an angry blowout. If that incident goes unaddressed, what happens? They're still going to need to process it, try and make sense of it, but maybe not in a constructive way. If they believe they were treated unfairly or violated and that it's the other person's fault, what do you suppose will happen?"

"They'll share what happened with others looking for consolation or validation," said Melissa.

"Right. They'll explain their version and express their feelings looking for support. And those listeners often feel like they need to support that person or pressured to take sides. Gossip starts to happen. That's only human. Before you know it, there are opposing camps, and that tension permeates the social climate.

"Resentments get activated. People get bitter. Old grudges surface and people start texting and even take to social media. That one disagreement or argument takes on a life of its own. Over time, people shut down, stop interacting with so-and-so, don't feel safe, and don't want to come to work anymore. That's how entrenchment happens. Your tsunami metaphor is not unrealistic."

Method

"This is a great discussion," I said. "I want to move us into talking about the actual method and how it was applied, the practice. Before we do that, I want to refer back to this idea of a ritual and the three stages of change. Rick's violation was the breach. His assault represented a breaking or transgression of social norms, values, and even principles that we assume others should also ascribe to such as safety, justice, civility, respect for others, decency, and co-habitation. I'm sure there are others."

Brad interjected, "Interdependence."

I added, "Interdependence, co-reliance, etc. The process of determining whether those norms and values are still valid, if they still matter, or really mean anything is what happens in the middle stage of 'betwixt and between.' There was no guarantee that those norms and values would be rearticulated, reclaimed, or reasserted for Maria and Leo, or the community.

"What about Rick? If he had gone to jail, those norms might've been referenced implicitly through enforcement or punishment, but we've all suggested that the educational piece, the experience of those norms being revalued, reconstituted, or reestablished by others, probably wouldn't have happened for him.

"When he made the decision to participate in this process, though he couldn't have known it would happen, that group essentially told him what it takes to be a member of the community. I would argue that Maria and Leo wouldn't have experienced those values being rearticulated and reasserted by 'the community' on their behalf if that group hadn't met.

"If Rick had just gone to jail, or if either they or he had declined to participate, they wouldn't have had the opportunity to understand that what he did to them was a result of what was done to him. There would've been any number of questions that would've remained unanswered.

"All of that information, the underlying reasons for why this 'breach' happened and what needed to happen to reassert those values moving forward, is what Rick's reparative contract, or agreement, was designed to accomplish.

"My point is that the restorative conversation, the method, and application facilitates the second and third stage. That's what makes it resemble a ritual. It conducts the middle stage, where people come together to discuss something that happened and decide whether those norms and values are still important, and the third stage of reintegration or reincorporation is where those values and principles are put into very concrete terms and measurable actions," I said.

"The reparative contract," said Devonte.

"The reparative contract," I agreed. "There are reasons why I've been so adamant about calling this a type of ritual. For a ritual to actually be a ritual that consistently accomplishes the important changes we've been talking about, and not just a meaningless or superficial occurrence, it has to have certain things in place.

"First, it has to be of a serious nature that addresses serious issues. Emile Durkheim (1858–1917) was a French sociologist who suggested that a ritual is more than just a casual occurrence. It is an *intentional occurrence that serves a serious purpose* or addresses serious matters that affect social life and social relationships. This is what a restorative encounter does. It is essentially a 'time-out or a time-away from time' to talk about a troubling event and talk about 'what could be, or should be, or might be.'[4]

"Second, it has to occur regularly. When it occurs regularly, it gains in importance or significance, and reliability within the community or organization. What this means is that if you are looking to make a significant and sustainable shift in how people treat each other in a collective like a family, workplace, school, or classroom, you have to implement this process of coming together and working through what happened on a consistent basis.

"You have to embed it or integrate it into your culture and social environment. When that happens, the process, the method, becomes predictable even though the outcome is unique to the context of the disruption. The more you do it, the more it matters, and the more people come to rely upon it for transformation.

"In the Rick and Leo case, it was the restorative justice program and the courts that established this consistency within the community by regularly conducting these encounters. The more you do it, the more people will trust it, and learn how to resolve issues civilly. The people who participated as community members in this particular circle knew the process and knew how to contribute to making it effective. They contributed to the seriousness.

"Third, a ritual has to have a structure to it. It has a beginning, middle, and end. That structure is what gives form to, or ushers, the change that happens in the relationships and awareness of the people involved.

"This structure indicates my last point. It takes expertise to conduct it. It takes training. The facilitator has to know what they're doing and be clear about what each step is supposed to accomplish. If they don't—like the example of the facilitator who brought a 'talking rock' into the circle to regulate turn-taking—people won't take it seriously and it won't achieve what it's capable of in terms of vitality and reconstituting interpersonal and social relationships if it is in any way superficial.

"In my experience, the schools or workplaces that fail in their attempt to use this method and its various practices and achieve what it can in terms of shifting a social climate toward respect and consideration do so because (a) they don't embed it or integrate it into their culture on a consistent basis, (b) they don't probe deep enough into the underlying reasons for why something happened, and (c) they don't continually improve their craft as facilitators. Patchwork attempts, or 'let's just shake hands and move on' thinking doesn't work. It just doesn't."

"You're saying that for this to actually work, you have to take a whole-institution or systems approach to implementation?" asked Brad.

I replied, "That's exactly what I'm saying. It's not just a practice that you do one time to address only one issue like misconduct. It's a way of communicating that embodies a way of thinking that you want people to develop and embrace. If you do that, then people will begin to think and interact in restorative terms.

"They'll instinctively begin to think in terms of relationships, impact, underlying reasons, and motivations, needs, and solutions, and they'll know how to resolve situations before they erupt or spiral into grudges, resentments, gossip, and blow-ups. You're developing people's capacity to have restorative conversations. I know that sounds idealistic, but that's been my experience," I said. "Satisfaction with the process leads to a desire for more of these conversations.

"I'll explain more about implementation in the next chapter. I'd like to turn now to what I call 'restorative communication.' The good news is that we don't have to reinvent the wheel. There are aspects of communication and interaction that are inherently restorative. We just have to develop those skills and understand what purpose or function they serve in restoration. We have to emphasize those aspects of communication that are restorative and relationship-centric.

"I don't know about you, but I never learned how to resolve disagreements or conflict or resolve issues growing up. My conflict style was either to overpower and 'win,' or run for the hills. It's kind of ironic that the one thing that distinguishes us as a species, one that relies so much on communication, isn't taught as a subject in schools like math or reading. We teach public speaking and how to persuade, but we don't teach civil interaction, how to listen, or how to resolve conflict. We take communication for granted until it becomes a problem.

"Is it any wonder that our public and political discourse, amplified by social media, is so infected with invectives, insults, hate, contempt, and abuse? We don't understand just how destructive this way of communicating is. Words matter. Like I said, they can build bridges or start wars. Words can be tools or weapons."

The Word *Restore*—An Exercise

"I want to try an exercise with you. It's simple and holistic," I said.

Barb interjected. "When I hear the word 'holistic,' I think of tie-dye, macrame, and granola bars."

"You're not gonna make us hold a rock, are you?" quipped Aaron.

The group erupted in significant laughter.

"No, he's going to tell us to separate the rock's behavior from the rock," said Barb.

"The underlying issue of the rock is dirt," said Devonte.

"Okay, here we go…" I said.

"We're going to restore the rock's relationship with itself and the community," added Brad. "My question is, which came first? The rock or the community?"

"The dirt," said Devonte.

"Doesn't the community make the rock?" asked Kris.

"The rock doesn't know it's a rock until it encounters itself through the eyes of other rocks," said Devonte.

"How do you restore a rock? Isn't the rock always a rock?" asked Barb.

"You can't restore a rock," added Aaron. "You can only hold it accountable for how it's impacted the dirt."

"You could change your relationship with the rock," said Kris. "A rock is either a tool or a weapon."

"I have empathy for the rock," said Joan.

"Good lord. Clearly, I had this coming to me. Did you all meet and rehearse this? Let me know when you're back on planet Earth," I said.

"The earth is a rock," concluded Melissa.

After we all calmed down, I said, "Seriously. It's just a simple exercise to help you reconnect with the power of a word. Close your eyes. Take about three really deep and slow breaths. On your third exhale, silently and slowly introduce the word 'restore' to yourself. Allow yourself to be private and intimate with the word. Try not to resist what comes up for you. Let it be. Do that for about ten to twenty more breaths," I said.

After several long moments passed, I said, "I'd like to know what came up for you."

Kris started. "I don't know if it was the laughter before or the word, but I felt a release of tension. Like a relaxation, letting go of stress. I didn't realize I was carrying that stress. It was like 'ahhhh … restore.'"

Joan spoke next. "I felt a wave of warmth come over me. I felt a sense of peace, protected, safe."

Barb spoke. "I felt a wave of sadness, almost heaviness."

"I did too," added Melissa. "I felt sad for the people I work with. What came up for me was how much I care about them."

"Barb, can you share more about what the heaviness is about?"

"Maybe what I felt was a heavy truth. I think I've been in denial about how much what's happening affects me. Especially the assault on women's reproductive health. It's depressing. People feel beat up. The pandemic, the hatred, the racism, the deceit, the mass killings, and school shootings. I think I've been in denial about how scared and depressed so many people are, including myself. I know we're all here to learn about restoration and make a difference. It just seems so overwhelming," she shared.

"I'm glad you and Melissa shared this, Barb, because I had the same heavy sadness come up for me. It was like a deep grief. But then I felt connected to all of you. I mean, we didn't know each other before we started this workshop, but I feel like we've connected with each other because we all share a desire to do something about what's happening. To make a difference. I think it's also because, in a sense, we're all participating in each other's stories," said Devonte. "Toward the end of the breathing, I felt a settling," he added.

"This is great," said Brad. "I had similar thoughts and feelings that you're all describing. What came to me was that here we are talking about restoration and how to do it, but doing so is, in a sense, restorative. These discussions give me hope. I'm more committed to teaching my staff how to do this. I'm going to do this exercise with them. I also had a deep sense of gratitude for all of you being here."

There was a moment of silence as we let what Brad said sink in.

Aaron spoke. "What came up for me was a deep satisfaction in the work I do with the environment. Environmental restoration is what I do. What came up for me was a sense that I'm doing exactly what I was meant to do in this life. I felt a kind of joy. Maybe it's the environment that is restoring me. I feel the connection with all of you, too. This isn't what I expected before we started. I think I also realized how certain areas of my life, my relationships, need some restoration."

I added, "Thank you for opening up and sharing your experience. I was going to wait until our last meeting to share this with all of you, but when we conclude our workshop, our time together, I'll mail each of you a rock."

"Like a touchstone," said Brad.

"Maybe. It might not know it's a touchstone until you touch it," I said.

Laughter and groans.

"Seriously, now. The reason I asked us to do this exercise is because it emphasizes two aspects of restorative communication. First, the ability of communication to 'constitute' or create an embodied/felt experience. Second, the concept of 'performativity.' In the case of restorative communication, the process enacts 'an experience of restoration' while people are deciding what restoration will be as an outcome," I said.

"So, it's both experience and outcome?" asked Brad.

"Exactly," I said.

Restorative Approach to Communication

"In the previous discussion, we talked about the concept of a 'restorative worldview' or paradigm. This way of looking, this lens, sees the world, both human and natural, as being *constituted by relationships*. Restorative communication puts that worldview into action. Simply put, if both people and relationships matter, restoration matters, and this foregrounds the role of communication in restoration.

"What exactly is 'restorative' communication? The obvious answer is that it is communication that restores relationships, or at the very least, restores a collective understanding about what happened. But as you pointed out, there are other things that are being restored like accountability, trust, dignity, and connection. Before we look at how those aspects of relationship are restored through communication, I want to start with something more basic, which is what restoration has to say about communication.

"First, restoration is an approach to communication that emphasizes the role that language and interaction plays in *constituting the meaning and experience of our personal and social relationships.*[5] This means that communication is much more than just the exchange or transmission of content, information, or ideas.

"The language we use and the manner in which we use it also constructs ("constitutes") the value and importance of the relationship and our experience of that relationship. This means that words don't just reflect our reality but have the power to create it. This is critical to understand because it means that restorative communication has the power to create a type of 'relational reality.'

"Second, restorative communication is *'performative.'* I'll explain what this means later. Right now, I want us to focus on the constitutive aspect of communication. These are two high-dollar words but bear with me. They're not as complicated as they sound.

"When schools, workplaces, families, or couples ask me to help, it's usually because their relationships have become adversarial and toxic. The first thing I ask is, 'How are you speaking to and about each other? What is the language you're using?' I explain that culture is a manifestation of communication.

"Whatever beliefs, values, ethics, morals, or principles we profess to aspire to or have become real and tangible in how we interact with each other and how we talk about each other," I said. "We'll talk a bit more about culture and communication later in our discussion."

Brad commented, "You can't call yourself a civil society if you don't have civil discourse."

"That's exactly my point; or a civil organization," I agreed. "I remember going into one workplace where there were posters on the walls proclaiming 'tolerance, diversity, respect, inclusivity, and consideration,' but every Friday a group of managers would get together for a happy hour and gossip, talk smack, about their subordinates.

"That type of derisive communication predisposed them to then treat individuals on their teams as 'less than,' and 'problems.' The posters on the wall were pretty but impotent. It was the derogatory communication that was constituting an environment of resentment.

"My point is that if we really want to create a social environment where people feel safe, valued, and respected, then we have to speak with and about each other in ways that are respectful, considerate, and welcoming. Words have meaning and the manner is as important as the message. Because communication has the power to create our experience, and 'make present' what we mean to each other, we can't take communication for granted.

"Inasmuch as communication has an effect on our conduct, our communication is also a type of conduct in itself. Restorative communication is focused not only on 'getting the story straight' or 'solving a problem.' It's also explicitly concerned with restoring the meaning of the relationship between the individuals and the group."

Joan commented, "If we want more empathy, which is one of our school's stated cultural values, we have to interact and speak in ways that are empathic."

"Yes. It's that simple. But the challenge is that ways of communicating with and about each other become habits or patterns. They become norms and they get hardwired into our brains. To break that unconscious pattern—which is what restorative communication does—you have to start by telling the truth about what people are saying to and about each other, which is the content, and account for the damage it's doing to people on an emotional and psychological level, to relationships, and to the social climate. That's the relational component. The point is that communication creates our experience of each other."

Joan responded, "Change your talk and your mind will follow."

"Great point," I said. "Let's take the example of Rick. What role did his father's language play in Rick's relationship with Latinos and eventual assault of Leo?"

Devonte answered, "His father used derogatory language, which constituted racism and led to Rick's relating to Leo with hate."

"That's exactly it. If we dig a little deeper, how would you describe the relationship between Rick and his father based on what his father was telling him about Latinos?" I asked.

Brad answered, "I'm glad you asked this. His father was using him. I couldn't put into words what I was thinking about their relationship. This makes it clear."

"What do you mean?" I asked.

"It was kind of like an emotional or psychological incestual relationship. He was using Rick to console his own humiliation, prove his point, and justify his hate," Brad replied. "In terms of constitution, like Devonte said, it was his labeling that constituted a relationship of shared racism within their relationship as well. I'm guessing that hate and animosity wouldn't have 'been constituted in their relationship,' to use your term, if his father hadn't continually spoken that way about Latinos to Rick. To that, I would add that the language his dad used, in turn, resulted in constituting an eventual relationship of them/us, or offender/offended between Rick and Leo. It constituted an act of dehumanization," he added.

"I couldn't have said that any better. This is a great segue," I said. "How did restorative communication—here I'm talking about the process of coming together and the discussion that ensued—'reconstitute' relationships? If we describe the relationship between Rick and Leo as initially one of offender/survivor, and characterized by an act of violence before our circle met, how would you describe the relationship between them, and perhaps their relationship with others in the circle as representatives of the community, after the process?"

Aaron spoke. "I see where you're going with this. You asked us what was being restored. If this circle hadn't happened, the meaning of the relationship between Rick and Leo would've remained constituted by what Rick did and what he said. In terms of identity, Rick was an abuser and Leo was the abused. Rick's relationship with the community would've remained disconnected. I think Leo's relationship with the community would've remained disconnected on a certain level too.

"What Rick did essentially isolated both of them. But as a result of the dialogue that happened with others in the circle, the accountability and repair, the meaning of those relationships was changed or reconstituted. To use your words, instead of 'this happened to them,' it became 'this happened to us.' You also mentioned power. The process reconstituted, or redistributed, power," he said.

"That's it," I said. "Let's review some of your observations about what was 'restored.' You mentioned accountability, understanding, dignity, trust, empathy, compassion, connection, remorse, and forgiveness. Each of these are meaningful experiences that we have within the context of both interpersonal and social relationships. All of the characteristics you pointed out were 'constituted,' or 'made present,' as a result of the interaction, dialogue, and the communication process used," I said.

Kris interjected. "But those attributes, or perspectives and feelings are also very personal. Does that mean that the interaction reconstituted the meaning of any relationship the individuals had with themselves?" she asked.

"That's a great question," I replied. "I don't think we can answer that because those experiences on an individual level are subjective. They're private. We can make observations, but only assumptions, and that's dangerous. We'd have to ask the participants about their experience and whether they thought any relationship they had with themselves was any different, if even for a brief moment.

"But since you brought it up, let's look at how the relationship we have with ourselves, the way we regard ourselves and what we think about ourselves, our core beliefs about who we are is, constituted by the conversation we have with ourselves," I added.

"Like self-talk," said Kris.

"Yeah. A friend of mine said something really insightful about self-talk. She said, 'I have conversations all day long and sometimes they're with other people!'"

Laughter.

"Typically, the conversation we have with ourselves is silent and more in the purview of cognitive psychology. Restoration looks at it a bit differently. Restoration just assumes that the way we talk to ourselves constitutes the quality or experience of our relationship with ourselves. It recognizes the communication we have with ourselves.

"If we speak to ourselves in condemning or toxic ways, judging or harshly criticizing and blaming ourselves, then that relationship can be characterized as intropunitive," I said.

"We silently punish ourselves. We prosecute, judge, and enforce retribution. It's kind of like resenting ourselves for who we are," I added. "Or we just numb ourselves. Try to shut the critical voice up. That's one of the reasons why I go fly fishing. The river is louder than the voices in my head!"

Brad spoke up. "That's why we say in recovery that resentment is like drinking poison and expecting the other person to die."

Kris said, "What makes it so insidious is that because we're so often unaware of that running dialogue, we don't even stop and ask if what we're saying to ourselves about ourselves is accurate or true."

"Or constructive," I added.

"So, does restorative communication, the process, work on an individual level? Can it reconstitute the relationship we have with ourselves?" asked Kris.

"In my experience, yes. I'll explain that in one of our later discussions, but we're getting off track here. Intrapersonal restorative communication—the process of changing the way we relate to ourselves to experience empathy, accountability, dignity, connection, compassion, forgiveness, humility, respect, etc., is what therapy is designed to facilitate.

"However, as an organizational tool, just like the structured process we use to resolve conflicts with others, it can also work on a personal level to resolve conflict with ourselves and repair the harm we've caused ourselves. It can be a therapeutic tool that points to issues we might need professional help with, such as unresolved trauma. I can explain more about this later. Right now, I want to get us back into talking about restoration and communication.

"I realize we're wading into some deep conceptual waters about communication. What I'm trying to illustrate is that there are some things happening in restorative communication and interaction that have profound implications, not only for people involved in a particular violation or incident, but also for social relationships that constitute a community. So, we're working on both a micro and macro level of relationships."

"It is pretty heady stuff," said Brad. "But this is resonating with me."

Melissa said, "It makes me realize how little I know about communication. This is complex, but it's helping me grasp how relationships and communication are intertwined. Like you said, as our communication goes, so goes our relationships."

"I'm starting to see the relationship between restorative communication and civil society," said Devonte.

"That's exactly it. Restorative communication is a type of civil discourse," I said.

"Let me keep going on this," I said. "I think this next concept will help us make the connection between the experience of restorative communication happening in Rick's and Leo's circle and what that means on a much larger, or macro level of social change.

"If you remember, when all of us began this group conversation, we lamented about the social climate of animosity, contempt, and retaliation that seems to have become socially permissible. Brad, you pointed out that our political discourse has sunk to new levels of toxicity and dehumanization. Kris, you suggested that our collective nervous system is shot. Barb, you mentioned that the animosity and lack of respect between nurses and physicians motivated you to retire early.

"Joan, you described a lack of empathy and controlling leadership style of your school's director. Devonte, you pointed out the ongoing attempt to ban and suppress education about diversity, the history of racism, and gender identity. We came together out of a shared frustration and desire to do something about this in our respective workplaces and communities. We're all looking for a solution that would make a positive shift. All of these are symptoms of broken relationships.

"The constitutive function of communication tells us that the experience and meaning of our relationships is constructed in the way we interact. If we want to make a difference, a positive shift, repair broken relationships, then we have to change the way we speak with, to, and about each other. Where does that shift begin to happen? The social climate of contempt we're all faced with is happening on such a massive scale, how could we ever hope to make a difference?"

The Little Girl on the Beach

"Have you all heard the parable of the little girl walking along the shore who comes upon thousands and thousands of starfish washed up on the beach? She starts to pick the starfish up one by one and put them back into the sea. An old man comes along and says to her, 'Little girl, there are thousands and thousands of starfish here. How can you possibly think you can make a difference?' The little girl picks another starfish up, puts it back into the sea, and says, 'I made a difference for that one.'

"On a macro social scale, each one of our respective workplaces, schools, and communities is a beach. Within these respective sites, imagine that each destructive interaction is a stranding of a starfish. Let's say that the starfish represents a relationship. The use of restorative communication and interaction is the act of putting a starfish back into the ocean.

"Let me take this metaphor a bit further. Think about the pebble in the pond and how it ripples out and then ripples back. The values, principles, and various communication practices of restoration ripple out. In my experience over the last twenty-plus years, when people experience a restorative conversation to resolve their differences, they start to embrace the method and develop the skills to apply it in other areas of their lives, in other conversations. They start putting starfish back into the ocean. That's how it ripples out," I said.

"But that takes programming," said Brad.

"Yes. The programming is how you implement the practices and support those conversations, how you teach people to use restorative communication, and how you make sure those conversations happen consistently," I replied. "With consistency comes fluency.

"Let me move onto the next concept. I used to rack my brain trying to understand exactly what it is that makes this method of communication so effective in resolving conflicts and reducing their reoccurrence. For example, when I built the restorative justice program at the university, we went from processing twelve cases per year to over 400 with a less than 1% recidivism rate. How or why did that happen? It happened one conversation at a time, but it also happened because we built a program that coordinated the facilitation of those discussions on a continual basis.

"You systematized it," said Aaron.

"Yes. Some of the students who came through our program as offenders ended up becoming facilitators. We ended up training law school students who wanted to learn this method. Why? What was it that inspired them? The city conducted an independent study of various programs addressing the tensions between permanent residents in the community, the police, the university, and students.

"There had been riots, continuous property damage, drunken fights, trash violations, etc. They concluded that our program was a valuable asset to the community. The statements made by community members were 'fund it,' 'support it,' and 'celebrate it.'[6]

"I asked, 'Why do people find this practice so satisfying?' Was it because offenders were held accountable without punishment? Was it because they made amends to the community members they had harmed? Was it because they actually repaired that harm? Was it because those who had been harmed had the opportunity to speak their truth, tell their story, express the harm they had experienced? Was it because offenders expressed sincere remorse? Or was it because we found a way to uncover and address underlying issues in a student's life like drug and alcohol abuse and/or unresolved traumas? In fact, it was all of these.

"When I started to deconstruct and interpret what was happening in these conversations in terms of communication and interaction, I came to realize that satisfaction came from both the experience that people were having during the conversations, and also the eventual outcomes called 'restoration,' which included repair, amends, professional support, community service, etc.

> **"People who study restorative justice sometimes ask, 'Is restoration a process or an outcome?' It's both. An experience of restoration can happen while determining what restoration is going to be."**

"This is what happened in the case of Leo and Rick's circle. The communication term for that is *performativity* or performative communication, when language or a communication process enacts what it is attempting to define or describe.

"I know this seems unnecessarily academic and theoretical. But, in terms of understanding how restorative communication works—and how we can more effectively practice it—we have to trust that there is something powerful and transformative happening for people just by the simple fact of coming together and talking with each other in this restorative way about something troubling that has happened."

"Reconstitution of the meaning of relationships," observed Devonte.

"Yes, and re-storying the meaning of what happened as well as their relationship to that event. In Rick and Leo's case, the meaning of the incident went from being about hate to about accountability and repair. The other aspect of performativity has to do with what is called the reflexive, interventional, and potentially reintegrative function of personal narrative that happens during the restorative encounter.

"This means that when people come together and share their accounts of what happened, they're not only creating or 'constituting' a way of knowing or interpreting what happened, but they're also reflexively constituting a way of knowing about themselves as part of a community.[7]

"In the example of Leo and Rick's circle, as everyone accounted for their experience of the event, they not only were constructing personal and social knowledge of what happened, but they also were reflexively performing an act of personal, cultural, and social identity constitution. Who am I, and who are we, in relation to this assault and in relation to the racial context? Who do we now choose to be, or who can we be now that we know what happened, why it happened, and we have a choice about how to proceed? Who, or what, is our community?

"I've always said that restoration is about reconciling with the past to clear the way forward for a better future. In my opinion, this has profound implications for how we approach, process, and re-comprehend history. I think one of the reasons why certain people are so afraid of Critical Race Theory and gender identity education is because they think it threatens their own personal, cultural, and social identity.

"They're afraid of being changed. The question is, 'Who are we, really, if we accept or acknowledge that structural racism is real and has historical roots in slavery?' Who will we be if we acknowledge that transgender or gender fluid people are human beings who deserve respect and dignity?"

"And that our ancestors may have been slave owners," shared Devonte.

"Exactly," I said. "What if the narrative we've abided by, exalted for generations, and relied on to tell us who we are is exposed as a myth or false narrative? What then?"

"Encountering the face of the Other might change our own," said Barb.

"That's it. Look, I realize I've taken us way down into the esoteric belly of restoration in communication terms, but I wanted you to grasp what is happening and what is at stake in restorative communication. I'm sure I sound like a mad scientist," I admitted.

"Pay no attention to the man behind the curtain," quipped Aaron.

"Touché," I said. "My point is that there is a lot going on in these discussions that we need to be aware of. It is about making peace and resolving conflicts, but it's also about reclaiming or reconstituting our dignity and humanity in the process. And it is fully an intervention in destructive or antisocial ways of thinking and believing.

"People come together, talk openly and frankly about what's happening/happened, acknowledge the impact, explore why it's happening, identify needs, and then put a plan in place to meet those needs and repair any harm. That's the restorative process.

"Restorative communication is simply a way of communicating and interacting that functions to connect or reconnect people in service of resolving an incident, issue, or problem. But in that connecting or reconnecting, we're presented with an opportunity to discover what we're capable of becoming in terms of being human.

"To go back to the image of a pebble in the pond, think about the ripple effect these conversations would have, this way of communicating would have on relationships in your workplace or organization or school if they were happening on a consistent basis," I said.

"It would shift the culture one conversation at a time," said Melissa. "One starfish at a time."

"Your connection of communication with culture is critically important, Melissa. This connection is one that is typically overlooked. I want to expand on that because if we change the way we communicate, especially when there is disagreement, conflict, or an incident of destructive interaction, we can change a culture. Communication and culture go hand in hand," I said.

Culture and Restorative Communication

"Throughout our discussion, we've been emphasizing that communication is more than just the content of the message. It's about recognizing the relationship-level of meaning that permeates every interaction. Honoring the relationship context of communication requires being *conscientious* about how our communication impacts others and determines the quality of our relationships. When people interact in ways that are conscientious, the culture of the family, organization, school, or business becomes a 'conscientious culture.'

"Anthropologists tell us that 'culture' can be understood as a set of shared beliefs, values, ideals, and norms. Cultural values can be either implicit (unstated but understood) or explicit (regularly communicated). Either way, the beliefs, values, and ideals that a family or an organization professes is intended to orient organizational members' thinking, behavior, and relationships. 'Culture' is often defined as 'who we are,' 'what we stand for,' and 'what defines us.'

"In communication terms, culture is a verb. It is in constant enactment or reenactment in the way people communicate. Cultural values and beliefs become real, evident, and tangible (felt) in the way the organization communicates to its members, and the way members communicate with each other on a daily basis.

"As I suggested, if an organization professes the values of fairness, respect, consideration, responsibility-taking, tolerance, and other ideals, these values don't exist if not consistently practiced in all levels of interaction. Culture is always in a dynamic state.

"As we covered in our third discussion, provocatively, culture can be either a tool or a weapon. If the communication that occurs between and about people is considerate, respect-based, mutually supportive, and positive, then the culture is positive and manifests as a safe, welcoming, and productive social climate.

"Communication is a tool. Social climate is a product of culture enacted in language, communication, and interaction.

> **If we want a climate where people feel valued and appreciated, the communication and interaction that enacts a culture of appreciation has to be consistently non-judgmental, non-retributive, pro-relationship, and compassionate.**

"Conversely, if the communication between members is negative, deficit focused, punitive and retributive, evaluative, judgmental, dismissive, or condescending, then words and conversations can become weapons which not only disregard positive cultural values, but also make a mockery of them and create a climate of cynicism, mistrust, and bitterness," I said.

Brad commented, "This is what is happening in our political discourse, but also in our communities and certainly on social media."

"Exactly," I agreed. "On an organizational level, when the professed cultural values of that organization don't match what is happening between members, those members begin to reject the culture—but do so 'underground.' This is when gossip happens. Gossip becomes the underground protest narrative or hidden script that people use in an attempt to regain power against the false narrative of the culture.

"Let me give you an example. I was working with a fifty-member organization that was experiencing what they described as 'chronic mistrust.' Members had longstanding grievances against each other. Meetings where important decisions needed to be made, and policy and strategies discussed, devolved into passive-aggressiveness, silence, blaming sessions, and toxic resentment.

"The organization had been through five directors in seven years. Each director tried earnestly to turn the culture around, but eventually left or was replaced because the climate didn't change. People wouldn't let go of their grudges. 'I'll change if they change' was the sentiment. The members remained polarized and new employees were forced to take sides for their own protection.

"The bitterness eventually spilled over into conversations that members were having with clients. Clients left. Employees left. Sick days for mental health were maxed out by members. Gossip was rampant and corrosive. Members even began attacking each other and the organization on social media.

"The board of directors were divided about what to do. Some wanted to clean house, fire the problem people. Others wanted to crack down and suspend people for engaging in toxic gossip. Some saw it as a training issue. I suggested that 'an organization is an organism.' It's a living, breathing entity consisting of interdependent parts. Those parts are the people, and their social well-being is dependent on the health of their relationships. Restore the relationships, heal the social organism.

"I suggested we take a two-prong approach—work on both the macro level of relationships as well as the micro level of interpersonal relationships. The macro level involved assembling the entire organization, all fifty members, in a large circle once a week for one month at sixty minutes each. In those assemblies, we went through the restorative process. The micro level involved facilitating the restorative process to address both one-on-one conflicts, as well as small group/team conflicts," I explained.

"You took a 'whole-organization' approach," said Brad.

"Yes. A whole-organization approach is a cultural approach. In the first large assembly, I asked each person to express what kind of a workplace climate they wanted. This was the first time they had ever gathered together to envision what was possible. They all wanted the same things. They wanted to feel good about coming to work. They wanted a climate where it was emotionally and psychologically safe. They wanted collaboration and cooperation. They wanted to feel valued and appreciated by each other and the leadership. They wanted people in the community (and their clients) to respect them.

"I asked them, 'What role would communication, the way you interact with each other, play in creating that ideal environment?' They were pretty stumped by the question," I said.

"You were trying to get them to see that how they were communicating was constituting their social environment," said Melissa.

"Yes, and how communication was influencing their experience of each other. As I said, we take communication for granted, so we don't realize it's the problem. We inhabit the relational spaces we create with our words and how we listen.

"That question also served to orient them toward a possibility for making positive change. But I didn't dwell on that question because in my experience, taking personal and collective ownership for making that change doesn't happen unless and until we first realize and acknowledge the damage, the hurt we're causing ourselves and each other with negative, demeaning, and deficit-focused language and interaction."

"From pain comes the motivation and commitment to change," said Brad.

"Beautifully said," I replied.

"That's basically what you did in the case of Rick," said Aaron. "You pointed to the impact."

"The process enabled that. I just followed the script," I clarified.

"I asked them, 'Imagine you were looking at your organization as a blanket and each thread of that blanket was an interaction. As objective as you can be, how would you describe the communication that is getting in the way of creating the kind of workplace blanket you want to wrap yourselves in?'

"This was essentially the first question in the restorative process, which is to ask, 'what's happening?' This question helped them focus on destructive patterns, or communication behaviors, that were harmful. I asked them to provide some examples.

"Some of their responses included the following:

- 'Our blanket is ripped.'
- 'Some of us just don't like each other and don't want to talk to each other.'
- 'People have long-standing grudges.'
- 'People sabotage other people's efforts.'
- 'People gossip and spread rumors.'
- 'We never talk about what's really happening because people are afraid to speak up.'
- 'People avoid each other.'
- 'We can't make decisions.'
- 'We need a new blanket.'
- 'We don't mend the fabric when it's torn.'

"That last comment about 'not mending' the rips held the key because it gave me the chance to offer a solution," I said.

"Restorative communication," said Joan.

"Yes. The five-step restorative process, the various practices, or applications, but most importantly, the restorative approach to relationships which emphasizes respect-based communication. I explained the steps, but I created an easy to remember acronym, 'S.H.A.R.E.,' and printed it out so they could refer to it.

- **SPEAK your truth about what happened.**
- **HEAR from others who have been directly and indirectly impacted.**
- **ACKNOWLEDGE what that impact was/is.**
- **RECOGNIZE the underlying issues and needs.**
- **ENROLL in a concrete and measurable plan of reparative/restorative action to address those issues and meet those needs.**

"I explained the steps, what they're designed to accomplish, and that this was the process we'd be adopting/implementing over the next two months to help them resolve long-standing interpersonal and group-based conflicts. I said, 'The goal is to give you the tools and skills you need so that you can make the positive shift you want to happen.'

"This first large group assembly/circle took about ninety minutes. I gave them some homework to do before our next large-group meeting. After I explained the process, the steps, I asked them to take the S.H.A.R.E. process home, set aside some quiet time, and go through each of the steps. Pick an incident where you said something that now, thinking back, you regret, or wasn't constructive or considerate of someone else's feelings. I emphasized, 'This isn't about blaming yourself.' It's about taking an objective look at how what we say and how we say it impacts our relationships and taking ownership.

"I gave them an example. I shared that I was once on a team of restorative facilitators and one the other facilitators did something during a conference that I didn't approve of. I was the co-facilitator in this conference. When we were discussing that conference in a team meeting, I was silent. When I was asked to share my thoughts about that conference I said, 'I'll pass.' After our team meeting, this facilitator approached me and said, 'I feel like you're judging me.' I replied sarcastically, 'My admiration is under control.' It was an inappropriate, smart-ass thing to say, and I regretted it almost immediately. When I said it, they walked away.

"Using myself as an example, I explained to our large group, 'What I just did was the first step. I told the truth, if only to myself at that point, about what happened, about what I said.' Then I thought about who might've been impacted by what I said. That's the second step. Obviously, the other facilitator was directly impacted.

"But others on our team were probably impacted indirectly because what I had said understandably got back to some of the other facilitators. With my passive-aggressive silence and that one unmindful remark, I had impacted the entire team. The impact rippled out.

"The next step—acknowledging the impact—compelled me to really think about exactly how I had impacted the other facilitator and the team. I had to hold myself accountable by putting myself in their shoes. How would I feel if someone said that to me? I might feel hurt, betrayed, or angry. I might feel defensive. I might feel that trust had been broken and not feel safe to express my opinion or share about my experience as a facilitator in team meetings. I might avoid interacting with me.

"What I said was not respectful, dismissed the other facilitator's dignity, and this would no doubt plant a seed of mistrust in the team. So, that one sarcastic remark negatively impacted the other facilitator, our relationship, and my relationship with the team. It was also a violation of the values and respect-based principles that we agreed to abide by as facilitators to protect our relationships and nurture an environment where we could learn from our mistakes, develop, and evolve in our craft.

"I then had to ask myself, 'Why did I say this?' Were there underlying issues, reasons, or motivations for me making this comment? What was going on with me? Was there an underlying need I was trying to meet? And what needs or obligations were created as a result of my callous remark? This is the fourth step of the S.H.A.R.E. process—recognize the needs.

"I told our assembly that 'clearly, I was sitting in judgment of this other facilitator.' I explained that I had co-facilitated a conference with this facilitator and they had brought a rock in from the parking lot and started the conference by passing the rock around the circle and asking each participant to share 'what came up for them.'

"I shared that when this happened, in that moment, I felt embarrassed. Because I was the co-facilitator, I thought that what my teammate did made both of us look foolish, and dismissed the seriousness of the incident we were there to address.

"Second, on a certain level I felt excluded because (a) it was out of the ordinary, and (b) I wasn't consulted beforehand. Because I wasn't consulted, I also felt disrespected. Third, and this is where my ego kicked in, I had been advocating for the restorative process in the face of constant objections that the process was 'touchy-feely' and superficial. So, when the facilitator produced the rock and asked the question, 'What comes up for you?' my immediate thought was, 'You've got to be kidding me.' I judged the facilitator for not being respectful of the process.

"All of these underlying issues or 'reasons' pointed to unmet needs. I realized I have a need to be consulted with before another facilitator/team member does something that is out of the ordinary and going to directly impact my participation as a professional. Second, I have a need for closer collaboration with another facilitator before any group restorative conference. Third, I have a need for any other facilitator I work with to fully understand the seriousness of the process. We're dealing with serious matters that have impacted people's well-being. I need other facilitators to take this as seriously as I do.

"At the same time, what I said, the sarcastic remark, created needs and obligations. First, I needed to take responsibility for my comment by acknowledging how it might have impacted the other facilitator and our facilitation team. Second, this meant I needed to listen to their truth about how I had impacted them. Third, there was a need for repair. This meant, among other things, apologizing for my remark.

"But fourth, I also had a need to speak my own truth about how the other facilitator's action with the rock impacted me. I needed to explain how seriously I took these conferences and our role in creating a safe space for open dialogue. Lastly, there was a need for the team to address this and restore a spirit of connection, collaboration, and safety.

"The last step—'enroll in a plan of concrete action'—meant going through the restorative process at our next team meeting. When we did, the air was cleared. The aforementioned needs were met, and obligations for maintaining good relations were fulfilled. In addition to the incident being resolved on an interpersonal relationship level within the group and between me and the other facilitator, a new policy item was implemented whereby facilitators working on a case would meet the day before to clarify exactly how the opening of any conference would be conducted," I explained to our small discussion group.

Kris asked, "I'm curious why you asked people to go through the S.H.A.R.E. process on their own, and pick an incident where they said or did something and not someone else?"

"Great question. First, I wanted them to have a personal connection to, or interior experience of, the process. I wanted them to feel it. How many times do we learn about a new process or method, or are inspired, but don't really embrace it on a personal level? Right before I met with the entire group, I overheard a comment, 'Bet we have to sit through another boring PowerPoint about conflict.' The last thing they needed was a bunch of knowledge or academic theory being thrown at them. I didn't use a PowerPoint.

"What they needed was a more intimate experience. To be frank, I wanted to take the process out of the intellectual or conceptual realm, and into the experiential realm of their feelings and consciousness. I didn't want them to just go home and think about it, which let's face it, typically doesn't happen. I wanted them to actually do it and feel it. That experience not only fosters a deeper understanding of how it works but can also lead to actually taking personal ownership of it," I said.

"Out of the head and into the heart," said Kris.

"Exactly. Intimate and personal experience rather than intellectual and professional engagement. Second, the reason why I asked them to pick an incident where they had done or said something they regretted was because as a collective, they were stuck in a destructive pattern of blaming others. I wanted them to begin to take personal ownership of their own communication behavior and think about how they might be contributing to the toxic social climate. I wanted them to see their part," I said.

"Hold a mirror up to themselves. Hold themselves personally accountable," said Brad.

"Yes, but in a way that was psychologically and emotionally safe for them by doing it on their own in private. When we met the next time, I didn't ask them to share about the incident they picked or what they had said or done. That wouldn't have been safe. Instead, I asked them, 'What became clear for you about the power of communication and words, and the role of communication in constituting our experience of our relationships?'

"Pretty much everyone recognized how we take communication for granted and don't think about the impact that what we say has on others. I made the comment that the old phrase 'sticks and stones will break our bones, but words will never hurt us' is false. Words stick with us and can continue to hurt us long after a broken bone has healed. Why is it that we can remember insults for years? Sometimes, a lifetime. Words matter.

"The reason I used myself as an example was about vulnerability. In my experience, the restorative process, the encounter, takes us right to the edge between vulnerability and defensiveness. Remember when I said that restoration is risky business? It's risky because there's nothing more vulnerable than to expose our imperfectness by saying, 'What I did or said was wrong. I am responsible for the harm I caused. I regret what I did, and will do what I can to repair that harm,'" I said.

"I have no defense," said Devonte.

"I have no defense and I'm appealing to your mercy. 'Tell me how I can repair this.'"

> **"Vulnerability is a leap of faith into trusting in the humanity of others. We trust that they will identify with our imperfectness and understand rather than condemn."**

"What I find tragic is that defensiveness not only continues the cycle of blame and disconnection but also exacerbates it. Defensiveness suppresses vital experiences that are critical to resolution: accountability, connection, empathy, compassion, repair, and pardon.

"In this particular organization, there was no safe space to be vulnerable; to accept imperfectness and acknowledge faults. There was no mercy. And yet, that's the very thing that would help them heal their relationships and start to shift their culture. But here's the thing—and this is important—it's not their fault. They didn't consciously or purposely set out to create an organizational culture where it would be unsafe to be vulnerable. It's much deeper and bigger than that," I said.

"It's our culture in general," said Brad.

"Can you say more about that?" I asked.

"Vulnerability is a sign of weakness to be taken advantage of. If you expose your own vulnerability, you risk being attacked. Especially in a win-at-all-costs cultural mindset. Like you said, it's a paradigm. If you're vulnerable, you lose. Is it any wonder people are afraid to admit their mistakes? I think as a culture we also equate making mistakes with shame, and that shame or fear of exposure is what keeps us from telling the truth," Brad replied.

Devonte asked, "What was their conduct policy like? Was it retributive?"

"That's a great question. Yes. The year before I started working with them, the director and the executive team rewrote the policy to include increasing levels of sanctions for destructive conflicts which involved cursing and angry outbursts. It was basically a 'three strikes and you're out' policy," I said.

"Sounds like they were trying to coercively regulate people's resentments," said Devonte. "Old Testament justice," he added.

"That's a great point. Leadership was trying to force a change in how people felt with the threat of enforcement. It didn't work. It made things worse. It just fueled further grievance. One of the exercises we did was a 'feeling rules inventory.' Feeling rules tell us what we have a right to feel, what we 'should' feel in any particular situation, and what an appropriate expression is. One well-known gender-based rule is, 'Real men don't cry.'

"Feeling rules begin in the family, and parents often differ in how they teach children to process their emotions. Feeling rules are often transgenerational. The value we place on emotions and how we process them are handed down to us. Some parents teach children to 'control' their feelings by telling them what they should and shouldn't feel in certain situations. The inventory I gave them asked them to think about rules about feelings that might have existed in their family:

- What message did you receive, or do you give, about emotions?
- When you had strong feelings, did you feel safe expressing them? Were they discussed?
- How was affection expressed?
- How was anger addressed?
- How successful do you think your family is/was in processing emotions?

"Feeling rules also exist in the workplace. People who have power and status in a workplace are permitted to 'express negative emotions in rude and disrespectful ways toward people with less power and status.'[8] Subordinates can become 'venting targets' because people in power believe they have the right to express anger, frustration, or coldness.

"Conversely, employees learn that it isn't acceptable for them to express the same emotions. This means that feeling rules become ways of controlling people, enforcing authority, and reinforcing status. When this emotional power imbalance exists, the workplace climate is not safe. This, in turn, impacts employee satisfaction and productivity," I said.

"There's no safe space to be vulnerable," said Melissa.

"That's exactly it," I replied. "We did an inventory of feeling rules in their workplace:

- Do you feel safe expressing your feelings?
- Are there those who seem to have more permission to emote than others?
- What role does unexpressed emotion have in any gossip?
- How do you respond when someone is experiencing strong emotion?
- Do you think the expression of emotions is handled constructively?

"Human beings are emotional beings, but we're not born understanding what emotions mean or how to process them. When we don't take the time to fully understand emotions and develop ways to work with them, they can wreak havoc on communication.

"Minor conflict can become toxic conflict. Decision-making discussions can devolve into protecting self-interest and heated arguments about territory. Resentment can exist as an undertone, and gossip can flourish. One thing is clear—any family or cultural rule that attempts to suppress or deny emotions gets us into trouble," I said.

"And emotional suppression leads to suppression of voice," said Devonte.

"I think so," I said. "And if people don't have the freedom to express how they feel and don't feel safe speaking up, then what motivation do they have to contribute their perspectives or ideas for problem-solving? There's no feedback."

Brad asked, "What did people say when they did the workplace inventory?"

"More than anything, they realized that there was no safe space to process strong feelings about issues or conflicts or how they were treating each other," I said.

"Chronic emotional indigestion. No wonder people are grumpy with each other," quipped Barb.

Hearty laugh.

"Suffocation," I added. "No safety equals no vibrancy. The organism can't breathe. There's another challenge that is more on the paradigmatic level. In the workplace, for the most part, fact, logic, and reason are exalted, and feelings are often seen as an obstacle to progress. The message is that emotions get in the way of getting things done.

"This hierarchy of reason over emotion has been around ever since Plato. Plato described emotion and reason as 'two horses pulling a cart in opposite directions.' Therefore, if you want to move in one clear direction (progress), you should cut the reins of the emotional horse. Ideally, you have to find a way to enable people to have and express their feelings, but not let emotion dominate the interaction or impede progress," I said.

Individual Accountability and Collective Enrollment

"I want to keep going with the example of this organization. In our second large-group circle, I asked them what became clear for them when they did the S.H.A.R.E. exercise on their own. Generally speaking, they made the connection between things they had said to and about each other and how that constituted an atmosphere of contentiousness.

"Several members commented that the exercise helped them see their part in creating that atmosphere. This was an important step toward taking personal ownership of communication behavior," I explained.

"Personal accountability," commented Aaron.

"Yes. For the most part, they were able to realize how one destructive conflict or demeaning statement was impacting others beyond the person they were in conflict with or disapproved of. Some explained that they were 'taking their resentments and regret home with them.'

"I asked them, 'What came up for you when you acknowledged that impact?' Some reported feeling a sense of regret for things they had said and ways they had handled a conflict. In my experience, regret can be a powerful motivation to pursue repair and restoration of the relationship.

"But where the proverbial 'rubber met the road' was when we discussed the fourth step of the S.H.A.R.E. process, which is to 'recognize the underlying issues and needs.' Generally speaking, the underlying issue was a lack of justice. People had done things and said things to and about each other that constituted a sense of violation of personal boundaries, disregard for emotional safety, and toxic disrespect. As one member admitted, 'Someone will drop a f*** you or f*** them bomb and walk away, and it never gets addressed.'

"Because there was no follow-up, no accountability, the seeds of resentment kept getting planted and retaliation became the only means of seeking justice. That was the entrenched pattern. And it certainly didn't help that management was imposing punishment through write-ups and scolding. It was like pouring salt on a wound. Predictably, employees turned their animosity toward management and leadership. No wonder they had such a high turnover rate for directors.

"One of the exercises we did was to 'name the needs.' I had them break out into small groups and share the needs they had identified when they worked through the S.H.A.R.E. process at home. One member from each small group made the list and then presented that list to the larger circle when we reassembled.

"What do you suppose happened?" I asked our discussion group.

"They all had the same needs," said Melissa.

"Yes. They all had a need to be treated with respect; to feel appreciated and valued; to feel safe, etc. But the one thing everyone needed that was missing was accountability. So, I asked them, 'what does accountability look like for all of you?' They settled on three aspects." I explained:

- Not letting things slide. Addressing them as soon as they happen.
- Accountability for the damage caused to people's feelings and morale.
- Meaningful repair, expectations established, and conditions set to keep it from happening again.

"That's the S.H.A.R.E. process," said Brad.

"It is. Strategically, by explaining the steps of S.H.A.R.E. at our very first assembly, and having them do the homework on their own, what I was doing was orienting them toward how to resolve their issues on their own. I gave them S.H.A.R.E. as a lens with a language to understand and talk about what was happening and what they could do about it," I said.

"So, you followed the process itself as a training method?" asked Devonte.

"I did. I used it to guide our discussion about what was happening, what they could do, and demonstrated how it works while I was explaining it."

"Performative training," said Brad.

"Yes. At least, that was my goal," I replied.

"Do restoration while teaching about restoration," added Joan.

"Give people an experience of S.H.A.R.E. while sharing about S.H.A.R.E.," I said. "I can't believe I just said that," I chuckled.

"Thanks for sharing," quipped Barb.

"What happened? Did they turn things around? How did you help them moving forward?" asked Melissa.

"If you remember, I suggested they take a two-prong approach. The first prong was to use S.H.A.R.E. to work through longstanding individual or interpersonal grudges and conflicts. This took about two months. The first month, I facilitated almost all of the meetings, the circles. But I included a co-facilitator so they could do it moving forward. The second month, I was the co-facilitator.

"As you can imagine, with such pent-up tensions, many of these circles were emotional. People spoke their truth, heard each other, expressed and acknowledged each other's feelings, actually started to forgive each other, and made agreements. For the most part, those agreements included coming right back together when the agreements were broken.

"As typically happens, people started to have these conversations on their own without the need for a facilitator. One of the techniques we developed out of these agreements was how to confront gossip when it's happening. I won't go into detail, but one of the techniques was to remind the person of 'our agreement' to create a safe space.

"The second prong was to take a more systematic or whole-organization approach with a type of informal restorative communication program. I'll explain this in more detail in our discussion about implementation, but essentially, this programmatic approach included the formation of a core team of facilitators, the creation of a relationship-centric communication conduct agreement by members, and ongoing training in restorative communication skills and practices.

"I used a 'train-the-trainer' model. I trained the core team in basic interpersonal communication skills, but also a more advanced method of interacting with someone who is struggling with unresolved traumas. I'll explain more in our next discussion, but this method is called "S.H.I.F.T.," which is about recognizing, understanding, and engaging with someone on a deeper level in the moment, when their nervous system is dysregulated," I explained.

"Co-regulation," commented Kris.

"Yes. 'Trauma-responsive restorative communication' is the more technical name for it. Like I said, we'll cover this in our next discussion. Before we finish our current discussion session, I want to give you a template that I gave them to help them create their own policy around communication. They used it as a reference. The goal was to give them some principles that could serve as guidelines to help them achieve respect-based interaction," I said.

The Seven Principles of Restorative Communication: The 7 R's [10]

A principle is a basic truth, ideal, or tenet that we rely on to guide our behavior. Most often, principles are based on a fundamental belief about what constitutes correct, moral, and/or ethical behavior.

In communication terms, a principle is essentially a ground rule which, if followed, ensures the correct, moral and/or ethical treatment of others (and us) in the act of communicating. A principle of communication, if intentionally enacted, directs communication behavior—the manner in which we interact with each other and with ourselves.

To be a conscientious communicator is to be consciously aware that communication is more than just the delivery of information or transaction. To be conscientious is to be rigorously aware that the way we communicate creates the experience of our relationships and each other. With self-awareness, intention, and practice, these principles become highly effective communication habits which influence social climate.

RELATIONSHIP

Conscientious communication begins with the principle of relationship. In fact, all the principles of conscientious communication are built on this first fundamental principle. The principle of relationship emphasizes the primary role that communication plays in creating and maintaining the experience of the relationships for communicators. Positive communication builds positive relationships. Negative communication degrades relationships. This principle places the health of the relationship—achieved and sustained by constructive communication—as the primary objective.

RECOGNITION OF INHERENT DIGNITY

The second principle is a Recognition of the Inherent Dignity ("ID") of life. Recognition of Inherent Dignity is a basic regard for the sanctity of an individual life. We may not agree with, like, or respect what another person says or does, but they are valuable simply because they have a beating heart.

The same is true of ourselves. Strategically, to recognize this principle compels us to distinguish between a person's inherent value, and their opinions and behavior. Behavior is something that people do. Valuable is something that people innately are.

RESPECT

Because every human being is born with inherent value, they deserve a baseline of respect. We may not respect what a person says or does, but we can be respectful in the way we communicate with them—and about them. This can be difficult to do when someone pushes our buttons, acts egregiously, and/or offends us. But respect-based communication is the relational life-blood of any healthy family or organization.

Respectful communication is the framework that protects people and preserves both interpersonal and social relationships. The personal benefit of communicating respectfully with others is that in doing so, we performatively reaffirm our own inherent dignity.

RESPONSIBILITY

Every individual is personally responsible for how their communication behavior impacts others. Responsibility means taking ownership for one's own communication habits with no excuses. We can think of this principle as our personal code of communication conduct. As leaders or parents, we can model this in our own communication as well as support others in our family or organization to do the same.

Taking responsibility for our communication means taking responsibility for the ongoing health of our relationships. When we miss the mark and communicate in an unhealthy or unconstructive way, we need to take responsibility for how we impacted others and our relationship with them. We do this by abiding by the following three principles: Reconciliation, Repair, and Reintegration.

RECONCILIATION

Taking responsibility for our communication and the health of relationships requires a non-negotiable commitment to reconciliation in order to reestablish harmony and "good relations" between individuals and/or groups. Without a commitment to reconcile, the consequences of a negative interaction are not addressed. As a result, a valuable learning opportunity is lost, people's feelings are not expressed, and resentment can build, thereby impacting future interaction.

Reconciliation enables accountability and the opportunity for reiteration of our values. Reconciling demonstrates our recommitment to the principles of conscientious communication. Reconciliation is perhaps the single most important principle in the prevention of future conflict.

REPAIR

Reconciliation often requires repair. To repair is to take ultimate personal responsibility for how what we've said may have harmed others. The principle of repair establishes that in order for relationships to be returned to a place of mutual respect and stability, any harm experienced as a result of negative interaction needs to be concretely addressed.

Repair can involve anything from a sincere apology, to a "reparative action plan" to address the underlying thinking, attitudes, and behaviors that led to destructive interaction. Repair should also include developing better ways to communicate through training and education.

REINTEGRATION

The principle of reintegration emphasizes the social reality of interdependence. Every individual is an integral member of the family, organization, and community and therefore needs to contribute—via healthy communication—to the social fabric. Abiding by the principle of reintegration compels us to constantly recognize our responsibility for the well-being of the whole, and consistently contribute to the health of relationships through constructive communication.

Reintegration requires that we (a) repair when needed, (b) accept limitations of others, and (c) strive to develop constructive personal communication skills. Reintegration is a constant process realized when healthy communication is restored.

I asked our discussion group, "How do you think the S.H.A.R.E. process would work with people's emotions in your workplace?"

Melissa said, "The obvious is that it would give people a safe space to talk."

"That could be risky," said Kris.

"What do you mean?" I asked.

"People's emotions can get out of hand. Feelings, especially if they run deep, could take over the discussion," she said.

"Especially if they've never been expressed before," added Brad.

"Or like you said, if they don't even really know how they're feeling, or haven't learned how to constructively express them," said Kris.

"I'd like to add to what you just said Kris," said Devonte. "I see S.H.A.R.E. as an opportunity for social-emotional competency building. I was thinking about this in the case of Leo and Rick."

"What is that?" asked Brad.

Devonte replied, "Social-emotional competency refers to our ability to recognize what we're feeling and thinking, process it through self-management, be aware of other people's feelings and perspectives, and the ability to make responsible decisions and build healthy relationships.

"These competencies were identified by a nonprofit organization called CASEL, which stands for the Collaborative for Academic, Social, and Emotional Learning.[9] Schools and teachers try to develop these competencies in students. It's a pedagogy that came from the field of child development and the recognition of early childhood attachment styles with caregivers and their influence on mental health and relationships. But the development of these competencies can happen throughout a person's life. It's not just for kids," he said.

"This is eye-opening," said Brad. "These competencies are either missing or underdeveloped in our patients," he said.

"They're underdeveloped in politicians," quipped Barb.

"Amen," said Brad.

"Who is your typical patient?" I asked.

"Young men in their twenties," Brad replied.

"Are the deficits a consequence of their addictions, or is addiction a consequence of these deficiencies?" I asked.

"I think it's both. If these competencies were sufficiently developed at a younger age, they might have the awareness and skills to deal with adversity and social pressures instead of choosing drugs or alcohol to cope; to escape. Once addicted, the possibility of developing these skills is disabled. I've never heard of CASEL, but these capacities are what we're trying to develop during the recovery process," said Brad.

Devonte added, "The more these capacities are developed in people, the healthier communities and society we'll have. I like what Aaron said earlier about social capital. I see S.H.A.R.E. as an investment in social justice and civil society with social-emotional capital."

Aaron added, "The more social-emotionally aware the individual, the more competent the society."

Devonte continued, "Yeah, and the stakes are extraordinarily, dangerously high right now. When I look at the hateful tantrums, racism, and violent rhetoric of ultra-right-wing politicians and groups, I see people who lack competency in these areas. Zero civility. Zero capacity to participate in democratic discourse. Zero emotional intelligence, let alone regulation.

"This is deeper than character or morality. It's a developmental issue. When I look at the former president, I see a social-emotional disability with roots in childhood attachment disorder. It's not just a lack of awareness, it's an inherent incapacity. It's a mental health issue.

"If these competencies aren't developed at an early age, then our evolution as a civil society not only stops but devolves into narcissism. I think democracy requires these competencies."

There was a moment of silence in our group. What Devonte said was profound.

"I don't mean to take us off track," he added.

"You didn't take us off track. You took us deeper into the hardcore truth about why social-emotional competency is critical. I needed to hear what you said," I replied. "I think we all did. Does anyone have something to add?"

Brad spoke. "First, I just want to acknowledge what Devonte just shared. Your observations lifted my spirit. I feel the same way, but I couldn't articulate it. I can see how this applies to our recovery center.

"The classrooms are the group meetings we have with patients. The 'school' is our center. Certainly, what's learned by our patients and, hopefully, the constructive changes they make in their behavior seeps out and into their families."

"I see it too," said Melissa. "We have brilliant, extraordinary surgeons with exceptional decision-making, but some are lacking emotional self-management, social awareness, and relationship skills. I'm anxious to see how we can implement S.H.A.R.E. to develop these aptitudes or competencies in a corporate environment with adults who might not have had the benefit of this learning in schools."

"Or their families of origin," added Brad.

"I want to steer us back to restorative communication, and specifically, the S.H.A.R.E. conversation process. Building on what Devonte shared, how relevant might this process be to developing these competencies? We can look at each competency and explore if or how S.H.A.R.E. might facilitate, or 'embody,' an experience of that competency for participants. I'm making three assumptions here.

"First, that learning is experiential. Second, social-emotional development is not limited to children or young people. It can happen throughout our lives. Third, I'm assuming that any incident of destructive conflict, interaction, or 'breach in pro-relationship norms' is not only an opportunity for using the S.H.A.R.E. process, but also potentially an opportunity for social-emotional awareness-building. We can use Rick's case as an example," I suggested. "Devonte, what do you think?"

Devonte spoke. "It's obvious that Rick was lacking in both self-awareness and self-management when he assaulted Leo. At a bare minimum, if he had those two competencies, he wouldn't have done what he did. He would've had a capacity in that moment for making the connection between what he was imagining, its influence on what he was feeling, which was paranoid and afraid. Then instead of exploding in rage and acting out his fantasy, he would have found a way to stop himself, calm or self-soothe himself, and let it go. He could've thought, 'Maybe I'm wrong.' He could've called the police. He could've made any number of different choices besides what he did," said Devonte.

"He could've recognized that he was triggered," said Kris.

Devonte continued, "At the least. It's also clear that he had no social awareness. He certainly had no capacity for thinking about how he was going to impact the other driver. He had no awareness of the other driver's vulnerability, let alone humanity.

"What he did also demonstrates that he lacked sufficient awareness that what he was about to do was not only unethical, but also illegal. He didn't stop and think, 'If I do this, I might go to jail.' He certainly wasn't thinking about his son. He had no mechanism for restraint.

"As for relationship skills, I think what is most tragic about Rick's case is that he had no awareness, couldn't even question the pressure that his dad was putting on him to conform to his racist attitudes.

"You take all of these deficiencies together, and the result is a person with no capacity for any responsible decision-making. He had no ability, no capacity, no social-emotional competency. I don't know if we can say that these competencies were developed during the conversation, but the lack of those competencies was exposed and the possibility for development was presented. They weren't explicitly talked about, but it seems to me that the restorative process, or 'S.H.A.R.E.' as we're calling it, addressed each of these areas of development.

"The circle made the connection between what he was thinking, believing, and feeling, his rage, and what he did, his actions, his behavior. They pointed out that in that moment, he had no control, no ability to 'regulate,' or even notice that he was out of control. They also pointed out the consequences of his being out of control. They also made the connection between what his dad was telling him and the consequences of that.

"But like Kris said, I think the most powerful example, maybe even transformative or developmental moment of this process in terms of social awareness, had to do with empathy. Rick was a chronically empathy-deficient guy. But he got a heavy dose of it during this process. He was able to see the depth of harm he caused Leo and Maria, feel remorse and a desire to repair what he did, but he also got to experience what it feels like when people feel and demonstrate empathy for you.

"I think this helped him be vulnerable. They didn't shame him. They held him accountable, but they embraced him and created a plan of restoration for him," explained Devonte.

"They demonstrated mercy," said Melissa.

"Yeah. They forgave him and gave him a chance to redeem himself. This leads to my last point, which is that his reparative contract essentially laid out a concrete plan for developing these competencies, or capacities through therapy which might address his trauma and give him the skills to confront his father.

"Seems to me that his attendance at the race-relations meetings would lead to developing his understanding of pro-social norms around diversity. I think the fact that Leo, Tim, and John went with him to his sentencing was a clear demonstration of inclusion," said Devonte.

"I want to take a moment and acknowledge your contribution to our discussion. What you just gave me, and I think all of us, was a depth of understanding about how restorative communication intersects with social-emotional competency building and what the consequences are when these competencies are missing. You made the connection for me," I added.

"Amen to that," said Barb.

"I second that, Devonte," said Brad.

"Thank you. I'm as frustrated as all of us. But I'm beginning to see how to make a difference," said Devonte. "My takeaway from this discussion is that if we want to change the world, we have to change how we communicate with each other."

"One conversation at a time," said Aaron.

"It's time to close our discussion. We've covered a lot of ground. We looked at the role that communication plays in constructing relationships, explored the function of restorative communication, and learned about a specific group communication practice called 'S.H.A.R.E.'"

I continued, "One underlying issue that we haven't explored is relational trauma. Conflict and destructive interaction can both activate and be activated by unhealed abuse and/or other traumatic experiences. While S.H.A.R.E. is both a group practice and a method for resolving an interpersonal conflict between two people, what do you do when a person is experiencing extreme agitation, emotional distress, or withdrawal? What do you do in that moment?" I asked.

"I ask this because it is inevitable that people will not be able to participate in a S.H.A.R.E. conversation if they are experiencing a type of traumatic stress—whether that stress is a result of trauma that happened long ago, or as a direct result of a toxic interaction."

"Like what Leo experienced with Rick," said Aaron.

"Yes. In those moments when a person is caught in the grips of a traumatic experience, we need a way to engage with them, help them, and gain their trust. Because if we don't do that, assembling in a group circle to discuss what happened and achieve a resolution or reconciliation risks retraumatizing that person or persons.

"What we're going to look at next is a restorative communication technique called S.H.I.F.T. that is trauma-responsive."

Closing Thoughts about Restorative Communication

What can we say about "restorative communication" in summary?

- *Restorative communication*, the process of encounter, is *performative*. By this, we mean that the restorative discussion provides for an *experience of restoration* during the interactive process as people are determining what the outcome called "restoration" will be.
- *An approach* to interaction that emphasizes the constitutive role of language and communication in human relationships.
- Communication is not just the delivery/transaction of information.
  - Communication creates our experience of interpersonal and social relationships on an emotional, psychological, physical, and even spiritual level.
  - Communication constitutes and substantiates the meaning of the relationship in the context of interaction (communicating with), but also in the act of framing (communicating about).
- *An ethic* of communication based on certain humanistic principles.
  - Recognition of the inherent dignity of life.
  - Respect for others' experiences and perspectives.
  - Personal and collective responsibility for relationships through respect-based interaction.
- *A pragmatic* process which:
  - Organizes and guides interaction through questions.
  - Creates the possibility for a shared understanding of an issue.
  - Exposes underlying issues, conditions, differences, reasons, causes, and impacts.
  - Produces collective agreement and accountability.
- *A method/skill* which:
  - Can be learned.
  - Can be applied in any circumstance of interpersonal and/or group interaction:

- ◆ Deliberation
- ◆ Decision-making
- ◆ Conflict management
- ◆ Conduct management (performance reviews and correction)
- *An organizational cultural asset* which:
  - Operationalizes positive cultural values of respect, responsibility, and continuous relationship-building on a day-to-day basis.
  - Instills and sustains relational resilience.
  - Establishes and maintains a positive organizational climate.

Primarily, when the restorative approach to communication is enacted, there is a *restoration of healthy, respect-based interaction* between individuals and groups.

Because restorative communication is a principled process which embodies the ethics of deep listening, respect, concern for others, responsibility, accountability, and inclusion, there is a *restoration of civil discourse* between members throughout the family or organization. Restorative discourse is about voice, listening, and exchange versus suppression, silence, and transaction.

Restorative communication—the individual dialogue practices—reminds people of their humanness and fosters compassion for our shared human condition. It's not "me and mine" or "you and yours." It's about us and ours. Conflict becomes an opportunity for collaboration.

Secondarily, when the restorative approach and method of communication is applied in any/all discussions around important issues, conflicts, decisions, and policy fulfillment, people feel seen and heard by each other, respected for their unique perspectives, and *realize their individual and collective responsibility for maintaining positive relations.* One of the outcomes of the restorative process is the *constant reinforcement of the need for relational trust*—a keystone of social-emotional resilience.

Third, when the restorative process becomes the way in which members communicate with each other on a daily basis to move through disagreements, arguments, and conflicts, then cultural values of respect, consideration, diversity of perspective, mutual understanding, and support become *actualized* on an experiential basis. Participants in restorative dialogues feel and see those values being practiced and applied.

The day-to-day enactment of this culture, in turn, fosters an overall positive and progressive workplace (or family) climate. People know they have a voice, that their perspective matters, and that they feel heard. With such culture and climate in place, people feel safe, and *morale and productivity increase.* People want to come to work and want to contribute as much as possible to each other, and the success of the family, organization, and/or business.

Lastly, the hallmark of any successful organization (or society) is *resilience.* Resilience is not just an economic capacity, but also an organizational capacity. The more resilient the people and their relationships are, the more capable the organization is of meeting any adversity—both internal and external—successfully. Effective communication—communication practices and processes which reinforce *inter*dependence—builds organizational resilience. Restorative communication makes communication an asset rather than an issue or liability.

Any family, group, or organization is a living organism consisting of relationships. The healthier the relationships, the healthier the organism. If the relationships between people are mired in dysfunctional communication patterns, unresolved conflict, gossip, lack of respect, lack of voice, inadequate and/or incomplete explanations for decisions, lack of clear boundaries, incapacity for and lack of continuous feedback, deficit-focused criticism, favoritism, suppressed opinions, etc., then the organism takes the hit. The community takes a hit, and society "keeps the score," to use Bessel van der Kolk's phrase.[11]

CHAPTER SIX
Co-Regulation
Through Connection

Traumatized human beings recover in the context of relationships [...] The role of those relationships is to provide safety, including safety from feeling ashamed, admonished, judged, and to bolster the courage to tolerate, face, and process the reality of what has happened. [1]

— Bessel van der Kolk, M.D.

When our group reconvened, I provided a quick recap. "In our very first discussion, we listed some of the crises we're all facing. Those crises run the gamut from environmental to social, local to global, personal to political. We described the cumulative effect of all of the crises we face as producing a social atmosphere of pervasive threat resulting in a type of 'existential anxiety.'

"Kris, you mentioned that 'our collective nervous system is shot.' I think this statement is important and the research would bear this out with regard to how the toxic political climate is impacting mental health.

"For example, Smith (2022) conducted two surveys to 'assess how political engagement affects physical, psychological and social health among adults in the United States, to establish whether those health impacts increased or decreased across the period of the Trump administration.' [2]

"The first survey was conducted in March 2017 (N=800) shortly after Donald Trump's inauguration. The second survey was taken in November 2020 (N=700) approximately two weeks prior to the 2020 election. It's worth quoting the findings from this study:

Results suggest that a large numbers of adults—depending on the health item, estimates run from tens of millions to more than a hundred million—attribute a range of significant physical, psychological and social health costs to politics, that those numbers stayed high and in some cases almost certainly increased over the course of the Trump administration, and that the 2020 election and its aftermath increased rather than decreased those negative health impacts.[3]

Based on the 2019–20 Census Bureau population estimates, the resident population of the United States included approximately 255 million adults at the time of the 2020 survey. Based on that number, the findings from the pre-election survey suggest that somewhere between a fifth and a third of adults—roughly 50 to 85 million people—blame politics for causing fatigue, lost sleep, feelings of anger, loss of temper, as well as triggering compulsive behaviors (e.g., difficulty in stopping thinking about politics and consuming political information), and difficulties in impulse control [...] A quarter of Americans reported seriously considering moving because of politics, and an estimated 40 percent—more than 100 million—consistently identify politics as a significant source of stress in their lives. Astonishingly, all three surveys consistently indicate that around five percent of adults report having suicidal thoughts because of politics—that's an estimated 12 million people.[4]

"When you add in the post-traumatic stress of the pandemic, school and mass shootings, the rise in white supremacy and race-based hatred and violence, the insurrection, the reality of global warming and its consequences, the war in Ukraine, Gaza, and other geopolitical threats, it's no wonder there has been a significant increase in clinically diagnosable mental health conditions such as depression and anxiety," I said.

> **"All of this shows up in our families, schools, workplaces, etc. So, when it does, and we can see it, what do we do as 'restorative practitioners'? How do we engage with someone who is exhibiting signs of this stress?"**

"With the technique we'll be covering, we're not only recognizing the other person's symptoms or signs, but we're recognizing their humanity by connecting with them on an empathic and intuitive heart-centric level to help them shift out of a state of feeling isolated and alone in their distress," I said.

"You're talking about trauma and dysregulation," said Kris.

"Dysregulation is a technical description, or clinical term, yes. I prefer the term 'distress' because it humanizes the immediate experience. Dysregulation is a condition that a person may have over time. Distress is a more accessible layperson's term. Who doesn't know what it feels like to experience distress? Similarly, distress can be situational and not pathological. The communication technique we're going to discuss is an effective intervention method regardless of the context because it works on a physiological level. But I'm getting ahead of myself here.

"Similarly, trauma is a descriptive term we can use to describe what a person has been through or is experiencing. Unresolved or unhealed trauma may be the underlying cause of the distress. PTSD might explain why they're in distress. But just like the term 'dysregulation,' trauma is a multi-faceted and highly subjective term that exists on a spectrum. When that person is right in front of you, what they are experiencing is physical, emotional, and psychological distress. How do you engage with that person?

"In this discussion, we're going to follow the lead of the little girl on the beach. We may not be able to restore or regulate the collective nervous system—in other words, all the starfish—but we can develop the communication skills to help the person standing right in front of us who is showing signs of distress. Once again, it's all about relationship and a quality or depth of connection.

"The signs of distress are recognizable or observable," I said. "If you're not a therapist or trauma specialist, what do you do? We can still help. We can identify, or 'spot the signs' that they are struggling, and connect. To see dysregulation as an experience of distress, and trauma as a potential reason, provides a lens to understand what that person needs right then and there.

"Technically speaking, this method is about co-regulating a person's emotions and nervous system when they're in a state of arousal. But in that moment, when a person is feeling scared, terrified, hyper-agitated, or checked-out and numb, it's really about connecting with them on a gut-level, heart-centric level of communication. That interaction, that communication technique, physically and literally embodies the message, 'You're not alone, you're safe with me, I'm right here with you in this moment, and we'll get through this together.' "

"This sounds a lot like victim's advocacy, which requires deep listening," said Kris.

"Victim advocacy is one context," I replied. "And yes, this is about deep listening, deep noticing, deep attention, and deep breathing. But the technique is also a progressive process. By that I mean that the goal is to not just feel empathy and to console, but also to guide that person through the distress. It's one-on-one restorative communication with a very specific purpose. It is very much a type of advocacy."

"It sounds like therapy," said Barb.

"I think it's more accurate to say it is therapeutic. This is an interaction technique designed to help that person feel safe and reclaim a sense of self-management in the moment," I said.

"Before you explain the technique, can you clarify the difference between this technique and the S.H.A.R.E. process?" asked Brad.

"Yes," I replied. "S.H.A.R.E. is essentially a group communication process used to address an event or incident that has negatively impacted people and their relationships. In this regard, you're using S.H.A.R.E. to guide a discussion about something that has happened. But that process, the questions and the steps, can also be used in a one-on-one dialogue with someone in order to understand what happened, who was impacted, how they were impacted, etc."

"Like in your pre-encounter interviews with individuals who were involved or impacted," said Melissa.

"Exactly. This technique—the S.H.I.F.T. trauma-responsive technique is most effective in a one-on-one dialogue technique where you are working face-to-face with a person who is showing signs of emotional or psychological distress," I explained.

"So, I can see how these two techniques can work together," said Brad. "For instance, if someone is seriously distressed as a result of something that has happened, and you're preparing them for the S.H.A.R.E. group discussion, you might use S.H.I.F.T. to help them be able to participate in that discussion."

"Yes. Think back to my initial pre-encounter conversation with Leo. He was hyper-aroused, seriously upset by what happened to him. What he needed from me in that moment was emotional support, empathy, validation, and reassurance that I would protect and support him when and if we moved forward with the S.H.A.R.E. process.

"If I hadn't established that deeper connection with him, I doubt he would've changed his mind about participating," I explained. "But I'm getting ahead of myself here. Later in our discussion, I'll provide an example that will more clearly illustrate how S.H.I.F.T. works within the context of the S.H.A.R.E. process."

"But you don't necessarily have to prepare for, or be in the middle of, the S.H.A.R.E. process to use this technique. Is that right?" asked Kris.

"That's right. S.H.I.F.T. can be used in any situation where you're working with someone who is distressed," I confirmed.

About S.H.I.F.T.

S.H.I.F.T. is the acronym for the technique that also describes what we're attempting to do. We're attempting to help shift that person's perspective about what they're experiencing.

- **SPOT the signs that indicate a person is in distress.**
- **HOLD a space of safety and empathy for them.**
- **IDENTIFY what they're experiencing.**
- **FOCUS on what they need.**
- **TAKE restorative action with them.**

"One way to think about the S.H.I.F.T. technique is as a type of 'intentional empathy,' or 'empathy as a relational tool for connection and recovery,'" I added.

"What's being restored?" asked Melissa.

"The short answer is connection. The experience of distress can be isolating. What this technique does is give you the ability to engage and connect on a level that reduces that sense and perception of isolation. The more complex answer has to do with co-regulation," I said. "Let me ask you. When you're experiencing distress, when you're either highly agitated or feeling completely overwhelmed, what is likely happening in your body?"

Barb responded, "Your breathing is shallow. Your heart is racing. Your muscles are tight. Your nervous system is being flooded with adrenaline and cortisol. That's the classic fight/flight/freeze survival experience."

"Right," I said. "So, if you're interceding, what are you attempting to do in response to that?"

"Soothe and restore a sense of calm," said Kris.

"Right. It's about reducing nervous system arousal," I said. "That includes both hyperarousal, which is extreme agitation, as well as hypoarousal, which is the exact opposite, lethargic and numb. What we're attempting to do is help that person make a shift from a state of fight/flight/freeze and into a state of feeling safe and present. This is deep empathy.

"I don't want to do a deep dive into the science because I want us to focus more on the technique. I'll just say that studies of the neurophysiology and neurobiology of trauma and the nervous system indicate that we can use both nonverbal and verbal communication techniques to co-regulate a person's nervous system.[5] S.H.I.F.T. is a restorative communication technique that intervenes, co-regulates, and helps a person feel cared for ... and cared about."

"Affective language," said Brad. "Language that creates a change in an emotional state."

"Exactly. We can do this because of specialized brain cells in our prefrontal cortex called mirror neurons," I said. "Bessel van der Kolk explains, 'We pick up not only another person's movement but her emotional state and intentions as well.'[6] He explains, 'A kind face or a soothing voice can dramatically alter the way we feel. When the message we receive from another person is, "You're safe with me," we relax. Being able to feel safe with other people is probably the single most important aspect of mental health.'[7] Van der Kolk (2014), Rizzolatti and Craighorn (2004), and Marco Iacoboni (2005) suggest that mirror neurons are the neural basis for empathy.

"This means that if we are present, calm, settled, grounded, open, and listening compassionately, we can have a profound effect in co-regulating the distressed person's nervous system. Nurses do this exceptionally well," I said.

"We try to," said Barb.

"Stephen W. Porges (2011) explains:

Similar to several other mammals, humans are a social species. Being a social species explicitly emphasizes that human survival is dependent on coregulating our neurophysiological state via social interaction.

The dependence of an infant on the mother is an archetypical example of this dependency and even illustrates the bidirectionality of the social interaction; the mother is not only regulating the infant, but the infant is reciprocally regulating the mother.

The features of co-regulation, reciprocity, connectedness, and trust resonate through the mammalian nervous system and optimize homeostatic function providing a neurobiological link between our mental and physical health.[8]

"With a kind face, deep and steady breathing, relaxed posture, and calm tone and tempo of voice, the other person's neurophysiological state can begin to attune to ours, and we can help shift someone from a state of both hyperarousal and hypoarousal—and initiate a more balanced nervous system. Conversely, if we're in an agitated state, anxious and/or stressed, the other person's nervous system will mimic ours," I said.

"So, you really have to be centered and calm before you engage," commented Kris.

"That's crucial. And it goes the other way, too. Our nervous system can get hijacked by the other person's. Think about someone who you interact with consistently that stresses you out. What happens in your body when you're getting ready to interact with them?" I asked.

"Heart races, adrenaline floods, shallow breathing," said Joan.

"Right. The history of our interaction with that person has pre-conditioned us to prepare for stress. In fact, we start getting anxious at even the thought of having to interact with them. That's a type of neural pre-attunement," I said. "If we dread having to talk with someone, that's why.

"I should add that when this happens, we can lose our sense of self. If we freeze, we swallow our voice. Joan, you mentioned that the director of your school uses passive aggression and intimidation as methods of control," I said.

"And isolation. She separates people and then interrogates them," Joan added. "It keeps people on edge and in fear and so they don't speak up."

"So, what we see is how one person can intentionally take another person's nervous system hostage for the purpose of establishing their own power and control. That's how bullying works," I offered. "We can also see how simple disagreements can quickly escalate into emotionally charged conflict. If two people's agitated nervous systems are engaged, the interaction can get out of control and destructive," I added.

"What you're saying is that we project our emotional state onto others," said Aaron.

"Yes. I think it's inevitable. The question is are we intentional in what state we want others to experience. We can become either aggressive, defensive, and retaliatory, or completely withdrawn. We covered this in Chapter 3. The point is that we need a communication technique, a simple, easy-to-remember go-to method that we can use either before things get out of control, which is preemptive or proactive, as well as after something upsetting has happened to help restore emotional and nervous system equilibrium," I explained.

"This is not some new discovery or sophisticated technique. It really is intuitive. Think about the support we give to someone we care about who is upset. I call it 'gentling.' We listen, we soothe, we nurture, we console and help them strategize. That's what we're doing with S.H.I.F.T. We're just taking our natural inclination for empathy and compassion and breaking it down into steps with the intention of restoring that person's sense of self-management or self-regulation.

"One of the remarkable gifts of neuroscience and *f*MRI brain scanning is that we now know what's happening between the brain, mind, and body when a person is experiencing different states of arousal. It's this research that has not only led to understanding the neurobiology, psychology, and physiology of trauma, but also how unresolved trauma impacts our ability to interact. Stephen W. Porges (2011) termed this our 'social engagement system.'[9] This research indicates that different types of communication and interaction can either aggravate or mitigate traumatic stress.

"But the wisdom of co-regulation is ancient and innate. We're wired for connection. It's what bonds us. It's as much a survival mechanism as is fight/flight/freeze. I would argue that it also facilitates collaboration," I said.

"It's not a character issue. It's the stress that is happening in the person," said Kris.

"Exactly. That realization is critical because it keeps us away from judging them for being a certain way and more effective in using our empathy and understanding to engage with them. It's not them. It's what they're experiencing.

"Let me give you some context to explain how this technique evolved from a need to keep people participating in restorative justice circles. When people come together in a circle to work through something traumatic that has happened, such as a crime or violation, that discussion can be retraumatizing. It can reactivate their embodied experience of what happened," I said.

"Like the case with Leo and Rick," said Melissa.

"Yes. This is why it is critically important that you prepare people before convening a circle. That pre-circle interview or conversation is a determining factor in how successful the circle is in working through the event. That one-on-one conversation before the group conversation is as important as the circle encounter. If the facilitator doesn't understand the depth or level of trauma and anxiety people have experienced, the discussion in the circle can be as traumatic," I explained. "Similar to PTSD, people can relive the experience of the violation."

"Revictimization," said Brad. "This is why you included a victim advocate and trauma specialist in Leo's circle."

"Yes. Because circles can be retraumatizing, and not just for the offender or survivor. Think about Tim's experience with his son. Before we convened, Tim and I talked about his capacity to participate. We worked through potential triggers.

"As a facilitator, you have to understand what that person is experiencing, spot the signs, and have a way of effectively engaging with them to help them feel safe and therefore able to move forward. And if something happens during the circle, if someone gets activated, you have to have a way of pausing the circle, take a break, and work with that person one-on-one to help them be able to continue.

"That's how this technique developed for me and why it is absolutely critical that we understand the experience of trauma, what's going on in a person's nervous system, and most important, have the communication skills to work with it when it presents.

"Those skills are transferable. By this I mean that it's not just a criminal violation or restorative justice circle encounter where this technique is useful. Anytime you see someone who appears to be struggling, you can use this technique to connect with them and help them," I said.

"Like at work," said Melissa.

"Yeah, or in our families," I agreed.

I added, "Let me give you a couple of examples. I'll start with a restorative justice example and then provide some examples from other contexts or situations. In this first example, I used the S.H.I.F.T. technique both in the pre-circle interview when I was preparing a family to participate in the group circle, and then during the circle when one of the parents became highly activated. This example will illustrate how critically important it is to spot the signs of traumatic stress, differentiate it, and engage with it to help a person move forward."

The Case of Loose Marbles

"I once facilitated a case where a 12-year-old boy ('Andy') and his friends were rolling marbles out onto a busy street. They were competing with each other to see if they could roll one completely under a car as it drove by. One driver called the police. The police came. The other boys ran off. The officer questioned Andy, drove him home, and issued a ticket to the parents and explained he'd be referring the case to restorative justice."

Spotting the Signs

"When I met with Andy and his parents at their home to find out what happened and prepare them for the circle conference, Andy's mother seemed understandably worried. She said that she thought her son was 'bullied into doing it.' Andy's father was sitting in his office with the door open, listening to us, but didn't come out of his office until the very end of our conversation.

"When he did, he was understandably upset too. He completely dominated the conversation. 'This is terrible, I can't believe he did this; this is not what we expect of him,' etc. He essentially ambushed his son in front of me. It felt that way to me. I'm sure it felt heart-crushingly worse for Andy.

"Andy and his mother were sitting next to each other on their couch. The father sat on the very edge of a chair apart from the couch. As soon as the father started to speak, the mother moved closer to Andy and put her arm around him. Andy never said a word. He was 'checked-out,' no expression on his face. In fact, he hardly moved," I explained.

I asked our group, "Based on what I described, what do you think I was seeing in terms of nervous system arousal and relationships?"

Kris answered. "The father was hyper-aroused. Andy was hypo-aroused. The mother was trying to protect her son from the father. She was shielding him. She was hyper-aroused too.

Melissa spoke. "All three of them were in defense mode. The boy was frozen. The mother was in a kind of defensive-aggressive fight mode. And the father was in both fight and flight mode."

"Why do you say, 'both fight and flight' with the father?" I asked.

"Because he blamed his son, which was aggressive, but defended himself with 'this is not what we expect,'" said Melissa. "That statement was a kind of passive-aggressive face-saving. My sense is that he was feeling some shame."

"I'm curious. What did each of you notice come up in yourself when I described what happened?" I asked.

"You mean, how did our own nervous system react?" asked Brad.

"Either that or anything else going on inside of you. Was there any impulse?" I clarified.

Joan spoke. "I zeroed in on what Andy was experiencing. I wanted to protect him."

"I identified with the mother," said Kris. "I felt a pit in my stomach. I guess I would describe what I was feeling was tightness."

"The father pushed my buttons," said Barb. "What went through my head was, 'Don't you realize you caused this?' I wanted to smack him upside the head and say, 'Wake up!'"

"Thanks for being honest," I said. "Aaron, what came up for you?" I asked.

"As you were describing this, I was thinking about how the S.H.A.R.E. process would work for this family. Not for what the boy did but what his father was doing to his son. I thought of Rick's case," he said.

"I did too," said Devonte.

"In what way?" I asked both.

"The underlying issue here is the father's self-centeredness. It seemed he was more concerned with how his son's behavior impacted him. It's the ripple effect. Maybe his son's actions were a statement of 'I'll show you.' I don't know," said Aaron.

"I thought the same thing," said Devonte. "Like Joan, I wanted to put my arms around this kid. Like Barb, I wanted to confront the dad. I also thought about what the mother said about the other boys. With his dad being so critical and punitive, this poor kid needed some acceptance and approval from somewhere.

"Maybe he was hanging out with the other boys and going along with them to get their approval; to feel accepted. I see this all the time at my school where kids bond with each other because they don't get approval and acceptance at home. Like Aaron said, it's the ripple effect."

"That's a really good point," I said.

"What did you do?" asked Devonte.

"Well, first, I gave you this example so you could notice and acknowledge your own reaction. This is crucial because if we're not aware of what's going on in us, with our own emotional reaction and judgments to what's happening, we won't be as effective in helping the other person. We can lose our objectivity and fall into evaluation.

"In this case, like all of you, I had a strong reaction to what both the mother and the father said. When the mother said her son was being bullied, my very first thought was, 'Let's find the boys and address the bullying.' Bullying is something that activates a strong emotional response in me because of my own childhood history with it. I call it my 'protector' impulse.

"Also like you, when the father blamed and criticized his son, my impulse was to confront him. In fact, like Barb, the thought, 'Don't you realize what you're doing?' popped into my head. I was already in protector mode, and this impulse only got stronger.

"What I did was take several deep breaths to slow my own heart rate down. I could feel the adrenaline in my nervous system. Those deep breaths helped me to let go of the story in my own head, maintain composure, and remain centered."

"Self-awareness and self-regulation," said Kris.

"Yes. The first step in the S.H.I.F.T. technique is 'Spot the Signs' of any emotional distress—not only in the other person, but also in yourself. What are you seeing? What are you noticing? What are you sensing?

"I should add that emotions are different than feelings. Rita Carter (2010) explained that 'emotions are a set of body-rooted survival mechanisms that have evolved to turn us away from danger and propel us forward to things that may be of benefit.' [10]

"The point is that an emotion begins with a physiological response to stimulus. It helps to think of 'stimulus' as information received from the exterior world through our senses (sight, sound, touch, and smell) and processed by our brain. As our brain processes this information, it becomes an emotion. But emotion can also begin from an internal stimulus such as a memory, a belief we have, or self-talk.

"We think of emotion as a feeling, but this is only half of the truth. When something happens or somebody does or says something to us and we feel something in response, what we're really experiencing is a sensation in our body's nervous system that is filtered first through our evolutionarily older 'survival brain' and then through various other parts of our brain with which we attach meaning to in the process. That sensational response is historically informed. It can seem 'familiar.'

"For example, in the case of anger, it would be much more accurate to say, 'I'm experiencing an increased heart rate, a surge of cortisol and adrenaline in my vascular system, a rise in my body's temperature, and a tenseness in my body.' Saying this would be more accurate physiologically but would no doubt result in us being assigned to an office way far away on a distant planet.

"Here's a table I put together to help correlate nervous system state with some of the signs and specific goals of S.H.I.F.T.

NERVOUS SYSTEM CONDITION	SYMPTOMATIC EXPERIENCE	S.H.I.F.T. GOAL
Fight/Flight Hyper-arousal Sympathetic Nervous System	Rage, Anger, Panic, Fear, Irritation, Anxiety, Frustration, Worry, Concern	To calm, soothe, reassure, empathize with, deescalate
Freeze Hypo-arousal Dorsal Vagal Complex Parasympathetic Nervous System	Dissociation, Numbness, Depressed, Helplessness, Shame/Shutdown/ Hopeless, Nonresponsive, Trapped/ Withdrawn	To connect, empathize with, reassure, draw out, encourage, support

"These are just a few of the signs. However subtle, what I noticed arising in myself was some sadness and perhaps a touch of anger with how the father was treating his son. In truth, I was also feeling some anxiety and thinking, 'How am I going to move through this?' To reassure myself, I took some long, deep breaths and let go of any story in my head. I centered myself, 'boots on the ground and butt in the seat.'

"The mother was showing signs of anxiety, fear, worry, concern, maybe some panic, and perhaps irritation, etc. She was in a state of arousal. Those signs were evident in her facial expressions, her wide red eyes. Her voice was high-pitched. She was speaking from her throat as opposed to her diaphragm. She was fidgety.

"Her move closer to her son and putting her arm around the boy when the father appeared was clear indication of fear and protection. What she needed from me was reassurance, empathy, understanding, and clarity about the restorative process and impending circle. She needed to trust me, and I needed her trust.

"The father was showing signs of anger, irritation, fear, frustration, and perhaps some shame and helplessness. These signs were evident in what he said, his body language sitting on the edge of the chair, gestures, and facial expressions. His brow was furrowed. His breathing was shallow, and his speech was rapid. He hardly took a breath between statements.

"What he needed from me was similar to what his wife needed, empathy and under-standing, not judgment or confrontation. He needed to be heard and reassured. I needed his trust, or at least enough of it to listen to what I had to say.

"Andy was essentially motionless, expressionless. He didn't appear to react to what his mother was saying about the other boys, nor when she put her arm around him. But—and this was key—when I made eye contact with him, he didn't look away. I couldn't fully interpret it, but it was obvious he was paying attention to me.

"However, when his dad came in and started his explanations, I made eye contact with him again, and he looked down at the floor. That told me all I needed to know. I made the decision to ask, 'Do you mind if I speak with "Andy" for a few moments?' I told them I'd explain the process after he and I talked.

"The point I'm making here is that this first step—'spot the signs'—is crucial," I said. "It's about observing and recognizing what the signs might be telling you about what's going on for the other person. If you miss the signs, you'll miss an opportunity and po-tentially make things worse."

"You were hyper-focused on their body language," said Melissa.

"And their breathing, facial expressions, and pitch and tone of voice as well as pace of speech. It will tell you a lot about what might be going on under the surface. It will clue you into their experience. And the more you do this, the more intuitive you'll be-come, and the more can be revealed and thus, the more effective you'll be in helping them. Whatever revelation that is will help you move to the next step, which is to 'hold a space of emotional and psychological safety' for them. This step is about engagement, and where co-regulation can begin to happen."

Holding Space

"'Holding a space' means that on an energetic level, you are remaining calm, cen-tered, gentle, and creating an interactional space of safety," I explained. "It's about your presence."

Kris commented, "It's a vibration you're emitting. Following the mirror-neurons dynamic, you're essentially lending them your own nervous system."

"That's a great way to put it. It is an energy. It is a vibration. Conceptually, we're lending our own emotional stability and calm nervous system to them. We use our centeredness and sincere concern as an instrument of regulation. The way you do that is with your own relaxed body language, deep and steady breathing, calm and gentle voice, kind facial expression and eyes.

> "Empathy is not only an altruistic feeling. It's also a powerful co-regula-tion skill. It sends the message—both verbally and nonverbally—that the person who is struggling matters, that we care, and that they're not alone."

"One of the ways I remind myself of this step is to remember a line from the Peace Prayer of Saint Francis: 'Make me an instrument of peace.' In this context, you're using your body as an instrument of peace. Your voice and body are powerful instruments of co-regulation.

"The other important piece, or skill, to this step of 'holding space' is what you say. It's important to acknowledge what they're experiencing. This does two things. First, it lets them know that you're really listening to them. Feeling heard is one of the most powerful experiences we can have. Active listening sends the message, 'you matter' and 'I care.' Second, it validates their experience.

"In this case, I responded to both the mother and father by saying, 'I can see that this is upsetting,' and, 'I can understand why you would be concerned about what happened.' These two statements validated their experience. The most powerful statements I made were, 'I can see how much you care about Andy,' and, 'I can see how much you love your son.' When I said that, both of them relaxed. It was subtle, but noticeable. These statements helped me gain their trust. When I said this, Andy made eye contact with me.

"You were attempting to co-regulate all three of them," said Melissa.

"Yes, I was creating, or 'holding,' a space of safety and concern. But the boy needed something more that I couldn't give him with his parents present. I needed to connect with him one-on-one to put him at ease and gain his trust. His parents' nervous systems were distracting, so I made a request. I asked, 'Do you mind if I speak with Andy alone for a few minutes to ask him about what happened?' and then expressed a need: 'I need to hear from him how he's doing with this and let him know it's going to be okay.'

Devonte replied, "By telling them what your intention was, you were also putting them more at ease."

"Yes. No surprises. No secrets. I was sending the message, 'All of this is going to be okay.' It was a strategic statement of reassurance for them, but also a co-regulation statement for Andy. Once they left the room, I smiled a bit to acknowledge some breathing room. He relaxed. For the first time he shifted in his chair. I relaxed, too.

"The third step of S.H.I.F.T. is to identify the feelings. Asking someone how or what they are feeling helps them shift attention from the sensations of being overwhelmed and scared in that moment, and toward self-awareness. Just the simple act of asking someone to try and name what they're feeling often has the redirecting effect of either calming them or drawing them out. This step also reiterates, or further emphasizes, that they matter, what they're experiencing matters, what they're feeling matters, and that someone cares.

"One of the ways to do this is to use 'I'm wondering if' statements or 'I imagine that' statements. Because Andy was only twelve years old, I changed this to, 'I bet this is all pretty scary.' He nodded. When he acknowledged my statement, I said, 'Yeah, I know what that feels like.' But to really gain his trust and put him at ease, I told him a personal story.

"You were bridging," said Melissa.

"Yes. I did it to put myself on his level. Kind of like an 'I've been in your shoes' statement. I did this with both Leo and Rick, too.

"I told him about a time when I was his age and I was with a group of boys, and we were throwing snowballs at cars driving by. I said, 'One of the drivers was a neighbor who recognized me and told my parents.' I said, 'I was terrified, really scared.' I then asked him, 'I'm wondering if that's how you're feeling, kind of scared about what's going to happen when we all meet. I bet it was scary when the policeman told your parents. Was that scary for you?'

"For the first time he spoke: 'Yeah.' I validated with, 'I get it. I would've been scared too.' I asked him if he had ever seen the movie *Pinocchio*. He said, 'Yes.' I told him I was sure I was going to be sent to Donkey Island. When I told him this, he chuckled. That chuckle let me know I had reached him. I told him a story.

"I then asked him, 'So, I'm curious about what happened.' Notice that I didn't say, 'Tell me what happened,' or, 'Tell me what you did,' which would've come across as evaluative. I said, 'I'm curious,' which was more of an invitation."

Identifying Feelings

"I asked him how he felt about the other boys not getting caught. He said, 'It's not fair.' I validated with, 'I agree,' I said, 'that sucks.' He asked me, 'Did the other boys get in trouble when you got caught?' I said, 'No.' He said, 'That sucks.' I said, 'Yeah, it did, but I learned not to go along with someone when they're doing something dumb.' He said, 'Like throwing snowballs at cars.' 'Bingo,' I said.

"He then asked me two really important questions. He asked, 'What happened to you?' I told him I had to apologize to my neighbor and shovel her sidewalk.' He asked, 'What did you tell your friends?'

"I replied, 'I told them the truth. I told them I got caught and had to apologize and shovel her sidewalk.' 'What did they say?' he asked. 'They made fun of me, called me a pussy,' I said. I added, 'That didn't make me feel good, so I stopped hanging out with them. It wasn't easy at first, but I got over it. I started hanging out with other friends.'

"I asked him, 'What would you do different if you could?' He said, 'Not do it.' I said, 'Yeah, that's what I thought about what I did too. It wasn't worth it.'

"He said, 'I knew we shouldn't have done it.' I said, 'It's great that you knew that. I thought the same thing when we started throwing snowballs at cars.'

" 'But you did it anyway,' he said. 'Yes, I was afraid of being made fun of by the other boys,' I said."

Focus on Needs

"The fourth step of S.H.I.F.T. is to focus on the person's needs. If feelings are expressions of needs being met or unmet, what do you suppose Andy was needing?" I asked the group.

Aaron spoke. "You kind of met his need to not feel shame because of what he did."

"I'm glad you mentioned shame because offenders often feel shame about what they did. That feeling of shame is often an underlying reason why offenders make excuses, deny, or diminish the severity of what they did, or even just completely check out of the conversation.

"Rick's case is a great example of this. It's critically important for facilitators to understand what shame looks like and how to work with it both before a group encounter, and also in the pre-circle interview," I added.

Barb said, "He probably also needed to feel like he had someone on his side based on how his parents were reacting. I mean, his mother was essentially blaming him for hanging out with those boys, and his father was blaming him for failing to meet his expectations or standards."

"He needed someone to champion him," said Brad.

"These are great observations," I said. "What do you suppose he was he needing specifically from me moving forward with the eventual circle?"

"I think he needed to know you were going to be his advocate," said Joan. "He needed to feel safe with you."

"Exactly," I said. "He needed to feel like I had his back, and I was going to represent him and protect him. He couldn't know this because he's a kid, but as adults, we do and that's a critical realization as a facilitator."

"And a parent," interjected Kris.

"Yeah. And it's not just kids. We all need that when we make mistakes and are in fear, feeling guilt or shame. So, what he needed from me right then when I was talking with him was for me to reassure him that I wasn't going to allow him to be shamed by others—especially his parents—for making a mistake. He needed understanding and pardon, not judgment and punishment."

I added, "This whole process of S.H.I.F.T. is about connection, safety, and trust."

"What did you say to him about the circle?" asked Melissa.

"The first thing I did was acknowledge his courage and honesty. I said, 'I really respect you telling me what happened. That's not easy to do when we know we've made a mistake. That takes a lot of courage, and I admire you for that.' I also told him I understand what it's like to feel like we have to go along with other boys in order to get their approval. I told him I did the same thing with the snowballs.

"I then asked him, 'Are you a bit scared about what's going to happen when we all meet in our circle?' He said, 'Yes.' He asked me if the officer was going to be there. I said, 'Yes, but that's because he cares about you. He's not going to scold you.'

"I added, 'No one is going to scold you.' I then used some humor. I said, 'You're probably going to have to shovel a truckload of marbles.' He chuckled and smiled kind of sheepishly, so I knew he was doing fine.

"I explained that we were just going to sit around in a circle and ask him what happened. I said, 'This is your chance to tell us whose idea it was to roll the marbles under the cars.' He said, 'Johnny.' I said, 'Great; we need to know that.'

"I told him the driver who called the police will be there, but he just wants you to know how scared he was when he saw a marble bouncing across the street. The reason I said this was to prepare him for feeling some empathy for the driver. Then I said, 'We're just all going to figure out how we can help you make a better decision next time you feel pressured by others to go along with a bad idea.'

"I asked him, 'How does that all sound?' He just said, 'Okay.' But then he added, 'My dad's really pissed off at me.' I told him, 'Yeah, my dad was pissed at me too, but I realized he was just scared too, because he cared about me and wanted me to make better choices.'

"I offered, 'Maybe you can apologize to him for scaring him. That's what I did with my dad.' I asked him, 'What do you say we bring your parents back in so I can explain how our circle is going to work? You good with that?' He said, 'Yeah.' He was fine. His whole demeanor had shifted.

"So, you co-regulated him back into a sense of self-management or self-composure," commented Kris.

"In a manner of speaking, I think so," I said. "At the least, his fear of me was diminished."

"So was his shame," said Brad.

"I think what we did was re-story what happened, what he did. I reframed it as an understandable error in judgment rather than a catastrophic failure of character or reflection of self-worth," I said.

"You did that by sharing your own experience, your own story," said Devonte. "You got down on his level. Doing that dissolved the power-over status inherent by your position or role of authority."

"That's a great observation," I replied. "The last thing someone who is afraid or feeling shame needs is for us to come in and say, 'You need to do this,' or give advice. They don't need us to try and save them or feel sorry for them. We're trying to help them regain their own power, their own sense of 'okay-ness.'

> **"When we try to tell someone what they need, they lose the valuable opportunity to discover for themselves what they need. Telling someone what they need can shut them down … and send them back into feeling overwhelmed and alone. It can reactivate them."**

"But when we facilitate a person discovering for themselves what they need, show them that they can meet that need, we give them freedom (autonomy), and we gain their trust. It sends the message, 'I'm here to assist. Not tell you what to do.'"

Take Action

"The last step of S.H.I.F.T. is taking action with the other person. The key word here is *with*. Helping someone take action to meet their needs as opposed to telling them what you're going to do to meet their needs is a step into self-manageability, self-empowerment, and a sense of autonomy.

"The act of partnering with them to brainstorm ideas to meet their needs helps them trust that they have the ability to help themselves, that they can meet their needs, and that they can ask for help and support from you. Considering that when you begin the S.H.I.F.T. process the person is feeling shut down or overwhelmed, supporting them to take action instills a sense of control over their experience.

"Notice I didn't say, 'I'm going to bring your parents back in.' I asked him if it was okay if I did. That request demonstrated partnership and shared power with him rather than control. I also didn't tell him, 'You need to apologize.' I suggested it was something he could do. This is an example of what the fifth step of the S.H.I.F.T. technique is: 'Taking action *with* the other person.'

"Reflecting on this specific interaction and the use of S.H.I.F.T., what was being constituted?" I asked.

"Respect," said Brad.

"Dignity," said Melissa. "You didn't treat him as an offender. You treated him as a young human being who made a mistake."

"Safety," said Kris.

"I think what was being constituted was an experience of social-emotional learning," said Devonte. "You helped him become aware of and understand what he was thinking and feeling about what he did. By using your own story, I think you pointed out how our need for inclusion can lead to going along with others when we shouldn't. I think this recognized the power of social pressure and how it can result in inappropriate behavior.

"You also mentioned how what he did impacted the driver. To me, this constitutes a reflection on responsible decision-making and recognizing others. How did the rest of the pre-circle interview go?" he asked.

"Thinking back, this is where I might have made a mistake, or done something different. When his parents came back in, I told them I thought they had a remarkable son. I then explained how the circle would go, the steps, who would be there, and that working together, we would create a plan for helping him make better decisions if faced with the same situation in the future.

"When I said this, the father said, 'Good, because he makes terrible decisions.' I cringed. The mother and Andy took the emotional hit. Everything in me wanted to confront that statement, but I didn't because I didn't want to make him the center of attention. Simply put, I didn't want to give him any airtime. I had made the connection with their son, and that was my main objective," I explained.

"Your admiration for him was under control," chuckled Barb.

"For what he said anyway," I replied. "I took a long, deep breath and just said kind of lamely, 'Well, our goal is for all of us to help him make better ones. For his sake.'"

The Circle

"During the circle when we were discussing how people were impacted, the father got seriously activated. He started beating himself up, saying, 'I've been a terrible father.' I paused the circle.

"As gently as I could, I said, 'Why don't we take a short break and get some water.' I went over to the father, sat down next to him, and quietly said, 'I can see this is really difficult. Why don't we get some fresh air?' As we walked out of the room, I passed by his wife and son, put my hand on Andy's shoulder, and said, 'It's going to be okay.'

"What was I doing in terms of S.H.I.F.T.?" I asked our group.

"The first two steps. You spotted the signs and then began the process of holding a space by pausing the conference," said Melissa.

"Yes. The signs were obvious but what's challenging in this technique is actually taking the initiative to intervene; to engage. That takes a bit of courage. I could've intervened right there in the circle. I could've cut him off and said, 'Thank you for sharing,' and moved on, or I could've just been silent. I could've just slid the box of Kleenex over to him.

"I made the decision to pause the circle and work one-on-one with the father for several reasons. First, I didn't want him to become the focus of the circle. We were there to help his son. However, helping his son meant helping him too. He mattered too. His harsh criticism of himself was a sign of a deep hurt, and I didn't want to lose the opportunity to connect with him and maybe steer him toward getting some help.

"When we talk about 'underlying issues,' my sense was that his self-condemnation was tied directly to how critical he was of his son. That much seemed obvious. Second, and maybe this was idealistic on my part, I wanted to give him the chance to step up for himself and demonstrate reclaiming his composure for his son. His son needed him to be present for him.

"When we stepped outside, he was struggling. He put his face in his hands. I said, 'Why don't we sit down?' There was a bench outside. I kept it very simple. The first thing I did was just sit there with him and remain calm and present.

"He was trying to calm himself down. He said, 'I'm sorry. I don't know what's going on.' As calmly and gently as I could, I said, 'It's okay. You're a father who cares deeply about his son. I'm a dad, too. It's easy to blame ourselves when they make mistakes.' I let that sink in," I told the group.

"You were bridging with him as a strategy for co-regulation," said Kris.

"Yes. And I was using my voice, breathing, and relaxed body as an instrument, and I was putting myself on his level as a strategy for creating a safe space for him. I was destigmatizing his experience. We create that space by expressing empathy and compassion. When we do that, the other person has the opportunity to sense that they're not alone in their distress. It's about connecting.

"But I also identified what he was feeling and then validated those feelings as 'understandable,' given the responsibility of being a father. Keep in mind that this only took about two minutes, and after this interaction, he started to calm down almost immediately.

"After a moment, he regained his composure and said, 'Thanks, I know we need to get back.' But rather than just get up and leave, I said, 'We do, but let's just take a minute and figure out how we can give you what you need, and what your son might be needing from all of us.'"

"Third step, focus in on needs," said Kris.

"That's it. As a facilitator of this technique, what you're trying for is a shift in their focus from the consuming experience of being stuck or feeling overwhelmed to 'What do I really need?' It redirects their attention. It's a step into the beginning of self-awareness, self-determination, or self-management.'

"Kind of like a shift from a belief that 'I can't do anything' to asking the question, 'What can I do?' asked Kris.

"That's exactly it. But we don't tell them what they need. Even if we think we know, our goal is to help them discover what they need," I said. "The challenge is that most often, they don't know what they need or how to even find out what they need, especially when they're in distress or highly activated.

"I asked him, 'What would you like your son to learn from this incident?' Without hesitation, he said, 'To make better choices and not let these other boys lead him into doing stupid things. He's better than this.' When he said this, it was a sign that he had shifted from feeling consumed by his own emotions toward thinking rationally, objectively, and lovingly about his son's well-being and the situation.

"I asked him, 'Do you think he was looking for their approval?' He said, 'Yes.' I said, 'So, it sounds like you'd like him to have enough self-awareness or self-esteem to not need that approval. Is that right?' He said, 'Yes. I want him to stick up for himself.'

"I said, 'It sounds to me like you are deeply concerned about his well-being, and this incident was scary for you. Is that fair to say?' He replied, 'This was scary. I really thought he was going to be arrested. What would've happened if he caused a wreck?'

"I asked him, 'Have you shared with him how this scared you?' He said, 'No.' I said, 'Maybe that's something you could share with him. Because that fear is a reflection of how much you love him, don't you think?' 'Yeah,' he replied."

I said to the group, "At this point, I was feeling anxious to get back in the circle, but I needed to address one more issue with him that might help him personally. I said, 'I'm just curious, when you were his age and you did something wrong, how were you disciplined?' He was honest. 'I got yelled at. If it was really bad, I got spanked or whipped with a belt.' I said, 'That's the way I was disciplined too.'

"I asked him, 'How did that make you feel?' 'Ashamed of what I did,' he said. I said, 'Me too. I'm not a therapist but maybe there's a connection between how traumatic this experience with your son has been for you, and what happened to you when you were his age.' I added, 'Might be something to look at.'"

I said to the group, "That last interaction was the fifth step of S.H.I.F.T., which is to take action, or at least present the possibility of taking action to pursue healing any potential root cause of a trauma."

Melissa commented, "You really have to know what you're doing with this technique. You have to know about trauma and the nervous system. You can't just all of a sudden do this."

I said, "I'm really glad you brought this up. You're absolutely right. For some people, it's just intuitive. But even intuition needs technique and craft. And it's messy, imperfect, and quite frankly, doesn't always work. But we have to try because the stakes are so high.

"I've found that the more I learn about trauma and how our brain, mind, and body struggle to process it, the more compassionate objectivity I have, and the more effective I'll be in supporting someone when they're in distress. Like we've been saying, it's not a matter of character, it's a matter of mental and emotional health and well-being.

"S.H.I.F.T. is about meeting the other person's needs 'in that moment' in order to help them shift their perspective about what they're experiencing, as well as their experience of what they're perceiving. Like I said, it's about progressive connection, co-regulation, and trust."

"How did the rest of the circle go?" asked Aaron.

"Andy's dad apologized for 'getting so emotional,' but he acknowledged that he was afraid. He also apologized to Andy for being angry with him. He even explained that when he got in trouble as a kid, his dad whipped him with a belt. When he said this, his wife exhaled and relaxed. At least, that's what appeared to me.

"Andy said, 'I'm sorry Grandpa hit you.' His dad said, 'He didn't know any better.' But then Andy said something very moving. He said, 'Thanks for not hitting me.' That just about had us all in tears, including the officer.

"The driver of the car shared how scared he was when he saw the marbles flying across the street. We talked about how it could've caused a wreck. Andy apologized sincerely. The police officer shared a story about how he once broke a neighbor's window with a slingshot when he was a kid. He told Andy, 'My dad was really pissed at me.' The message the officer was sending was, 'We all make mistakes,' and 'I've been in your shoes.'

"One of the more noticeable shifts that happened toward the end of the circle was with Andy's mother. Her entire demeanor had shifted. She was relaxed. Her face was relaxed, and she just seemed relieved based on her posture," I said.

"Her son was treated with compassion," said Joan.

"Yes. And so was her husband," I added.

"The reparative agreement called for family counseling. We gave Andy some suggestions about what he could do and say if he's with a bunch of kids who are doing something destructive or dangerous. His dad said, 'I need to find a way to set aside more time for us.' I'll add that when the circle was over, I went over to Andy and said, 'No Donkey Island for either of us.'"

"I'm curious. How did you develop this technique?" asked Brad.

"First, I can't claim ownership of the technique itself. Personally, I don't think anyone can because it's a capacity for a depth of connection that we have as a human being. We're wired for social connection. How we communicate determines the meaning and quality of that connection. Think about what a mother does to soothe her child when the child is in distress. A loving father does the same thing. A loving friend or partner does it too. I think it's innate.

"Barb, you said nurses are hardwired to do this professionally. Victim advocates, crisis intervention and emergency response people do it. What I did was break it down into steps, understand what those steps were doing, and provide an acronym so people can remember it and do it without having to think too much about it.

"The story of how this technique developed for me professionally has to do with needing a way to keep people moving through the restorative process. Not just in a justice setting, but also in organizational settings and families. Crime and conflict are both emotionally charged. People get hurt and sometimes that hurt is traumatic in itself, but it's also based in a person's history. I needed a way to work with that hurt in the moment to keep them moving forward.

"But the deeper story is much more personal. The need to soothe the other person was a matter of survival. So, when I say it's intuitive, what I mean is that I had to find a way to keep myself safe in a threatening situation. It's not something I share in my trainings because I don't like to divert people's attention away from the technique to my story. I'll share it with you because we've connected on such a deep level in our discussions.

"My mother was physically and emotionally abused as a child by her father. She experienced horrendous trauma growing up. As a result, she suffered from PTSD. When she would get triggered, she had no choice but to do what was done to her.

"I somehow instinctively knew that the best way to keep myself safe was to calm her and soothe her. It often didn't work, but there were times it did. It wasn't conscious on my part. I was a kid. I also used it when faced with bullying. So, when I was faced with clients who were dysregulated, it came naturally to work with them in a way that would soothe and reassure them.

"The science of trauma helped me to understand what was happening with this technique, which I didn't even know was a 'technique' until I started to deconstruct what the heck I was doing. It's all about a quality and depth of connection that happens in interpersonal communication and interaction. What we're doing is working with that person on the level of their nervous system. We do that with profound empathy, but also with purpose and craft. It's performative interaction.

"What this means is that the technique really has unlimited applications and contexts. Thus far, we've mainly focused on restorative justice applications, but because it is simply an interaction technique, it can be used in any circumstance or situation when someone is feeling completely overwhelmed.

"I want to share another case with you to illustrate how S.H.I.F.T. works in practice," I said. "The following conversation took place over the phone and lasted about ten minutes. The context was pandemic fatigue. I wrote about this case in a white paper, so I'll just paste it here."

Moving Through a Breaking Point

I have a friend who is an eighth-grade teacher. Her passion for teaching, her devotion to her craft, her love for her students and her ability to relate to them have always been an inspiration to me.

She is also one of the most resilient people I have ever known. Over the years I've seen her bounce back from personal loss and crisis. She always seemed to turn adversity into wisdom.

In the height of the pandemic, she called me late at night in tears: "I don't think I can go on. I do my very best to stay positive and upbeat. When I try to reassure my students that 'we're going to get through this and it's going to be okay'—they just don't believe me. I don't believe me.

"Things aren't normal. Masks aren't normal. Staying six feet away from each other isn't normal. One day we're in class, the next we're online. And there is so much animosity in our nation. I get angry when people tell me, 'Things will return to normal.' I'm at a breaking point."

Strategic Empathy

"Listening to Lori, my teacher friend, I had a choice to make. I could immediately launch into an explanation of how she could strategically use S.H.A.R.E. in her class to talk about the impact of COVID and the current social climate on her students' emotions and spirits. She had already been using S.H.A.R.E. to guide student discussions about subject matter (teaching circles), used it to create a class respect agreement, and to address in-class disruptions. She knew the S.H.A.R.E. process as well as anyone. Certainly, I would help her strategize how to use S.H.A.R.E. to help her students talk about their experience of the pandemic. This could wait. Right now, it was about *her* spirit.

What my friend was experiencing was *pandemic fatigue*, a trauma—an experience that overwhelms, and in this case, exhausts our ability to cope. I would also argue that the current social climate, in part because of the political animosity happening, is also a type of existential trauma fog. It's not any one event, but a climate rife with fear and uncertainty. Certainly, it has been and continues to be exhausting.

"What she needed from me *in this moment* was not Dr. B. the consultant, but Will the fellow teacher and friend who cares about her. She needed me to *hold her experience with her*, empathize with her, and be her advocate.

> **No doctor can write a prescription for friendship and love.**
> **—Bessel van der Kolk**

"But it's been my experience that empathy, while soothing, achieves its greatest potential when it leads to taking action that heals. Empathy, I believe, is the seed for advocacy. She needed me to help her S.H.I.F.T. from her current state of feeling overwhelmed and depleted, to a place of self-compassion and hope. First things first."

SPOT the Signs of Overwhelm

"Without being a trauma specialist or psychologist, how might we know when it's trauma? What makes trauma exceptional? What do we look for? What are the signs? In the extreme, a person may be abnormally agitated and hyper, or completely withdrawn or frozen.

"In this case, when my friend said, 'I don't think I can go on,' it was a clear sign. I'd never heard her say anything this despondent. She was crying—not out of sadness or grief, but out of despair, anger, and emotional exhaustion. It was a cry for help.

"Spotting the signs of trauma can be learned. That's what being 'trauma-informed' teaches us. But we also need to know how to respond when we see it. That's why the S.H.I.F.T. technique can be described as 'trauma-*responsive* communication.' It's a way of interacting with someone who appears distraught or highly anxious (dysregulated) in order to help them 'come back' to the present moment, back into their body (regulate), and then gain some awareness and perspective.

"At the very least, we can help them realize that what they're experiencing is 'not them,' but something that is happening to them. We can also help them see that they have options about how to work with what they're experiencing right then. The goal of this technique is to help someone move from feeling incapacitated and powerless, to feeling cared for and ultimately, empowered.

HOLD Their Experience with Them

"Lori, I'm really sorry you're feeling overwhelmed. This is an extraordinarily tough time for teachers. You're not alone. We'll get through this together, okay?" I affirmed.

I explained to our group, "Holding a person's experience with them means several things. First, it means not trying to change the way they are feeling or thinking. We allow them to 'be where they are' without trying to fix them. This is about trust. It's about them, not us. Second, it means providing a stabilizing presence for them. We do this by maintaining our own state of calmness, compassion, and empathy for what they're experiencing.

"We stay *lovingly present.*

"When we hold another person's experience of distress with them, we're essentially doing the same thing. We're not physically holding them, but we're holding them in *how we communicate* with them in such a way as to co-regulate, soothe, and calm. It's our own deep and steady breathing, empathic listening, *gentle voice*, gestures, facial expressions, perspective, and language. We're engaging in a heart-centric way.

"When we feel safe and cared for, the brain produces oxytocin (the 'feel good' chemical), and the pituitary gland secretes endorphins. It's nature's way of soothing.

"When we do this, we're *working with nature's inherent way of restoring equilibrium* through empathic attunement. We're using our own nervous system and state of calm as an instrument of peace."

IDENTIFY Feelings with Them

"Empathy is opening ourselves to understanding and caring about another person's experience. Empathic *inquiry* is slightly different. It is asking questions to help the other person identify/recognize and express what *they* are experiencing and feeling—and then validating that experience and those feelings.

"I asked Lori, 'Tell me more about how the stress of the pandemic is impacting you physically.'

"She replied, 'There's just this heavy feeling of doom. I feel it in my stomach and my chest. It's there when I go to bed. It's there when I wake up. It's exhausting. It feels like there's nowhere I can go to get away from this worry.'

" 'I get it. Does it feel like there's no safe place to recharge your spirit?' I asked.

" 'That's exactly it,' she replied. 'I'm lethargic, and you know me, that's not a term people would ever use to describe me. I seem to have lost my optimism.'

" 'That's completely understandable, my friend. This thing that we're facing can consume us. We're only human and our spirit is worn out. Are you able to sleep?' I asked.

" 'Not like I used to,' she replied. 'I can't seem to not worry or think about all the stuff I need to do. I never signed up to teach online and I'm pissed off. They expect us to do both at the same time. People have no idea how hard it is to do both! They think we can just switch on a moment's notice and not lose a beat with students. And then parents blame us for their students falling behind. And I don't feel like I'm very capable, and I've never felt that before.'

" 'Lori—everything you're saying and feeling is absolutely understandable. It's understandable that you're feeling exhausted and it's completely normal, and I think healthy, that you feel angry. People don't understand that moving to online teaching requires learning a new technology—on the run. And on top of that, you're striving valiantly to make things emotionally okay for your students, yes?' I asked.

" 'Yes! We're not only having to make sure students don't fall behind but provide emotional support for them. They feel the stress and fear at home and carry it into the classroom. Nobody understands this except another teacher,' she exclaimed.

" 'I get it. And when they're physically in school, you have to make sure they wear their masks and stay apart. Yes?' I asked.

" 'Yes, and it's exhausting, and I feel angry,' she added.

" 'You're not alone in feeling that. I feel it too. I get angry too. It's traumatic. And that trauma has been compounded by the uncertainty of school openings and closures,' I replied.

" 'Yes,' she said. 'It's overwhelming.'

" 'It is,' I said. 'And no one can fully understand what you're going through except another teacher.'

" 'Exactly,' she said. 'My heart goes out to frontline healthcare workers.'

" 'Yes,' I said. 'Mine too. And teachers are a kind of frontline social-trauma responders for kids. Yes?' I asked.

" 'I never thought of it that way. Yes,' she replied.

" 'So, Lori, would you be willing to try something with me? Let's try letting this heaviness just be in us for a moment. Where is it in your body?' I asked.

" 'My stomach,' she said.

" 'Close your eyes and take some slow, deep breaths with me and allow yourself to feel it. See if you can breathe deeply into where you feel that heaviness,' I said.

"A moment later, I gently asked her, 'If this heaviness could speak in a child's voice, what would it say?'

" 'It would say, "I'm scared," ' she replied. 'It would say, "Please take care of me." '

" 'That's really beautiful, Lori. Thank you for sharing this with me,' I said. 'It sounds like the heaviness is making a request. Yes?'

" 'Yes. It's asking me to let go of it,' she replied.

" 'I think so. So, let me ask you. You said earlier that you don't think you can go on. Is that really true?' I asked.

" 'Of course not. You know me. I guess I just need to vent. But I need to find a way to take care of myself. I'm giving so much to others, there's nothing left for me at the end of the day,' she said.

" 'I hear you. Would you be willing to let me partner with you to find a way to do it differently?' I asked.

"She laughed. 'I knew you were going to say that!' "

FOCUS on Needs

"When trauma overwhelms our ability to cope, it can leave us incapacitated to even *recognize* what we need to be able to cope.

"Impact creates needs. Name the impact—specifically, and you can potentially discover the physical, emotional, mental, and even spiritual needs.

"And *it's not that Lori didn't know what she needed.* But in those moments when we're caught in the grips, it's extremely helpful to have a friend or colleague who can help us recognize and validate those needs.

" 'How about if we review how you're being impacted to figure out what you need?' I asked Lori.

" 'Well, the stress isn't going to go away,' she commented.

" 'The circumstances causing that stress may not, but we can make changes in how we work with that stress,' I said. 'We can start by making our own mental health and well-being the priority,' I added. 'We can nurture ourselves.'

"After I repeated back how Lori was being impacted by the 'existential trauma' of being a teacher (and a human!), I asked her, 'What do you need?'

"We made a short list. Rest; time away from all of it each evening (sanctuary); exercise; a way to release anger; reaching out to someone regularly/daily; centering on self-compassion each morning; and other needs.

" 'How are we going to make sure you meet your needs?' I asked Lori. We both brainstormed some ideas and then created a plan of restorative action."

TAKE ACTION. What Can You Agree to Do to Meet Your Needs?

"The value of partnership in this step has to do with self-care, accountability, and follow-through. This is where a 'support buddy' or 'empathy buddy' helps immensely; someone who is committed to helping us follow through on our agreements with ourselves to maintain health and well-being.

"Lori's plan of restorative action included the following:
- A 20-minute walk immediately after her last class (either in-person or online classes she was teaching)
- 20 minutes of reading something spiritual and soothing right before bed
- 15 minutes of meditation in the morning focused on feeling loved
- Use of a 'slam ball' in her garage when she was feeling angry
- A 5-minute daily call to a colleague just to check in; or with me if needed

" 'I don't know if I can do all of these every day,' she said.

" 'And when that happens—because of course it will, it's a great opportunity to say something kind to yourself. Like, "I'm doing the best I can," ' I said.

" 'I knew you were going to say that!' she replied.

" 'It's the truth, right?' I said."

I asked our group, "What sticks out for you about this technique?"

Melissa replied, "The objectivity piece. The more we understand what's happening inside the other person, the less chance there is that we'll get sucked into their trauma. That's not easy for me because I have my own trauma that gets activated when I'm faced with someone who's angry or hyper-aroused. Like you said, it's easy for our own nervous systems to get hijacked. What do you do when the other person is attacking you verbally?"

"Honor yourself. Extend dignity to yourself. Pay attention to your nervous system and then protect yourself by withdrawing immediately. That withdrawal starts with taking deep breaths. Statements I've found effective are:

- I can see that you are very upset/angry.
- I'm willing to work through this with you, but not this moment.
- I will not allow myself to be disrespected or abused.
- Let me know when you're ready to discuss this.

"And then walk away. Your safety takes priority over any attempt to resolve or reconcile. This is a type of verbal aikido. It's a communicative martial art. You're taking their energy and returning it to them with a statement of willingness but with conditions for reengagement.

"Another 'trick' I use is to make a slight shift toward the side of the person. Maybe half a step. This gets me physically out of the way of their projection. It's a self-protection maneuver. It's about personal space. I also take a step back from the individual. It's very subtle but noticeable. It sends the nonverbal message, 'I'm not going to be a target.'

"After you walk away, get some support from someone immediately so you can let them co-regulate you. Doing this is an affirmation of your own dignity and nonnegotiable need to be treated with respect. You can't co-regulate someone when your own nervous system is under assault," I said. "It's critically important to remember that other people's reactions or responses—even if we have a part to play in what happened—are their reality and ultimately, their responsibility. Same with us," I added.

"The point is that we have to have a technique that we use that we don't have to think about in that moment. It needs to be automatic," I said.

Devonte added, "You can't reason with someone who's being unreasonable."

"Great point," I said. "And when and if you do come back together to address the issue, use the S.H.A.R.E. process and have someone else facilitate it. Ask a supportive colleague to participate and be your advocate. Because chances are the person who came unglued has impacted others, maybe in the same way.

"What else sticks out for you about S.H.I.F.T.?" I asked the group.

"It seems complicated," said Kris. "You said it's intuitive and becomes second nature with practice, but how do we get good at it?"

"Great question. The acronym helps. Spot the signs. Hold the space. Identify feelings. Focus on needs. Take action. I suggest practicing it with a friend, partner, or colleague when both of you are not in the midst of an upheaval," I suggested. "Pick an event or incident that was stressful and then go through the steps. See if you can soothe and calm each other."

"Practice the chords of the instrument before playing the concert," said Aaron.

"Yeah. Let's do one now. Joan, would you be willing to do this with me? You mentioned the situation with the director of your school. Would you be willing to let us support you?" I asked.

"Oh boy," she said.

"What just came up for you?" I asked.

"Dread and sadness," she said.

"Where is that feeling of dread?" I asked.

"In my stomach," she said. "I feel sick to my stomach."

"See if you can breathe into where that is," I said. "Take some deep breaths that reach all the way down into your stomach. I'll do it with you. In fact, let's all do it."

After a few breaths, Joan said, "I'm just so tired of this. Everyone is. It's exhausting."

"I bet. It's understandable that you would feel exhausted. It sounds like people don't feel safe," I said.

"They don't. Nobody does. It's like the fox guarding the hen house," she said.

"That's a great analogy. No wonder people feel on edge," I said. "I'm wondering if you feel angry about this."

"I do feel angry. I've worked there for over twenty years with exceptional and visionary leadership. Our social climate, our culture, has always been caring, supportive, and safe. That's why parents send their kids to us. We've always been a strong community. Our strength was our connection with each other. That's being denigrated. People, teachers, are afraid of her. Everyone comes to me for support, and it makes me angry that they don't feel safe," she said.

"That's a really stressful position to be in, Joan," I said.

"It's so frustrating," she said. "I feel like I'm taking up too much of our time here," she added.

Barb said, "You're not. This is the work. I can relate to what you're experiencing."

"Me too," said Devonte.

"This is the work," I said. "I want to ask, where are we in the S.H.I.F.T. process?"

"Helping Joan identify what she's feeling," said Kris.

"Yes," I said. "And importantly, just letting Joan vent. This step is about supportive listening. Listening for the sake of advocacy."

"Holding the space," said Barb.

"Yes. Empathic listening," I said. "Making it safe to let it out. Notice some of the statements I've used like 'breathe into that feeling,' 'it's understandable,' 'I'm wondering if you're feeling…'"

Barb said, "'I can relate.' All of these are connecting statements, language strategies to help Joan feel safe to feel and express what she's feeling."

"I do feel safe here," said Joan.

"I do too," said Kris.

"I have a question, Joan," said Melissa. "Have you expressed how you feel to any of your colleagues? Is there anyone you feel safe enough to let this out?"

"No," she said. "We support one another, but we feel powerless when it comes to preserving the culture that makes us who we are. Our culture has been our guiding light and inspiration. It's been heartbreaking to the see the unique relational culture we've worked so hard to create, be replaced by a hierarchy of power."

"Who is there to support you, Joan?" I asked. When I said this, Joan's eyes started to water.

"I'm sorry. I don't want to make this a therapy session about me," she said.

"You're not," said Brad. "This is what matters. You matter to us. This is sacred stuff. I feel honored that you're sharing this with us."

"I do too," said Devonte. "Let us love on you."

Devonte's statement "let us love on you" issued a huge shift in our experience of each other. After a moment, Joan took a big, deep breath and said, "Thank you. I've been holding all of that in. Thank you for caring about me. We've been through a lot. It's ironic but your support and my feeling of safety is exactly what our culture has always been about."

I gently asked, "Joan, how can we best support you through all of this?"

"Just sharing this with you is a huge relief. I feel everyone's love and concern," she said.

"Maybe we can help you figure out what you might be needing moving forward," I said.

"I knew you were going to say that!" she chuckled.

"So, that's the taking action step," commented Barb.

"Yes," I said. "Feelings reveal needs. Needs require action to be met."

Turning back to Joan, I said, "I want to return to the situation with your school director. You mentioned to me that you have an upcoming conversation scheduled with her. Is that still happening?" I asked.

"Ugh. Here comes the dread again," she said.

"That's understandable. But now you're not alone in this. You have our support. We can help you prepare for this talk with her," I said.

"What is your biggest fear?" I asked.

"I have two fears. The first is losing my job, not because I would need to find another job but because I love the people I work with, the teachers, the parents, the kids.

I've worked there for twenty-five years and I'm proud of the contribution I've made to our culture. Our mission is to foster an environment where people feel valued, accepted, celebrated for their uniqueness, and most of all—kindness. I've contributed to this. I've 'held that space' for two decades. That's why people send their kids to our school. Those values used to apply to us. Now they don't.

"That's my biggest fear, that she's dismantling our culture. Like I said, people don't feel safe. They have no voice. We have no representation. She changed our organizational structure so that any and all complaints or concerns come to her. How do you do that when she's the source of the dissatisfaction?

"We used to have a practice called 'tough conversations' where everyone would gather in a circle and work through challenges. She stopped that. The latest contract she created for teachers and staff stipulates that she can fire you for any reason, at any time at her discretion, and you will lose all of your benefits," Joan explained. "This is about justice. This issue is why I enrolled in this discussion. To try and figure out how to restore justice and save our culture."

"What you describe sounds oppressive," I said.

"It *is* oppressive. The impact on people's spirits is profound. People feel trapped, and so it feels false to those of us who have intentionally created an environment of love. The other feeling that comes up for me is anger. What she's doing is unethical and destructive—and no one can do anything about it," she said.

"That's not leadership," interjected Melissa. "No wonder you're feeling dread."

Joan continued. "People tell me that I should just 'keep my head down' and that there's nothing I can do about it," she said. "I feel stuck. Everything in me wants to confront her in this upcoming conversation, but if I do, she'd probably fire me on the spot. Then what?"

"Let's see if we can unpack this and help you prepare for this conversation," I said.

"Quick question," said Barb. "Where are we in the S.H.I.F.T. process?" she asked.

"We're moving into focusing on needs. Joan has identified and expressed not only what she's feeling, but also what others are also feeling. What are those feelings? Frustration, hurt, fear, anger, exhaustion. Joan, do I have this right?" I asked.

"Yes, and deep, deep sadness," she said. "I feel sad. I feel loss. It feels as if our culture is dying. It hurts."

"Thank you for trusting us, Joan. Thank you for being vulnerable and sharing this with us," I said.

"I feel safe here," she added.

"Underneath each of these feelings is a need. Feelings point to needs. Once we understand what those needs are, we can strategize a way to meet those needs. I like the statement, 'needs are nonnegotiable.'

"In this case, there are two contexts. First, there's the micro context of what Joan needs and what she can do to meet those needs in her upcoming conversation with the director. Second, there's the larger, macro, or social-cultural context of what everyone needs and what can be done to meet those needs. This includes the director," I said.

"Wait. Why do you include the director when she's the problem?" asked Barb.

"Great question. Let me ask all of you. Why include what she might be needing?" I asked.

"I think I can answer that," said Joan. "It's the first of the 7 Principles you gave us; recognition of inherent dignity. Like it or not, she's part of our community. If we profess that we're a community where it's safe to make mistakes and everyone is valuable and deserves respect and dignity, we have to include her."

"I'm sorry, but that sounds touchy-feely," said Barb.

"What would you suggest?" I asked Barb.

"Schedule a meeting with the board of directors and the faculty without the director and tell them what she's doing. She needs to be held accountable," said Barb.

"That's certainly one course of action," I said. "Joan, what do you think of this strategy?" I asked.

"I thought about that. I agree about the need for accountability. Right now, there is no accountability. I also agree that the board needs to know what's going on. But not to necessarily issue a decree or judgment, but to understand how this style and the organizational changes are impacting morale and our relationships. And realistically, people wouldn't feel safe coming forward. The faculty doesn't have a relationship with the board. The risk of retaliation from our director is real. I'm trying to figure out what a restorative approach would look like. We desperately need this program and these practices but there's no way our director would ever allow it," said Joan.

"Because of her own fear," said Barb.

"I think the deeper truth is that she's afraid of people having a forum to air their grievances," said Joan.

"She sounds pretty fragile," said Kris.

"She's operating out of a different paradigm. It feels like it's fear and control centered," said Joan.

"And because you see that, you have empathy for her," I mentioned.

"I do. You said something in one of our earlier discussions about empathy and accountability going hand-in-hand. How does that apply here?" asked Joan.

"We can have empathy for a person's incapacity or underlying issues that we may sense even if they don't, but still hold the behavior accountable for its destructive impact," I said.

"Separate the behavior from the individual. Right?" asked Barb.

"As a restorative communication principle, yes," I said. "If we can separate what a person is doing from their inherent value as a human being, what happens?" I asked. "More directly, what does that do for us?"

Kris answered. "It gives us objectivity, which keeps us from being sucked into the drama or being manipulated."

"Yes. It's an interior boundary we're setting for ourselves. It's subtle, but powerful because it keeps us from getting our own nervous system hijacked. Like we've said, it's not 'them.' It's the emotional state they're in, the story they're acting out, or the paradigm they're acting out of," I said. "But it's also a social boundary. That boundary says, 'This behavior is not who we are or what we aspire to be. We care for you as a member, but this behavior is destroying us as a community.'"

"It enables you to maintain your own dignity and demonstrate self-respect," said Devonte.

"And that's really the point," I said. "Joan, what upsets you the most about how your director is treating you in this situation?" I asked. "If it helps, use 'I feel' statements."

"I feel angry and hurt that my integrity is under assault. I feel threatened. I feel disrespected. I feel mistrusted. I feel disvalued and unappreciated. I feel unheard," she said.

"Okay. It sounds like you're very clear. Let's translate these feelings into what you're needing. For example, if you feel threatened, it means you have a need to feel safe," I explained. "What are your needs?"

"I have a need to be treated with respect. I have a need to feel like I'm valued. I have a need to feel like I'm being heard. I have a need to feel like I can speak my truth about what I see happening to our school. I have a need for our faculty and staff to be treated with respect," Joan said.

"This is great. How does it feel to identify and vocalize what you need?" I asked.

"Empowering. But now my fear and anxiety about confronting her is coming back up again," she said.

"That's understandable. That fear and anxiety is the mechanism that this style of leadership depends on to secure power," I said.

"Like bullying," said Barb.

"Exactly," I said. "We covered this in our third discussion."

"That's messed up," said Barb.

"It is. But here's the thing. In my experience, it's not sustainable. That style of leadership doesn't last. Eventually, people either revolt or leave. The question is always, 'How much damage will that leadership style cause to people, relationships, and the organization, community, or society before it is confronted, rejected, and/or removed?'"

Brad commented, "This is eye-opening. This is exactly what's happening in our country. This is what you were saying when we talked about the threat of retribution and violence."

"Yeah. Like we discussed, the power-centric strategy is designed to activate our fears to suppress our voice and then manipulate our thinking. What Joan is experiencing with the director is a micro example of how power-by-threat of retribution works.

"How can we support Joan to speak her truth and reassert her need to be treated with respect in her upcoming meeting with the director, but do so in a way that also honors her core value of empathy and consideration?

"Joan, if your director was sitting right here in our discussion group, what statement can you make that would express your need to be respected but in a way that also demonstrates your need to recognize or acknowledge her humanity?" I asked.

"I respect you, but I don't respect what you're doing or how you've treated me?" asked Joan.

"You're on the right track. My hunch is that she would only hear the 'I don't respect what you're doing,'" I said. "Selective or defensive listening," I added.

"Lead with a statement of empathy and then follow with your truth," I coached. "Empathy disarms defensiveness and creates a space for us to speak our truth with dignity. This was the genius of Martin Luther King, Jr. Nonviolent communication."

"I avoid conflict at all costs. I've never been good at standing up for myself. I feel sick to my stomach," she said.

Gently, I asked, "Joan, I'm curious if you've ever experienced abuse?"

"Yes" she said softly. "When I was a teenager."

"I'm sorry to hear that, my friend. It's understandable that this would be scary. The experience of abuse is traumatic. It doesn't just go away after the abuse is over. It can stay inside of us. This person, your director, is acting abusively however implicitly or passively. Can you see that?" I asked.

"Yeah," she said.

"That young person that still lives inside of us might've had no one there to protect us or stand up for us. Now they do. They have us. What is being asked of you in this situation?" I asked.

"To step in," she said. "To stand up for myself."

"I think you might be onto something there. And it's really scary if we've never done it before. Joan, you have a right to speak up for yourself. You have a right to be treated with respect. You have a right to feel safe. You matter. Maybe this is an opportunity for you to step up for yourself in a way you're not used to," I suggested. "What do you think?"

"If I don't confront her, I'll be profoundly disappointed in myself. I'll be depressed and that will impact my health," she said.

"Your anger at being treated this way is invaluable. It's your truth and it shows us where our boundaries are and have been violated. That's where we get our courage to act not only on our behalf, but also on the behalf of others. Our anger gives us our energy and conviction. It's an asset.

"What you just demonstrated in crafting what to say to your director is your own courage and dignity stepping up. You demonstrated your dignity by being empathic, and you affirmed your dignity by asserting, 'I'm not okay with what's happening.' That's how empathy and accountability can work together. How does it feel to hear this?" I asked.

"Validating," she said. "I still feel some dread but it's not crippling. And truth is, my integrity and my values are more important than her insecurities. It's kind of like that feeling you get when you feel nauseated. You know you need to throw up and that you'll feel better once you do, but it's such a pain in the ass that you wait until you absolutely have to," she said.

"That's hilarious! Time to upchuck," said Barb.

"What a great analogy," said Kris.

"Way to go, Joan!" said Melissa.

"And we're here for you. We have no expectations, Joan. I think I can speak for all of us that any one of us is just a phone call away," I said.

"Amen to that," said Devonte.

"Absolutely," said Aaron.

"If you have to throw up during the meeting, make sure you do it on her desk," said Barb.

"Geez, Barb," I replied.

"Just vomiting my truth," she said. "You said retribution has its place, right?"

"Retributive vomiting," said Kris.

> Social isolation and loneliness have been shown to have a wide range of negative physical/health consequences. Feeling lonely, for example, causes our cortisol levels to soar, a hormonal outcome that causes wide-ranging damage to the body and mind. In fact, acute loneliness is seen as every bit as stressful as being physically attacked. Human beings are wired to be in groups, and, when we aren't for too long, we feel alienated and insecure. Loneliness and social isolation is increasingly a public health epidemic in America.[11]
>
> I think there's a lot of people out there who are suffering quietly and don't really know why. For a subset of those people—the reason why is loneliness. That's the thing. It's like turning the light on. Once you see it, then you know, and then you can act.[12]
>
> —Bradley Riew

Closing Comments: The Ripple Effect of S.H.I.F.T.

I explained to our group, "When you stop and think about the negative impact that the myriad of social crises we're facing has on our collective nervous system and psychological well-being, the pervasive atmosphere of threat, a technique like S.H.I.F.T. can be an antidote. It's simply an interpersonal communication technique that helps us meaningfully connect with each other, support each other, and constitute an act of humanity in the moment. I refer to both S.H.A.R.E. and S.H.I.F.T. as rehumanizing conversations."

"This is a type of deep noticing of the Other," said Brad.

"I really like that. With S.H.I.F.T., we notice each other's struggle, we engage and create a safe emotional and psychological space of care and concern. Empathy is the motivation for creating that space, but it is also the technique for establishing that connection.

"When we're struggling with an overwhelming experience and feel someone's empathy and concern for us, our nervous system and body gets the opportunity to relax, and our perspective about 'who, what, and where' we are can begin to shift. The message is simple but profound—*I'm not alone*. Taking action with and on behalf of each other confirms that empathy and compassion are not just 'feel goods,' but also holistic restorative solutions.

"And we don't have to wait. For homework, before our next discussion, I suggest you all practice this technique in a conversation with someone who you care about and appears to be struggling with something happening in their lives.

"It's the starfish principle. How do we shift 'the world' toward a relationship-centric paradigm? One conversation at a time. Think about the ripple effect. What would be an outcome if a family, group, workplace, or any collective would start practicing this? What would the cumulative effect be?

"The thing about restoration is that we often don't know what needs restoration until we're into the process. We have to trust that it will emerge and be prepared to recognize it and move into it," I said. "It's a leap of faith."

Barb replied, "This is all very inspiring, but how do you get everyone else to start picking up the starfish too?"

"That's what we'll cover in our next discussion," I said. "It's all about implementation, and implementation takes planning, organization and collaboration, training, and sustainability. You need to put a system in place to make sure the starfish are getting regularly picked up and tossed back in the ocean."

"I still say you need a wheelbarrow," quipped Barb.

"Programming is that wheelbarrow," I said.

"But to wrap up this discussion and while we're on the story of the little girl on the beach, imagine that when the old man encountered the little girl, he could see that she was seriously distressed, upset, and feeling completely overwhelmed and perhaps incapacitated by the prospect of returning thousands of starfish back to the ocean.

"Imagine that the old man was trained in both the S.H.I.F.T. technique and the S.H.A.R.E. process. What would he do?" I asked.

Kris responded, "He's already spotted the signs that indicated she was stressed, so his next move would be to engage with her and seek to soothe and reassure her."

"Yes, exactly. Those are the first two steps of S.H.I.F.T.—spot and hold," I said. "He would engage with statements like, 'I can see this is upsetting for you.' This is an empathic statement which connects him to her. He might ask her, 'Would you be willing to let me help you?' This statement signifies him 'holding a space' of empathy and concern for her and creates a space for possible collaboration," I said.

"Assuming she agreed to let him help her, his next statement might be, 'I can see how much you care for each starfish, and I'm wondering if you're feeling worried *we* won't be able to return all of the starfish back to the ocean and some won't make it,'" I said.

"That's the third step. Identifying her feelings with her," said Kris.

"Yes. But notice that he said *we* won't be able to return all of the starfish, and some might die. By using 'we' instead of 'you,' he has now formed a partnership with her, and this helps the little girl not feel so alone in her fears or her mission," I said.

"So, he's continuing to co-regulate her nervous system and emotions," added Kris.

"Exactly. She's no longer alone in her experience. She now has an advocate. He might then move into focusing on needs, which is the fourth step of S.H.I.F.T. She needs help, both of them need help. So, he asks her, 'What do you think about us asking others to help us?' He doesn't tell her, 'We need to get others to help.' He asks her if she thinks it would help. Again, with this technique, we're not taking control of fixing the problem. We're continuing to strengthen the partnership," I said.

"And providing her with the opportunity to take action for herself in partnership with him," said Kris.

"I think so," I said. "It's about shifting her perspective from 'I'll never be able' to 'now I see a way I can.' This is about shifting someone from feeling helpless in their situation to feeling empowered to take action on their own behalf."

"And on behalf of the starfish," added Aaron.

"In this case, for sure," I said. "Let's say that she agrees that they need help. What would be his next move?"

"He would say, 'I know some people we could get to help us' and then ask her, 'Do you know anyone who might help us?'" said Kris.

"Exactly!" I said.

"They would then formulate a concrete plan to ask those people to come and help," said Kris.

"And make damn sure they all brought wheelbarrows!" exhorted Barb.

"Last question for you," I said. "Where would S.H.A.R.E. fit into this scenario?" I asked.

"I can answer that," said Aaron. "You would schedule a community gathering to discuss what happened, acknowledge the impact not only to the community but the tidal ecosystem, recognize what is needed to collaboratively respond when this happens again, and put a plan of action in place so that when it does, everyone shows up to return the starfish," he said.

"You're missing something," said Barb.

"With their wheelbarrows!" said Aaron.

CHAPTER SEVEN
Taking Restorative Action

Never doubt that a small group of thoughtful, committed citizens
can change the world: indeed, it's the only thing that ever has.
—Margaret Mead

"Before we dig into this discussion on implementation, I want to check in with Joan about her conversation with the director. How did that go?" I asked.

"I think it went well. When I met with her, I basically did a combo of S.H.A.R.E. and S.H.I.F.T. I started with S.H.I.F.T. because I could tell she was tense. Rigid. But when I saw that, I just took a few deep breaths and reminded myself 'her reality isn't about me.'

"I asked her how she was doing, and I think my question startled her because she broke eye contact with me. She answered kind of flatly, 'Fine.' I told her I really appreciated her taking the time to meet with me."

Barb interjected, "Even though she's the one that scheduled it."

"Yes," said Joan.

"Nice move," said Kris.

"How did she respond to thanking her?" I asked.

"I think she was surprised," said Joan.

"Verbal aikido," said Brad.

"What do you mean?" I asked.

"Well, Joan took whatever negative power energy the director was projecting and returned it with gratitude. That's pretty disarming," he said.

"It also constituted an act of dignity," I said.

"So, that's what you mean in the first of the 7 Principles of restorative communication. Joan was recognizing the inherent dignity of the director by acknowledging her with a statement of gratitude before they even started," said Kris.

"Exactly. Expressing gratitude was a demonstration of respect. It also initiated a space, or tone, of civility," I said.

"But that's who I am," said Joan. "That's where I come from."

"So, in a sense, expressing gratitude right from the start was a type of 'speaking your truth'?" I asked.

"That is my truth," she said.

"How did the conversation go from there?" I asked.

"I think I kind of took control of the conversation. I told her, 'I can see how important it is to you that we continue to grow as a school. I know you care deeply about our sustainability. I can only imagine how difficult it must be to have so much responsibility for our future on your shoulders," explained Joan.

"How did she respond to this?" I asked.

"I could tell that she was struggling with what I was saying because her body language changed," said Joan. "She seemed to tense up a bit, which kind of surprised me because I was expressing respect and empathy."

"Acknowledging her experience with empathy is exactly what I'm talking about with regard to the relationship-centric nature of restorative communication. Restorative communication is intentional communication. We do it for a reason. We have to move into and through resistance. Your statement constituted inclusivity and compassion," I said. "Anybody else want to comment?" I asked the group.

"I don't see what you did as control, Joan," said Devonte. "I think it was more about working with her discomfort and creating an emotionally safe space. You were embracing her."

"I like that. A space of embrace," said Kris.

"I was hyper-aware of her nervous system and body language. To be honest, I was protecting myself by trying to regulate hers from the start," said Joan.

"Did it work?" asked Melissa.

"It did for me because I felt comfortable in my own skin. I was alert but relaxed," she said.

"What happened next?" I asked.

"I told her my truth. I said, 'I'm deeply concerned that our culture is shifting away from our core values of kindness, transparency, and mutuality," said Joan.

"How did she respond?" I asked.

"She tensed up," said Joan.

"When I sensed her tenseness, I realized she was taking what I was saying as a criticism of her. She was taking it personally," said Joan.

"How did you respond when you sensed this?" I asked.

"My first thought was, 'There's an underlying issue here that may be rooted in an unresolved woundedness or hurt.' Then I felt a flood of compassion for her. I said, 'I'm wondering if you feel like we understand how difficult your position as our leader is? I'm wondering if you feel supported by everyone?'"

"Wow. You really embraced her," said Melissa.

I asked the group, "What part of the S.H.I.F.T. technique was Joan using?"

"Identifying the feelings," said Aaron.

"I think it was both holding a space of empathy, which really lasts during the whole encounter, as well as identifying feelings or giving her the opportunity to identify her feelings. The steps of S.H.I.F.T. are fluid. How did she respond when you said this?" I asked.

"She was quiet. I think my acknowledgment of her possible feelings helped her feel safe with me. This is going to sound crazy, but that shift was palpable. I now understand the 'holding space' part because it's something that is tangible. It's like a huge exhale. You can feel it."

"That's the co-regulation part," said Kris.

"And she looked tired. I realized the weight she must feel as a director. She said, 'Leaders don't get to feel.' When she said this, I immediately thought of feeling rules," said Joan.

"That's a powerful admission. How did you respond?" I asked.

"I took a chance," said Joan. "I said, 'That's not fair to you because you're only human. I want you to know that you matter to me and not just because you're my boss. Your feelings are very important to me.' I added, 'I can speak for everyone else too. We all care about you. That's what makes our community so special.'"

"Holy shit," said Barb. "You nailed this."

"I just spoke from my heart," said Joan.

"How did she respond when you told her everyone cared about her?" I asked.

"She was silent. I could tell that what I said touched her," said Joan.

"How did the rest of the conversation go? Did you address her treatment of you?" I asked.

"That was the tough part. I'm good at being kind, but like I shared, sticking up for myself is stressful," said Joan. "I just don't like conflict."

"I don't know if this was S.H.I.F.T. or S.H.A.R.E., but I said, 'I need you to know that I don't feel like you trust me. Because I don't feel like you trust me, I don't feel like you respect me.'"

"How did she respond?" I asked.

"She apologized," said Joan.

"Was she sincere?" asked Barb.

"It felt sincere," said Joan.

"Okay, let's see if we can unpack this," I said. "This is a great example of how S.H.I.F.T. and S.H.A.R.E. can work together. At the start, it was S.H.I.F.T. because you spotted the signs of her defensiveness, or tension, in her body and facial expressions. You recognized that this was an expression of a type of distress that probably had roots elsewhere.

"But you responded with empathy, and in doing so, you created and held a space of compassion and concern. That 'space' and your expression of empathy for her helped disarm her. How would you describe your tone of voice?" I asked.

"I remembered what you told us about the sound of our voice and so I consciously tried to be very gentle and soothing. I spoke calmly and unrushed," said Joan.

"Do you think that had an effect?" I asked.

"Absolutely. But not only for her. It helped me stay centered. Speaking that way kept me calm," she said.

"That's what you were telling us about restoration being performative," commented Brad.

"Yes."

> **Restorative communication utilizes the performative aspect of language and interaction. It does what it says. It constitutes what it calls for. In trying to become an 'instrument of peace,' we experience peace ourselves.**

"Joan, what you also did that was in line with S.H.I.F.T. was identify what she was feeling and then focused on what she might be needing, which was to feel valued and included. Where it became S.H.A.R.E. was when you talked about her mistrust of you. You spoke your truth about what happened, shared how it impacted you, and stated that you have a need to be trusted and respected. Does this sound accurate?" I asked.

"It does," she said.

"What action came out of this conversation?" I asked. "Both S.H.I.F.T. and S.H.A.R.E. culminate in an agreement to take some type of action moving forward," I said. "Did this happen?" I asked.

"At this point in our conversation, I felt like I had connected with her, so I suggested we start having more conversations like this. I said, 'Everyone needs to know how difficult your job is,'" said Joan.

"How did she respond?" I asked.

"I think she felt a bit embarrassed. She said, 'It's not that big of a deal,' but I disagreed and said, 'It *is* a big deal because you matter, and your feelings matter, and people need to know. I suggest that we talk about the changes we see happening in our culture at our next faculty meeting.' I told her I thought it would help reconnect us. She agreed. But then I took a big chance and told her, 'You're our leader, but you're also one of us,'" said Joan.

"You ended the conversation with a connecting statement," I said.

"I thanked her for her willingness to talk with me and then I gave her a hug," said Joan.

"You started with the hurt and ended it with a hug," said Kris. "How did she receive your hug?"

"She was stiff," said Joan.

"One step at a time," said Brad.

"Way to go, Joan," said Melissa.

"Well, we'll see," said Joan. "It's a start."

"I really appreciate you sharing this with us Joan," I said. "It's pretty remarkable. Instead of going in and immediately talking about what she did to you, which would have put her on the defensive, your focus was on what was happening with her. That ability to be objectively aware, but also engaged, is what S.H.I.F.T. is about. S.H.I.F.T. is about operating on two levels: the objective, problem-solving level but also the emotional or feeling level.

"I think what we see is that restoration starts with a conversation and then, ideally, proceeds into the next conversation. You started with S.H.I.F.T. and then proceeded with S.H.A.R.E.

"What I've found is that the more we have these gut-level conversations, the more connected we become and the more willing we are to have more of these conversations about what is unspoken but exists, nevertheless. Both methods are a way to talk through emotionally charged issues.

"This seems like a good moment to segue into talking about implementation. How do you integrate these conversations using S.H.A.R.E. and S.H.I.F.T. into the social fabric?" I asked.

Our Intention

"Let's think back on why we came together. First, we share a deep concern about an increasing level of contempt and animosity permeating our larger cultural and social experience. Joan, I think you said it best when you commented that 'the world has become a meaner place to live.' We described this as a type of existential social trauma.

"Second, we see and feel the destructive impact this is having on our children, families, schools, colleagues, and respective workplaces. Brad, you pointed out the destructive impact of dehumanizing political rhetoric. Aaron, you expressed our shared frustration about our continual disregard of the environment.

"To use Bessel van der Kolk's phrase, 'our bodies are keeping the score.' The environment is our body and it's keeping the score. Devonte, you said something that stuck with me. You commented that 'toxic social interaction is poisoning our collective soul.' Our collective social spirit is hurting.

"The claim I've been making is that all of this is a matter of broken relationships. Generally speaking, we are 'out of right relationship' with ourselves, each other, our history, our planet, and the natural world.' We've forgotten the inescapable reality of interdependence. As a result, our relationships have become transactional and adversarial, and our communication has devolved into toxic dismissiveness. Without a meaningful realization of interdependence, we end up using our words to denigrate and desecrate 'the other,' falsely thinking that our personal security is dependent upon seizing power over the other.

"The argument I've been making is that if we want to make a positive change, if we want to facilitate a cultural shift toward a relationship-centric paradigm which would reassert the principle of interdependence, we have to change the way we communicate with and about each other. We have to realize that words matter, and that our communication constitutes our experience of ourselves and each other. As we speak, so we go. We inhabit the relational spaces we create with our words.

"What we've done thus far is explore a restorative paradigm. The restorative paradigm is a way of looking at life through the lens of relationship. It is a relationship-centric paradigm constituted by restorative communication and interaction.

"The principles of restorative communication are a recognition of inherent dignity, mutual respect, civility and engagement, responsibility-taking, repair, and reconciliation. As we've recognized, these principles seem to be missing in our world right now.

"These principles are rehumanizing. If we're sick and tired of dehumanization, the restorative response is to rehumanize. Restorative communication accomplishes this.

"So, now the question is, 'How can we integrate this way of communicating into our respective immediate social environments on a consistent basis?'" I asked.

"The practices," said Brad.

"Weaving them into the social fabric," commented Melissa.

"Yes. It's helpful to remember that the practices are the situations, contexts, or applications. In other words, where does restorative communication, restorative conversation happen? Critically important, who is going to coordinate, support, and facilitate the implementation and sustainability of those practices, and how does that happen? We can't rely solely on the individual. It takes a collective effort."

> **For "restoration" to accomplish what it's capable of in any environment, it takes a whole-system approach, programming. It is programming that embeds and sustains the range of restorative communication practices into a "site."**

Foundation and Scaffolding: People, Policy, Program, Practices

"Each of you are working in distinctive sites, or 'communities.' Brad, your community is a recovery center. Melissa, yours is a healthcare facility. Kris, your site is a mental-health nonprofit organization. Devonte, yours is a high school. Joan, yours is an elementary school. Barb, now that you're retired, you expressed an interest in becoming a consultant and trainer in workplace relationships for hospitals.

"Aaron, your sites are the communities you work with to implement environmental restoration practices. All of us share a sense of some value or solution in a restorative approach. While the model I'm going to present may not directly apply to your community engagement, in the next session I'm going to focus on environmental restoration because as I'll explain, it is our relationship with the environment that, I think, has the most to teach us about restoration.

"There are several things to keep in mind about implementing these practices. First, if the goal is to make a positive and sustainable shift in how people regard and treat each other, then you have to give them the communication skills and practices to make that shift. Making a positive, pro-relationship shift in culture and social climate requires replacing destructive patterns of communication and interaction," I said.

"So, the goal is to get people thinking and speaking in restorative terms," commented Brad.

"Yes," I said. "The goal is to get people using restorative communication on their own, proactively in their everyday interactions with each other, and not wait until there is a more serious conflict or incident of misconduct."

"You're talking about the principles of conscientious interaction," commented Melissa.

"Yes," I said. "You want those principles to become active, real, tangible, and present in how people interact. Let me give you an example. What do you do when a colleague comes to you and starts to gossip about another person? How do you respond? What do you say?" I asked. "Joan, what would you say?"

"I'd stop them and say, 'It hurts to hear this,'" she said.

"Okay. You expressed the impact. That's the third step of S.H.A.R.E. Anyone else?" I asked.

"I would say, 'It sounds like you need to have a conversation with the other person. Would you like me to facilitate that?'" said Kris.

"I like that," I said. "It's proactive, carries the message of accountability, and encourages the person who is gossiping to take personal ownership and responsibility for their relationship with the person they are gossiping about. You're also setting a boundary that says, 'I won't participate in gossip,' and you're pointing to the possibility of a S.H.A.R.E. encounter."

"Yeah, but then that person will just go to someone else and probably gossip about you," said Barb.

"Right, so the issue of gossiping needs to be addressed on a collective level. One of the practices we'll talk about later in this discussion is the creation of a collective Respect Agreement which outlines how people agree to treat each other. If that agreement was in place, you could remind the person of your collective commitment to not gossip about each other," I explained.

"This example leads to a second thing to keep in mind with implementation. Again, if the goal is to shift the culture toward a more positive and relationship-centric social climate, then patchwork attempts at adoption or implementation don't work. The patterns won't change on an everyday level of interaction.

"I've seen schools and workplaces only use the basic restorative justice process to address misconduct. It's reactive and not proactive. What typically happens is that there is an introductory training in that one practice or model. But restorative communication is more than just a conflict or misconduct response. It's a way of communicating that emphasizes the value of the relationship, and that's not limited to incidents of conflict and misconduct.

"This points to another problem with patchwork implementation. The skills and any range of practices or applications fade without some type of programmatic foundation or support to ensure that the conversations happen consistently in a range of contexts. We'll explore those contexts later in this discussion," I said.

Melissa commented, "This reminds me of one of the biggest issues we have with professional development sessions. People get excited and motivated to use new skills, but that inspiration is not sustainable if there is no ongoing support."

"Kind of like going to a self-improvement seminar. You get excited but the excitement is short-lived," said Barb.

"That's it," I said. "It's a Band-Aid feel-good approach. Unconstructive patterns of communication are hard to change because it involves a change in behavior. We're asking people to shift how they have conversations and dialogues about challenging issues and in a range of circumstances including conflict and harmful conduct."

"Change is scary," said Kris.

"It can be, and that's understandable. And that's why you have to take a whole-system or whole-community approach," I said. "A programmatic approach ensures those conversations are consistently happening and measures their effectiveness and satisfaction in resolving issues.

"In one elementary school I trained, the faculty didn't want to use restorative practices with the students. Three months after the training, the practice faded away. In one high school I trained, they didn't want to use restorative practices with faculty. Restoration failed. But in one school, they took a whole-school approach. They took it to heart, and they took it seriously. They used it with both students, adults, and even parents. They implemented a program, and the relational climate changed. Quite frankly, people felt relieved that they now had a way to resolve issues and conflicts that everyone agreed to apply.

"One other thing to realize is that even though the particular site may be different such as a school or a workplace, the basic components are the same: *People, Policy, Practices, and Program: the 4 P's.*"

People

"Think about three to five people in your community/site who really want to see a positive shift happen in how people treat each other, your social climate. These are people who care deeply about the relational culture of the community/organization, are tired of the status quo of interaction, know it can be changed, and are committed to making that change happen.

"These people are your greatest asset. They are your early adopters, your change agents, your stewards, your cohorts. This small team will be responsible for implementing the program, facilitating the practices, keeping track of how conflicts and issues are resolved, and conducting ongoing training in restorative communication," I explained.

"This is a train-the-trainer model," said Brad.

"Yes. It's all about self-sustainability and growing expertise from within. The name of this group is up to the team. One elementary school where I helped implement this program called their group a 'Restorative Council.' One hospital I'm working with calls their group the 'Ambassador Team.'

"It's important that this team reflect the diversity of roles in the organization. For example, in a school this group might consist of both teachers and administrators as well as counselors. In a hospital or healthcare facility, this group can consist of nurses, physicians, techs, and administrators. Brad, in your recovery center, the group might consist of counselors, techs, and an administrator.

"When I put this program into a university, the group initially consisted of the school's ombudsman, a campus police officer, a career guidance counselor, and municipal court officials. Once the program was up and running, we didn't need such a large advisory group. Two people administered the program itself, which after two years was processing roughly 400 incidents per year, and we only needed a facilitation team.

"The basic roles and responsibilities include meeting at least once a week to review incidents, schedule and conduct preliminary interviews with participants, identify and discuss any underlying issues participants might be facing, schedule and facilitate restorative conversations, monitor restorative agreements, seek continuous feedback from participants about their experience, and eventually conduct trainings in restorative communication practices," I explained.

"Like S.H.A.R.E. and S.H.I.F.T.," said Melissa.

"Those are just two basic scripts, but they are the essential steps to any restorative practice.

"There's one other responsibility your group will need to fulfill, and that is the creation of a policy for the program and the documents you'll need to keep track of incidents."

Policy

"In a previous discussion, we talked about paradigms. We distinguished between a retributive paradigm and a restorative paradigm. Policies are where these two paradigms collide. If an organization or school pursues restorative communication practices and commits to building a type of program to support those practices, they'll need to create a policy for the program that explains how incidents and conflicts are processed. A problem arises when an organization or school begins to create a policy for a restorative program, but the existing conduct policy is punitive. Let me explain this.

"Discipline policies are formal proclamations from the organization. The vast majority of discipline policies that exist in organizations (schools, workplaces, etc.) are 'institutional-centric' or power-centric edicts that reflect the same retributive principles that drive our justice system. For the most part they don't define, characterize, or promote positive behavioral norms. They don't establish relational goals. They don't inspire.

"Punitive policies tell you what happens if you don't behave. If you break the rules, you get punished. Similar to the criminal justice system, as misconduct increases in seriousness, so too does the punitive consequence. Both are deficit-focused systems of behavioral management. They do more harm and don't repair the harm that exists. This is especially damaging to individuals who carry the seeds of trauma.

"If we really want a positive cultural shift in our workplaces and schools which will, in turn, manifest as a safe climate, then we have to begin by reevaluating official behavioral policies.

> **"A punitive policy focuses on negative attributes and emphasizes behavioral deficits while ignoring character assets and fails to address the real underlying issues compelling antisocial behavior—like trauma."**

"Punishment may reauthorize a rule and relieve or remove an immediate problem through force and exclusion, but it doesn't explore or seek to repair what might be causing the person to act out.

"If a child or an adult feels bad about themselves, reprimanding or scolding them only reinforces a pre-existing negative self-image. In this regard, a retributive policy compounds and facilitates more trauma.

"Conversely, a restorative behavioral policy communicates positive pro-social behavioral aspirations like respect, responsibility, accountability, repair, and commitment to community. When these behavioral ideals are not met, the response should be designed to remind, reintroduce, encourage, reaffirm, and reclaim the inherent value of the individual to the community.

"These restorative principles teach individuals that they are an integral part of a larger community, and that the well-being of all community members is everyone's responsibility. More importantly, restorative communication practices are designed to discover and address the underlying thinking and issues that may be compelling the antisocial behavior—like traumatic stress.

"Simply put, a restorative culture is one with a defined set of behavioral responses that emphasize relationship-building and connection. When interactions, incidents, and situations occur that disrupt social harmony and compromise the learning or working environment, rather than excoriate, punish, and exclude, a restorative response embraces each conflict or act of misconduct as an opportunity for reflection and socioemotional learning.

"The policy explains the restorative approach as a method, the range of contexts and issues where the method will be used, the various practices, and how incidents will be processed by the program. I like to look at the policy as a relationship manual or teaching document that sets forth positive aspirations or expectations as much as an explanation of the parameters of the program. Here's an excerpt from a typical policy:

> *When an incident or conflict happens that disrupts the relational harmony of the social environment, our policy is to speak with everyone who was involved or impacted, hear their perspective, understand why it happened, determine what people need to resolve the incident (including repair), and co-create an agreement to nurture constructive changes.*

"Notice that the above statement is 'asset-focused.' It articulates a positive and relationship-centric response to an incident rather than a coercive one. In doing so, it establishes a positive communication norm in how the organization/school responds to incidents, conflicts, or conduct issues.

"Even though workplaces and schools are implementing restorative practices, their existing employee or student conduct polices often remain sanction-oriented and deficit-focused. I refer to sanction-oriented conduct policies as 'or-else edicts.' They explain how the school or organization will sanction and punish people based on an established hierarchy of violation seriousness, but not how it will help people resolve issues, learn, and grow from any incident or conflict.

"It's also been my experience that in the desire to embrace restorative practices, workplace or school conduct policies are not as specific as they need to be in terms of articulating the philosophy or reasoning of restoration, explaining exactly how incidents are actually processed, and how behavior is held accountable with dignity. People need this clarity and specificity.

> **"A conduct policy should be a living document that shines a light on what's possible, rather than simply explaining the sanctions for breaking the rules."**

"It should promote positive behavioral norms and clear expectations for all community members—including the leaders. When a policy sets forth positive behaviors and positive responses that the whole community can aspire to, it reminds people not only about what's expected, but also what's possible in terms of human dignity. Most conduct policies explain what happens when people fall short, but don't inspire what's possible or remind them of their inherent goodness.

"A conduct policy is essentially a collective agreement about how we commit to work with each other to continually establish a physically, emotionally, and psychologically safe environment. The policy articulates the structure and steps of deepening engagement when there's conflict or misconduct," I explained.

"This is the circle rippling back toward the center where the incident happened," commented Kris.

"Exactly. A policy should remind members of their responsibility for each other … not threaten them with exclusion when they fail. A policy lays out the processes, methods, and practices for working through the conflict or misconduct in a way that restores relationships and membership," I explained.

"Are you suggesting that this policy replaces whatever conduct policy already exists?" asked Brad.

"Not necessarily," I said. "But at the least, retributive or punitive responses to conduct should be guided by one question—are we trying to control behavior by force and threat, or are we attempting to work with conduct through engagement with the goal of intervention and growth?"

"You're taking a prosocial-emotional approach to a conduct policy," said Melissa.

"I like that. I'm taking a relationship-centric approach that embodies a prosocial-emotional awareness and development.

"As we've been discussing throughout our conversations, this is a radically different approach to accountability and one that people, leaders, and organizations find very difficult to change. I'm not saying that there aren't incidents or situations where the only option to protect the community is to separate from an individual. Those boundaries are necessary. But even that process of separation can be restorative and use restorative language. In those cases, the question is, 'Can we move through this separation with grace and dignity?' " I said.

"What you're saying is that there's a restorative approach to ending a relationship." commented Kris.

"Yes. I'll give you two quick examples. In one family-run business it became clear that the negativity and bitterness of one of the employees was impacting the rest of the company. This employee had worked there for a couple of years, and it became known that the employee was a survivor of a physically abusive relationship. The owners had tried several approaches from writing the employee up to suspension.

"Instead of just saying 'we tried, you're fired,' the owners approached the employee by saying, 'It's clear to us that you're not happy here. We know you're struggling to come to terms with what happened to you. We believe you have many interests and talents, and we'd like to see you pursue those.'

"They offered to help this employee get access to professional help and pay for it, and enroll in retraining and education that would fit her interests at a local community college. If the employee enrolled, the company would pay the first year's tuition.

"They didn't have to do that. While this may seem like a bad financial decision and exorbitantly generous, the dignity and respect this decision communicated paid huge dividends in the workplace climate and the reputation of the owners as caring people. This employee ended up turning her life around. The owners got to feel good about how they handled it. As one of the owners told me, 'It was the right thing to do.'"

"In another example, a school needed to separate from a student. But instead of just summarily expelling the student, they facilitated the enrollment of the student at another school where that student's needs would be better met. They worked closely with the parents during that transition.

"My point is that this approach to policy is a 'needs-based approach,' and one that is fundamentally relationship-centric and grounded in humanistic principles."

"This sounds like a trauma-informed approach to policy," said Kris.

"I'm glad you brought this up. In my opinion it is. Most policies ignore the reality of trauma, and thus miss the opportunity for a potentially transformative experience not only for the person who is struggling, but also for the organization—even if it is ultimately necessary to separate.

> **"There is a direct relationship between the level of trauma experienced and the level of harm caused. Simply put, the more traumatized the individual, the more harm they are likely to cause to themselves or others, and the more skillful we need to be in how we engage with them. A policy should lay out that engagement."**

"The logic is straightforward. The sooner we can recognize the existence of trauma in a student's or employee's life, and the sooner we engage with them from that perspective, the better chance we have of intervening and possibly preventing escalation. This could very well save not only their lives, but also the lives of others.

"Some people argue that it's not the responsibility of a school or workplace to facilitate the healing of trauma-based issues. I disagree for two reasons. First, schools and workplaces are where we spend the majority of our in-person social interaction time. For most students, school is the first social experience they have. That experience profoundly and unavoidably informs the rest of their social life.

"If we don't help them navigate this social terrain with the necessary emotional and relational skills to care for themselves and each other, and work through conflicts, how can we expect them to navigate the much larger world where trauma is inevitable? The more they know and understand what trauma is, how it motivates behavior, and how to work with it, the better off our world will be.

"Second, we have no other option. If we want a more empathic world, we have to start by implementing empathic practices in schools and workplaces. If we want people to start taking responsibility and holding themselves accountable, we have to have practices that not only separate accountability from shame and condemnation but also point toward intervention, repair, and healing."

"Accountability with compassion," added Melissa.

"I think so. Accountability can be empowering. Let me show you a framework that I've used with both schools and workplaces when they're reimagining their conduct policies. Educators, especially counselors and learning specialists, are very familiar with this. This framework is based on the Multi-Tiered System of Support (MTSS) developed by the Center on Positive Behavioral Interventions and Supports.[1]

"This is a data-driven, trauma-informed problem-solving framework to improve outcomes for students, but I've found that this evaluative structure for levels of conflict and misconduct can be valuable for workplaces as well. Especially when reviewing conduct policies.

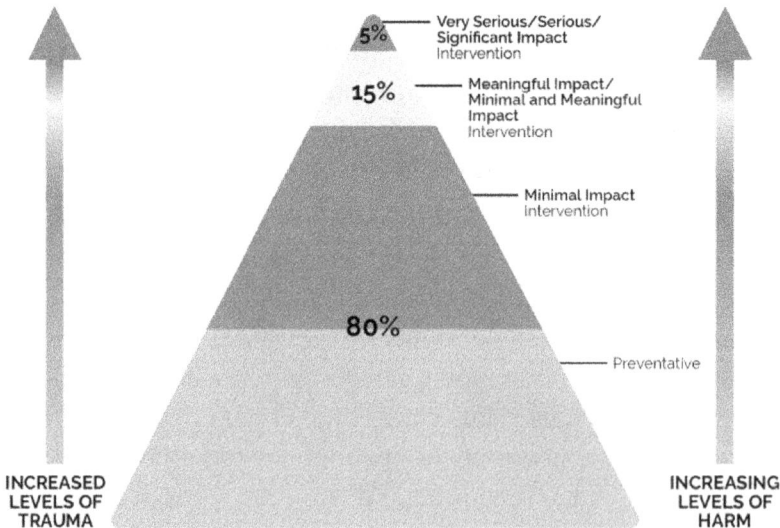

"As the level of trauma increases, the level of harm and impact increases and so does the need for a more focused and intensive engagement. When you base your conduct or conflict response on the harmful impact on people and relationships rather than what rule or code was broken, which is what restorative practices do, you avoid the thinking that misconduct requires punishment.

"As we've been discussing, restoration uses the level of harm to ask increasingly much deeper questions in the pursuit of discovering underlying issues and needs. The response is determined by those issues and needs rather than attempting to control the behavior through admonishment, coercion, and exclusion. Here's a section from a policy I wrote for a client:

> *The goal of the restorative response is to engage with an employee(s) when an incident has occurred. This means that the more serious or impactful the incident was/is, the tighter the circle of concern and response needs to be from all of us.*

"Let me ask you a question. Can you see where the basic scripts of S.H.A.R.E. and S.H.I.F.T. can be implemented?"

"The context changes but the method of engagement, the questions, and discussion remain consistent," said Brad.

"Yes. What happened or is happening? What is the impact on people and relationships? What are the underlying needs? What needs to be restored? What is our agreement? What do we now choose to do?" I restated.

"What also changes is the agreement," added Brad.

"Yes. Can you speak more about that?" I asked.

"Looking at this chart, 80% of the time the agreement might be as simple as an apology or a commitment to stop gossiping. This could happen using S.H.A.R.E. as the practice either in a one-on-one conversation with an individual, or between two individuals with a facilitator," he said.

"Or simply becoming aware of the negative impact," added Kris.

"But in the minimal intervention stage, you might set aside time to go through S.H.A.R.E. with a small group to include others who were impacted. Like the case with Rick and Leo, that agreement might include some type of counseling?" Brad asked.

"It could. But keep in mind that there is great value simply by people assembling in a circle to talk about something that has happened or is happening," I said.

"This is the performativity you were talking about. Restoration can happen in the course of people determining what a restorative agreement needs to be," said Devonte.

"Yes. It's about the encounter, the discussion, and the connection. S.H.A.R.E. is just the script that guides people through problem-solving, informed by how people are feeling about what happened and discovering their needs," I said.

"In the top 20%, the agreement would definitely include some type of professional help like what happened with Rick," said Brad.

"Yes. The degree of impact was very serious, and the trauma that was revealed required professional support," I said.

"Rick's case was both an intervention but also preventative," added Brad.

"Yes," I said. "In the case with Andy's father, the S.H.I.F.T. discussion was an intervention in that moment, but also preventative in that we kept his trauma from overwhelming the circle. I would argue that the S.H.A.R.E. process used in the circle was also an intervention, as well as preventative," I added.

"The point here is that a restorative conduct policy should correlate and articulate types of conduct with the seriousness of their impact on people and relationships, not on what rule was broken. It should also explain the process of engagement and expected outcomes. When you build a policy this way, people who read that policy understand not only how the organization or school determines seriousness based on impact, but also what to expect as a response. A policy should establish an ethos for the organization.

"Here's an example of how one former client's organization described three levels of impact:

> DEGREES OF IMPACT: 'Impact' refers to how the employee's, supervisor's, or executive's actions have negatively impacted (a) another employee, supervisor, executive, or client; (b) other employees, supervisors, executives, or clients; (c) the larger social climate of the workplace. We identify impact as: *physical, emotional, and psychological well-being; safe social climate; personal and company property.*
>
> 1. MINIMAL: The employee's, supervisor's, or executive's actions and behavior were disruptive and maybe inconsiderate but didn't result in any significant harm to anyone. This incident is usually addressed with a one-on-one S.H.A.R.E. dialogue.
>
> 2. MEANINGFUL: The employee's, supervisor's, or executive's actions and behavior have become a pattern and/or have caused significant disruption to the social environment, and resulted in identifiable harm to another employee, employees, team, or the workplace climate. This incident is typically addressed with a group S.H.A.R.E. conversation, facilitated by a member of the Ambassador Team, and conducted with others who were impacted. This group conversation produces an agreement stipulating reparative actions to be taken by the employee, supervisor, or executive.
>
> 3. SERIOUS: The employee's, supervisor's, or executive's actions and behavior have caused significant harm to others and the workplace. The

automatic response is a S.H.A.R.E. group conference with those impacted, as well as subsequent meetings with the person who harmed, and may or may not result in a requirement for professional counseling, suspension, and/or permanent separation between the employee, supervisor, or executive and the organization.

"The policy also needs to explain the process of that response, how it is coordinated and administered. That takes us to the third 'P,' which is Program," I said.

Program

"What I'm calling a 'program' is simply the administration and coordination of how incidents are processed. This coordination includes documentation, initial interviews with participants, scheduling group conversations, facilitating those conversations, monitoring agreements created during the conversations, maintenance of satisfaction surveys, and producing reports about the effectiveness of the program and its practices.

"This same organization explained their documentation as such:

> Consistent and accurate documentation is crucial to ensuring the continual authenticity, depth, stability, and effectiveness of our approach to helping resolve incidents, issues, and/or conflicts. Documentation serves an important organizational function that keeps our approach and practices *consistently meeting the needs of everyone involved.*
>
> Like the policy, the purpose of documentation is to *train our focus* toward possibilities for human growth and development. In fact, the entire program is geared toward taking a moment of disruption, interpreting it as a window into a member's experience, and an opportunity for mutual understanding and respect, community-building, and mastering the communication skills to effect positive 'change.'
>
> Fundamentally, documents are designed to help 'separate the behavior from the individual.' Behavior is what people do, not who they are. When we take this approach, we can hold the behavior accountable for its impact on others and explore why it happened while honoring the inherent dignity of life within the human being.
>
> *Documentation is not about keeping a record of bad behavior.*
>
> Documentation is about enabling our Ambassador Team to work closely with our members to address an incident in an expedient and thoughtful way that supports both individual and collective relationship-building. The particular documents we maintain are:
>
> A. An *Incident Report* that participants complete prior to restorative engagement.

B. A *Confidentiality Form* that protects people's privacy and ensures the content of conversations is kept strictly confidential.

C. A *Process Explanation Sheet* that explains the S.H.A.R.E. process and helps participants understand what to expect.

D. A *Process Status Sheet* that documents where the incident is in terms of the process of being resolved.

E. An *Agreement Form* that participants create, commit to, and sign during the group conversations.

F. A *Participant Satisfaction Survey* that asks for participants' feedback on their experience with the conversation and suggestions for improvement.

G. A *Program Data Collection Sheet* to measure the overall effectiveness of the restorative program and S.H.A.R.E. in resolving issues and conflicts to the satisfaction of participants and the organization.

H. A *Program and Facilitation Manual* to conduct training of facilitators and general ongoing training in restorative communication methods for members.

The documents are just tools. Not every incident will need every document. The Incident Report, Status Sheet, and Agreement Form are the most important in terms of tracking progress.

"Does this documentation go into the employee's file?" asked Brad.

"That's a good question. It's up to the organization. In my opinion, the only documentation that should go into an employee's file is a notice that they have participated in a restorative conversation concerning a specific incident or matter. The records of their participation should be kept with the program. I suggest this for two reasons. First, the program is primarily concerned with tracking categories of incidents, their resolution, and participants' satisfaction with the process. It's a different consideration.

"Second, and most important, this helps keep participation in these discussions safe. If employees know that what they are discussing in these conversations will not be used against them, they are more inclined to be open, frank, and honest in how they feel," I said.

"So, the program maintains some autonomy," commented Brad.

"Yes," I said. "That autonomy is important in terms of instilling confidence in people and helping them understand that they need to take ownership of the incident and its resolution. However, and this is important, it needs to be explained that if there is some type of litigation resulting from an incident, the program is required to surrender its records if subpoenaed. This should be explained in the Confidentiality Form," I said.

"That also protects the organization," said Brad.

"Yes" I replied.

"In general, it's a program facilitated by the people, for the people," commented Devonte.

"I like that. It's a 'community-based' program. This reminds me, membership on the Ambassador Team should always be volunteer and rotating every six months or so. This serves to distribute responsibility and raise the overall mastery of the approach and practices," I commented.

"So, after a while you have people who are capable facilitators as just part of the workforce," said Brad.

"Yes. And that is how you embed restorative communication in the workplace, which serves as a preventative mechanism," I replied.

"And get people thinking about impact before they say or do something," said Devonte.

"Ideally," I said.

"What happens if people don't fulfill their agreements or if it happens again?" asked Melissa.

"Another great question. If an agreement isn't fulfilled, it's time for another conversation. The 'what happened' is that the agreement wasn't honored. Why? What are/were the underlying reasons? What was/is the impact of that agreement not being honored? What's our new agreement? The same discussion is about why it happened again. Maybe the agreement needs to include some professional help in addition to additional repair," I added.

Practices

"We've already discussed the steps of S.H.A.R.E. and the S.H.I.F.T. technique. Though the example I used of S.H.I.F.T. was in a one-on-one interaction, it can also be used in a group setting when that group has shared in an experience of a traumatic, upsetting, or distressful event," I said.

"Group co-regulation," commented Kris.

"Yes, and it can be very powerful. One person facilitates the steps, but the group acknowledges what they've experienced, what the signs are that they see that indicate the experience has been overwhelming, creates and holds its own space of physical, emotional, and psychological safety, acknowledges the impact, recognizes what everyone needs, and takes action to provide mutual support. But you're right on target with the nature of group co-regulation," I explained.

Brad spoke. "This is similar to what we do when there's been an overdose in our facility. But this makes me rethink how we conduct our large group meetings to explain what happened to our other clients. This is more experiential or process-based and less about providing information."

"That's a good distinction. It's not about telling people what they might be experiencing or how they should think about what happened. It's about asking people. Even though people need information to understand what happened and understand what other people think or know about what happened, what you're really trying to do is create a safe space for people to process and share how it impacted them, how they're experiencing it, and help them discover what they need.

"It's a facilitated process rather than a directive process. Instead of saying, 'You might or might not be experiencing or feeling this,' you're asking, 'I'm wondering if any of us might be having any feelings or thoughts about this such as …'

"Brad, when you do your process, do you do it in a circle?" I asked.

"No. We do it in a large dining hall," he said.

"So, people are sitting at tables?" I asked.

"Yes," he replied.

"I suggest doing it in a circle. A circle is a 'performative or experiential symbol' that communicates 'we're in this together and we're safe here,'" I added. "It helps with group co-regulation. The restorative circle encounter is designed to be a space of relational sanctuary. As a physical space, the circle configuration ensures a 'suspension of status.' No one person is in front or behind any other. All members face the center and each other.

"The circle is probably the single most powerful operational symbol of inclusion, equality, and community. I mentioned this earlier. It doesn't just represent or symbolize community; it creates the experience of community viscerally by nature of its geometry. The circle space provides the experience it represents.

"I want to turn to contexts or scenarios where S.H.A.R.E. can be used. Because S.H.A.R.E. is simply a guided conversation practice, it can be used in a wide range of circumstances from low-level impact to high-level impact incidents or events, and from one-on-one dialogues to small or large group gatherings. It is both preventative as well as interventive. Any time there is an incident, event, conflict, issue, or situation that needs to be addressed, S.H.A.R.E. can be used to guide the discussion. I realize I'm casting a wide net here, but bear with me.

"Because of S.H.A.R.E.'s focus on inviting people's perspectives, achieving a shared understanding of an event or issue, acknowledgment of impact, recognition of needs, and the collaborative creation and enactment of a plan of action, it is an effective step-by-step decision-making tool. It simply breaks down an issue into manageable, thorough, and progressive mini-discussions guided by questions."

"You're saying it can be used as a decision-making tool. How does that work?" asked Aaron.

"Let me give you a simple example. I once worked with a board of directors who needed to make a change in a policy. That change would require the implementation of a new human resources program, which would affect the entire organization. They had selected two possible programs but couldn't reach a consensus about which program to implement. Heated arguments ensued, and people got frustrated and threatened to quit the board. The discussions devolved into blaming, accusations, and territorialism. They had lost objectivity and emotion overpowered rational thinking.

"We took each potential program and went through the steps. If we implement program A, what will be the impact? We looked at both potentially negative and positive impacts. We looked at several categories of impact such as financial, administrative, operations, required training, people's resistance or buy-in, workplace relationships, and morale. We identified needs. What needs would program A meet? What needs would not be met? What would be needed to implement the program? We did the same with program B.

"We did this over the course of one day. They chose program B. In my opinion, there were several reasons why they were able to break the deadlock and reach a consensus in a short amount of time. First, and probably most important, agreeing to follow the process was an initial act which demonstrated a willingness to collaborate. This kept them from entering into the discussion based solely on their own positionality and self-interest. I explained to them, 'We don't know the outcome, but we trust that whatever outcome we arrive at will have been thoroughly discussed.'"

"Trust the process," said Aaron.

"Yes, and trust in each other's desire to do what was best for the organization. Before that, they didn't have a process and so the discussions always deteriorated into a fight where each person argued from their own personal perspective and interest. By agreeing to trust the process, they were implicitly committing to collaboration.

"Second, and though they didn't fully realize it, they were creating a criteria they could use for determining what would constitute a rational decision that would provide the most benefit. By identifying and acknowledging the potential but real impacts of either program, and recognizing the needs that would be met, left unmet, or created as a result of either program, they gained some objectivity.

"Essentially, what happened was that the S.H.A.R.E. process constrained self-interest without denying it in service of making the wisest, most rational decision. Each person's perspective and contribution was valued and appreciated. There was a shared understanding of why the particular program chosen was being chosen.

"I want to list a series of typical or common situations where you can use S.H.A.R.E. Schools that have implemented restorative practices will recognize these. It's been my experience that some of these practices can also be adopted in families as well as workplaces. As I've emphasized, the core practice of people coming together to address an issue by going through the steps of S.H.A.R.E. is valuable, effective, progressive, and relevant for any circumstance that involves human relationships."

Speak your Truth—*Hear* from Others—*Acknowledge* the Impact—
Recognize Needs—*Enroll* in a Plan of Restorative Action

Practice	Context – Purpose
Respect Agreement	List of 5–10 guiding principles that members create and agree to honor with regard to how they treat each other both in general, and when there is disagreement or conflict. Agreement is referenced on an ongoing basis (i.e., 'how are we doing with our agreement?') and when an incident of disrespect occurs (i.e., 'which principle did we fail to uphold?'). Preventative practice.
Daily/Weekly Check-In	Quick empathic connection tool. Helps members of a class, team, small group express and recognize any challenges members might be struggling with and need support for from group. Preventative and potentially interventive.
One-on-One Dialogue	Conducted with an individual who was involved in, experienced, or witnessed an incident of incivility and/or violation of principles of 'right relationship.' Precursor to Group Circle or Facilitated Dialogue between two people. Preventative and interventive.
Facilitated Dialogue	This is a facilitated dialogue between two people who are engaged in a low-impact disagreement or conflict. Typically evokes each person taking responsibility for their part (i.e., apologizing) and produces an informal verbal agreement to 'make things right.' Preventative and potentially interventive (de-escalation).
Group Circle	Facilitated group encounter to address an incident, destructive conflict, pattern of destructive interaction, etc. This is the core restorative group practice. Attended by those directly involved and/or impacted by the incident. Interventive and preventative.
Support Circle	Facilitated group encounter to provide emotional support for an individual who has experienced a traumatic incident. If an offender was involved, they do not attend. Interventive (see page 223).
Accountability Circle	Facilitated group encounter where participants express the harm caused to the collective/community as a result of uncivil behavior or actions. If a survivor was involved, they do not attend. Interventive (see page 224).
Decision-Making Circle	Facilitated group encounter where participants collaboratively determine the criteria for what constitutes a wise decision.
Teaching Circle	Facilitated group discussion about a subject, topic, or issue using S.H.A.R.E.
Recognition Circle	Facilitated small or large group encounter where members acknowledge and celebrate contributions made by a particular member or group.

"Each of these practices can help in resolving issues and building relationships not only in schools, but families, workplaces, and the larger community as well.

"I want to explain the Support Circle and Accountability Circle in more detail."

Support Circle

"I'll give you a story. I went to a conference on restorative practices, and people were asking about how to approach bullying using the restorative process. One school administrator explained, 'We bring the victim and the offender into a circle and work through what happened as quickly as we can.' People cringed when they heard this.

> **"Bullying is essentially an act of relational terrorism. I define bullying as the repeated use of threat, violence, or social exclusion in order to intimidate, belittle, demean, and dominate another human being for the purpose of the offender's self-interest and/or self-gratification."**

"This applies to both schools and workplaces. When a person has experienced bullying, the first thing they need to experience is the community embracing them and protecting them. The survivor/victim needs to know that their experience is being taken seriously, that they matter, and that the community will confront the aggressor, and hold the behavior accountable.

"The Support Circle creates a safe space for the survivor to explain what happened, express how they feel, how it impacted them, and experience collective support and protection from the community—without the offender being in the circle. The message the circle gives the survivor is, 'This didn't happen because of you, but because of the thinking and behavior of the other person—and we won't tolerate this.'

"Bullying is isolating. A Support Circle prevents that. If you try to just 'bring the person who bullied and the person who was bullied into a circle immediately, you risk retraumatization. All it takes is one glance from the offender to revictimize.

"A Support Circle creates relational sanctuary and addresses isolation, humiliation, shame, and fear. The survivor is supported to process what happened on an emotional level and have their experience taken seriously by others committed to their safety. In this process of sharing and caring, the survivor's story becomes 'our story too,' part of a larger narrative of 'this affected us as well, you're not alone, and we're going to address it,'" I explained.

Kris commented, "I can see a Support Circle working in any number of situations where someone needs support, not just bullying. I'm thinking about someone who has experienced any traumatic event that may have happened outside the organization."

"Or even if the entire workplace or school has experienced a trauma, like a suicide or a shooting," added Brad.

"Yes. It's simply a way for people to gather together and use these steps to constitute connection and caring," I said.

Accountability Circle

"The Accountability Circle is conducted with the offender, without the survivor present, in order to directly hold the offender's behavior accountable. This is how the community intervenes and takes ownership of the incident and the behavior. They are the ones who need to express two things.

"First, that 'This behavior not only impacted the other person, but all of us.' That impact needs to be articulated. When this happens, the person who bullied comes to realize that the person they bullied is not alone, has the support of others, and that the bullying didn't just violate another person, but an entire community.

"Second, that 'This behavior will not be tolerated in our community.' However, and this is critically important, the offender—as a human being—is not condemned or shamed. Instead, the underlying thinking, reasons, and motivations for the bullying should be explored and addressed in the reparative agreement. What repair does the offender need to make? What support does the offender need to make the necessary changes and ensure that it doesn't happen again? What are the consequences if it does?

"Whether or not there is an additional/eventual Group Circle assembled for both, should be given careful and substantial consideration by the Ambassador Team or Restorative Council. It's been my experience that when these two practices are implemented, over time, incidents of bullying are consistently addressed. That consistency can foster a larger culture of respect and transparency. Your thoughts?" I asked the group.

"This just seems like such common sense," said Barb.

"I think it is," I replied. "The question is, 'How seriously will a community take the issue of bullying or harassment?' and 'How willing are they to actually take action to confront it?' When I was a kid, bullying was treated as 'just a normal part of growing up' and 'kids will be kids.' Now we know just how traumatizing it is, and how it can impact a person's mental health throughout their entire life—and not just the survivor, but also the person who bullied.

"The effects of childhood bullying don't disappear after childhood. Those effects show up in our families, workplaces, communities, and society. If not acknowledged, confronted, and repaired when it happens, then what happened on the playground can kill long after it has occurred.

"Both the Accountability Circle and Support Circle are restorative ways to address it when it happens in schools, but also in workplaces. The only question is how seriously will we take it? What do you think about what I'm saying here?" I asked.

"Of course, my mind goes to the bigger picture of what's happening in our politics. Bullying seems to have become an acceptable way of getting elected," said Brad.

"Yeah, but it doesn't last. People get to the point where they reject it. The only question is how much damage has to be done before they do, and how the rejection of that way of treating others is handled," said Devonte.

"Well said," I affirmed. "With the exception of natural disasters or accidents, people traumatize people. I believe our news media and entertainment take advantage of trauma. They have a vested interest in keeping collective PTSD going.

"This is why it's so critical that we implement restorative practices and programming to support those practices in schools and workplaces. Restorative practices are a way to hold antisocial thinking and behavior accountable, but with the intention of transforming the belief system or trauma motivating it one conversation at a time. Restorative communication is a way to replace hateful rhetoric with civil discourse in those social places and spaces where we spend most of our day-to-day lives.

"When accountability and empathy converge, hearts and minds align. The wisdom embodied in these practices gives people a way to reject hatred without violence. That's been my experience. I may sound 'pollyannish,' but that's my take."

> **Cultures are malleable. Cultures foster or undermine health and well-being and encourage or discourage our highest human nature. A society can intentionally foster greater capacities in its citizens. Through the beliefs we select, and the practice we embody, we can choose to cultivate a more empathic and communal mindset—fulfilling our human essence.**
>
> **—Darcia Narvaez (2014)[2]**

Summary: People, Policy, Program, and Practices

"Let's summarize what implementation looks like if the intention is to take a systems approach.

"First, you need cohorts, people who want to see change and are committed to helping you do the work of implementation. These 'early adopters' serve several purposes. They review the existing behavioral policy, and they make any changes in that policy to reflect and promote restorative values and principles more accurately.

"Second, that policy needs to clearly articulate the components of the new 'restorative program,' which explains how incidents are processed, documented, the specific practices used like S.H.A.R.E. and S.H.I.F.T., and what the expected outcomes of the practices are.

"Third, your team of cohorts will also create the necessary documents and procedures to process and respond to incidents. They won't have to do this from scratch because those documents and scripts, etc., can be provided by me or should be provided by any consultant who has built programs before.

"So, your new Ambassador Team or Restorative Council are the program builders. They are also your facilitation team, so they'll become trained in the various practices, be able to train others in the practices and skills, and need to meet on a regular basis to discuss incidents and continuously improve.

"Lastly, there are the individual communication practices or applications of the restorative method. We listed and described a few of those practices above, but regardless of the context or specific practice, the core restorative script for those practices is S.H.A.R.E.

"Here is a visual model for how to grow a restorative culture:"

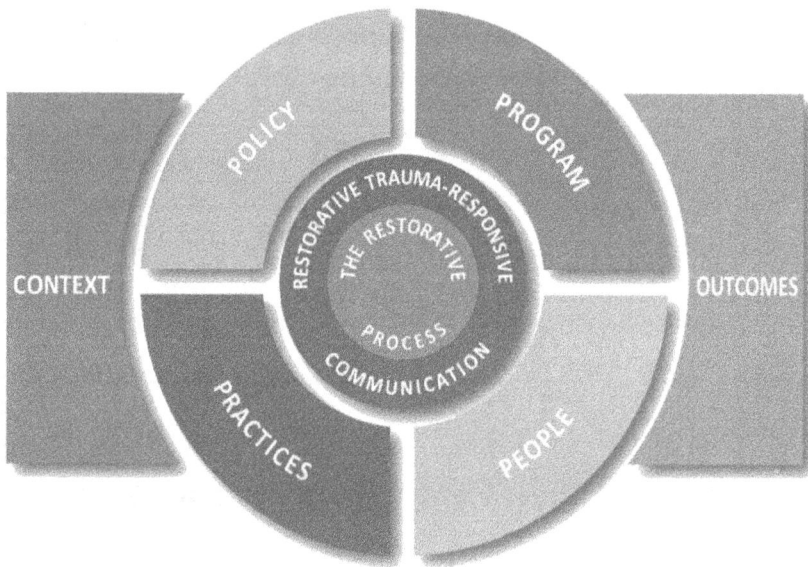

"You can see that at the center of this model is the S.H.A.R.E. restorative process: What happened? Who was impacted? What was that impact? What, if any, are the underlying reasons, beliefs, motivations, or issues that resulted in what happened? What are the needs? What needs to happen to address any underlying issues?

"What needs to happen to repair the harm? What is our agreement? What actions do we agree to take to restore people, relationships, civility, respect, and dignity? What do we need to do to make sure people and relationships matter?

"As we've covered substantially, S.H.A.R.E. is simply an acronym that helps people remember the steps of the restorative process. As we've discussed, this process can be conducted in a one-on-one dialogue or a group encounter.

"S.H.I.F.T. is a restorative trauma-responsive communication technique used to help an individual process a traumatic experience in that moment. Looking at this model, the reason why S.H.A.R.E. (the restorative process) is in the center, and S.H.I.F.T. (restorative trauma-responsive communication) surrounds S.H.A.R.E. is because it is often the case that people will get triggered or emotionally activated and need more support on an individual face-to-face encounter. But both S.H.A.R.E. and S.H.I.F.T. are components of trauma-responsive communication.

" 'Practices' refers to the particular applications of both S.H.A.R.E. and S.H.I.F.T.

" 'Programming' refers to how those practices are coordinated and facilitated. 'People' refers to the core group of people who coordinate the programming, facilitate the practices, and conduct ongoing training in restorative communication, but also review the existing conduct policies and make changes to ensure that restoration is the institutionalized response to incidents.

" 'Contexts' refers not only to the circumstances of the actual incidents in a particular site, but also the 'social spaces and places' where restorative cultures can be grown. It could be a family, school, organization, justice system, workplace, church, recovery center, etc.

"The outcomes are what we've covered consistently: civility, accountability, responsibility, respect and rehumanization, reparation and reconciliation, mutual understanding, empathy and compassion, connection, inclusion, reintegration, and in my experience—regeneration."

"Restoration," commented Kris.

"One starfish at a time," I said.

"The systems approach is the wheelbarrow," said Barb.

"Amen," I said.

CHAPTER EIGHT
Interdependence:
Starfish, Lakes, and Mothers

The most powerful agents in any culture are those that shape the imagination of the people. The imagination shapes childrearing practices, the type of adults the children become, and the type of culture adults create for their children.[1]

In a society where children are immersed in media, those who tell the stories about what human life is and should be like are those who create the media; their world-views and interests shape children's minds about social and moral life.[2]

When our group reconvened for our next discussion, I asked, "Why bother with restoration, restorative justice, or restorative communication? Why put forth the effort? I ask this because when we look unflinchingly at the seemingly insurmountable social and environmental crises we face, it's understandable that we might feel despondent.

"In the spirit of transparency, there are moments when I feel an overwhelming amount of discouragement. I ask myself, 'Why bother with restoration when nothing seems to change and so much needs restoration?'

"This was the question the old man asked the little girl on the beach tossing starfish back into the ocean. The old man was asking, 'Why bother?' But for her, the question of *why* didn't make sense because it was so obvious to her that the question never crossed her mind.

"If I read more into this story, I see the intersection of meaning and mattering. For her, every single starfish mattered. For her, the act of picking up a single starfish and putting it back into the ocean was meaningful. She was making a difference, but she was also participating as an integral member of a larger ecosystem. She was innately connected.

"The old man, on the other hand, by even asking the question, symbolizes our doubts, cynicisms, and disconnection from meaning and mattering. He questioned whether what she was doing was meaningful, or if it really mattered given the immensity of the problem. 'Well, it mattered to that one,' she told the old man. She contested his story. She was, really, the elder here.

"She should've thrown him into the ocean," said Barb. "But that would've been retributive," she added.

We chuckled, but then I offered, "She did have a choice. She could've said, 'You're right,' and stopped doing what she was doing. She also could've argued with him. If she had done either, what would've been the impact?"

Devonte replied, "If she changed her mind to agree with the old man, she would've become like the old man, just as disconnected. Something soulful would've died too."

"If she had taken the time to stand there and argue with him, starfish would've died," said Aaron. "And starfish are a keystone species, the center of a whole tidal ecosystem."

"I'm certain there is a much deeper and relevant symbolism to what you're pointing out, Aaron. The point I'm making with this story, and which I think helps us to grasp a concept like 'moral imagination,' is that she had no doubt she could make a difference, no doubt she was doing the right thing, and had a logical solution and a plan of action: restore the starfish. Her compulsion came from a deep sense of responsibility. Without that sense of responsibility, restoration wouldn't have happened.

"There's one other point to this story. The fact that the old man asked the little girl 'why' represents hope and the possibility for a shift in his paradigm and ours. It's a moment of potential moral imagination expansion. I like to think that he started helping toss the starfish back into the ocean."

Moral (Re)Imagination

"I'm interested in this term 'moral imagination.' What exactly does that mean, and how does it apply to restorative communication?" asked Brad.

"I'll do my best," I replied. "It has to do with the capacity or ability to imagine an ethical or moral response to a given situation or circumstance that may or may not be typical or reflect existing social norms, practices, principles, or standards. Like moral thinking outside of the box. The little girl's actions were not typical to the old man. He couldn't see the morality of what she was doing.

"For example, as we talked about in Chapter 3, from a retributive perspective, the ethical or 'just' response to a transgression like crime or misconduct requires a determination of guilt, judgment, and the determination of an 'appropriate' sanction or punishment. Accountability is fulfilled when punishment is applied. That's the longstanding justice norm. I don't think it is unreasonable to suggest that retributive justice and the application of punishment is an enforcement of a moral edict," I said.

"Kind of like 'thou shalt not or else,'" said Brad.

"But would that norm be considered moral or even ethical, in Rick's case? What about Andy? In both of these instances, would punishment be the correct moral response? What the restorative encounter did was provide the participants with the opportunity to imagine a different but equally moral response and a different interpretation of accountability, one that reflected the humanistic values of empathy, compassion, repair, and forgiveness. In essence, the groups reimagined and performed a different understanding of what constitutes a moral response. That response was more nuanced because it took Rick's history into consideration.

"I want to make another point. If we believe we know the outcome before we actually come together and discuss what happened, hear from people, and discover what might be the most 'appropriate or humane' response to resolve the situation, there's no space for moral imagination. The restorative discussion opens that collaborative space of discovery. Restoration is an example of interaction searching for moral reimagining.

"This is what happened in the case with Rick and Leo. Out of the realization of the harm and suffering experienced by Leo and Maria, any immorality of what Rick did was revealed in context. Out of the story of Rick's history came the possibility for reimagining how he might learn or develop what constitutes the moral and ethical treatment of others, especially people of color.

"The message was not 'you shouldn't have done this because it's immoral.' The message was, 'You shouldn't have done this because of the damage and harm your thinking and actions caused others and yourself.' That message emerged from the context of what happened and its impact," I said.

"The immorality of threatening someone's life with a gun was revealed as 'immoral' because of the pain and anguish caused to Leo and his wife," said Melissa.

"And the community. I realize this may sound like semantics, theoretical, or way too heady and philosophical, but I want to say one other thing about the restorative process, restorative communication as a practice of moral reimagining.

"Historically, both nationally and globally, we've relied upon religious texts, stories, orthodoxy, and traditions to teach us about morals, how to treat each other, and how to be in 'right relationship.' We've relied upon religious leaders to interpret those moral precepts, their reasoning, and show us their relevance. But that influence is in steady decline. In a national survey conducted by the Pew Research Center (2017), the data revealed a trend toward 'religious disaffiliation' that continues to rise," I offered.

> **The data shows that just like rates of religious affiliation, rates of religious attendance are declining. The religiously unaffiliated are on the rise among younger people and most groups of older adults; their growth is most pronounced among young adults.** [3]

"That's because religions have lost their relevance to younger generations. The sad part, from my perspective working with young men in recovery, is that the very idea of spirituality, the possibility of having a transcendent experience, never gets explored. Their cynicism about religion keeps them from pursuing a deeper reality," said Brad.

"I have to admit that I have the same cynicism. Religions have become political tools. To use your word about rhetoric, God is used as a trope. Religious leaders have abused their religious authority. It's a spiritual felony," added Melissa.

"To that I would suggest that social media has become the new church; a place where people, especially young people, congregate and are being taught about social and moral life, to use Narvaez's quote. The question is, 'If we can no longer rely upon religions to teach about universal values and principles,' where or how is that void going to be filled? Because those values and principles are critical components of civility. If religions are losing their relevance, where do we learn about 'doing unto others,' accountability, ethics, repentance, forgiveness and charity of spirit, amends-making, and redemption?

"I've been arguing for twenty years that the restorative approach and the discussions that ensue embody timeless and universal moral principles of right relationship. But it doesn't dictate those principles. Instead, it uses a moment of social discord, transgression, or conflict to facilitate an experience of those principles organically. The values and principles are emergent. That scares people," I said.

"People come to these moral revelations through their experience of the process of talking about their hurts, their wounds, and then work together to make amends and restore relationships—not only with each other, but also with themselves in the process.

"Restorative communication gives us the ability to discover and consider moral possibilities that extend beyond any given circumstance and recognize or discover deeper truths and ethical responses that may or may not be evident until we go through the process of collective investigation," I concluded.

"I have a question for you, Will," said Kris. "You've been doing this for twenty years. Why do you keep picking up the starfish?"

"I know what it feels like to be the starfish," I chuckled. "I know the conviction of the little girl. But I also know what it's like to be that cynical old man."

> **What postmodern science is telling us—that the universe is a whole and that all things, living and nonliving, are interrelated and interdependent—has been, for most of the world's history, common knowledge. We, a postindustrial, urbanized people, alienated from our own bodies and from the body of the earth, have to learn it, and most often it's a strange knowledge. We are ruining the space, and when this occurs, justice issues emerge centrally and painfully.** [4]
>
> **—Sallie McFague (1993)**

Lake Restoration

"I want to give you two cases that I think exemplify what we've been talking about. The first is an example of how we can look to the environment to teach us about restoration. The second is an example of how the restorative process activates moral imagination.

John's Story

In 1999, my wife and I bought a small cottage on a nice 165-acre lake in Michigan. I grew up on Androscoggin Lake in Wayne, Maine, and I wanted to share that experience and my deep love of lakes with our daughter.

When we purchased the property, the water was clear, the surface clean, and there was a nice gravel bottom off of our shoreline. Right around that time, Eurasian water milfoil invaded our lake. Within a season, the milfoil had taken over large sections of the lake.

Our Lake Association knew we had to take immediate action. We hired experts and did what we were told. We initiated an aggressive herbicide program for the lake. At first, the program was successful. We got the milfoil under control. We thought the problem was solved. We were wrong.

By 2003, my wife and I finally moved to the lake after restoring the cottage. We couldn't wait to enjoy the lake. Unfortunately, on our daughter's first swim in the lake, we discovered that our once-nice gravel-bottom shoreline was now plagued by over a foot of black, smelly, greasy muck. Her bathing suit was so black after a few minutes in the water that my wife pulled her out and immediately took her up to the house for a bath. We had to throw her bathing suit away.

Needless to say, this was heart-wrenching. We had just spent lots of money purchasing this property and lots of time, effort, and money rebuilding the cottage. After all of that, we couldn't even go for a swim in the lake where just four years prior we had a clean gravel bottom and clear water. I started to project what the lake might look like in 5–10 years. I realized that our lake property would not be the legacy I had planned on passing on to my children and their children. I had to do something about it.

—John Tucci

"John took action. Unwilling to accept the condition of his lake, and the status quo methodology of toxic aquatic herbicides, he began his search for a better way. That search became a lifelong mission and the formation of Lake-Savers, which has since restored over fifty freshwater lakes and reservoirs worldwide.

"John's story is similar to early restorative justice pioneers who were unwilling to accept the status quo of retributive thinking and methods in juvenile justice. In both cases, the existing paradigms were not only not working, but doing more damage and making matters worse.

"As John realized, poisoning aquatic weeds is a cultural, behavioral response to the condition of the lake, which doesn't address the underlying reasons why weeds and algae take over a lake in the first place.

"The search for a better way of justice led criminologists and sociologists to Indigenous peoples' worldviews and practices of restorative justice. John's search led him to ask, 'What does a lake need to be restored?' In both cases, the restoration of relationships was the answer.

"John's method of *restoring a lake's inherent biological capacity to continuously restore itself* should deeply inform our understanding of restorative justice and the restoration of human beings and human relationships.

"Without getting into too much scientific detail, freshwater lakes and reservoirs are in a state of crisis because of human behavior. The waste generated by industrial, agricultural, and residential development ends up in the watersheds which flow into lakes. As a result, 48% of all North American lakes are polluted with pesticides, phosphates, and nitrates (fertilizers), as well as untreated human and animal waste.

"As John says, 'The fertilizers we use to grow green crops and lawns grows green lakes.' This is the 'why.' Not only is the lake negatively impacted, but so are the people depending on the lake for fresh water, recreation, livelihood, and in John's case, a joyful experience he had as a young boy and wanted to pass on to his daughter.

"As fertilizers feed the lake, weeds and algae grow exponentially and begin to literally choke the lake, using up its oxygen. Explosive weed and algae growth are symptoms of a much deeper problem. Their cyclical growth, death, and decomposition create an inordinate demand for dissolved oxygen. Dissolved oxygen is *the* critical component of the ecosystem that supports oxygen-dependent bacteria (aerobic bacteria).

"Aerobic bacteria break down any organic matter and nutrients and convert them into microscopic organisms that form the basis of the food web. This process is similar to the human digestive system, which requires aerobic bacteria to break down food and convert it into energy on the cellular level.

"Over time, as those weeds and algae continue in their cycle of death and re-growth, the bottom of the lake becomes layered with dead organic matter, a compost pile that continuously 'self-fertilizes' the lake. The bottom of the lake becomes a nutrient dump.

"When this happens, dissolved oxygen levels plummet even further; aerobic bacteria levels decline, and anaerobic bacteria take over. Anaerobic bacteria are bacteria that do not require oxygen to live. They do not break down nutrients as quickly as aerobic bacteria, nor do they convert those nutrients into beneficial micro-organisms for the food web. Therefore, the nutrients which would normally be converted by aerobic bacteria into microscopic organisms that form the basis of the entire food web (fish) instead fuel further weed growth.

"It's a vicious downward cycle that results in the failure of the entire ecosystem. Without intervention, the lake will become irreversibly eutrophic, potentially toxic, and eventually die.

"Here's where it gets interesting in terms of restoration. The typical human response is to dump aquacides into the lake to kill the weeds; in other words, treat the symptom. But treating the symptoms by poisoning the weeds only makes the lake worse because the dead weeds end up on the bottom of the lake and exacerbate the problem of nutrient overloading and oxygen depletion. *The real issue is the lack of oxygen.*

"Logically, if you restore dissolved oxygen to the bottom of the lake, aerobic bacteria will thrive, anaerobic bacteria will decline, and the lake will be able to process/convert the nutrients *like nature intended*, controlling/limiting the growth of weeds and algae. That's nature's restorative way.

"What John is doing is repairing the broken 'parts' by restoring dissolved oxygen to the lake bottom. When dissolved oxygen is restored, aerobic bacteria are also restored, thereby restoring the lake's inherent ability to process nutrients and sustain itself in the face of ongoing nutrient pollution. By restoring the broken microbiological parts, he's restoring balance to the natural and interdependent web of microbiotic relationships that constitute a healthy eco-system.

"We may scratch our head and wonder, 'What does restoring a lake have to do with justice?' If 'justice' for a lake means returning it back to the healthy condition it was in prior to the violation of nutrient overloading by human behavior, then justice for human beings means returning individuals to a healthy condition intended by nature.

"If restoration is the ultimate act of justice for the lake, I believe the same is true for a human being. If justice for a lake (or any natural environment) requires giving that lake what it needs to recover and heal, then authentic justice for people (and communities) requires giving them what they need to recover and heal.

"Treating the symptoms by dumping poison into the lake will not restore the lake. In fact, it'll make it worse. You have to get oxygen to the bottom where the problem is. The same is true in the case of a human being who may be suffering from unresolved physical, emotional, and psychological traumas. With humans, the toxic sediment is the memorialization of the trauma hardwired into the subconscious. Punishing them only compounds that trauma."

Lessons

"What does John's approach teach us about restoration? First, *to restore is to return something (or someone) to an ideal, original, or intended condition.* With a lake, the ideal condition is the condition the lake was in before humans polluted it. The work of lake restoration requires repairing the ecosystem's ability to process nutrients. So fundamentally, to restore is to *repair*.

"Second, and this is critical to an understanding of restorative justice and human restoration, restoration assumes that if a broken part is part of a larger whole, or system, the system is also not functioning as it could or should. The contribution the broken part is designed to make to the system is missing. In essence, the relationship between a broken part and the larger organism is 'not right,' not what it could or should be.

"Restoration, therefore, emphasizes *relationship* restoration, assuming that if you repair the broken part (e.g., dissolved oxygen), you will also restore the relationship between the part and the system. Reciprocity will be restored. In the case of lakes, what is broken or missing is dissolved oxygen at the lake bottom. When dissolved oxygen levels are restored, all the relationships that constitute a lake's ecosystem will begin to function as nature intended.

"Third, because restoration recognizes the role a broken part plays in the demise of a larger system, restoration also emphasizes *interdependence*. The health and well-being of the system is dependent upon the health and contribution of each part. Logically, if you restore each and all of the parts, you'll restore the inherent relationships between them, and eventually, the larger system. You'll restore interdependence between the parts.

"Fourth, in recognizing and emphasizing interdependence, the process of restoration accomplishes *reintegration*. As a damaged part is repaired and its relationship to the larger system restored, the part is reintegrated back into the system. The part is returned to the system as an integral, contributing, and therefore necessary part of a healthy, fully functioning whole."

> • **Restoration requires repairing the broken parts.**
>
> • **Comprehensive repair restores relationships.**
>
> • **Complete restoration accomplishes reintegration and reestablishes interdependence.**
>
> • **Restoration results in the return of a system to an ideal or originally intended condition—a fully functioning whole.**
>
> • **Restoration requires restoring an ecosystem's capacity to continually restore itself.**

"Poisoning the lake is really a human-centric or ego-centric solution. People want the weeds and algae gone—immediately. A clean, clear lake is good for property values, recreation, and 'shore appeal.' The priority is on the human experience of the lake. The potentially irreparable harm to the ecosystem is a secondary consideration (for most).

"John's approach is what I would call 'lake-centric' or 'eco-centric.' His method places the health of the ecosystem/lake as the primary concern. He's saving the lake for the lake's sake.

"Symbolically, the lake is the survivor of environmentally destructive human behavior. Restorative environmental justice places the needs of the ecosystem first."

Cross-Cultural Compassion: When Mothers Meet

"I want to share another story with you that I think illustrates both moral reimagining and interdependence.

"Every day for the past year, Rhonda Smith (40) came home to eat lunch with her husband, who was battling cancer. Coming home for lunch was an opportunity for her to connect with him and provide care. When her husband passed, she continued her daily ritual of coming home for lunch. Often, she would use this time to grieve.

"Rhonda and her daughter, Tiffany, were doing the best they could to support each other in their great loss. 'He was our rock,' both would say. Tiffany was in her last year of high school and looking forward to fulfilling her father's dream of entering college.

"Just down the street from Rhonda and Tiffany's house lived Tina Romero (36), her two young boys (4-year-old twins), and teenage daughter, Maria (16). Tina had also experienced the loss of her husband in the last year. Her husband went to work at his construction job one day, and never came back. He was an abusive man and before he left, he took what little money the family had out of the bank. Tina found out a month later that her husband had returned to Mexico, abandoning his family with no intention of returning.

"His abandonment resulted in extreme financial hardship for Tina and her children. She had to rely on the charity of friends and her church to make ends meet and was working nights as an office cleaner. She relied on Maria to come straight home from school each day to take care of her brothers.

"Rhonda's and Tina's worlds converged one day when Rhonda came home during her lunch break. The minute she stepped into her house, she sensed 'something was not right.' The house was cold. At first, she thought the heater had stopped working. Then she thought maybe a window had been left open. Then, she heard what sounded like someone upstairs. She knew her daughter, Tiffany, was still at school. Rhonda quietly closed the door, went to a neighbor's house, and called 911.

"Moments later, two police cars arrived with four officers. Two went to the back of the house, and two entered through the front door with guns drawn. As they entered, they called out, 'Police department!' At that moment, the two officers at the back of the house observed a young woman exiting through a window with a backpack. It was Maria.

"As the police handcuffed Maria and placed her in the back of the patrol car, Rhonda recognized her. She told the officer, 'She lives down the street.'

"Maria was charged with breaking and entering—a felony. Under juvenile criminal law, she was facing fines, restitution, detention, probation, counseling, and a record. When Maria and her mother went before the judge, he referred Maria's case to restorative justice because this was Maria's first offense, she admitted to what she had done, and in the judge's estimation, prosecuting Maria and punishing her with fines and detention would cause undue hardship on her mother. The judge was giving Maria a chance.

"However, whether Maria would have that chance also depended on the willingness of Rhonda to meet with Maria and her mother. Understandably, oftentimes, survivors have no desire to meet the person(s) who has offended them. Meeting face-to-face with the offender can retraumatize the person who was harmed.

"In this case, Rhonda (and her daughter, Tiffany) agreed to meet for two important reasons that survivors often express. First, they wanted to understand why she had broken into *their* home. "Why us?" Second, they wanted Maria to understand how what she did had impacted them.

"After meeting with both Rhonda and Tiffany, it was Tiffany who was the most traumatized. She was understandably angry and felt 'completely violated' that someone who lived in her neighborhood, and knew her, would break into their home, rummage through her closet and dresser, and steal the Walkman her father had given her. She wanted to make sure Maria understood how violated she felt. Rhonda wanted to know why Maria did what she did—'What were you thinking?'

"When I met with Tina and Maria, Tina explained that she felt betrayed and ashamed of what Maria did. 'Didn't she understand how hard it was just to get by?' Tina was also consumed with a traumatizing fear that Maria's crime risked Tina being deported. 'What would happen to my children?' She was also very angry at the example Maria was setting for her younger brothers. Tina explained (pleaded, really) that 'this is not who we are.' I could tell she had not slept for days.

"Maria was terrified of meeting Rhonda and Tiffany (and the officer). She was afraid of their anger, afraid that her mother would be deported, ashamed to admit what she did, and asked me if there was a chance that she would be arrested again.

"Three weeks after the break-in, Rhonda and Tiffany, Maria and her mother, Tina, the arresting police officer, a Spanish interpreter, a victim's advocate for Tiffany and Rhonda, my co-facilitator, and I all convened in a circle. After explaining the agenda for the meeting, I asked Maria to tell us exactly what she did.

"She explained that she was coming home from school and when she passed by Rhonda and Tiffany's house, she 'just wanted to see' what the inside of the house looked like.

"I asked Maria, 'Did you know who Rhonda and Tiffany were?'

"She replied, 'I knew who Tiffany was from school. I knew she lived there.'

"Maria explained that she knew they weren't home and so she went to the back of the house to look through one of the windows. When she discovered that the window wasn't locked, she slid it open and crawled through it into the house.

"I asked her, 'Right when you saw that the window was open, did you think that what you were doing was wrong or that it was against the law?' I had asked her to think about this question when I met with her before we convened in the circle.

"She replied, 'I knew I was doing something bad. I didn't mean to hurt anybody.'

"I pressed her. 'So even though you had the thought that you were doing something wrong, you decided to go ahead and crawl through the window?'

"She said, 'I didn't think anyone would know.'

"I asked her, 'So, you didn't think you would get caught?'

"'I didn't think anyone was watching. I was just going to look around. I wasn't going to steal anything,' she repeated.

"I asked her, 'After you crawled through the window, what did you do?'

"She explained, 'I just started looking around at all the nice furniture. Then I went upstairs and looked in the bedrooms. I saw that Tiffany had a lot of nice things.'

"I pressed her again. 'What made you decide to take some of her things?'

"'I wasn't going to take anything. When I heard someone come in the front door. I just kind of freaked out and started stuffing things into the backpack,' she said.

"'Maria, that sounds a bit like an excuse. Are you saying that you would not have taken anything if someone—Rhonda—hadn't come home right then? I'm having a hard time believing that,' I said. 'I mean, if you didn't plan to steal anything, why did you all of a sudden start stuffing things into the backpack? Why didn't you just try to sneak back out through the window?' I gently pressed.

"'I didn't mean to steal anything when I snuck into the house. I swear! I don't know why I started stealing things,' she said. When she said this, she started to cry. 'I'm really sorry. I did a very bad thing,' she added."

Quick Reflection

I said to the group, "It's been my experience that in moments like this, when real and raw feelings begin to surface, the story of what happened fades, and the felt facts of the human experience of what happened emerge. There is a palpable shift that happens in the atmosphere of the circle.

"Facilitators often describe this moment as 'a drop from the head to the heart,' when the exposure of someone's pain and remorse redirects the focus of others from needing to know the details of what happened, and toward the human experience of what happened. It is as if the undeniable reality of emotional and psychological pain connects people, and displaces for a brief moment, the importance of needing to know why.

"However, it is the responsibility of the facilitator to not let the expression of remorse or feelings of offender guilt in any way distract or divert attention away from the victim's experience. If this happens, the circle becomes about the offender's experience, and not the pain and suffering of the victim. This can lead to revictimization and retraumatizing."

Back to the Encounter

"I thanked Maria for being honest and vulnerable. I turned to Tiffany.

"'Tiffany, would you be willing to share how what Maria did impacted you?' I asked. I had helped Tiffany prepare for this in my earlier conversation with her and Rhonda.

"Tiffany began, 'I need you to know how violated I felt when I found out that you had gone through my things. When I went to my room and saw that you went through my closet, dresser drawers, and desk, I was outraged. I have never felt so violated in my life. To imagine someone that you don't know rummaging through my personal possessions is traumatizing.

"'But you knew who I was. You knew that was my stuff. And honestly, I don't believe that you didn't plan on stealing anything. I just don't believe it. You may not have thought it was a big deal or that I wouldn't care because I have nice things—but it *is* a big deal! You did this to me.

"'But what hurt me the most was that you took my Walkman. My dad gave me that Walkman just before he died. I don't know that I can ever forgive you for that. I'm really angry. And the fact that you live down the street from me and we go to the same school really bothers me. I mean, am I going to have to look over my shoulder at school? Are you going to get your friends to gang up on me? I'm sorry, but I'm really pissed off.'

"I let several moments go by before I said anything. I looked around the circle. Rhonda and the victim advocate both put their arms around Tiffany, who began to sob. Rhonda had tears streaming down her face. The officer too was visibly moved. He had removed his glasses and was rubbing his eyes.

"Maria sat completely motionless, staring down at the floor in front of her. Tina was looking straight at Tiffany and Rhonda, and tears were streaming down her face as well. But my sense was that her tears were coming not from a place of shame, but sorrow and empathy for Tiffany as perhaps only another mother can feel. Her tears started when Tiffany mentioned her father.

"Finally, I took a deep breath and spoke to Tiffany.

"'We can all see how what happened, what Maria did, was traumatic for you, Tiffany. I want to thank you for being willing to come here and express how you were impacted by this. It takes a lot of courage.'

"I turned next to Maria. 'Maria, I'm wondering if there is anything you would like to say to Tiffany.'

"After a moment, Maria looked up and said, 'I am sorry for what I did. I hope that you can forgive me sometime. My friends won't bother you because I don't really have any friends anyway. And I would never say anything bad about you if I did.'

"Tiffany took a breath, sat up straight, and said, "I believe that you are sorry. And I probably would not feel so devastated by what you did if it wasn't for losing my father.'

"I turned to Tina next. 'Ms. Romero, would you be willing to share how what Maria did has impacted you?'

"Tina took a deep breath and began. 'When the officer came to our house and I saw Maria in the back of the car, I thought maybe somebody had done something to her. The girls at school have been really mean to her since my husband left us. But when the policeman told me she was caught breaking into a house, I couldn't believe it. I thought, "How could she do this?" I was afraid that I would be arrested too and sent back to Mexico, and I thought, "What would happen to my children?" I thought Maria would go to jail.'

"She continued. 'I blame myself for this. Maria and I don't see each other a lot now that I go to work right when she gets home from school. I need her to take care of her brothers so I can go to work. And I work on the weekends too. She's had to help me too much.

"'I am ashamed of what she did. I'll do whatever I can to repay you for what she stole. I'm sorry you lost your father (to Tiffany) and your husband (to Rhonda). I'm just so sorry,' she concluded.

"The officer added, 'We'll return your Walkman and anything else that was stolen, Tiffany. We just need to wait and see what the judge decides to do. But you will get your things back.'

"He then turned to Ms. Romero. 'Ms. Romero, our policy is to not contact Immigration unless the person who committed the crime is here illegally.'

"I turned next to Rhonda. 'Would you be willing to share how what happened has affected you?'

"Rhonda replied, 'First, I have a question for Maria. 'Did you know that my husband, Tiffany's father, had died before you broke into our house?'

"Maria responded, 'No.'

"Rhonda asked, 'If you had known, would you still have broken into our house?'

"Maria responded, 'No. I never would have had done that.'

"Rhonda continued. 'I need you to know that when I came home and heard you upstairs, I was really scared. I thought of my husband and how he wasn't there to protect Tiffany and me. When the police came and caught you crawling out of our window, I felt so unsafe in my own home.

"'Like Tiffany, I felt so violated that someone would do this to us, and I wondered if you did this because you knew my husband had died. I believe you when you say you didn't know, but I want you to know how terrifying it was for us what you did. Breaking into our home, for whatever reason, was an invasion of the one place where Tiffany and I feel safe.

"'But I also want you to know that we are good people. My husband was a very kind man. If he were here, he would not want to see you go to jail. He would forgive you, but he would want you to learn from this and use it to become a better person.'

"When Rhonda said this, Maria began to cry.

" 'I want to ask you, what have you learned from this?' Rhonda asked.

"After a moment, Maria replied, 'What I did really hurt you and your daughter.'

" 'Yes,' Rhonda replied. 'Who else did you hurt?'

" 'My mother,' replied Maria.

" 'Yes,' replied Rhonda. 'Who else?'

" 'My brothers,' said Maria.

" 'Yes,' said Rhonda. 'I bet they were scared when they saw you in the police car. Who else did you hurt?'

" 'I don't know,' said Maria. 'The police?'

" 'Yourself, Maria. You hurt yourself,' Rhonda said. 'Have you thought about what would happen if you got a criminal record and had to go to juvenile detention? You would have a very hard time getting any kind of a job, and you probably wouldn't be able to finish school. And what would your mother do?

" 'Maria, I know that you too have lost your father, and I'm sorry for you and your mother. I understand how hard that is. I understand how painful and scary that is. But I also see how strong your mother is. And I also see how strong you can be by coming home from school to take care of your brothers. That takes a lot of courage.'

"Maria was looking down.

" 'Maria, can you look at me?' asked Rhonda. Maria looked up at Rhonda.

" 'Maria, I forgive you. You made a very poor choice that hurt people, but I forgive you,' said Rhonda. 'And I want to see you use this experience to make some changes.' "

Repair

"We turned next to figuring out what Maria needed to do to repair the harm she had caused to Rhonda, Tiffany, and her mother. We created a 'Reparative Agreement.' The Reparative Agreement is essentially a contract between the offender and the restorative justice program that serves as a representative of the court.

"If the offender completes the items/actions stipulated on the contract, the judge takes that completion into consideration when determining what to do with the offender's case. If the offender completes the contract, their case is typically suspended for a year, and usually dismissed. If offenders don't complete the contract, the case proceeds through conventional prosecution and punishment.

"In typical fashion, those who were harmed determine what they need the offender to do to repair the harm to them. In addition, because the larger community is also considered as a 'harmed entity,' the offender is required to perform some type of community service.

"With the exception of the officer (who received a call and had to leave), I asked everyone in our circle to suggest things that Maria could do to make things right.

"I started with Tiffany. She said that she didn't need Maria to do anything. She said that more than anything (in addition to the return of her things), she wanted Maria to understand how angry she was and 'don't expect me to be all friendly when we see each other at school.'

"I turned next to Tina, who said to Tiffany and Rhonda, 'I need you to know how sorry I am that Maria did this.' To Maria, she said, 'I need you to never do anything like this ever again. I need you to take responsibility for how scared your little brothers are that you could be put in jail. I need you to set a better example for them. I also need you to always come straight home from school and help me.'

"Finally, we came to Rhonda. I asked her, 'What do you think needs to happen to make things right?'

"She said, 'I think "making things right," to use your term, goes beyond Maria needing to do anything to repair any harm that happened to us. I think the real repair needs to happen for her and Tina. We didn't talk about it, but Tina's husband, I think, is the real offender here. Ms. Romero, Will shared with me that he abandoned you and your kids a few months ago. I would like to see what we can do to help you and Maria.'

"'Well,' I said, 'whatever we all decide needs to be measurable. In other words, we need to come up with three to five actions that Maria can take within a certain amount of time, which can be put into her contract. The courts will need to see this. But we get to decide—including Maria and Tina, what those five actions are.'"

"I continued, 'One way to think about this is short-term and long-term. What are some actions that can be taken to make things right in the short-term, and what are some actions that can be taken to make things right in the long-term, over time?'

"I added, 'Making things right is not only about repair, but also about meeting needs. So, we might ask ourselves, 'What are some needs, that if met, will ensure meaningful change?'"

The Agreement

"Our discussion lasted about thirty minutes. The following needs were identified, and concrete actions put into the agreement to meet those needs.

"First, both Rhonda and Tina agreed that one of the reasons why Maria broke into Rhonda and Tiffany's house (and not someone else's) was because she wanted what she thought they had: prosperity, security, and success. Rhonda suggested, and Tina agreed, that Maria needed to set some goals and a plan to meet those goals.

"Rhonda asked Maria, 'Do you have any desire to go to college?'"

I explained to our discussion group, "Because part of my job as a facilitator is to discover any positive attributes an offender might have that could be built upon, I offered that 'Maria was making above average grades at her high school.' It just so happened that Rhonda worked for the local community college as an administrator.

"She suggested that Maria speak with an advisor at the college to determine what grades she would need to get to be accepted. She also suggested that there were financial aid programs and scholarships that Maria and Tina could take advantage of.

"The agreement stipulated that:

- Maria would meet with an advisor the following week. Rhonda agreed to attend that meeting to support Maria.
- Rhonda agreed to help Maria find a tutor who would work with her once a week to help her raise her grades. Rhonda offered to pay for the tutor.

"Second, Tina needed a plan to become a naturalized citizen and ensure that she wouldn't be deported.

- Rhonda agreed to put Tina in touch with someone Rhonda knew, who could guide her in this process.
- Rhonda agreed to pay the initial application fee.

"Third, to enable Maria to meet each week with a tutor, Rhonda offered to watch the boys at her house for two hours each week.

"Fourth, Maria and Tina agreed to attend family counseling offered by the county. I agreed to make the initial call to the agency and provide the contact information to Tina. The agency had child care on site. Maria and Tina agreed to attend counseling once a week on the weekend when Tina was not working.

"Lastly, I agreed to put Tina in touch with a battered women's outreach program I had previous experience with, to apply for emergency financial assistance.

"Six months later, I checked in with both Rhonda and Tina. The agreement was being fulfilled."

Group Reflection

I asked our group, "After hearing about these two cases, what came up for you?"

Aaron replied, "In the first case, John was taking an Indigenous approach to restoration. He was essentially asking the lake what it needed, and the lake was answering. That seems like such an obvious first step, but I also think it demonstrates a type of humility."

"Say more about that?" I asked.

"Well, he tried the conventional approach, which was to poison the weeds but when that didn't work for the good of the lake, he was humble enough to actually allow the lake to speak for itself and then give the lake what it needs to restore itself. I can see why you chose this case to explain how an ecosystem is an original model for the restorative process.

"He was essentially discovering the S.H.A.R.E. process organically. The lake spoke its biological truth. He identified the impact, recognized the core need for dissolved oxygen, and then enacted a plan of restorative action. He was also taking a whole-lake approach. I can see why you emphasize the need for programming in a workplace or school. I get the whole-workplace or whole-school concept. This is exactly what I try to get communities to see when they're facing an environmental degradation," said Aaron.

"I think he's also facilitating a restoration of the relationship between the lake community and the lake through education," I said.

"What about the second case?" I asked. "What do you think about this concept of moral reimagining?"

Melissa spoke. "Once again, I'm blown away. I know that you're selecting cases that are exemplary, but these examples are inspiring. The word that comes up for me is mercy. Rhonda was merciful. I think that's probably one of the most powerful moral expressions we can have as human beings. And it wasn't just mercy. It was a deep empathy and compassion," she said.

"Compassion in action," agreed Kris.

"Yeah. And compassion that arose out of the circumstances of Maria and her mother. It was a recognition of their shared losses. Rhonda lost her husband. Maria's mother lost hers. Both daughters lost their fathers. That acknowledgment opened the possibility for empathy to happen. What would've happened if this conversation hadn't happened?" asked Melissa.

"Think about John's work with lakes. He's acting out of a deep sense of compassion for the lake itself," I said. "Think about how restorative practices in schools and workplaces would help not only systematizing this type of accountability but also empathy, compassion, and understanding of human imperfection. We are conditioned to focus so heavily on the harmdoing and its impact that we miss the opportunity for teaching about the value of mercy," I added.

"If you put a restorative program and its practices in either schools or workplaces, you're giving people a chance to experience the convergence of accountability with empathy and mercy."

Joan spoke next. "I thought of the quote you gave us from Darcia Narvaez about how culture and media shape the moral imagination of children. I think about the images of children and mothers being separated at the border and put in cages. Think about how those images shape the way our children view the world and society. I see what you're saying now about how a restorative process is type of moral reimagining. I imagine what would happen if these conversations were happening in our school.

"We never talk about mercy. We give lip service to the virtues of empathy and respect. We talk about it, but we don't do it. We also talk about diversity and inclusion, but we don't recruit children of color or faculty of color. In truth, I feel shame about this."

"I see this as a case of moral reimagining happening through cross-cultural restorative communication," said Devonte. "I'm starting to sound like you. I'd like to use this case in my class to teach about immigration and social justice."

"Barb, what do you think?" I asked.

"I knew you were going to ask me to chime in. I want to find Maria's father, sit his ass down in a circle of mothers, and make him morally reimagine himself!" she said.

Hearty laughter.

"Brad, what do you think?" I asked.

Brad replied, "I see now why the title for our conversation is 'the restoration of meaning and mattering' and why you asked the question 'who or what decides?' Like all of us, I was deeply moved by this story. In this case, the restorative conversation enabled these women and their daughters to matter.

"To use your words, the meaning of the incident, the break-in, was reconstituted by the interaction, by the process. It shifted from being just 'a crime' to an opportunity for a heartfelt encounter. I think the depth of that heartfelt experience is what makes this approach extraordinary. From a spiritual perspective, it's as if whatever God or a Higher Power is, was given an opportunity to become manifest organically or holistically," he said.

"That's an interesting observation. The restoration of a person's spirit is a subject we will explore in the rest of our conversations," I said.

Summary

In this eighth discussion, we started with the question, "Why bother with restoration when any singular restorative action seems so infinitesimal in the face of apparently insurmountable social and environmental crises?"

Returning to the parable of the little girl on the beach, for her, returning even one starfish to the ocean mattered not only to that particular starfish, but also to the entire tidal ecosystem. Concurrently, her actions were not only meaningful to the ecosystem, but also for her on a personal level.

She recognized each starfish as an integral member of a larger system. Simultaneously, returning each starfish was a demonstration of her own membership and participation in that larger ecosystem. She too was an integral member and, as such, felt compelled to contribute.

That sense of responsibility contested the old man's (and perhaps our own) complacency and cynicism—why bother? That thought never entered the little girl's mind. For her, taking responsibility was just the right, or moral, thing to do in that circumstance.

Her example led us into a discussion about the concept of "moral imagination"—a possibility for discovering and sensing what is the right or necessary action to take to restore relationships. That possibility emerges or presents itself only through the context of the circumstance, and our engagement and interaction with those who are suffering as the result of an incident. In essence, we might not know what the right/moral response is in any given situation unless and until we engage and interact with each other.

As we saw in the case of Rhonda and her daughter, Tina, and Maria, the "right or correct" response to the incident emerged when each expressed and recognized not only the harm caused, but also the personal impact. The restorative process facilitated that discovery, but also presented the opportunity for empathy to be expressed. It was that empathy that motivated imagining "the right thing to do" in that situation—if restoration was in fact the goal.

Both the parable of the little girl and the case of the mothers and daughters also demonstrated a type of Indigenous wisdom about the nature and inescapable reality of interdependence. Though I didn't mention this in our discussion, I was reminded of the statement made by Chief Justice Robert Yazzie in an earlier discussion about restorative justice: "It doesn't matter if I caused the harm, I am responsible for repairing it."

The little girl didn't cause the starfish to be stranded, but she felt responsible for restoring them back to the ocean. Rhonda didn't cause the harm Tina had experienced from her husband abandoning them, but she felt compelled to address it by supporting Tina to get assistance in becoming a naturalized citizen and securing a tutor for Maria. The possibility for that happening would not have happened had this encounter and discussion not occurred.

Lastly, we looked to John Tucci's work with restoring freshwater lakes and reservoirs as an example of the pragmatism of restoration with regard to the recognition of interdependence. Recognizing the interrelatedness of integral parts which constitute a lake ecosystem, John chose to contest the norm of treating the symptoms of lake decline by poisoning the weeds. Instead, he searched for the underlying causes of eutrophication, discovered a critical integral and missing part (dissolved oxygen), and developed a technology to restore dissolved oxygen to the lake ecosystem.

As an example of a type of Indigenous wisdom, he asked the lake what it needed, and the lake responded. This took humility. Simply put, he not only didn't cause the problem, but he also took actions that demonstrated a sense of moral responsibility and compassion for the well-being of all lakes. He did the "one small thing" that would impact a much larger problem of ecosystem deterioration. He is restoring each lake's inherent capacity to continuously restore itself. In essence, he is "restoring restorativity." He is restoring the larger problem of North American lake decline, one lake at a time.

To me, that is the most eloquent example of restoration. But how do you restore an individual's inherent capacity to continuously restore themselves? Is that even possible?

CHAPTER NINE
Restoration as Realization

After a first generation of survivors experiences trauma, they are able to transfer their trauma to their children and further generations of off-spring via complex post-traumatic stress disorder mechanisms.[1]

Freedom is what you do with what's been done to you.
—Jean-Paul Sartre

When our group reconvened for the second-to-last discussion, I explained that in these last two discussions, we'd be looking more closely at trauma from the perspective of restoration.

"At the beginning of our discussions, I suggested that looking through the lens of restoration can take us as deep and far back in time as we're willing to go. Because restoration begins with an incident where harm happened to people and relationships, initiates a search for the underlying reasons that led to why something that happened such as a violation, identifies and acknowledges what the negative (life-destructive) impacts were, and what we might do to repair, heal, and move forward with a new awareness—it is uniquely qualified as a way to understand relational trauma.

"This includes individual or personal trauma, and both intergenerational and transgenerational trauma. Inasmuch as restoration is a frame or lens, if trauma is an underlying issue, how might restoration work to address it?

"Put another way, 'How does what happened back then, maybe generations ago, continue to harm us now, and continue to degrade our relationships?' Once we understand that, we're confronted with the question, 'What are we going to do about it?' Where does our responsibility for what happened back then begin, and end? Are we responsible for the harm our ancestors caused? What if that harm continues across generations? Shouldn't we at least know? What does this knowledge give us? More importantly, what are the consequences of not knowing?

"I also suggested at the beginning of our discussion that looking through the restorative lens is risky because it may reveal things about ourselves, our families, and our inherited cultural history that we may not want to see.

"Restoration reveals the ugliness, the abuse, the brutality of racism and discrimination, the hatred and violence, the atrocities, and in sum, the dark side of our ancestors that remains unresolved in ourselves today. But restoration also gives us a way forward. At the very least, it gives us a way to understand, and hopefully accept, how things that happened long ago continue to negatively impact us now.

"Kris, you asked me, 'How can the restorative process work on a personal level?' Inasmuch as I've attempted in our group discussions to explore the restorative paradigm, its practices, and provide examples of how it works in various *social* contexts, this last question challenged me. Should I share my own radically imperfect journey with personal and familial restoration?

"At first, doing so seemed like a big risk. I had to wrestle with the voice that said, 'It wasn't that bad. It happened a long time ago. Get over it; you're being self-indulgent," or even worse, 'Who cares?' "

Brad interjected, "If any of us do that, if we let that voice be the final say, then whatever trauma we've experienced will have won. And isn't the whole point of the restorative process to speak our truth? The deeper and broader truth is that if our story helps even one other person to recover from their own, then what we went through has a purpose and meaning beyond our own experience. Its purpose is bigger than us. This is especially true in recovery from drug and alcohol abuse."

He continued, "And to be blunt about it, I don't fully trust someone telling me how to do something unless they've done it themselves. If they haven't done it, it's just a theory. When someone has been where we have been, and has experienced what we have experienced, they speak our language of adversity and suffering. They understand.

"They have access to us on a much deeper and personal level than someone who dictates from a podium, an altar, or from behind a desk saying, 'Do it like this.' For me, it's a matter of trust. This reminds me of a statement Ghandi once made that 'to believe in something, and not to live it, is dishonest,' " said Brad.

Barb added, "Totally agree. I need to see how to do something from someone who has actually done it. To me, that's where authentic expertise comes from. Don't tell me about it. Show me how you did it. I learned to be a nurse from other nurses."

Kris added, "What motivated you to use the restorative process on yourself?"

I replied, "Let me give you some background first, and then I'll explain how I pursued restoration on a personal level to conduct what I refer to as 'trauma-tracking.' Trauma-tracking is where you trace the history of traumatic experiences. You look at your own first, and then backtrack through your immediate family's experiences, back through the generations, and potentially its ancestral origins. It's a process of detective awakening."

"This is kind of like what we did with the origins of retribution," commented Aaron. "We tracked the retributive mindset all the way back to its mythic origins."

"Yes, and tried to understand how that paradigm remains, even on a personal level," I replied.

Melissa asked, "With trauma-tracking, you're talking about intergenerational trauma?"

"Yes," I replied. "And transgenerational trauma. Let me provide some descriptions of trauma before I launch into my own story."

Individual Trauma

"The determination of whether an event/incident/injury is traumatic is dependent upon the individual's subjective experience of the event and/or conditions. What may be traumatic to one person may not be for another. Trauma by definition is an experience that overwhelms our capacity to cope on a physical/material, emotional, psychological, spiritual, and interpersonal relationship level. This is true for individuals, families, and communities.

"Trauma can be understood as a single event, series of events, or consistent and persistent experiences of overwhelming encounter(s). It can be impersonal (not intentional, e.g., natural disaster) or personal (intentionally committed by one/others to harm the individual(s)).

"Neuroscience tells us that trauma impacts, alters, diminishes, and often degrades healthy neurological brain chemistry and cognitive as well as social-emotional function. In the case of childhood trauma, it inhibits neurological development.[2]

Relational Interpersonal Trauma

"The study of relational trauma took a major leap forward with the CDC–Kaiser Permanente ACE study (Adverse Childhood Experience) conducted between 1995 and 1997.[3] This groundbreaking study concluded that adverse/traumatic childhood experiences (neglect, abuse, etc.) lead to the adult onset of chronic diseases, depression and other mental illness, violence and being a victim of violence, incarceration, etc.

"Subsequent studies generated by the ACE survey concluded that relational trauma is dynamic and cumulative. That is, individuals attempting to cope with unresolved relational trauma develop destructive coping behaviors that not only compound their trauma but also result in traumatizing others in relationship with them.

"This realization influenced behavioral treatment approaches. Substance abuse, alcoholism, domestic violence, attention disorders, etc., began to be framed by professionals as symptoms of deeper issues—potentially unresolved historically based relational trauma (neglect/abuse).

"With the ACE study and increasing attention paid to the relational context of trauma, the phenomena of intergenerational and transgenerational trauma moved from the category of theory to empirical realization. We now know that unresolved trauma from previous generations gets transferred in numerous ways.

> **"Traumatic events from hundreds of years ago and those occurring in the present day affect successive generations of families and individual family members."** [4]

"The transference of historical trauma happens in a multitude of ways and on multiple levels of experience (individual/collective—internalized/external realities):

Materially: Through economic marginalization, deprivation and poverty, confiscation of homelands, property ownership, economic opportunity, and security.

Physically: Substandard health services, lack of access to health services, inadequate nutrition and education about nutrition, higher mortality rates (suicide and homicide), unmet basic health needs, lack of personal safety, domestic violence, overwhelming stress, and anxiety which degrades physical health.

Neurological & Epigenetic: Recurring incidents of trauma (neglect/abuse) and pervasive untreated PTSD disable normal brain function. The behavioral symptoms of trauma, as well as environmental conditions, influence gene expression and propensity for mental health issues (depression, aggression, dysregulation, etc.).

Psychological: Negative thought patterns, destructive cognitive patterns, abandonment, entrenched hopelessness, mindsets of futility, resentment, bitterness, fatalistic worldviews, shame-based core beliefs, denial, etc.

Emotional: Deep sorrow, unprocessed grief, anger and rage, self-hatred, despair, dissociation, etc.

Spiritual: Historical prohibition of culturally specific spiritual traditions and practices results in personal and collective disconnection from healing effects of sacred sources/beings tied to creation myths. This is especially true for Indigenous peoples. This break in relationship with culturally specific numinous sources produces existential angst and/or ontological woundedness (spiritual violation) on the personal and communal level, etc. Religion can also be traumatizing when leaders use religious authority to abuse or shame members.

Social: Social structures can induce/activate trauma when they are not trauma-informed and empathically responsive. Social services fail to recognize trauma, focus only on symptoms and not causes. Distressed families, distressed schools with trauma-uninformed staff, punitive behavior policies in schools, nonresponsive healthcare agencies, law enforcement and judicial system, discrimination by lending institutions, etc.

Cultural: When Indigenous cultural narratives that reflect positive beliefs, norms, values, and identity are replaced with popular culture and Euro-American values of consumerism and "every man for himself" paradigms, then this indoctrination and assimilation suppresses (and I would argue violates) communal identity, language, heritage, and dismisses culturally specific worldviews. Historical narratives taught in schools which cast aspersions on Indigenous people and people of color become in-substantiating within those communities. Children's perception of self and culture is distorted by white history. Simply put, history books can be traumatizing."

Devonte asked, "Can you unpack this a bit more? You're talking about colonialism?"

"Yes," I said. "I'll explain more when I get into my own story, but think about how colonialism, conquest, and enslavement, and then the continuous denial that those things actually happened, or that they were justified, led to erasing the cultural history of Indigenous ways and continue to impact successive generations."

"Holocaust deniers," said Aaron.

"Exactly. Think about how the current effort to ban books about slavery, the atrocities committed against Native peoples, and the Holocaust manifests and reifies white privilege and structural racism. This is a type of transgenerational cultural trauma," I said. "When people, white people, say that slavery benefited the enslaved, how does that impact people of color and their children?"

"It's cultural gaslighting," said Devonte.

"It is. And think about how that deceit, denial, and censoring or revisionist narratives of history become inscribed in cultural memory. It's like saying, 'What you know happened to your ancestors didn't happen,'" I said.

"And what your ancestors did wasn't that bad," added Devonte.

"Yes. What we see when we look through the restorative lens is the depth, severity, and pervasiveness of personal and collective trauma. Generationally transferred trauma becomes an entrenched/internalized cultural narrative which, in turn, becomes a self-fulfilling prophecy and which ultimately holds individuals, families, and communities hostage.

"This narrative continues when the truth of trauma is never told—when it is not named for what it is, where it comes from, why it happens, and how it gets passed down. Neither is its destructive impact on both personal and collective levels realized.

"Think about the denial that the Tulsa Race Massacre happened. Think about what it must feel like when you know your ancestors, your grandparents, were murdered because of the color of their skin. Think about how that discounting or denial continues to impact current generations," I said.

"The impact is never acknowledged because it's not taught in schools," said Devonte.

"Right. If I was teaching a history lesson about the massacre, I would follow the 5 steps. We would first be very clear about exactly what happened, the facts. Second, we would recognize all the people who were impacted—including successive generations. Third, we would discover exactly what that impact was and still is on numerous levels. This would give us the opportunity to identify the underlying racist thinking and beliefs that motivated the massacre.

"Fourth, we would ask, 'What is needed to repair this historical harm?' Lastly, we would ask, 'What responsibility needs to be taken and by whom, and what needs to be repaired?' I would then ask the class to come up with suggestions for reparative actions," I said.

"The reparative plan could be a homework assignment," said Devonte.

"At the very least, the story would've been meaningfully told. What happened and the people who experienced it will have mattered."

"People, white people, don't want that story to be told," said Devonte.

"And that's how denial and the lack of truth keeps all of us hostage—including them. If we deny what happened then, it's a short step to denying what's happening now," I said.

"Those who don't know their own history are destined to repeat it," said Aaron.

"Or continue to suffer because their history, experience, humanity, and identity are never acknowledged," I agreed.

"I want to shift us back into appreciating the intersection of restoration with personal and generational trauma. The question is, 'How can the restorative process be used to heal an individual's trauma by connecting it with intergenerational and transgenerational trauma?' Kris, you asked me what motivated me to try to understand this intersection. I'll do my best to share what happened," I said.

Background

"In 2001, I was in the beginning of a doctoral program in Communication. I was looking for a meaningful subject that I could research. I chose bullying. Actually, bullying chose me. I wanted to understand it, why it happens, what happens to victims, research how it was being addressed in schools.

"The Columbine High School shooting had happened a couple of years before and when it was suggested that the two boys who committed the atrocity might have been victims of bullying bent on retaliation—I was horrified, sickened, and outraged by what they did. If bullying played a part, it was about the entrenched insanity of toxic revenge and mental illness that bullying can cause. Like the vast majority of us who witnessed this, I asked, 'Why didn't we see this coming, and what could've been done to prevent it?' I don't mean the school itself, but societally."

"This is why you're so adamant about spotting the signs in the S.H.I.F.T. technique," commented Melissa.

"Yes. We have to spot, engage, and intervene. I reached out to Dr. Beverly Title. Dr. Title had built a nationally recognized bully-proofing program for middle schools. When I explained my interest in bullying and my academic background in Native American studies, she suggested I look into restorative justice, which at that time was a relatively unknown type of tribal justice which, as I've explained, emerged from the ceremonial peacemaking practices of Navajo people and other tribal communities. As Beverly explained, 'It's a type of justice that focuses on repair, healing, and the restoration of the survivor rather than retaliation.' This is when the light went on for me.

"After participating in that first restorative justice circle conference, I found my research site. More important, and though I didn't consciously comprehend it at the time, I found a justice I had been longing for on a personal level for my entire life—a type of justice and accountability that didn't include revenge, retaliation, and retribution.

"Two months after attending this first conference, I became certified as a restorative justice facilitator. The following year, I was hired to expand a fledgling restorative justice pilot program at the university. Working with the municipal court system, the police, university officials, and a committed community of residents we expanded this program from processing twelve cases per year to four hundred-plus. I trained a team of thirty facilitators. The program became nationally recognized, and I was nominated for a community leadership award by the university's *Institute for Ethical Civic Engagement* in recognition of that work.

"During the time of my directorship and while conducting research for the dissertation, I developed and taught a senior seminar in restorative justice for the university and taught courses in Peace and Conflict Studies and Conflict Management. I presented a workshop on gender bias at an annual International Restorative Justice Conference.

"I completed my research, finally finished the doctorate, and was asked to testify in front of the House of Representatives of Colorado in support of legislation that would establish restorative civil justice practices statewide. I was a keynote speaker at a conference on the intersection of mental health and restorative justice.

"But here's the thing. As much as I was immersing myself in the world of restorative justice, facilitating face-to-face encounters between survivors and offenders, and helping others to resolve violations peacefully, my personal life was crumbling. I was recently divorced and struggling with depression.

> **The more cases I facilitated, the more circles I sat in, the more I was confronted with how little restoration had happened in my own life.**

"Every circle, every book, every conversation reminded me of that. I was a good actor. Those that did know I was struggling didn't understand. I didn't understand either. I couldn't just fix it by changing my mind. I quit the gym. I quit mountain climbing. I quit fly fishing. The grass started to die.

"I came home after teaching one day, curled up on the floor in the fetal position. I was done, emotionally paralyzed. I couldn't see any reason to keep going with the exception of my daughter. People who suffer from depression understand this experience," I said.

"I understand it. I've struggled with depression most of my life," said Melissa.

"Me too," said Kris. "I know the fetal position well."

"I know I have too. It's like you're psychologically paralyzed," said Aaron.

"It's like you have a hole in your soul," said Brad.

"Thanks for acknowledging your own struggle," I said. "I was forty-two years old, I needed what restorative justice promises: accountability, repair, forgiveness, and healing. But in my case, and as is the case with adult survivors of childhood relational trauma, there was absolutely no possibility of confronting those who had been abusive face-to-face in a restorative justice conference—even though I had kept in constant contact with them in my head for over thirty years.

"I didn't let this deter me. I reasoned, 'Why can't the restorative process used in restorative justice be applied on a personal level?'

"As we've discussed, restoration is a logical, pragmatic process. That process is a powerful tool in helping survivors organize and address a violation in a reconstructive way that leads to restoration and closure. Even though an offender is not present—for whatever reason—doesn't mean a person can't use the process for themselves.

"Just like the restoration of a lake, the lake can be restored without the involvement of those who have polluted it. It would certainly help if those 'offenders' could be held accountable for repair, which might change their behavior, and maybe prevent them from reoffending, but the damage done can be repaired regardless.

"Applied on a personal level, if I'm a survivor, the process gives me the opportunity to recount what happened, identify specifically how I was impacted/harmed, which in turn, concretely establishes exactly what needs to be healed or repaired. I'm reminded of a powerful statement by Bessel van der Kolk, M.D., in his book *The Body Keeps Score* (2014):[5]

> **"People cannot put events behind until they are able to acknowledge what has happened and start to recognize the invisible demons they're struggling with."**

"When people ask me, 'Why go back?', I offer that it's the only way to reconcile what happened once and for all within yourself. Simply saying, 'What's done is done. Let's leave well enough alone,' only allows what happened then, to continue in a haunting loop now.

"Aaron, your recollection of Santayana's quote that 'those who don't know their own history are condemned to repeat it' is especially true for people who have suffered any type of abuse. Unaddressed trauma becomes a phantom. To slay a phantom, you have to face it. Phantoms disappear when faced. Their 'existence' and power depend on remaining hidden in the subconscious.

"Think about a child shaking with fear in bed because she thinks there's a monster under it. The parent comes in, turns the light on, looks under the bed with the child, and says, 'See ... no monster.' The tragedy with unaddressed childhood relational abuse is that there was no one there to turn the lights on and look under the bed with you.

"By making the commitment to go back and unflinchingly face what happened, you're turning the light on in yourself. You are doing the work of a warrior. You're choosing to make a stand and not be the victim anymore. It's having the courage and commitment to settle an account.

"From a restorative perspective, it's going back into the scene of a violation in order to gather experiential evidence. It's a pragmatic first step. There's a purpose to it. It's reconstructive reporting. It's not wasteful wallowing in self-pity. In fact, it's the exact opposite. It's the first step out of self-pity and into reality."

As I explained to our group, "In the majority of cases I've facilitated over the years, one of the most liberating and empowering experiences for survivors is being given the opportunity to tell their story of what happened and how it impacted them in a group of concerned others. We saw this in the case of Leo and Maria. There's a reason for this.

"When we are violated, we are overpowered—especially children. One of the immediate consequences is a loss of voice. In the terror and humiliation of a degradation, we get silenced. The story—our story—gets suppressed. We swallow it. The longer we go without speaking it out loud, the louder it gets in our subconscious, and the more it has neurological control of us.

"As I explained in one of our earlier discussions, the reason why telling our story is so important is because the human mind processes experience in terms of narrative. Narrative is the mind's continuous attempt to make sense of experience. Story is a reconstructive attempt to interpret, organize, rationalize, explain, and reason.

"If our story remains in silence, if there is no action taken in response, it remains an interior monologue. Conversely, telling our story with the intention of taking further action—to purposely explore how we were impacted and then take reparative action— enables us to effectively utilize our story in a constructive way.

"This is what psychotherapy is supposed to facilitate. In my experience, the challenge with most talk therapies is that they don't access the neurological functions engaged with our initial attempt to rationalize and make sense. At least, that's been my experience with talk therapy. The story is the beginning of the restorative process, but it is only a beginning.

"In a typical criminal justice process, the case begins with a police report. The report is a matter-of-fact, unembellished account of what happened, who was involved, and a description of what they did. Think of this as your police report. If it was in court, this would be your testimony. It helps to put what happened down on paper in concrete terms: 'This is what happened to me.' In essence, it makes it real.

"When I facilitate restorative conferences, I encourage survivors to provide a matter-of-fact account with as much detail as possible. 'Show us the documentary movie scene-by-scene.' Because in this case, we're recovering from an event that may have happened long ago, perhaps when we were children, it's important to be as detailed as possible, and account for all the times you can remember being bullied, assaulted, abused, etc. How old were you? Where did it happen? Who did it? What did they do? Were there any witnesses? What happened after? Did anyone intercede on your behalf? Who didn't intercede?"

Kris asked, "You journaled?"

"Yes. I wrote it all down," I said. "It made it real for me."

"Writing it down was restorative in itself," she added.

"Yes," I said.

The Story

"Here's my story. When I was a kid, I endured repeated and often violent bullying. It didn't just happen at one school but all through elementary, middle, and high school: both private and public. I wasn't just 'picked on.' Other boys (and girls) taunted me, called me names, made fun of the way I looked, talked, and walked, spread vicious rumors about me, threatened me, hit me, kicked me, threw rocks at me, ganged up on me, and beat me up.

"When I was nine years old, when the bullying began, my dad sat me down at the kitchen table and told me, 'You have to draw a line in the sand and if somebody crosses it, do whatever you have to do to defend yourself.' I wanted to do that, but I couldn't. It wasn't that I wasn't physically capable of defending myself because I was an athlete. I had no problem with aggression and violence on the football field. It was a sport.

"The reason I couldn't defend myself on the playground was because bullying paralyzed me psychologically and emotionally. I froze. For me, it was life or death. I couldn't understand why other kids hated me so much. I was convinced there was something fundamentally wrong with me. I was sure I was inherently bad, not likeable, not worthy. Certainly, I was a 'coward'. It wasn't until I started to apply the restorative process on a personal level that I discovered where this freeze response came from, but I'll save that for later because it involves trauma-tracking.

"In sixth grade, I developed a bad stutter. Couldn't get the words out. It's an impact and the only reason I mention it here is because it fueled further bullying. The same boys would snicker whenever I got called on in class and, of course, mimic me on the playground or in the hallways. They would mimic my walk and mimic my stuttering at the same time, and other kids thought it was hilarious. I couldn't make myself small enough.

"It got so bad in seventh grade that I switched to a public middle school in eighth grade. Here I became the target of a gang of three boys whose methods were more violent. They pushed me into lockers, spit on me, threw rocks, and one day jumped me in an alley and hit me in the back of the head with a brick.

"Nowadays, of course, this might be reported, and criminal charges filed. Back then, telling anyone about what was happening was out of the question. I was too afraid of more severe retaliation, and too ashamed to admit I was afraid.

"And so, I left again. Like I mentioned earlier, I went to a boys' Catholic boarding school in another state. All I wanted to do was play sports and study. I was a good enough student when I applied myself, and I was a good football and basketball player.

"My brother was a football coach. I knew how to be aggressive. I knew how to block, hit, and tackle. Like I said, this kind of physical violence I could handle. But on the first day of football tryouts, a boy who I had never met came to me and said, 'You're a faggot and you're not going to be on this team.'

"On the field that day during a drill called 'bull in the ring,' I held my own against this boy. I hit him as hard as he hit me. I think he was surprised. The next day, another boy (who I had never met but was also on the football team) confronted me in the hall and said, 'I heard you wanted to kick my ass.' I quit the football team.

"For the next four years, I endured more of the same, but it wasn't only me. I remember countless rat-tail towel fights in the showers. The weakest boys got it the worst. The weakest boys always got the worst of all the bullying, and it was systemic. Not once did I ever even hear the word *bullying* mentioned.

"I received another moniker for my funny walk, 'cobber.' That became my nickname, and it wasn't used in any endearing way. Boys would imitate my walk in the dining hall, in the school halls, wherever there was an audience. One night I arrived back at my room from a basketball game in another town. It was about 2:00 a.m. I walked into the room, opened the closet door, and taped on the mirror was a note that read, 'Hey cobber … how does it feel to go 0/13? You suck!' The games were always broadcast on the local radio station and piped through the loudspeakers at the school. It was the worst game of my high school career and the second worst night of my life at the school.

"Finally, however, I exploded with rage. The priests came running down the hall and forced their way into the room. 'What's your problem?!' The incident was never resolved, never even addressed. But I was left alone, finally.

"My senior year the basketball team won our league title. During warmups for the league championship game, a group of students in the stands began chanting, 'Pretty boy, pretty boy.' And just like I had always done, I took it in. This time, however, I channeled the rage into my highest scoring game of the season. This was a prophetic 'I'll show you' moment, as I realized years later.

"When I graduated from high school, I thought it was over; something that happened and wouldn't happen again. I was wrong. The bullying was now inside of me. It was a festering existential psychic wound that impacted me most of my adult life. It poisoned my self-esteem, filled me with shame and rage, infected my relationships, degraded my physical health, pretty much ruined a promising acting career, and damn near killed me. I couldn't let it go because what happened back then wouldn't let me go. It had never been reconciled.

"It wasn't over. All those incidents, all those times of being bullied, punched in the face, kicked, spit on, hit by rocks, taunted, teased, threatened, chased, and excluded, were all inside of me. What I couldn't have known then was how deeply scarred bullying left me, and how destructively it impacted my relationship with myself, other people, and life itself."

"My God, Will," said Aaron.

"Yeah. It happened. But here's the thing. Inasmuch as this is what happened to me, my story is not exceptional. So, on a certain level, like Brad said, we have to think about all the children who experience this every day. Why do you think kids harm themselves, take their own lives, or bring guns to school? It's the pain of humiliation and for some, the inward rage of self-hatred and self-harming, and for others, the outward rage of retaliation," I said. "Think about the exponential damage of cyberbullying."

Barb said, "This really pisses me off. I was bullied for being different, for being gay. I couldn't wait to get the fuck out of my hometown. This makes me realize I've never really addressed it."

"I know the feeling," I said. "The problem is that we can carry that toxic crap around inside of us until we face it. That's what I tried to point out to Rick."

"Which is what you did using this process for yourself," added Kris.

"Yes. I thought I was beyond it until something triggered me and I would lash out," I said. "Inward rage became outward rage."

"Kids made fun of me for being a bookworm," said Melissa.

"This makes me think that we need to address bullying in our recovery clients," said Brad.

"It can be a life-defining traumatic experience," I said. "Especially when it's chronic."

"How does this relate to generationally transferred trauma?" asked Devonte.

"Great segue. Let me keep going," I said.

How Far Back?

"I'm often asked, 'How far back do you have to go?' The short answer is, 'As far back as you can.' In my case, a nagging question always existed: Why was I so paralyzed with fear? Other boys would fight back. For me, it was a matter of life or death. Objectively speaking it wasn't, but my emotional, psychological, and nervous system response made it so. I froze.

"I never understood why I could be so physically aggressive on the football field, or so unafraid of physical violence in sports but not on the playground. Why couldn't I defend myself? Why didn't I have enough sense of self to stand up for myself and draw that proverbial line in the sand? Why was I so terrified?

"The more investigation I did into where this freeze response came from and why it was there from the very first bullying episode, the more I came to realize that this freeze response was in place long before I was bullied in school. I was predisposed to feel terrified. Why? This is when I started to look into trauma, where it was in my own family and ancestry, and how it was generationally transferred.

"Before I explain what I found, let me first explain one of the false fears of going back and facing any type of abuse in the family. The phantom. It has to do with secrecy and exposure. We believe that we owe an allegiance to never reveal the darkness of our family. We believe that if we do, we are being disloyal and violating an unspoken rule of 'keeping it in the family.' We may not even know that what happened in our family was abuse. We think 'it's just life.'

"We believe that we will do immeasurable harm to our parents, siblings, or even the 'hallowed reputation' of our long-dead ancestors if we talk about the bad stuff that happened. We believe that no matter what, we are obligated to protect the family or ancestral myth at all costs—even to the point of denying anything bad ever happened. It is as if the family is saying, 'Don't tell anyone what you found under the bed.'

"And so, we implicitly commit to take the secret to the grave. Tragically, in the case of abuse, keeping the secret puts us, and quite possibly our family, in the grave quicker. Denial is lethal.

> **"As long as you keep secrets and suppress information, you are fundamentally at war with yourself."** [6]

"Where do these beliefs come from? It's fear and perhaps shame. We might be so ashamed of what happened, or afraid of being criticized and excluded from our family, that we refuse to know about it, let alone talk about it. We are terrified of a core belief that we are fundamentally not loveable.

"We believe that our 'sins' and the sins of our ancestors are so evil that we can never be forgiven and therefore prove we are unworthy of forgiveness. The Bible says, 'Honor your mother and your father,' right? We construe this to mean, 'Thou shalt never say anything bad about what they did.' "

> **What cannot be spoken to the [m]other cannot be told to the self.**
> **—John Bowlby (1991)**

"But the Bible also says, 'Hate the sin and not the sinner.' And this holds the restorative key to unlocking the door of secrecy of our ancestral and family past. If we don't talk about the sin, the sin will continue intergenerationally. And as I came to realize, if you don't talk about the sin, you'll never be able to forgive the sinner, or perhaps ourselves. Certainly, you won't stop the pattern of abuse.

"As I've been emphasizing, the restorative response is to separate the behavior from the individual. Separate the sin from the sinner. The behavior needs to be named, confronted, and understood. Focusing on the behavior (a) permits us to name the behavior, (b) talk about how that behavior impacted us and others, and (c) enables us to understand the underlying reasons and cultural inheritances as to why the person behaved the way they did. This puts the reality of the behavior into the context of inter- and transgenerational trauma, psychological and emotional health, and not a matter of worth or moral judgment.

"When it comes to talking about family and ancestors, separating the individual from how they behaved gives us the ability to let the truth set us free with dignity and without condemnation. I've found that this strategic accountability is the ultimate act of responsibility, but also a threshold into the third stage of reintegration, which is understanding how what happened then—the motivations and the reasons—might be a part of us now. I've found that this depth of accountability is the ultimate act of empathy for ourselves, but also an opening for forgiveness which leads to liberation."

"And redemption," said Devonte.

"Yes," I said.

Going Back

"When I started this process, I drove back by my childhood house long after my parents had moved. In fact, it was almost thirty years after I had left. When I turned into the neighborhood, passed the two schools I attended, and turned onto my street, I felt a knot in my stomach. The closer I came to the house, the more tense, anxious, and heavy I became. I parked just across the street and sat there, staring at the house and the memories, not only of the neighborhood but also what happened inside the house came flooding back.

"As far back as I could remember, my mother suffered from what I would call 'fits of darkness.' Something would happen and she would get triggered, or activated, and she would lash out and become abusive, both verbally and physically. After the abuse, she became defiant, and then depressively remorseful. It was a cycle.

"And yet, she was a remarkable woman, fiercely devoted to her children. She made sure her kids had the best education, a spiritual foundation, and instilled in them a belief that they could accomplish anything they set as goals. When my brother contracted polio, she made it her mission to rehabilitate him. He ended up becoming a football and track star. Her son's polio was not going to defeat him or her.

"She was successful in the realm of public service. She ran for public office and was a secretary to the state governor. This was no small feat for a woman, let alone a Hispanic woman in the late 1950s.

"But something would happen, and it was as if something came over her, consumed her, and she became someone else. There was never any discussion about it afterward. Each member of our family dealt with it as best they could in their own way. My response was to try to immediately reconnect, attach, make her feel better, make it better. The oppressive silence would go on for days, sometimes weeks.

"The first memory I have of being the target was when I was three or four years old. She and I were the only ones home. I must have done something wrong, something to upset her, but I can't remember what that was.

"We were standing in the kitchen, and she was yelling at me. She called me 'a little piece of shit,' and grabbed me by the ear and pulled me outside on the back porch. I remember crying and pleading with her not to whip me. A common response she gave was, 'I'll give you something to cry about.'

"She pulled my pants down around my ankles and then went over to a plum tree we had and pulled a switch off of it. She came back over to me and holding my wrists together out in front of me, began whipping the back of my legs ferociously with the switch. As she switched, she raged, telling me that I 'should be ashamed of myself.'

"She switched and switched, and then threw the switch in the flower bed and walked back into the house. I didn't follow her. No doubt I was in shock. The backs of my legs were on fire. I got as far away from the house as I could. I went and hid inside the doghouse.

"This scene with the switch was repeated often. It was never done when my dad was around or my sister. When I got bigger (five or six years old), she used a belt," I said.

"The tool became a weapon," said Aaron.

"Yes. When I was ten years old, in Cub Scouts and playing little league football, there was an incident that was profound both for me and my father. My mother was the Den Mother for my Cub Scout troop. Our troop had a meeting at our house and another boy and I were goofing around and not participating in the troop meeting. This other boy followed another weaker boy home and beat him up. The mother of the victim called my mother, and my mother called the bully's mother. The other boy blamed it on me, telling her that I told him to beat up this other boy.

"My dad and I were in my dad's truck. I was dressed in my football uniform, and we were just pulling out for him to take me to practice. My mother came running around the corner of the house with a piece of lumber in her hand. She was wearing her Den Mother uniform which made her look like a police officer. She opened the door of the truck and yanked me out screaming, 'You little piece of shit. I didn't raise you to be a bully!'

"She then proceeded to beat me on the back of the legs and back with the piece of wood. She hit me so hard the board broke in half. I didn't cry. I took it in. I got back in the truck, and we drove to the field in silence. Later that day in practice, I cracked another kid's ribs on a particularly rage-filled hit. She put it on me. My dad didn't intervene. I took all this out on someone else.

"One day after school, as I approached my house, there was an ambulance parked in front. Just as I ran up to the front yard, two attendants dressed in white were wheeling my mother out on a gurney. She was strapped down and crying, pleading, 'Please don't make me go!' I rushed up to her and she cried, 'Don't let them take me!'

"They loaded her into the back of the ambulance and drove away. I can still see her tortured face through the window. My dad was standing on the front porch and when I asked him where she was going, he replied, 'She's going away to rest for a while.' Decades later, I learned that she had tried to commit suicide.

"The accounts I give above gave me as clear a picture as I could put together by going back into my immediate family. And while they may be difficult to hear about, their recall serves a valuable purpose in the process of restoration. We simply have to get what happened out and down on paper. We have to face what happened. It's the only way."

> **"While trauma keeps us dumbfounded, the path out of it is paved with words, carefully assembled, piece by piece, until the whole story can be revealed.** [7]
>
> **"Silence about trauma also leads to death—the death of the soul. Silence reinforces the godforsaken isolation of trauma."** [8]

"Retelling our story of what happened is not easy. It activates long-buried but still potent emotional responses. This is unavoidable. But let me offer some solid encouragement based on my experience in this process of restoration.

"First, what we went through, what any victim of bullying and abuse experienced, had absolutely nothing to do with who we are. The bullies and abusers did it because there's something troubling inside of them though they may never come to recognize or accept it, address it, or experience remorse in later years.

"Second, the traumatic response to the abuse—no matter how long ago it happened—can be healed once and for all. That's why I'm including this story here. There is a restorative way through this."

What's the Impact?

"As I've explained in our discussions, in the restorative process the question of impact is divided into two parts: who was impacted and how? Which question comes first depends on the context in which restoration is practiced.

"For example, in cases where the harm caused to a single survivor resulted in ancillary indirect harm to family and friends of the survivor, it's important for the offender to realize that they didn't just impact one person, but also a network of people related to the survivor. And equally, those who care about the offender are negatively impacted as well. We've talked about this consistently in our discussions, and we saw this in the Leo and Rick case.

"For our purpose here, I'm opting for understanding the impact that relational abuse has on the individual first. I do so because once we have a clear picture of how hurt we were/are, we can also understand how the harm we experienced back then has/had a profound influence in the way we relate to others, and how others relate to us.

"In a typical (secular) restorative justice conference process, 'harm' is recognized as happening on a physical/material, emotional, and psychological level of experience. Prior to the encounter between the survivor, offender, and others involved, each are asked to think about how the violation impacted them in these specific ways.

"During the actual encounter, for example, the facilitator asks each person, 'How did this affect you physically? Were you physically hurt, or did you experience any stress?' or, 'What emotions did you experience? Were you afraid or angry?' or, 'What were you thinking during, just after, and since the violation?' (e.g., anxiety, bitterness, resentment, thoughts of retaliation). This is what I did with Leo. I typically ask the offender, 'What were you thinking just before the offense? What was going through your mind?' This is what I did with Rick.

"These categories are useful in a social context of determining harm resulting from a single incident of violation, but they do not fully reveal the depth of harm that can occur with severe violations such as relentless bullying or repeated abuse. They can, however, point to deeper wounds that either occurred or were activated as a result of the violation.

"But these deeper psychological and emotional harms are not typically addressed during a conventional restorative justice encounter. If there is a clear sign that a person (either survivor or offender) is suffering from a pre-existing mental health issue that requires professional care, the reparative agreement created during the conference can include pursuing counseling, therapy, or substance abuse rehabilitation," I explained.

"This is what happened with Rick," said Brad.

"Yes," I said.

"To more precisely comprehend the harm that occurs from relational trauma such as severe bullying and abuse, we have to identify where the survivor experiences the most profound harm—*the brain*. With children, the impact is even more debilitating because the brain is just starting to develop.

"Understanding how the brain is impacted by childhood bullying and abuse opens the possibility to *repair the brain and restore the person on the deepest level*. In fact, as I experienced, if we don't repair the damage caused there, personal restoration remains elusive and incomplete. The psychological, emotional, and physical harm caused by childhood abuse and severe bullying will continue to manifest symptomatically throughout a person's life. Our spirits are broken, and it degrades our health," I said.

"Death by despair," said Brad.

"That's a powerful way to put it. When I came to realize this as I searched for the root of my own troubles, I realized that throughout my entire life, the issues I was struggling with were not a matter of character, and not circumstantial, but existed on a much deeper subconscious level. I always knew that the bullying and abuse were somehow related, I just never realized that they had impacted my neurological development.

"When I began consuming the literature on relational trauma and the brain, scientific explanations began to demystify my own challenges. As I stated previously, the bullying and abuse were 'inside of me,' and attempts to resolve it from the 'outside-in' never worked. As I explained, conventional talk therapy simply didn't work.

> **"Psychologists usually try to help people use insight and understanding to manage their behavior. However, neuroscience research shows that very few psychological problems are the result of defects in understanding; most originate in pressures from deeper regions in the brain that drive our perception and attention. When the alarm bell of the emotional brain keeps signaling that you are in danger, no amount of insight will silence it."** [9]

"It never occurred to me that what I was experiencing throughout my adult life was neurologically based. I remember sitting in a psychiatrist's office a few days after unfurling from the fetal position on my living room floor. This was the first time I had ever seen a psychiatrist.

"After I gave him a brief history of my childhood, he said, 'You're suffering from PTSD' (Post-Traumatic Stress Disorder). I protested that I'd 'never been in a war.' He said, 'You were raised in a war zone, and you've been at war with yourself ever since.' His comment hit me square in the chest:

> *For the first time we could watch the brain as it processed memories, sensations, and emotions and begin to map the circuits of mind and consciousness.* [10]

"In the last fifteen to twenty years, advances in brain-imaging technology (fMRI) have provided neuroscientists with extraordinary revelations of how the brain functions when processing traumatic experiences and memories. Neuropsychologists can now see what the brain is doing when memories of traumatic events get triggered and, most important, design systematic therapies to directly address it.

"To understand how a traumatic event impacts the brain, we first have to know a little about brain anatomy, development, and function."

A Bit of Brain Science

"As I sought to understand how trauma impacts the brain, Bessel van der Kolk, M.D.'s book *The Body Keeps the Score* (2014) served as a type of scientific recovery guide for me. I'm going to walk you through how I tried to understand my own brain matter.

"Anatomically, the brain is divided into two hemispheres; right and left. The right hemisphere processes and stores information on an intuitive, emotional, visual, spatial, and tactual level. The right hemisphere develops in the womb so that when a child is born, they are immediately capable of responding to their mother's touch, voice, face, and love/affection.

"The left hemisphere processes information on a linguistic, sequential, and analytical level. The left hemisphere develops after birth and enables us to figure out how things work, how to coordinate our actions to accomplish tasks and goals and manage time. You might have heard it said that 'left-brain people' are predisposed to think logically and rationally. 'Right-brain people' are more intuitive and artistic.

"Both hemispheres store memory of past events differently. The left brain stores memories of facts, statistics, and vocabulary and explains our experiences and memories rationally. The right brain records sound, touch, smell, and the emotions they evoke. We might think of it as an emotional memory chip."

The Emotional Brain

"At the base of the two hemispheres are two 'evolutionarily older, and to some degree separate brains'; the more primitive reptilian brain (standard equipment on every new baby) is responsible for all the things that babies do: eat, sleep, wake, cry, breathe, sense temperature, get hungry, pee, and poop.[11]

"Directly above the reptilian brain is the mammalian brain, which develops after the baby is born. The mammalian brain consists of the limbic system. The limbic system is the seat of emotions, which monitors danger, judges what is pleasurable or scary, and determines what is or is not important for our survival. Van der Kolk (2004) describes the limbic system as the 'central command post for coping with the challenges of living within our complex social system.'[12] The limbic system is shaped by experiences and the baby's own genetic makeup (temperament):

> *Whatever happens to a baby contributes to the emotional and perceptual map of the world that its developing brain creates [...] If you feel safe and loved, your brain becomes specialized in exploration, play, and cooperation; if you are frightened and unwanted it specializes in managing fear and abandonment.*[13]

"He goes on to write, 'Because experience contributes profoundly to limbic system development, repeated experiences of feeling either loved or unwanted can become the "default setting"—the response most likely to occur.'

"Later experiences can modify early patterned responses in the limbic system for better ('a close friendship or a beautiful first love') or worse ('by a violent assault, relentless bullying, or neglect'). Taken together, van der Kolk designates the reptilian brain and the mammalian brain as the 'emotional brain ... the heart of the central nervous system,' which 'initiates preprogramed escape plans, like the fight or flight responses': [14]

> *These muscular and physiological reactions are automatic, set in motion without any thought or planning on our part, leaving our conscious, rational capacities to catch up later, often well after the threat is over.*" [15]

The Rational Brain

"The two frontal lobes of our brain constitute the bulk of our neocortex. We might think of the neocortex as 'the CEO' of our brain, making rational decisions about the information fed to it from the lower mammalian and reptilian brain. If we jump in fright when we think we see a coiled snake on the floor, but then realize it's only a rope, it's our neocortex that knows the difference and tells the other two brains to calm down: 'It's only a rope!'

"The neocortex begins to rapidly develop at age two. As it grows, our capacity for language (symbols), abstract thought, discernment, anticipation, planning, assigning meaning to experiences and events, self-reflection, awareness, making choices, collaborating, and empathizing with others increases.

"With regard to empathy, van der Kolk explains that neuroscientists discovered 'specialized cells,' called 'mirror neurons,' in the neocortex that enable us to 'pick up not only another person's movement but her emotional state and intentions as well' (59). This realization is what motivated me to develop the S.H.I.F.T. trauma-responsive communication technique:

> *When people are in sync with each other, they tend to stand or sit in similar ways, and their voices take on the same rhythms. But our mirror neurons also make us vulnerable to others' negativity, so that we respond to their anger with fury or are dragged down by their depression.* [16]

"As he emphasizes, 'Well-functioning frontal lobes are crucial for harmonious relationships with our fellow humans.' [17] Our neocortex is what enables us to comprehend and participate in cultural values and norms. It can stop us from doing something that violates those values that constitute appropriate behavior:

But it is exactly on that edge between impulse and acceptable behavior where most of our troubles begin. The more intense the visceral, sensory input from the emotional brain, the less capacity the rational brain has to put a damper on it.[18]

"At this point, I started to understand what can go wrong when experiences of abuse dominate. Parts of the brain charged with logically comprehending take a back seat to parts meant to protect from impending violence. Understanding how this happens and the consequences, or patterns that develop neurologically, helped me appreciate what predisposes a person to PTSD after abuse."

The Circuitry

"There are five essential components that communicate with each other and determine how we respond to external stimulus. The *thalamus* is our sensory receiver. Here, sensory information received by our eyes, nose, ears, and touch come together. The thalamus takes this sensory information, processes it into a type of unified, or coherent whole ('this is what is happening'), and then sends this information along two neural pathways. The first pathway is to the *amygdala*. Van der Kolk describes the amygdala as our 'alarm,' which determines if what is happening is a threat to our survival. Keep in mind that this happens in an instant.

"At the same time, the information received by the amygdala is shared with the *hippocampus* which correlates the incoming information with past experiences. If a threat is confirmed, the amygdala fires a message to the *hypothalamus*, which then secretes stress hormones (adrenaline, cortisol) that get carried into the nervous system. Heart rate increases, blood pressure rises, breathing accelerates, muscles tighten, and our body prepares for fighting or fleeing. We might call this our 'threat detection and response system.'

"If the hippocampus determines 'not a threat,' the amygdala is deactivated, and the information is passed on to the anterior cingulate, which determines whether our experience of threat is 'real versus perceived.' Information is then passed to the prefrontal cortex for a more 'refined interpretation.' If you remember, the prefrontal cortex is where our executive 'rational brain' resides:

If the interpretation of threat by the amygdala is too intense, and/or the filtering system from the higher areas of the brain are too weak, as often happens in PTSD, people lose control over automatic emergency responses, like prolonged startle or aggressive outbursts.[19]

"Finally, located in our executive brain is the *medial prefrontal cortex* (MPFC). Van der Kolk calls the MPFC 'the watchtower' because it is here where we perform our highest level of objective rationalization, interpretation, and potential detachment. Our

MPFC enables us to realize that 'other people's anger and threats are a function of their emotional states' and not our problem or because of something we did or are.

"When a child is a victim of abuse, the MPFC never gets the chance to develop normally. The thalamus is continually overloaded with traumatic sensory experience, the amygdala constantly fires its alarm, the body is continuously flooded with adrenaline, cortisol, and other stress hormones, and the young body and nervous system are in a constant state of crisis. The entire system is programmed to prepare for impending violence whether that threat is real or imagined."

> **"Terror increases the need for attachment, even if the source of comfort is also the source of terror."** [20]

The Abused and Bullied Brain

"When I first read this statement it all made sense. It explains why I couldn't fight back on the school playground or in the halls. For me, every instance was a matter of life and death. My developing mind-body connection was hardwired to freeze. The freeze I experienced when my mother raged, whipped, and switched me repeatedly before I was five years old took my entire nervous system hostage.

"I don't say this to be dramatic. It was what it was, and it did what it did. The point is, I didn't have any other option than to freeze. When the first bullying episode happened in elementary school, though new in terms of social experience, the threat response was already well-rehearsed by my nervous system. The bullying triggered a post-traumatic response already in place neurologically."

> **"If there's no way out, and there's nothing we can do to stave off the inevitable, we will activate the ultimate emergency system: the dorsal vagal complex (DVC). This system reaches down below the diaphragm to the stomach, kidneys, and intestines and drastically reduces metabolism throughout the body. Heart rate plunges (we feel our heart 'drop'), we can't breathe, and our gut stops working or empties (literally 'scaring the shit out of us'). This is the point at which we disengage, collapse, and freeze."** [21]

"In fact, throughout my adult life, my nervous system continued to keep me hostage. Any time something triggered me into feeling threatened, I relived the original abuse trauma as if it were happening for the first time.

"There's another consequence to being emotionally and physically abused by a primary caregiver, and it has to do with attachment. Because when we are children, we are completely dependent on our mother or primary caregiver for meeting our most basic affection, security, and survival needs, we instinctually bond with them on an emotional and psychological level. We have to or we won't survive. 'Children have a biological instinct to attach—they have no choice.' " [22]

> **"Whether their parents or caregivers are loving and caring or distant, insensitive, rejecting, or abusive, children will develop a coping style based on their attempt to get at least some of their needs met."** [23]

"It's nature's way. As a child, we don't have the brain circuitry established that would enable us to disassociate from them, rationally assign responsibility to the abuser—and detach. And if the abuser is the one we depend on for nurturing, we're trapped.

> **"Children in this situation have no one to turn to, and they are faced with a dilemma; their mothers are simultaneously necessary for survival and a source of fear."** [24]

"I'm oversimplifying this dynamic considerably and there's an entire field of research devoted to childhood attachment disorder. There are various ways in which children attach. My response was to take the hit, internalize it, disassociate from myself, and then try to reattach to her to feel safe again. Any sense of 'an autonomous self' didn't exist other than as an object of disgust in my mother's eyes in that moment, followed by her plea for emotional support.

"This sequence established an automatic attachment response that predisposed me to always seek safety and approval from the very person who was beating me.

"This dynamic of attachment to abuser also explained why whenever I was bullied, I sought their approval instead of defending myself and repelling them physically. Eventually, this would change but not for the better. Attachment manifested in retaliation and attack. Humiliation motivated retaliation through overwhelming violent response."

> **"We remember insults and injuries best: The adrenaline that we secrete to defend against potential threats helps to engrave those incidents into our minds."** [25]

"Van der Kolk explains that under normal circumstances, the left brain (rational) and right brain (emotional) collaborate to produce an 'integrated response.' We experience an emotion, and the left brain comprehends it. A traumatic event 'disconnects' other brain areas (hippocampus and thalamus) necessary for proper storage and integration of incoming sensory information. In essence, abuse 'breaks' the 'right relationships' between various parts of the brain:

As a result, the imprints of traumatic experiences are organized not as coherent log-ical narratives but in fragmented sensory and emotional traces: images, sounds, and physical sensations.[26]

"Because we can't comprehend what's happening in a traumatic moment, anytime we experience a similar sound (angry voice), image (angry face), or physical sensation (fear), the same neurological emergency response kicks in. And because the historical trauma hasn't been worked through therapeutically, we can't differentiate between 'that was then, and this is now.' That is what PTSD is:

The trauma may be over, but it keeps being replayed in continually recycling memo-ries and in a reorganized nervous system.[27]

"Every time we get triggered, we suffer from sensory overload as the hippocampus falters in its ability to regulate the amygdala, and the hypothalamus floods the nervous system with stress hormones. The nervous system is on fire. We can't turn the alarm off because we can't find the switch.

"We have no capacity for self-calming and self-soothing. We can't talk ourselves off the ledge because we're too consumed by the fight/flight/freeze reaction. Any interior dialogue we might rely upon in these traumatic moments to self-soothe—such as a con-versation with a higher power—is impossible.

"In a typical restorative justice conference, the facilitator reviews the discovered harms before the reparative plan of action is created. As I explained, harm is recognized as happening on a physical, material, emotional, and psychological level of experience.

"With an adult victim of childhood abuse, each of these areas of harm emanate from a traumatized brain. As happens with PTSD, the emotional, psychological, physical, and spiritual harms of the traumatic violation continue to manifest throughout life unless the traumatized brain is healed. We can't not feel that way, and we can't stop thinking that way. Our brains won't let us. We're not 'doing it,' it's doing us. It took me a long time to accept this.

"The problem is that when the traumatic event(s) happened, all the sensory informa-tion—the sights, sounds, hits, faces, and terror—became inscribed and memorialized in our emotional brain. As a child in a moment of parental abuse, the reptilian brain regis-tered the crisis, the just-developing mammalian brain egocentrically interpreted, 'It's my fault' (survival attachment), and this is as far as any processing went.

"The rational brain never had the chance to process it with any objectivity (detach-ment) because as a child, it wasn't developed yet. With repeated abuse, the neurological pathways, the relationships between thalamus, amygdala, and hypothalamus became hardwired in a trauma loop.

"We were programmed by the trauma. Anytime a similar sight, sound, physical sensation, or circumstance occurred, the memorialized threat circuit switched on, and the subsequent traumatic reaction kicked in. We never had a chance. All we could do was attempt to treat the symptoms with coping behaviors. Therefore, to repair the harm at its deepest level, we have to heal the original trauma by repairing the way the brain processes it."

"We enter the world prepared to have a spiritual life." [28]
—Lisa Miller

Neuro-Spiritual Violation

"Though spiritual harm is not typically recognized and addressed in conventional (institutional) restorative justice, I do so here. This harm is the deepest and most all-encompassing. Native communities tell us this, but we haven't figured out a way to address it in the secularized practice of restorative justice or restorative school discipline practices. However, in the emerging field of neurospirituality, modern neuroscience is providing scientific evidence that pursuing a relationship with a higher power or Greater Spirit restores what some scientists call 'the spiritual brain.'

"With the remarkable advancement in the technology of brain-scanning and science of neuropsychology comes the equally extraordinary ability to identify what the brain is doing when a person is engaged in such spiritual practices as prayer and meditation or experiencing transcendence—the sensing of the existence of a unifying presence or reality both within and beyond the apparent and that we are innately a part of.

"In her groundbreaking book *The Spiritual Child*, neuropsychologist Lisa Miller, Ph.D. (2015), provides scientific evidence that we are born with an innate capacity for 'transcendent knowing, relationship, and experience.' [29] She explains:

> *Spiritual development is a biological and psychological imperative from birth. Natural spirituality, the innate spiritual attunement of young children—unlike other lines of development—appears to begin whole and fully expressed.* [30]

"Miller defines spirituality as 'an inner sense of relationship to a higher power that is loving and guiding' and that regardless of the name we give this power (e.g., God, nature, spirit, universe, creator), 'the important point is that spirituality encompasses our awareness and relationship with this higher presence.' [31]

"Fundamentally, spirituality is experienced as a *relationship* with something other. She suggests that our innate capacity for transcendent experience exists prior to, and independent of, any religious indoctrination or enculturalization. In other words, we're genetically and biologically endowed to experience transcendence from the start. Religious practices may enhance and grow this spiritual capacity, but the capacity itself exists in the first breath (and maybe before).

"From a scientific perspective, she explains, 'In neuroimaging scans, we have found synchronization of the regions of the brain when in spiritual or contemplative practice':[32]

> *Research using MRI on people in active meditation shows activity of the middle pre-frontal cortex, a central structure that links to and regulates other brain regions such as the limbic system, such that our emotions, governed by the amygdala, are eased; when we meditate we feel less revved up for fight or flight.*

"While these studies were conducted of adults, Miller suggests that synchronization of neural pathways happening in adult spiritual practices is a natural process also occurring in brain development in infants and children, and which can be interpreted (observed) as happening in specific behaviors and relationships children engage in. This is why she concludes that 'spirituality is experienced through a biologically based faculty' and that we are 'born ready to use it.'

"In addition to her important assertion that we're biologically predisposed to spiritual awareness and experience, she emphasizes the *relational* aspect of transcendence and the crucial role parents play in growing a child's innate spiritual capacity. Mom and Dad are our first 'Gods,' and so our first experience of transcendence is in our relationship with them.

"This doesn't mean that even as children we don't/can't experience transcendence with and through others (people, animals, nature, etc.), but because they are our first caregivers on whom we are completely dependent for affection, security, and esteem, they represent our first opportunity for spiritual relationship—one that deeply informs our future experience of something 'other.'

"There are spiritually based behaviors that parents can model and encourage in their children to nurture brain synchronization found in adult spiritual experiences. Like a garden, the soil of transcendent capacity needs to be consciously and lovingly cultivated to produce spiritual fruit which will nurture and sustain the child in their growth and passage from infancy through adolescence and into adult life. This fruit is an inner resource that enables the child to navigate the inevitable tumultuous stages of encultura-tion, socialization, and individuation. The 'spiritual brain' requires tending:

> *As the child grows, natural spirituality integrates with the cognitive, social, emotion-al, and moral development, as well as physical change, to create a more complex set of equipment through which to experience transcendence and spirituality. Ultimately, if maintained and integrated with these other aspects of development, spirituality supports the child through the challenging developmental passage of adolescence.*[33]

"One of the most powerful (and simple) illustrations of the criticality of sowing the seeds of spirituality in children is Miller's table."[34]

Developmental Task	With Spiritual Core	Without Spiritual Core
Self Is	Inherent Worth	Abilities Based
Identity	Meaning and Purpose	Acquiring Success
Work	Calling and Contribution	Talents and Gains
Relationships	Sacred, Share Love, and Grow	Pleasing, Meet Needs
Path	Buoyed Up and Guided	Unsure, Instrumental
Place in World	Always Connected	Ultimately Alone
Existential Reality	Purposeful World	Random World
Nature of Reality	Love, Life-giving	Unknown
Good Events	Blessings	Deserved, Luck
Bad Events	Opportunities, Learning	Random, Failure

"Miller's observations of the lifelong impact of spiritual core development are significant. In simplest terms, nurturing a child's inborn capacity for spiritual experience and perception builds a lifelong reference point, an interior compass that establishes a baseline of emotional and psychological resilience, and instills a secure sense of self with which to navigate the inevitable challenges of being human.

"The strength or weakness of this spiritual core profoundly influences the child's ability to nurture themselves, avoid self-destructive behaviors, and make healthy, life-affirming choices. A weak spiritual foundation makes a child vulnerable to substance abuse and addiction, depression, and abusive relationships in later life.

"Childhood relational trauma not only obstructs this developmental capacity for transcendent experience but also *robs a child of resilience*. Without this inner resource, the child's ability to 'make sense of things' from a more enlightened (detached) perspective and successfully navigate the ups and downs of life with an inner awareness of strength is handicapped.

"This is essentially a violation of spiritual potentiality that destructively impacts *all aspects of experience* and those relationships that constitute a human life—physical, emotional, psychological, and social. In no uncertain terms, who the child thinks they are, why they belong, and what they fundamentally believe about what is most important in life—the big existential 'Why?'—is up for grabs.

"Without a sacred or transcendent awareness to orient by, a child is left to navigate the perilous journey of identity formation, looking for themselves in distorted socially constructed mirrors. They become prey to what popular culture tells them they should be, donning numerous masks in an attempt to fit in. I know this only too well."

The Birth of the False Self

"Van der Kolk, in his review of pediatrician and psychoanalyst Donald Winnicott (1960), explains that the ways a mother holds and interacts with her child 'lay the groundwork for a baby's sense of self—and, with that, a lifelong sense of identity.' [35] Quoting Winnicott, van der Kolk relates, 'If a mother cannot meet her baby's impulses and needs, the baby learns to become the mother's idea of what the baby is.' [36]

"While Winnicott's work is from the 1960s, his scholarship remains as relevant today, perhaps even more relevant with regard to advancements in neuropsychology and the science of trauma than it was when he first published his thesis."

> "The mother gazes at the baby in her arms, and the baby gazes at his mother's face and finds himself therein ... provided that the mother is really looking at the unique, small, helpless being and not projecting her own expectations, fears, and plans for the child. In that case, the child would find not himself in his mother's face, but rather the mother's own projections. This child would remain without a mirror, and for the rest of his life would be seeking this mirror in vain." [37]
>
> —D.W. Winnicott

"In this most impressionable and vulnerable infant state, our very first *sense* of self is given to us from our birth mother or from our original caregiver if we were adopted. If a mother physiologically communicates in any way other than with tenderness, affection, security, and love, the baby has no other option than to sense that rejection on a kinesthetic, nonverbal level. The baby attunes itself to the mother's disregard.

"There are two basic consequences to this neglectful transmission. First, without proper emotional attunement to a loving presence, we don't develop the capacity to soothe or calm ourselves in times of emotional distress. We can't regulate our emotions. We can't self-comfort naturally. 'Associating intense sensations with safety, comfort, and mastery is the foundation of self-regulation, self-soothing, and self-nurture.' [38]

"Addictions and other self-destructive behaviors can be understood as attempts to regulate and soothe the emotional and psychological torment of not being initially loved and cared for. Referring back to Miller's work with transcendence in children, an abused child is incapacitated to relate to a higher power which might provide emotional soothing."

> "How many mental health problems, from drug addiction to self-injurious behavior, start as attempts to cope with the unbearable physical pain of our emotions?" [39]

"Second, as our sense of self continues into other relationships, we develop what Winnicott (1960) defines as a 'false self.' If our first sense of self is not acceptable to our primary caregiver, we have no other option than to assume that core identity with others. If we have a core belief that we are fundamentally unworthy and unlovable, then who we come to think we are (subconsciously) informs who or how we think we need to be in the world in order to be 'acceptable.' It's not our fault. It's a matter of survival. We adapt. We unknowingly construct a false sense of self that becomes who we think we really are (Winnicott, 1965). It's a convoluted identity from the very start.

"One of the most insightful explanations I've found of the psychology of the false self comes from Thomas Keating, O.C.S.O. (1999). Keating explains:

We are thrust because of circumstances into the position of developing a homemade self that does not conform to reality. [...] The homemade self or the false self, as it is usually called, is programmed for human misery. [40]

"Keating offers a clear description of the false self and its motivations.

Everything entering into the world that makes survival and security, affection and esteem, and power and control our chief pursuits of happiness has to be judged on the basis of one question: Is it good for me? [41]

"Keating explains the false self as 'that drive (which) increases in proportion to the felt privations of that need that we suffered in early childhood' [42] (parentheses added). The continual attempt to meet the needs of survival and security, affection and esteem, and power and control puts us in opposition to others. We subconsciously attempt to manipulate, seduce, dominate, coerce, and generally use other people and circumstances to supply us with what we didn't get. When we don't get our way, we throw tantrums, act like victims, and blame others or situations for our misery."

"Can I interject something here?" asked Barb.

"Of course," I said.

"This sounds like narcissism, and it describes exactly how our former president is acting," she said.

"Maybe so. But the real question is, what emotional deprivations happened to him as a child that hardwired him to desperately demand so much attention from people without regard for them?"

"That's the empathic approach," said Brad.

"Is there any other way? Separate the behavior from the individual. It's also a detached approach. Let me keep going. When people closest to us pull away, we feel abandoned. It's a childish way to relate to life. The end result is that we don't ever learn what it means to be in right relationship with ourselves—or anyone else, for that matter. We don't take responsibility for ourselves. We will never take responsibility for the well-being of others.

"The false self is a constructed 'coping self' which develops throughout our lives in a vain pursuit of happiness which can never be recovered through status, cultural symbols, addictions, and/or human relationships. Cynthia Bourgeault (2004) equally writes:

Beginning in infancy (or even before) each of us, in response to perceived threats to our well-being, develops a false self; a set of protective behaviors driven at root by a sense of need and lack. The essence of the false self is driven, addictive energy, consisting of tremendous emotional investment in compensatory 'emotional programs for happiness.' [43]

"Keating, Bourgeault, and other scholars of Contemplative Practices have dedicated themselves to the recovery practice of 'the true self.' One of the primary survival techniques of the false self is through the development of coping behaviors.

"Rather than interpreting addictive behaviors as a sign of an immoral character (which is an evaluative, deficit-focused, and misdirected assumption), coping behaviors, I believe, are desperate attempts to find a place of security within the chaos of self-hatred."

"Again, this describes Trump," said Brad. "This would imply that the root cause of his demand for attention is fueled by his own self-hatred."

"Maybe so," I replied.

Destructive Coping

"It helps to think of destructive coping behaviors as desperate attempts to create a protected space both on the inside and the outside. The deeper the feelings of fear, condemnation, shame, abandonment, and hopelessness are, the thicker the wall needs to be between us, what happened to us and our pain, and between ourselves and others.

"The tragic truth is that as traumatized children, we never got the chance to know who we really are. We had to insulate in order to navigate a condemning world on the inside, and a perceived dangerous world on the outside.

"The irony of this strategy is that it keeps us from the very source of healing relational trauma—a safe place to reprocess our trauma in the presence of supportive others who will accept us not just in spite of our suffering, but because of our suffering."

"That's what we do in recovery meetings," said Brad.

"And it's also what we tried to do with Leo, Maria, and Rick," I said.

I added, "When I take an honest appraisal of how I attempted to cope with my own PTSD, it all makes sense. Neurologically, I tried to muffle the constant triggering and release of stress hormones by numbing out with alcohol, drugs, and adrenaline. Adrenaline was my drug of choice. Things slowed down when I was speeding.

"The first time I got on a pair of snow skis, I was addicted. It didn't matter that I didn't know how to turn or stop. I just wanted to go fast. That was the thrill, the adrenaline rush. Being on the edge of disaster was euphoric.

> **The faster I went, the further away from how I felt about myself I got. Broken thumbs, wrists, ribs, and concussions. None of it mattered.**

"Van der Kolk writes, 'Many abused and traumatized people feel alive in the face of actual danger—panic and rage are preferable to the opposite, shutting down and becoming dead to the world.'[44] I was a poster child.

"This morphed into winter mountain climbing. Anything I could do to get away from anyone and everything and especially myself. I climbed in the winter because it was more dangerous and the elements more extreme. The threat of avalanches was a thrill. And I didn't want to see anyone else. I was driven by a need for intense physical stimulation from the outside to override the raging storm on the inside.

"Cognitively, I was in a constant fight with negative core beliefs about my self-worth and lovability. I searched for acceptance with performance. I went to Italy and became a model. I went to L.A. and became an actor. With every show, inside I was seeking approval, recognition, acceptance, and vindication of all those who called me 'pretty boy.' The entire time I was trying to prove *to myself* I was worth it. It never worked. I was never convinced. I was asking the wrong person.

"Socially, I lived always on the lookout, scanning everyone and every conversation, hyper-alert for any threat, male or female. I could walk into any room and immediately sense people's moods by their faces, body language, and voice. I could tell who was on edge and what they were feeling. I was never still. That hyper-alertness was a survival skill I developed as a child.

> **"In my late teens and twenties, there were fights. This is where freeze transformed into fight. I went on autopilot. I should have walked away from each of them, but I couldn't. In that moment of threat, I had no objectivity. It took me years to forgive myself. This is why I've committed my life to peacemaking."**

"For seventeen years, I tried to numb myself and silence the brutal inner critic, and the deafening voice of self-condemnation and self-punishment that would just never shut up. I existed in a state of intro-retribution. I was essentially whipping myself inside. Anything to escape, but it was never enough. The hole inside didn't have a bottom. And wherever that was, its sediment was shame.

"When I finally broke, I came to realize the deepest harm of all. I had no faith. I had no faith in people, nor did I have any faith in any 'higher power.' As I mentioned above, I finally curled up on the floor in the fetal position and waited for the end. I was done fighting. The 'end' came, but it wasn't what I expected. I'll cover that in our next and final discussion.

"Throughout our discussions, I've explained that restoration is fundamentally about the restoration of relationships. In restorative justice, this means the restoration of interpersonal and social relationships damaged by a criminal violation.

"Restoring the relationship with ourselves is an inside job. Having completed the painful but necessary steps of accounting for what happened and how it negatively impacted us, we can now start the equally courageous work of repair which leads to *intra*-personal reconciliation, reintegration, and ultimately—*restoration*.

"But reconciliation, reintegration, and restoration of the relationship we have with ourselves requires reconciling and integrating the history of abuse and trauma we may have inherited from our ancestors. We have to know what happened to them, what they did, and how they transferred or transacted trauma through generations. That's how we can separate the abusive behavior from the individuals and make sense of why it happened."

Trauma-Tracking: Underlying Issues, Trans- & Intergenerational Trauma

"I want to share this piece from Kareem Abdul-Jabbar writing about the impact of not teaching kids about the dark side of U.S. history, our history:

> *This dumbing-down of our children is one of the greatest dangers to America's existence because democracy depends on an informed citizenry who can understand what we did right and wrong in our history in order to set a more successful course for the future.*[45]

"This reminds me of Darcia Narvaez's reflection on moral imagination. Critical thinking about structural racism, slavery, conquest and colonialism fosters moral imagination," I said.

"White people don't want to look in their closets," said Barb. "If they did, they might find a relative who's gay or Black. God forbid they might see themselves."

I replied, "The question in my mind is, 'Are we responsible for repairing the harm of our ancestors?' Each person has to answer that for themselves. If we are, then how responsible are we? What does that sense of responsibility compel us to do to make things right? If that makes us uncomfortable, we need to ask ourselves why. What are we so afraid of?

"More importantly, what's the cost of maintaining our own denial? Shouldn't we at least know and accept or acknowledge what our ancestors did?" I asked. "What's the impact if we don't? What are the underlying issues or beliefs that are driving our denial?"

"And how we still benefit from that," said Devonte.

"Exactly, and how others still suffer because of what our ancestors did generations ago," I said. "It is *that* story that can liberate us from our own collective smallness or self-centeredness."

"You're talking about transgenerational trauma," said Kris.

"I am. Think about growing up, being cast into a historical master narrative that says your people were hated, owned, and eradicated simply because they were a different color and spoke a different language or believed in a non-Christian God. That narrative is not only dehumanizing and traumatizing in itself but fosters suppression of voice, depression, and poverty of spirit in subsequent generations.

"That's what transgenerational trauma does. But it gets transferred *inter*generationally," I said. "The intergenerational part happens when the symptoms manifest in destructive coping, child abuse, domestic violence, alcoholism, and addictions.

"Since we're on this topic, let me share another story with you. When I started digging into my own ancestry, I did something I call 'transgenerational trauma-tracking.' On both sides of my family, I found people who were fighting for justice, and people who were committing atrocities. People who were kind, and people who were cruel.

"On my father's side, there were slave owners and men who fought in the Civil War on the Confederate side. But even within one family, there was a great-great-grandfather who sided with the Union even though he was from the south. Yet, his son was a Confederate. But that son eventually changed his mind, became a peacemaker, and intervened in a gun fight that ended up killing him.

"That knowledge is liberating for me because whether I like it or not, it's in me if only genetically. It also shows me that personal change, a paradigm shift, is possible even within one generation. It gives me a choice of which ancestor I feel aligned with, but I have to take ownership of both sides and both mindsets. I don't get to discard one side. It happened, and it's part of my family history.

"On my mother's side, which is the family history I know most about, I had a hard time finding heroes. The first ancestor was a soldier in Onate's colonizing army in 1598. He participated in the massacre of 800 Native American men, women, and children.[46] In 1833, another ancestor was a territorial governor of New Mexico when it was still a part of Mexico. He granted almost 16,500 acres land to seventy Spanish families.[47]

"One of those families was my great-great-great-grandfather who I learned was a 'Comanchero' and participated in kidnapping Native American children and selling them to wealthy Hispanic families and ranches. Some of that land was passed down through the generations to my brother, sister, and me. But that land always belonged to the same Native Americans whom the original ancestor had tried to eradicate.

"The Native Americans had been there for thousands of years before the Spanish showed up. It was their ancestral homeland. They came from that landscape. The Spanish, my ancestors, took it by force, doctrine, and imposed legal justifications for confiscation—all of it backed by violence and threat of violence. With the assistance of a friend, my brother, sister, and I returned our portion of the land to the Tribe.

"My point is that we have to know what our ancestors did. And we don't get to cherry-pick the stories. Where does racism and racial violence come from? It's a cultural inheritance. It gets transferred through families—our families and the structures and institutions our ancestors built. Those institutions are alive and well today.

"When I started to intergenerationally trauma-track in my own family's history, I came face-to-face with why my mother suffered so much and why she really had no alternative in those moments of her own PTSD.

"What I discovered was that my mother was brutalized by her father. When she was born in 1922, her mother wrote a letter of apology to my grandfather saying, 'Well, I guess you're pretty disappointed in me' (for not having a boy).

"For my mother's entire childhood and into her teens, she was physically abused, berated, and treated like a mistake. At the age of sixteen she became pregnant, and her father's response was to beat her and kick her. No one protected her. She once shared that she sewed single-edge razor blades into the soles of her shoes to protect herself at school from the bullies. She got tough at a very, very young age.

"It wasn't until I was in my late forties that I learned that her father was an alcoholic and that he once kept prostitutes in the back room of the bar he owned. No wonder my grandmother always seemed so detached, nervous, and forlorn. I could've stopped there, but I wanted to find out what happened to him and so I did some deeper digging/tracking into family cultural history. I had to separate him from what he did and ask, 'What happened to him?'

"My grandfather was born in a small village in New Mexico in 1889. If you remember, I mentioned his father who was a member of a religious brotherhood that practiced whipping and switching as a means of penance. This practice was also used as a means of disciplining children. I have no doubt that the cultural tradition of 'sacred whipping and switching for transgressions' was the way my grandfather was disciplined—and the way he 'disciplined' my mother. His mother and father gave him to a childless sister to raise. That was essentially the first abandonment. His 'real mother and father' lived just across the street, and he knew that he had been given away while his sisters and brothers weren't.

"When he was twelve years old, there was no education available in his village, and so he and a brother (who remained with the birth parents) were shipped off to an Indian boarding school in Oklahoma.[48] Because they were dark-skinned, they posed as Native Americans. Darkly ironic. While at the school, his brother died under suspicious circumstances. The consensus was that he was murdered. My grandfather made the journey back to New Mexico with his brother's body on the train.

"He went on to become the first family member to receive a formal education in Santa Fe, but it came at a cost. It was a time of radical cultural assimilation into a new American identity. Speaking Spanish in schools became a mark of 'the other.' He was essentially caught in a cultural collision zone where to escape the poverty of a small village, he had to assume a foreign, more American identity. He had to discard where he came from and develop a false persona to succeed.

"Because he was the first from the village to go to college, he was on his own, just like he was on the train ride back from Indian School. His response was to get tough. Be the bull. Take control. Dominate. Never show weakness. He eventually disparaged the people and the village from which he was born.

"These are not excuses. They at least track the trauma on cultural and historical terms.

"I turned next to asking, 'Why did the bullies bully?' Fully understanding that 'behavior isn't the individual' but an expression, or symptom, of either their own internal woundedness or exterior cultural inheritances liberated me to make rational sense of it all. These boys were not to blame.

"The reasons, as best as I could assemble, gave me an insight into 'offender' behavior that continues to inform my work as a restorative practitioner, and enlarge my heart as a human being. From what I could discover, the roots of abuse all had to do with *relational trauma* happening in a family, in a time of cultural transition, and generationally transferred.

"The boys who bullied me in grade school never had a chance. One boy was later killed in a drug deal. Another boy ended up in prison for murder. When I was working at a grocery store just after high school, I ran into the boy from my Cub Scout group who followed the other boy home, beat him up, and then blamed it on me. He had become a heroin addict. I could see the tracks on his arms, how emaciated he was, and that he was paying for his food with food stamps. He was only nineteen years old. I knew about his family. I knew he never finished high school. Any resentment I had toward him melted, and I just felt so sad.

"All three of these boys never escaped from the neighborhood. A fourth ended up with numerous felony convictions and also spent time in prison. Everybody knew everybody in that neighborhood and a friend of mine kept me informed over the years. Inasmuch as I escaped the neighborhood, these young men didn't. We all carried it with us, but to different destinations. I was lucky. Sports and academics saved my ass.

"As for the neighborhood itself, it was located between two military bases that were highly active during the Vietnam War. Many homes had a neatly folded American flag on the mantel, and a glossy photo of a handsome young man in uniform who never returned. One of the boys had lost two brothers.

"When I think through my heart about this time period and that neighborhood, I can't begin to imagine the trauma of parents and siblings having to deal with the loss of a son, brother, or father. Feeling so powerless, where else could the powerlessness felt at home be released except in school halls and the playground?

"Depression, domestic violence, alcoholism, and drug addiction were rampant. The entire neighborhood was traumatized.

"As for the bullies in high school, I came to realize that in very concrete ways, bullying was an implicit male cultural value. To be a bully was to publicly demonstrate machismo. It signified status in male social capital of power-over and power-by-violence. It was a celebrated archetype. To be a bully was to be esteemed in the eyes of a wounded male culture that raised its young men to believe that sensitive (nonviolent) boys are 'pussies and faggots.'"

> "This toxic socialization process is solidified in the compulsory utter-
> ing, 'Boys will be boys' when we highlight toughness while ignoring or
> shaming tenderness. This is an expired societal attitude and belief that
> perpetuates the problem, rather than naming it." [49]

"I'll close this story with this. When my mother passed at the age of eighty-eight, she was surrounded by her family. She had suffered from dementia for several years. When she passed, we were all standing around her bed and holding her hand.

"The night before she passed, I spent the night with her in the hospital. When she would moan, I would soothe her and caress her forehead. Though she and I never discussed what she had done, or what happened to her, in those final moments of passing it just didn't matter. Everything passed away in her last few breaths.

"I understood it wasn't her. In fact, our whole family knew it. We knew she loved us. She knew we loved her. She knew I loved her, and that's all that mattered. Tenderness had replaced torment. Love was the ultimate restorative mattering.

"However, the trauma that I experienced, even though I knew it was not intentional, still needed to be healed. I still harbored deep resentments that I tried to ignore. My brain needed to reprocess what happened, and so I undertook to take ownership of my own restoration. It was my responsibility—not hers, and not the bullies'.

"The last thing I'll repeat is that my story is not unique. There are millions of people suffering from the consequences of unresolved childhood trauma. Untreated, we live each day with one foot in the fearful future, the other in the painful past, neurologically torn apart inside, and never fully engaged in the present.

"Childhood relational trauma and bullying is coming out of the closet. The curtain of denial and ignorance is being pulled back, but in my mind, too damn slowly. With each school shooting we pull the curtain back a little more, but we never seem to ask the deeper questions which would point to terror existing in the minds of children. Why does it take a catastrophic event to talk about it?

"As soon as the media stops running the story, the underlying psychological issues that compel shooters and school violence—like trauma and PTSD—get superficially diagnosed, classified for public consumption, and that's the end of the story. We quickly move on to the politics of gun control. Urban massacres fade away. Bullying is old news. Childhood relational trauma never gets meaningfully discussed.

"We never look beneath the headline. We don't look under the bed. If we did, we would realize that childhood abuse, neglect, and trauma happening in families, schools, and communities is not just an 'issue,' it's an epidemic monster ripping the social fabric of our culture one child at a time.

"In my opinion, unresolved individual and collectively shared trauma gets used against us by political actors. Our trauma gets capitalized on. Power-seeking political actors weaponize our collective trauma and in doing so, ensure its perpetuation. This is why Scarry's rhetorical analysis of how stories traumatize to secure dominance is so important. The mechanics are the same.

"When I see politicians and other public personalities activating fear, spewing hatred, contempt, and blatant racism, I find myself wanting to sit down with them and ask, 'What happened to you?'"

Barb commented, "I want to confront them with 'What the fuck is wrong with you?'"

The group was silent.

Closing Discussion

I admitted to our group, "I've taken us way deep into the impact of trauma and tried to ground that impact in a context by using my own story. I'm wondering how what I've said has landed with you."

Brad said, "Can we talk a bit about your story? You covered a lot of ground."

"Agreed," said Barb. "We're not ready to toss you back into the ocean yet."

"For sure. I'm still trying to process it," added Melissa. "There's a lot of 'there' there."

"Sure," I said. "What stuck out for you?"

"Well, for starters, it takes courage to be that vulnerable," said Brad. "I'm wondering how you feel about that."

I replied, "As I said, at first it felt self-indulgent and disloyal. But in the end, it isn't about me, and the story is not unique.

"What I wanted to show with my story is what happens neurologically—and eventually, psychologically, emotionally, and behaviorally—when a child experiences any kind of beating. All I learned was fear, shame, and resentment. I was held hostage by my feeling of humiliation and its evolution into rage. It's an old adage, but if you kick a dog enough times, it will eventually bite you.

"Working through all of that actually brought our family closer together. It deepened our love and commitment to each other. As for me taking the risk to share it, yeah, that was my experience, but like you said, if it helps somebody else, it's worth it. If anything, it's a story of someone reaching a critical point of breaking from a past and getting stuck in the liminal stage for decades.

"The restorative process opened the door and shed light on what's possible during that space of betwixt and between. I like to think that some of my armor has rusted off. I'm convinced it can do that for others," I said.

Brad replied, "You telling your story gives me the courage to share mine. My old man was an alcoholic who beat his wife and kids almost daily. That's one of the reasons why I enlisted in the military and eventually became a cop. Both were disciplines with understandable rules and predictability. The reason I'm running a recovery center is directly related to my own struggles with addiction."

"Bingo," said Kris. "I became a trauma specialist so I could extract people from abusive situations. Trust me, your story isn't just yours. It's ours. As much as I'm doing what I do for others, I'm clear that on some level, I'm still always trying to heal my own trauma.

"I have a copy of van der Kolk's book on my desk. I've just about worn it out from underlining and making notes in the margins, and I've required my staff to read it. It demystifies trauma. I'm glad you relied on it so heavily in explaining the brain science of trauma. I need to read Miller's book," she added.

"But to see this stuff actually applied in a restorative framework, and especially on such a deep personal level, gives me tremendous hope. It also makes me realize how much restoration I need to do. So, thank you for sharing your story," she said.

"You're welcome," I said.

Brad added, "Your story also made me realize that we need to address the trauma of bullying in our clients. We also need to dial in on child abuse and family violence more deeply than we do.

"Most of our young men come from affluent families. It's hard for them to talk about their families because they're afraid of losing their financial support. That fear can keep them from looking at their families objectively. The family has coped by continuing to pay for expensive rehabs."

"I was bullied as a kid," said Aaron. "A lot of times it was violent. I was the 'nerdy science kid.' I'm not sure I ever recovered from that. It shows up now when I stand up in front of a community group and preach about the environment. I always seem to pick out the people in the audience who clearly disdain environmental restoration.

"I can see it in their faces. I take it personally. It triggers me. I get the hyper-alert part of your story. When they challenge me after my talk, if I'm honest with myself, I'm shaking. The way I cope is to 'put on my scientist hat' and bury them with statistics. My intellect is my armor, I guess."

"I get it," I said.

Devonte spoke. "I've had to develop a thick skin. I like your comment about having the skin of an elephant with the heart of a lion. You try to ignore it and live your life. But underneath, it burns like a deep resentment. It hurts. Some of those cuts don't heal. It makes you angry and it keeps you angry. I've often thought that if I ever let my rage out, it wouldn't stop. I get the 'hyper-alert' part. I'm hyper-alert every time I leave my house. I make sure my kids are too. How do I protect them from my own hyper-alertness? They shouldn't have to grow up that way. Maybe there's such a thing as transgenerational hyper-awareness.

"I've spent most of my life trying to rationalize it by saying, 'It's not about me, it's about them,' and, 'You have to be better than them,' and, 'Not all white people are racist.' But that only goes so far when everywhere you go, you have to look over your shoulder. It's an ever-present reality, and it's exhausting. And it never seems to change.

"I find a lot of truth in what you're saying about separating a person's behavior from their value as a human being. But how do you do that in the face of racism?" Devonte asked.

"Or transgender bashing," added Barb.

"Or anti-Semitism," said Aaron.

"Or anti-Muslimism," said Joan.

"Anti-humanism," I said.

We let what Devonte shared sink in.

"I guess the way I look at racism, anti-Semitism, genderism, or even bullying, for that matter, is as a type of cultural mental illness, insanity, or soul sickness. In my opinion, hate is an expression of self-hatred. The person who hates, feels the hate in themselves," I said.

"The performativity of hatred," said Devonte.

"Well said," I replied. "Brad, you looked like you wanted to add something?" I asked.

Brad shared, "One of the things I've realized after years of mentoring addicts and alcoholics is that substance abuse is an attempt to cope. But going this deep into how any experience of trauma, childhood or otherwise, impacts how our brain 'produces our mind' is pretty startling.

"I'm wondering how we can develop conversations and education around this in our program. I can now see how and why both S.H.A.R.E. and S.H.I.F.T. can be effective ways of interacting with trauma. I get it.

"I also want to commend you again for telling your story. It makes me think of how many men go to their graves early simply because they haven't felt safe saying. 'I feel fear.' Your story motivates me to look more deeply at why I became a cop," said Brad.

"Thanks Brad. I appreciate your acknowledgment," I said.

"That was my takeaway too," said Melissa. "How different would our world be if men acknowledged their vulnerability and were supported to talk about the terror they've experienced? What also struck me was the principle of separating behavior from the individual. That makes such perfect sense if we look at trauma as a kind of psychological and/or spiritual malady. It's not *us* but what happened to us. This realization has huge implications for how we move through conflict. But like Brad said, this shift in perspective and being able to apply it in a workplace is daunting."

"It all starts with education, and that's why we're having these discussions," I said. "The more we know, the more effective we'll be in recognizing the signs of trauma-driven behavior and directly, but empathically intervening with people experiencing destructive conflict. The more knowledge and understanding we have with trauma, the more effective we'll be at practicing S.H.I.F.T. and S.H.A.R.E."

"I'm feeling pretty heavy," said Joan. "This is serious stuff. Overwhelming. My go-to coping mechanism is to tell myself, 'It wasn't that bad,' and, 'It'll all work out.' What came up for me is how swallowing that, or discounting what happened to me with the sexual abuse I experienced, is still unresolved. I think on a certain level, I still hold the belief that what happened to me was my fault.

"I'm a people pleaser. It's one of my coping mechanisms. Listening to your story, I realize that this coping is a way to keep people from disapproving of me. Kind of like, if you knew my story, you would judge me. You would see how afraid I am. I can relate to your comment that you couldn't make yourself small enough. I can also relate to the false self concept."

"What are the consequences of that to you, Joan?" I asked.

"I hide. I become a chameleon. I don't speak my truth," she said.

"You did speak your truth to your director and look at the outcome!" said Barb. "You and I should hang out. I'm the exact opposite. I'll tell people exactly what I think whether they want to hear it or not!"

"Really?" asked Devonte. "That doesn't sound like you."

Serious laughter erupted.

I asked Barb, "What are the consequences of that to you?"

"Criminy. I knew you were going to ask that," said Barb. "I'm struck by the concept of a 'false self' too. Listening to Devonte I see how I've developed a kind of tough exterior to protect myself. People avoid me like a cactus."

"So maybe there's a happy medium," I suggested.

"What's that?" asked Barb.

"Make friends with your inner cactus," said Devonte. "Understand what triggers you."

"That statement triggers me," replied Barb.

More serious laughter.

"Okay," I said. "We need to wrap up this discussion. Give me one statement about what you'll take away from what we've talked about."

"I'm trying to understand how trauma applies to the environment," said Aaron.

"Like a family secret, why is it that people don't want to admit that global warming is real?" I asked.

"Because they might feel bad about their own behavior which contributes to it," said Aaron.

"I think you're onto something there," I said. "If I read you right, climate denial is a coping mechanism."

"What comes up for me is the thought that our reluctance to let go of fossil fuels is a type of transgenerational environmental trauma," he said.

"Wow," I said.

"Yeah," said Devonte. "That makes perfect sense."

"Devonte, what's your takeaway?" I asked.

"The concept of trauma-tracking really struck me. It made me think about why minorities and marginalized people, people of color who are historically and continually discriminated against—not only structurally, but too often violently—can't just 'rise above it all.' Like you said, we can't just 'change our minds' because our brains won't let us. My take is that we can't just change our collective minds without repairing and healing our own individual traumas.

"You also said that the history of suppression and discrimination—colonization—becomes internalized as a cultural narrative, the story we tell ourselves about ourselves. How do you break that? How do you change, or to use your term, 're-story' ourselves without violent confrontation? What happens when restorative communication is one-sided? We can't change what happened or its impact. How do you restore your relationship with the past when the past has been so traumatizing that we don't even know how that trauma is showing up? What happens when people just refuse to hear, or even listen?"

There was silence in our group.

"I wish I knew, Devonte," I replied. "What you're asking is how do we hold ourselves accountable for what has happened and its impact. The best I can do is share how I tried and continue to try to do that using restoration as a guide.

"I suggested that change happens one conversation at a time. But that seems so minuscule when it comes to confronting the massive history of injustice, global paradigms, worldviews, and institutions that fundamentally depend on marginalizing others to legitimize themselves. How do we do the small things to impact the big things?"

I added, "I go back to the story of the little girl on the beach. It helps me to think about social justice movements. When one person speaks up, others are motivated to do so too. There's a resonance, relating, and identification that takes on a life of its own. THAT is power distributed."

"Like Black Lives Matter," he said.

"Yes, or any movement begun with the motivation to achieve fairness and social justice. How do we take that message, that story, that truth, that pain and internalize it, own it, credit it, harvest it and institutionalize it to make real and sustainable changes? How do we build on that momentum? How does *that* become how we instinctively think not only about our history, but also how we make decisions about how to repair the damage of racism?

"We have to tell the truth of our history and challenge the history that we've been told. That challenge scares people who've relied upon that history to affirm their superiority," I said.

"When the old man on the beach wouldn't pick up the starfish, I fantasize that the little girl told him, 'Well, then get your fucking head out of the sand, and get the fuck out of the way,'" said Barb. "That's my inner cactus coming out."

More laughter.

"Yeah, it may seem insurmountable, but we have no other choice if we really want change to happen," I replied. "What else are we going to do but have these tension-filled conversations? It's about future generations and the future well-being of the planet."

"You're a hopeless liberal idealist," said Brad.

"I don't think this perspective is liberal. It's not an ideology. It's human and humane. When it comes to transgenerational trauma, that means being unafraid to tell the truth about what happened with our ancestors, and how what happened negatively impacted them and continues to impact us now. That's what trauma does. It's like a generational virus. The only antidote is truth."

"So, what exactly did restoration look like, or happen for you? Clearly, you've recognized the impact on such a deep neuropsychic level, but how did you restore that?" asked Kris.

"I'll explain that in our next and final discussion. It really is about neuro-spiritual restoration. The caveat is that this type of deep and personal 'restorative justice' is a continual process. It's a way rather than a final destination," I said.

"It's about the journey and not the arrival," commented Devonte.

"Amen," I said. "Or as my mother would say, '*Adelante!*' —Let's get on with it!"

CHAPTER TEN
A Story of Restoration

"I suggested in our very first discussion, and have repeated throughout, that to restore is to return someone or something (i.e., a relationship) to an *ideal, original, or intended* condition. What is this condition? In spiritual terms, we might say that this ideal condition is a connection with a greater reality that encompasses all of life. What is that greater reality and how might we know we're 'in it'?

"In many tribal wisdom traditions, human beings are considered *innately* a part of a greater Spirit. To be restored is to *experience* being reintegrated back into not only the community, but also a connection to a *Greater Spirit* from which we came. On the deepest level of experience, restoration restores our relationship with a Greater Spirit, Flow, reality, or 'Presence,' by collapsing our perceptual distance between us and 'all of it.' We realize we are a part of it rather than thinking we are apart from it.

"On an experiential level, this ideal condition is characterized by feelings of *belonging*, connectedness, inner peace, emotional balance, and psychological well-being. Diné (Navajo) people have characterized their experience and awareness as Hózhó (*Beauty*). To be in *right relationship* is to be cognizant of 'Beauty all around'—in the landscape, in relations with others, in ourselves, and with the stages of life. 'Beauty flows from the mind or inner form of the person.'[1] I feel reverence for this teaching.

"In this cultural context, Beauty is a *way of being* in right relationship with *all that is*. When a person doesn't believe or experience this, the effect is a feeling of isolation and exclusion. We might call it 'spiritual dissonance.' Indigenous wisdom traditions tell us that healing a person's broken spirit is crucial to restoring interpersonal and social/tribal relationships.

"I readily admit that while I might attempt to theoretically and/or conceptually grasp Indigenous peoples' restorative practices or this concept of 'Beauty' from an academic or philosophical perspective, I am inherently and unavoidably incapable of fully comprehending, let alone ever experiencing, the language, culture, and sacred mythology of Native Peoples within which ritual healing exists and receives its power of psychological healing. Their experience and understanding is theirs, and theirs alone.

"'Restoration' as proscribed and practiced by Indigenous people is a profoundly more comprehensive, complex, intricate, and sophisticated process grounded in cultural traditions than 'restoration' as pursued and understood in a conventional western restorative justice context and situated within a western Judeo-Christian worldview.

"Some scholars track the 'spiritual roots' of restoration in religious texts and traditions.[2] But limiting any discussion of spiritual restoration to religion reminds me of a well-known quote by the Buddha: 'It's not the finger pointing at the moon, it's the moon.' Unless we've stood on the moon, how can we know what an experience of the moon is? The best we can do is listen to the stories of those who've been there, and trust, try to identify with what they're describing—what it might have felt like to be there.

"I believe the same could be said about an experience of a restoration of spirit. We can't fully understand what that means until or unless we've experienced it, but we can ask people what they mean when they say, 'I've experienced a restoration of a relationship with myself and something much bigger than myself.'

"However, if we can learn from the wisdom of tribal restoration, it tells us that *intrapersonal* healing is a necessary element in the restoration of social relationships.

"I believe that the field of neuroscience is now beginning to explain in scientific terms what tribal healers intuitively know. First, that what we call consciousness and/or perceptual awareness is a manifestation of deeper subconscious states. No news there. Sigmund Freud theorized this and so did Carl Jung, but leading-edge neuropsychologists are now discerning the relationships between cognition and the experientially impacted subconscious memory—how the brain produces the mind and how the mind, our beliefs, thinking, stories, and memories, and the feelings they induce influences brain function.

"Second, ancient healers knew that accessing those deeper 'unseen' states holds the key to restoring a patient's relationship with themselves, the tribal community, and a perspective of life itself. Neuroscientists tell us that restoration involves restoring compromised neurological pathways between various parts of the brain that keep a person locked in subconsciously driven traumatism and reactive negativism.

"Third, ancient healers understood the transformative experiential effect of rhythmic patterning, drumbeats, chanting, mnemonic linguistics, and cadence. Today, neuroscience tells us that recovery from historical relational trauma can be accomplished through therapies that utilize rhythmic patterning such as EMDR, chanting, mindful breathing, and drumming.

"Simply put, both ancient healers and neuropsychology appear to be telling us that we can activate the brain's inherent capacity to heal itself under certain conditions. We can re-hardwire our brain and if accomplished, an *embodied* experience of profound peace, reconciliation, beauty, joy, and health become manifest. As Native people might describe it, 'right relationship with all that is.'"

Reparative Action

"Throughout our discussions, we've emphasized that restoration is fundamentally about the restoration of relationships.

"To repair the harm at its deepest level, we need to heal the original trauma by repairing the way the brain processes it. Healing, or reconciling trauma, is about restoring relationships between various parts of the brain that were negatively impacted by what happened. How do we do that? I have no 'definitive answer.' All I can do is relate how I pursued it and continue to."

A Story of Reparation

"As I explained, before I realized that the harm that I experienced had impacted my neurological functioning, I pursued an array of cognitive behavior-based approaches. But knowledge about psychology, woundedness, family dysfunction, and abuse never got at the *experiential core* of the trauma.

"Knowing more and 'changing my mind' didn't change how I was wired (or how I acted). I pursued pharmaceutical solutions too, and while they were effective in desensitizing the traumatic response, they only treated the symptoms and not the cause. They were bandages.

"What I needed was a *transformative* restorative experience that would disarm the neurological triggers of toxic emotional reactivity, stress, and self-defeating core beliefs. Simply put, I needed a new captain in charge of a restored nervous system.

"When I met with the psychiatrist after picking myself up off the floor, he said, 'I can give you some meds to take the edge off the intensity, but you need to deal with what happened to you.' He then explained that a new type of PTSD therapy was showing some promising results with Vietnam veterans. 'It's called Eye Movement Desensitization and Reprocessing (EMDR), and the way it works is that it enables the patient to reprocess traumatic memories and disarm the fight-or-flight reaction.'

"I asked, 'How long is this going to take, because I'm sick and tired of spending thousands of dollars on long, drawn-out navel-gazing bullshit sessions rehashing old dramas?' He said, 'People report experiencing remarkable recovery in a few sessions. But it's like any therapy—you'll get out of it what you put into it.'

"I left his office and went to the bookstore. The only book I could find was, as fortune had it, written by the discoverer and developer of EMDR, Francine Shapiro, Ph.D. (2001). Though the book was geared toward the clinician, it introduced me to the world of neuropsychology and a method of trauma transformation that seemed too good to be true.

The goal of EMDR is to achieve the most profound and comprehensive treatment effects possible in the shortest period of time, while maintaining client stability within a balanced system. [3]

"When I read this, I chuckled, 'Well, the client in this case is hardly stable, and I'd certainly like to know what a balanced system feels like.' But when I went online and read the following statement, I was encouraged.

The net effect is that clients conclude EMDR therapy feeling empowered by the very experiences that once debased them. Their wounds have not just closed, they have transformed. [4]

"This sounded authentically restorative. Though the evidence of success was more anecdotal than quantitative at that point in time, the testimonies of patients and certain procedural elements involved in the actual process convinced me to choose EMDR as the central reparative action to pursue.

"The procedural elements involved alternating, bilateral stimulation using rhythmic patterns of eye movements, tapping, and sound, and I immediately thought of Indigenous healing rituals which incorporate mnemonic rhythmic chanting of sacred song by the healer."

> **"It integrates the traumatic material. As our research showed, after EMDR, people thought of the trauma as a coherent event in the past, instead of experiencing sensations and images divorced from any context."** [5]

EMDR: Eye Movement Desensitization and Reprocessing

"Shapiro explains that one day while she was walking, she was having some disturbing thoughts that would come and go.

I noticed that when disturbing thoughts came into my mind, my eyes spontaneously started moving very rapidly back and forth in an upward diagonal [...] I started making the eye movements deliberately while concentrating on a variety of disturbing thoughts and memories, and I found that these thoughts also disappeared and lost their charge. [6]

"The correlation between eye movement and cognitive processing is well documented in research literature.[7] The more recent understanding of the similarity between the function of bilateral eye movement in EMDR in processing traumatic memory and the function of REM in sleep that occurs during dreams suggests 'if the bilateral stimulation of EMDR can alter brain states in a manner similar to that seen in REM sleep then there is now good evidence that EMDR should be able to take advantage of sleep-dependent processes, which may be blocked or ineffective in PTSD sufferers to allow effective memory processing and trauma resolution.' " [8]

> **"Hold that image in your mind and just watch my fingers moving back and forth," may very well reproduce what happens in the dreaming brain."** [9]

"What EMDR does is enroll the brain's inherent capacity for processing information and assigning meaning to it. When the traumatic event happened, processing was restricted to the thalamus-amygdala-hypothalamus 'crisis management network,' and never proceeded to the anterior cingulate where the threat could be secondarily signified, or passed on, to the frontal cortex where the information could be processed rationally.

"As a result, the trauma and its sensations became 'stored in the same form in which it was initially experienced, because the information-processing system has, for some reason, been blocked.' [10] Every time the memory was triggered, the physiological fight-or-flight network engaged. The meaning of the sensations—and any future similar sensations—was automatically interpreted as 'crisis.'

"Van de Kolk explains that with EMDR, 'the focus is on stimulating and opening the associative process.' [11] The associative process is the reprocessing of the memorialized traumatic sensations by connecting disparate neural networks between the emotional and rational brain.

"In layman's terms, the significance of the event to our brain needs to be reinterpreted and thus, have a new meaning attached—a new association. The traumatic event should become 'something that happened back then,' rather than 'something that is happening to me now.' If the correct associative process happens, we are desensitized to the memory, not by avoiding it, but by integrating it into a larger schema.

"Shapiro explains, 'When we ask the client to bring up a memory of the trauma, we may be establishing a link between consciousness (the present moment) and the site where the information is stored in the brain' (parentheses added): [12]

> *Specifically, there appears to be a neurological balance in a distinct physiological system that allows information to be processed to an 'adaptive resolution.' By adaptive resolution I mean that the connections to appropriate associations are made and that the experience is used constructively by the individual and is integrated into a positive emotional and cognitive schema.* [13]

How It Worked for Me

"After I decided to pursue EMDR, my next step was to create a concrete plan of reparative action. First, I committed wholeheartedly to the process. Whatever the EMDR protocol required, I was in. In truth, I committed to surrendering, no resistance. Like I said, I was done running and done fighting.

"Second, I spent a considerable amount of time with due diligence, finding what I considered to be the best EMDR practitioner. Third, I knew that the process was going to destabilize me and that I wasn't going to be firing on all cylinders. My elevator wasn't going to be going to all the floors.

"I enrolled a few close friends to keep tabs on me and even though I still had to teach classes, I lowered my own expectations of how effective I was going to be. I prepared lesson plans for the rest of the semester so that I wouldn't be scrambling about at the last minute. I also made damn sure I called friends on the phone to debrief after sessions. I had a support network in place. Fourth, I committed to keeping a detailed account journal of what I was about to go through.

> **The depth of darkness to which you can descend and still live is an exact measure of the height to which you can aspire to reach.**
> **—Laurens van der Post**

"I searched for a qualified practitioner. I had two criteria. First, the person needed to be either highly recommended or highly certified. I wasn't going to just hand my broken brain over to anybody. Second, I was going to trust my intuition. Recommended, qualified, or not, I wasn't going to waste any time, money, or vulnerability with someone I didn't immediately sense was (a) confident, (b) warm in demeanor, and (c) had worked with adult victims of childhood relational trauma. When it came to gender, I didn't have a preference. I just wanted the person to know what they were doing.

"The psychiatrist gave me the names of two therapists. In 2003, EMDR wasn't exactly mainstream and there weren't but a few therapists where I lived who were doing it. When I called each, I got their voice messaging. The first one's voice didn't sound too confident (at least on her machine). The second one sounded too young for me.

"When the EMDR Institute in California called me back with the name of a third therapist who was also a trainer, I was encouraged. I called, and my gut told me this was who I needed to work with. He gave me a brief history of EMDR and when he said, 'Trauma gets locked in the body as well as the brain,' I laughed and told him, 'Well, I got a lot of trauma-drama in me.' He didn't laugh, which impressed me. He sounded warm and said he had been doing this for ten years. His name was Keith.

"I scheduled an appointment for the following week. Keith told me to make a list of the ten most disturbing memories in my life. I explained that I was following the restorative process used in restorative justice and that the first step was explaining what happened in detail. Therefore, I had already assembled the most troubling memories. For once, I had done my homework before it was assigned.

"However, I asked him about the need to go back through each and every incident. "Is this really necessary?" I also explained that I was just beginning my education about EMDR and how trauma affects the brain. I stated that I wanted to understand the process as much as experience it. I told him I had read through Shapiro's text for clinicians. In that text, she indicated that EMDR was a 'time-free' psychotherapy, meaning that by reprocessing one particular memory, other memories are also reprocessed as 'clusters':

> *Since the information is linked associatively, many similar memories can be affected during the treatment session, and it is possible for the new positive affect and positive cognitions to generalize to all events clustered in the memory network.* [14]

"Keith explained, 'It's the traumatic response to the event that's getting reprocessed. So, if we can reprocess a particularly disturbing event, the hardwired traumatic response activated by other similar memories can be reprocessed as well. That's one of the reasons why this method works deeply in a shorter amount of time than conventional cognitive behavioral approaches.'"

I told the discussion group, "I've made the conscious decision to share the work I did in EMDR with all of you by providing the actual content from one of the sessions. My rationale for disclosing this is in alignment with the reason why we're having these discussions and committing them to this book—to encourage anyone to do their own work of deep restoration.

"The first session lasted ninety minutes. I thought it was going to be just an introductory meeting. I told Keith my story. I explained that I was recently divorced, had fallen into a depression, and 'couldn't get up off the floor.' I told him I thought I had abandonment issues and unresolved issues with bullying.

"He asked me about my current relationship with my parents. I said, 'They know I'm struggling but they don't understand. Hell, I don't understand either.'

"Keith said, 'Okay. Let's put what happened with your mother at the top of the list.' I immediately tightened up and he noticed this. I asked him, 'Do we really have to go there just yet?' Thinking back on this moment, I realize that I was hesitant to reveal a family secret.

"He said, 'Let's try this. Put your right hand gently over your heart and say, "I honor and have profound respect for my feelings."'

"I couldn't do it. He asked, 'What's coming up for you?' I told him, 'My mind is telling me, *This is stupid*, and *I won't believe it.*' He said, 'That's okay. We'll work with that.'

"He picked up a small wand and said, 'Keep your hand over your heart and follow the tip of the wand with your eyes.' He started moving it slowly back and forth about two feet in front of my face. 'See if you can say it now.' I did as Keith instructed. 'I honor and have profound respect for ... This is fucked up.' Keith asked, 'Is there an image that comes up for you?'

" 'Yeah,' I said. I took a deep breath and recalled the memory of the switching. At that point I couldn't continue watching the wand. My body was convulsing, and I doubled over in the chair. I could feel stinging on the back of my legs.

"When Keith began to wave a baton back and forth and I followed it with my eyes... something much, much deeper began to surface. It's hard to explain. There was a shift from my adult perspective—the man sitting there in the office talking about something that happened over forty years ago—to that of me as that child getting switched. I experienced an 'objective detachment.' It was happening to me as that little kid.

"The way I know this is because of the change in how I physically grieved and felt in my body. The grieving shifted from my shoulders down to my pelvis. As an adult, I close my eyes, cover my face with my hands, and usually 'swallow the sobbing' with no voice. I suppress it.

"As I followed the baton and the memory came vividly forward ... her face, my wrists, the feeling of the switch on my legs, her voice...I physically became the child, and in an instant, my face and chest opened up and my voice became that of a little boy. I was looking through *his* eyes. The convulsive grieving was coming from that little boy reliving the actual event rather than me as an adult reflecting about it intellectually and feeling conflicted.

"Keith said, 'Okay. Let's come back to present. Look over at that clock on the wall.' I looked up, and when I focused on the clock (which was a ridiculous cat with a swinging tail), I calmed down. He said, 'You're okay. We're just here in the office. Let's take a few deep breaths.'

"My entire body was shaking. I said, 'I was four years old, Keith.' This was me as an adult describing what happened. Keith replied, 'Okay, let's go with that,' and he started moving the wand again. I went right back into the scene.

"She was enraged. She wasn't punishing me—she was whipping the hell out of me, and I just stood there. I couldn't move. She had so much hatred in her face. She just kept switching me. She was yelling at me. She called me 'a little piece of shit' and told me I deserved it.

"The waving of the baton continued, keeping my conscious 'adult' mind busy while the child subconsciously came forward to tell his story. The grieving was the most intense and guttural convulsive grieving I had ever done in my life.

"Keith asked, 'What is he saying?' I said, 'Why are you doing this to me? I don't deserve this.' "

I told our group, "In that instant, with the voicing of that question and statement, something shifted. There was an instantaneous perceptual 'break' between her and me. She was 'over there,' away from me. It's hard to explain, but for the first time I saw her objectively as another human being standing apart from me, doing something violent.

"I was able to distinguish between 'me' and 'her' and in doing so, there was an immediate physical feeling of detachment, release, and separation. My entire body felt an instant release of tension and an extraordinary lightness. Like some heavy interior weight had been lifted. It was a feeling of physical liberation.

"Thinking about this moment later, I believe that what happened was that the trauma circuit of amygdala-to-hippocampus back to amygdala was interrupted and a new pathway from hippocampus-to-anterior cingulate was established regarding this specific memory. I'm not a neuroscientist, but I believe this is what was happening in my brain.

"In that instant, that little boy was no longer the reason why it was happening, trapped, and unable to move away. This liberating instant was organic or holistic. It just happened. It was that little boy that stepped away from her to question what was happening. He became his own 'self' instead of the object/reason for her rage. He was given objective discernment.

"This was the instant when I stopped being a victim and became a survivor. Some mind-body connection was made, some memory system was restored—that I physically felt, that enabled me to differentiate between me and her. I was no longer attached to her.

"Also, and this is hard to explain because it was a physical sensation, I didn't feel like there was any distance between the experience of that little boy and myself. We were the same person. I was him. There was no cognitive split. It was an instant of radical reintegration.

"Then another set began, and I went back in. Keith asked me, 'What is the belief you have about this?'

"I said, 'This has nothing to do with me, Keith. This is not about me.'

"I wasn't angry. I was simply clear about whose problem this really was. Even though I had known this intellectually as an adult, especially an adult who was trained in restoration, the child part of me needed to experience this, needed to come to this moment of empirical realization on his own.

"Keith stopped the wand and I once again returned to the office. My arms and legs were tingling, and I felt physically unburdened. We sat for a moment and what came to me was that I had just gotten a large piece of my 'self' back. I had ceased being a prisoner of the trauma. That little boy was the one that figured it out, not Will. I didn't have to retrieve him or rescue him from the scene…he retrieved himself. The scene lost its power over both of us because the memory became objectified. 'It' and I were not the same. It had let me go. I felt so at ease.

"I said, 'My God, this poor woman.' He said, 'Go with that,' and I began to follow the wand again.

"As I followed it with my eyes and the memory came forward, I saw her standing there apart from me and a tremendous feeling of compassion flooded me. I felt a warm wave of profound empathy come forth. I didn't manufacture this ... it emerged organically. And in that moment, as that child, I was able to see my mother in a moment of trouble and my heart opened up. It felt like my entire chest was expanding and I realized how deeply I loved her ... as a human being who was special in my life rather than a threat.

"It was the first time I experienced what I can only describe as a settling into the tangible presence of something profoundly 'other' and extraordinary. Perhaps this was a moment of experiential transcendence. I don't know. All I know is that I didn't conjure this. I didn't pursue this. I didn't rationalize or explain. I only knew it from sensing it, feeling it. I felt completely embraced, safe and secure, and fully present. Maybe my prefrontal cortex had now been activated.

"When we finished and I left the office, I stepped out into a very different world. Everything was more vivid. The sky; the cars passing by on the street; leaves of trees; colors; people walking by. I noticed and heard all of it. It was surreal. I felt an energized calm I had never experienced before.

"I walked a few blocks to meet a friend for coffee. She said, 'Something has changed with you. It's your shoulders. I have never seen you so at ease.'

"I shook my head. 'I have no idea what just happened. I think I came home to myself.'

"For the rest of that week, I felt pretty numb. Like I had been through a subconscious brain surgery. I would come home from teaching and just sit on my patio. I didn't have much energy, didn't eat much. I went for a few walks, watered the grass, and made a few calls, but for the most part I just sat on my back patio. I did wonder whether what I had experienced was real. I didn't spend too much trying to figure this out. I recorded what happened in the journal. I slept like a rock.

"Keith and I did about six sessions over two months. We worked through the bullying incidents, and the result was much the same. I organically detached and experienced compassion and forgiveness for them instead of rage and retaliatory resentment. They too were victims of numerous familial and cultural violations.

"Whatever happened in those moments during my sessions with Keith was a tangible experience of remarkable cognitive release on one level, and radical reintegration on another. Dissociated subconscious parts of myself and of past and present converged into one. The traumatized memories locked away for so long in a secret place were freed and allowed to become integrated as part of a larger narrative *history*."

"Can I interject?" asked Kris.

"Of course," I said.

"I'm struck by Langellier's concept that once a story is told, it becomes contestable. It seems to me that what EMDR was providing was a neurological contesting of the story you had about what happened to you. So, EMDR was enabling you to re-story the meaning of what happened. Is that right?" she asked.

"I never thought about that, but that makes sense," I said.

I continued, "The rip in the psychic fabric was mended when the relationship between the emotional brain and the rational brain was restored. They finally made peace with each other. The amygdala let go. The anterior cingulate was finally put in the game, and the prefrontal cortex got a fresh canvas to paint on. So, to answer your question, the re-storying was facilitated by reprocessing. Most important, it was organic. It wasn't forced.

"But the most extraordinary gift EMDR delivered was an experience of release followed by forgiveness. The reason I could never forgive was because that little boy never got justice, and the man went about trying to get it through force of will (no pun intended). I was always *fighting* for it. This is not an uncommon response for people who have been treated unjustly. Injustice is an experience of being overpowered and debased.

"The problem is that we convolute reclamation of power with force, with the need to retaliate, overpower, and punish the other who unjustly treated us. This is an understandable ego-driven power and the birth of retaliation and retribution. It comes from a place of woundedness," I said.

"And that is what makes us vulnerable to having that retributive impulse be manipulated for political power," said Brad.

"Yeah," I said. "The tragedy of this quest for power through overpowering is that in the end, we punish everybody, especially ourselves. We keep up the fight without tending to the cut to use Devonte's phrase. We don't sit with the pain and, therefore, we lose the transformational experience that honest grieving and forgiveness has to offer.

"Conversely, EMDR facilitated an experience of a different kind of power, one which can only come from *surrendering* to the emotional fact of what happened. With that surrender came detachment from the abusive act, the violence, and the people.

"This detachment is exactly what the restorative process is designed to provide and why I think EMDR is a method for 'deep restoration'—psychological detachment from the abusive act, or violation, by realizing, experiencing, and acknowledging that what an offender did was because of something troubling inside of them.

"We may have been the target, but it had nothing to do with us. Restoration is a boundary reclamation process. It forces us to take ultimate responsibility for our own experience. Experiencing that boundary-setting is a liberational act.

"EMDR extracted me from a subconsciously formed defensive posture and the power/powerlessness dichotomy. Once I stopped trying to draw a line in the sand, as my father suggested, I found myself sitting in the middle of a metaphorical circle which appeared on its own."

"That sounds like the deepest outcome of re-storying," said Aaron.

"I think so," I said.

> The nearly absolute dominance of materialism in the academic world has seriously constricted the sciences and hampered the development of the scientific study of mind and spirituality. Faith in this ideology, as an exclusive explanatory framework for reality, has compelled scientists to neglect the subjective dimension of human experience. This has led to a severely distorted and impoverished understanding of ourselves and our place in nature. (Manifesto for a Post-Materialist Science 2014) [15]

Subjective Knowledge of Restoration

"On a personal level of experience, restoration is subjective. How do you measure, quantify, prove, or contest when a person says, 'I've experienced a restoration of my relationship with myself, my community, and "all that is"'? What does that mean?

"If there is a spiritual dimension to restoration, how do you define or prove it? How do you measure spiritual restoration? How do you measure epiphany or awe? How do you prove the existence of, or connection with, an 'all-encompassing love,' 'higher power,' or greater reality? How do you quantify an experience of transcendence? What are the variables? What's the data? Where's the proof? How do you measure forgiveness?

"Referring to the statement above made by a collaborative of internationally recognized scientists, from a variety of scientific fields (biology, neuroscience, psychology, medicine, psychiatry), attempting to analyze any subjective experience of what we might call spiritual restoration challenges our western predilection for a materialist, proof-based, rational-centric demand for quantifiable data. Simply put, if we can't see it, define it, measure it, hold it in our hands, and prove its 'materiality,' how do we know it exists?

"The personal/spiritual or transcendent dimension of restoration confounds a conventional scientific paradigm which searches for objective empirical proof. It challenges the very foundation of what counts as 'knowledge.' It's a different, and I would argue, sensorial epistemology, an ancient way of embodied knowing and becoming only through an experience of deep reconnection.

"I admit to struggling not so much with this way of understanding restoration, but with translating that experiential and highly subjective understanding into any claim of 'knowledge.' I'm always left with more questions than answers. What is 'the matter' of restoration? What is its substance? Is there something 'essential'? Is there an 'it'? I need to go stand in a river again, and soon. Maybe the trout know.

"As an advocate for this way of looking at the world, through the lens of relationship, and working to implement communication practices and programming, I seem to always fall back on statistics as evidence that it works in social settings. When I'm asked, 'How do you know it works?', I say, 'Well, if you implement this way and these practices, *the studies* show a decrease in destructive conflict and an increase in satisfaction, etc.'

"How do you measure a personal experience of restoration? How do you quantify vulnerability, empathy, connection, or mercy? At a certain point, we have to take what people say about their experience as valid—if only for them. The more people describe their experience in similar ways, patterns develop, and the accounts become 'a way of knowing' and 'a way of trustful accepting.'"

> **"Hell is not so much a place as a state of consciousness in which one feels rejected by God, abandoned by everyone, and hateful to oneself."** [16]

Spirit Restoration

"One of the deepest wounds of childhood relational trauma is the installation of a core belief that the world is a dangerous and threatening place. And if people we rely upon for safety, such as our primary caregivers, are violent and abusive, how can we possibly believe that there is a loving energy that exists in the universe? People might tell us there is 'Something There' and that we belong to whatever 'that' is, but we don't believe it. Call it an existential mistrust. An original suspicion."

> **"And if we were raised in a religious tradition or environment that told us we were one step away from hell, we might have lived in fear of an existential threat, a wrathful and bodyless God lurking in the shadows. This was Scarry's point. With such threat, we might have turned our back on the whole concept of a God. A loving God may be a reality for others, but not for us."**

"And then we're condemned for not believing in that God," said Barb.

"Yes. And then that fear of condemnation gives rise to both internal condemnation and its manipulation rhetorically.

"Religions attempt to develop a human being's capacity for experiencing transcendence in terms, language, story, images, and rituals that humans can understand. Religion describes the experience of the transcendent as a relationship with a God (Higher Power) and offers suggestions (instructions) for how to consciously experience whatever 'God' is.

"But when the experience of transcendence is claimed as an exclusive product or property of a religious narrative, or doctrine, then the experience itself gets co-opted. It gets captured. The tool has started the conversion of the human longing for connecting with something bigger than ourselves into a weapon as Scarry indicated.

"When this happens, the darkest side of religiosity often rears its ugliest head—the exaltation of spiritual leaders and persecution of the nonbeliever in the name of God. It's a type of *relational spiritual abuse*. Kris, I like what you said about this being a spiritual felony committed by people.

"And yet, as we covered, Lisa Miller's research (and others) provides evidence that we are born hardwired with the capacity for a transcendent experience or awareness from the start. It's in our DNA. We're genetically predisposed to sense something both beyond as well as within. 'Out there' and 'in here.' How do we restore that awareness?

"I believe that this is where the restorative process asserts its deepest objective—to restore a person's connection with wonder, awe, and a feeling of reverence for life itself —'all that is.'"

> **"The great illusion we must all overcome is the illusion of separateness."** [17]

"EMDR facilitated brief moments of what I would call 'subconscious reintegration.' In those moments, I experienced detachment, release, repair, reconciliation, forgiveness, and compassion. The problem was that even after having gone through such a subconscious altering process which disarmed the trauma circuitry, the conscious belief system driven by the false sense of self that I had developed to protect the wounded kid in me remained.

"EMDR did its work in the deep neural landscape. Now, I needed some cognitive restoration. Old beliefs and patterns of thinking are hard to let go of. Simply put, I needed a re-cognition of my foundational belief system about the meaning of life. Why are we here? Why do we exist? The same old question—'What's the point?'"

Holding the False Self Accountable

"As I explained in our previous discussion, Thomas Keating (1999) and others describe the false self as a type of persona that we unconsciously develop in the pursuit of unmet early childhood needs of security and survival, affection and esteem, and power and control. Unconsciously looking to satisfy those instinctual needs as adults, we pursue their fulfillment in human relationships, and social-cultural symbols of status, success, wealth, competition, etc.

"We construct a compensatory personality. Much like an actor assumes a character, traumatized children and adults can assume a false persona to protect their woundedness. It's an unconscious strategy, a mask, a type of psychological armor. We unknowingly present, perform, persuade, manipulate, strive, and demand to attain what we think will make us acceptable, gain approval, feel safe, and 'be happy.'

"When we don't get what we think will make us happy, we get frustrated and as Keating states, 'off go the afflictive emotions' [18] such as bitterness, anger, resentment, judgment, depression, self-loathing, and abandonment," I said.

"Sorry to interrupt, but that describes what's happening with our former president," said Brad.

"Maybe so," I replied. "Looking through the lens of restoration, we have to ask what might've happened to him. This realization should empower us to unflinchingly hold the behavior accountable. Realize it is an expression of a wounded psyche and perhaps mental illness. Prevent the person from continuing to impact us with that behavior. We have to hold the addiction to negative attention accountable much like we would a child throwing a tantrum."

"Once again, that's a pretty compassionate approach," said Barb.

"And once again, is there really any other way?" I asked. "The more we judge and condemn, the more we attach, and the less we understand the woundedness that drives the behavior. We become subject to that behavior and not objective about the behavior which should motivate us to reject the behavior while maintaining our own dignity.

"The manner in which the false self is conducted and maintained is through a false belief system which fuels negative thought *patterns*. If we believe we're not worthy or acceptable from the very start, then we will look for confirmation in the circumstances and relationships that constitute our life.

"As survivors of childhood relational trauma, unrestored, what we believe about ourselves and what we tell ourselves is not the truth. It's distorted. We come by it honestly, but it is, in fact, not accurate. It's a false narrative, and we filter our daily life through it. To restore, we have to re-story ourselves. We have to dismantle the armor."

> **"How much false self are you willing to shed to find your True Self?"** is the lasting question.[19]

"First, we have to realize that the things we've been pursuing, in fact, won't make us feel whole (e.g., job, money, relationship, status, power, etc.). They may satiate what the ego (or society) tells us we need to be acceptable, but *they won't satisfy us on a spiritual level.*

"Second, we have to remove the mask and let go of our distorted sense of self. To do so, we have to *identify our false beliefs* and the *patterns of negative thought* they produce. Whenever we tell ourselves—unconsciously or not—that we're not enough, or that we have to be more or less than we are, it's the false self talking—and it's a lie.

"Third, we have to sit in the middle of the whirling emotional turmoil we've been running away from, let it surface, listen to it, feel it, express it, and let it go. The armor of the ego has been protecting us from this pain, but also keeping it in place. The wounded ego reinforces the lie. It has to because it has been in charge of our perceptions, protecting us.

"It doesn't go easily. Dying to the false self and the false narrative it produces *is* painful. Who are we if we're not our false self? There's no way around it. EMDR is one way to process that pain. When the ego stops defending or being in control, all the shame, self-loathing, feelings of abandonment, anger, remorse, and 'emotional sediment of a lifetime' begin to surface (Keating, 1999). It has a voice. What is it saying to us?

"This is why the ego wants to take back control. It doesn't want us to feel the pain. The ego wants to keep the lid on. The ego is running the show. Just as the roots of memorialized trauma exist in the subconscious, so do the motivations and well-rehearsed strategies of the false self, its false core beliefs, negative thought patterns, and its superficial goals.

"What I've found is that we have to surrender *all of it* into stillness and the Embrace of an Unconditional and All-Encompassing Love that we may not know or have experienced as existing *until we let go absolutely*. We have to trust that there's something Else behind the door, something bigger than us. This is the greatest act of the spiritual warrior—to surrender."

"That's exactly what we do in recovery," said Brad.

"This is not a quick fix like EMDR, but it's the only truly restorative conscious way. In this regard, pain proves the pathway to freedom. Ultimately, to be restored to the truth of ourselves and the Beauty that resides within and all around, we have to accept, and even embrace, our imperfectness. With humility, we have to allow the lie we've told ourselves and others about ourselves to surface and die. But first, we have to become aware of the lie," I said.

"And if the person can't come to that realization on their own?" asked Barb.

"Intervention," said Brad.

"The fact of the matter is simply this: transcendence is moving through…not around or over the pain. It's not about conquering. It's about conceding. As Richard Rohr suggests, it's about 'falling upward.' " [20]

All-Encompassing Love

I asked the group, "Where is this 'all-encompassing love' to be found? In my case, I wasn't interested in going back to a church. What I wanted was direct access with no mediator. I wanted an experience of the moon and not the finger pointing at it. I wanted an unobstructed connection.

"EMDR taught me that all I had to do was surrender. I didn't do anything special to experience what I did during EMDR except become willing, open, and completely vulnerable on an emotional and psychological level to the painful memories of what happened to me as a kid.

"What happened in those experiences was a tangible experience of 'a Presence' emerging of its own accord when my defenses were down. It's like one of those optical illusion posters. The image underneath appears only when you stop staring at it.

"To try and reexperience that, I tried various forms of mindful-based meditation. There's an immense body of research and literature about the benefits of meditation. Meditation lowers the heart rate, releases and reduces anxiety and stress, and sharpens the focus. It's good for the body and good for the brain.

"Because of the brain's neuroplasticity—the ability of the brain to create new neural pathways or discard others to adapt—with meditation, we can change the way our brains are hardwired. We can defragment our memory system. There is no doubt that we can become a less reactive, more compassionate, gentle, and present human being with a daily retreat into mindful awareness of these qualities. These qualities then become present in our interactions with others.

"As I tried to be mindful in meditation, however, there was something missing and this was the experience of the presence of an All-Encompassing Love. My mind was too, well, full. There wasn't any room. I didn't need to be more mind-full. I needed mind-less-ness.

"I was so focused on observing what I was thinking in order to think differently or not think that I wasn't able to surrender thinking altogether because I had nothing to surrender it to that I could trust. As such, I wasn't experiencing the Presence I had experienced in EMDR. I was stuck between a rock and the altar. I couldn't go back to church, and I couldn't just 'be the rock.'

"What I realized was that more than just a meditation practice, I needed a surrender practice which would allow for a relationship to emerge with a consoling, tender, and loving Energy. I needed a meditative *prayer* practice that would facilitate a consistent intimate encounter with a loving Presence. Call it a 'Sacred Original Parent.'

"I believe this might be something that any adult survivor of childhood relational trauma or neglect needs to consider. If a parent was abusive or emotionally absent, a relationship with a Higher Power or Presence can provide the loving internal embrace that was missing. If we're going to be surrendering our false self and its underlying emotional and psychological pain, I suggest we need some loving Presence to surrender it to. But we have to surrender before that Presence emerges. It's an enigma.

"For me, nonverbal prayer initiates that restorative encounter. Prayer is the interior performance of relationship with an unconditionally Loving Source. Prayer restores our original capacity for transcendent experience and sense of reverence by activating a feeling of consolation and trust. Prayer is performative.

"If we don't pursue this relationship with a Loving Source within ourselves, we will continue to seek it outwardly in relationships with others and the cultural status symbols, as Keating suggests. We'll do anything to fill this honest longing for acceptance and connection, but we'll seek it from sources that by nature can't provide it. Divine trust—the kind an unconditionally loving and affectionate parent enables—can only come from one place."

God?

"When I use the term 'God,' I do so nonexclusively. I'm not capable of defining what God is nor am I interested in assigning or limiting whatever concept of God *is* to any religion, image, narrative, doctrine, gender, persona, or human likeness. It's not the name that matters, but the experience of unconditional loving Energy that does. The need for a name fades as the experience emerges.

"Does this Presence or Energy really (objectively) exist, or is it a projection of a wishful and yearning imagination? I don't think it matters. I look at it as a spiritual technology for deep healing guided by reverence. Trying to figure out what 'God' is or isn't keeps us stuck in the intellect and away from the powerful experience of communion. 'God' becomes an artifact. The subjective experience is what matters in the process of healing relational trauma.

"Is the sense of this Presence a natural consequence of neurospiritual restoration, as Miller might suggest? I believe so. In fact, I think the two are coterminous, or co-occurring, and I think this is exactly what the neuroscience of spirituality is now proving."

> **"A great many researchers of various religious and non-religious backgrounds now believe that what we call the divine lives in our neural circuitry, and that science can now both evoke its presence and also help us understand it more fully."** [21]

"If Miller is correct in her assertion that we are born with the innate capacity for transcendent experience, and I believe she is, then removing the false self and reprocessing trauma memory restores this spiritual capacity on a neurological level.

"When these two components of restoration are working together—the brain and surrender to an unconditional Loving Source—I believe we are being primed for an experience that mystics call 'unification.' We become the Love we surrender to."

> **"Our brain-scan studies of contemplative forms of Buddhism and Christian meditation show that when activity in the parietal areas decreases, a sense of timelessness and spacelessness emerges. This allows the meditator to feel at one with the object of contemplation: with God, the universe, peacefulness, or any other object upon which he or she focuses."** [22]

"Keating characterizes this process as 'Divine Therapy,' and this makes perfect sense.[23] Typically, we go into conventional therapy (Cognitive Behavioral) to talk about our problems. We tell the therapist our story. We explain what's happening and maybe what happened in childhood. We dump our bag of accumulated psycho-emotional junk on the floor and the therapist separates it out, organizes it into categories, diagnoses it, and classifies it.

"The therapist suggests strategies, solutions, methods, and techniques to 'manage' our neurosis. It's a secular practice informed by diagnostic language and the conventional practice of psychotherapy. It takes time and a lot of money. The work that Keith and I did was fully grounded in neurological reprocessing and took only a month.

"Divine Therapy assumes that 'The Therapist' already knows our story. We don't need to explain anything. In fact, attempting to explain, think about, and/or manipulate the pain with cognitive methods keeps it locked in the ego's intellectual interpretation and away from the source of the dysfunction—our brain's inability thus far to effectively reprocess and release the emotional pain buried on a subconscious level. In this regard, language and intellect become barriers."

Neurospiritual Restoration:
The Brain Aligns with the Heart in Prayer

"The emerging field of research on what the brain is doing when engaged in spiritual experience is referred to as 'neurotheology.' I prefer the term *neurospirituality* because it widens the interpretive lens to include spiritual practices and experiences which may or may not include recognition of a God, Gods, or religion.

"Theology is the study of 'a God' and/or religious belief. While neuroscientists have focused primarily on practitioners within a tradition, I don't think it's fruitful to exclude other forms of contemplative practices—not necessarily grounded in a religious doctrine—that might engage neurological function similarly. For me, standing in a river repeatedly casting a fly is contemplative. The river is 'the presence.' The trout, however, are 'finny jokesters' and constant reminders that I'm not in control!

"In simplest terms, neurospiritual restoration implies that as we pursue a relationship with an All-Loving Presence, maybe in nature, the experience of this pursuit facilitates the restoration of the relationships between the various parts of the brain that keep us stuck in the past. Sensing this Presence brings Peace.

"As I stated above, for adult sufferers of unresolved childhood relational abuse or neglect, it is crucial that this presence embody a depth of love, experienced as unconditional tenderness, compassion, consolation, acceptance, and affection. These are the characteristic experiences of a child safely held in their caregiver's arms, complemented by the admiring gaze and protective embrace of a loving partner. It's an interior space of welcoming.

"In terms of the combined restoration of brain and spirit, if we need proof, the science bears this out:

> If you want to maintain a healthy anterior cingulate cortex, frontal cortex, and limbic system, by all means meditate and pray, but only on those concepts that bring you a sense of love, joy, optimism and hope.[24]

"What Andrew B. Newberg and other neuroscientists are telling us is that as we pray and meditate, we enact the restoration of relationships between various parts of the brain; relationships which have been violated by relational trauma. These words from Richard Rohr are profound, and so restoratively true:

When we don't know love, when we experience only the insecurity and fragility of the small self, we become restless, violent, and hateful. But in contemplation we move to a different space where we see the illusion of separateness. [25]

"Relationally traumatized children have no safe interior place of retreat. As adults looking for this place, contemplative prayer can provide this inner sanctuary where we can surrender our false self, allow the anguish to surface, and release it into the loving Presence of a Divine Caregiver. When this happens, the brain continues to heal. New neural pathways are created, and old ones discarded. The old false self begins to fade, and a more authentic self emerges, one that realizes its irrevocable place in the Great Heartbeat of the World.

"Perhaps this is what is meant by the biblical verse Matthew 18:3: 'Unless you turn and become like children, you will never enter the kingdom of heaven.' I interpret this to mean 'unless we allow ourselves to become completely vulnerable, we won't experience the presence of a divine loving embrace.' We have to fall before we can be caught."

"What happens if you don't catch fish?" asked Barb wryly.

"They have a God in their life and it ain't me," I said.

Closing Discussion

"I realize I've taken us deep, far, and wide into an esoteric landscape of restoration," I said. "We got together because we all wanted to see how restoration could matter in our workplaces and in our lives. While we've covered that, I took a risk and just 'let it all hang out' with what I've learned and experienced with restoration on a personal level. I'm wondering how this all sets with you. If there is a message in all of this, what is that message?" I asked.

Kris spoke. "It's going to take me awhile to unpack all of this. There's just so much to consider."

"Ya think?" said Barb. "When do we get your notes?"

"What notes?" I laughed.

Barb caught on and just smiled.

"I'll mail them with the rock," I said.

Laughter. It was a good release. Kindred spirits.

I continued. "Seriously. What's the message in all of this for you?" I asked. "Barb?"

"Okay. Two things. First, this entire discussion has made me realize that I've been confronting 'the world' with my defensiveness. That takes a lot for me to admit. Your comment about the false self being a type of armor really struck me. But second, and this is really my takeaway, there's a different way—a very pragmatic way—to address the things that people do that piss me off. This whole restorative process gives me a different way to look at those things and actually make a difference instead of just bitching about it.

"I really do love people. That's why I became a nurse. But my judgment of people, my 'evaluation' of them, to use your term, is what has kept me from experiencing joy. I've been so focused on other people's imperfections and deficits that I haven't looked at my own. That too, takes a lot for me to admit," she said.

I took a chance. "Barb, don't you think it's ironic that your name is 'Barb' and you've described yourself as a cactus?"

"Oh gawd!" she laughed.

"Even cactuses bloom," said Aaron.

Silence.

"Love that, Aaron. So, yeah, the message to me is that restoration is a way to bloom," said Barb. "But let's be clear. That ain't gonna happen overnight."

"Patience, grasshopper," said Brad.

"I hate grasshoppers," said Barb. "They're annoying."

"You really need to restore your relationship with grasshoppers," said Devonte.

More laughter.

"Devonte, what's your takeaway from all of our discussions?" I asked.

He thought for a minute. "I'm conflicted. I'm hopeful, but I'm a realist. The transgenerational piece and 'restoring the harm of our ancestors' is so obvious, but I seriously doubt it'll ever happen on a meaningful scale. I think we all agree it needs to happen and that's the argument you've been making, but I just can't see how white people's understanding of their own privilege and acceptance of another history is ever going to change. I don't mean to sound pessimistic, but that's how I feel. Every time we try to teach or enlighten youth in hopes of future change, books get banned, Black kids get shot by police for wearing hoodies.

"I'm tired of seeing people have to fight for their right to exist, to be learned about, and be treated as human beings. And not just Black people—any people who aren't white, male, so-called 'Christian,' and heterosexual. Any restorative shift that needs to happen is so massive, so tectonic, that it seems futile. And we seem to be going backward. We never seem to fully 'break from the past.'

Devonte continued. "But on a personal level, like you said, 'you found a justice you had been looking for your entire life.' This resonated with me. The possibility of a justice that restores gives me hope. Soothes me. I don't like my own retributive impulse. It's kept me feeling protected, but also exhausted. You reach a point where you've had enough. What then? Maybe it's time for me to do a little restorative soul-searching.

"So, the deeper message I get from our talks is that you just have to keep moving forward. Like we've said, one conversation, one interaction, one connection at a time. What you gave us, in addition to baring your own soul, which I found very moving, is a way to have that conversation. I intend to use the S.H.A.R.E. process as a discussion guide. I'm getting ready to teach a section on the history of immigration in America. You can ban a book, but you can't ban a conversation. And even if you do, or try to, that conversation is still going to happen—underground, on the streets, and in our homes.

"I guess what I'm saying is if there's any message of hope I received from our discussions, it's that there is a way, like Barb said. Connecting with all of you has also given me hope. It's been very meaningful and felt safe. I wish our conversations would continue," he finished.

Brad commented. "Thank you, Devonte. You always seem to say what's on my mind. It's sobering. We have a saying in recovery, 'We do the footwork and stay out of the results.' We've overused the allegory, but it's the little girl on the beach."

"Joan?" I asked. "What message did you find?"

"Authenticity and courage. Or maybe the courage to be authentic," she said.

She continued, "I had no idea what to expect we would talk about. I just wanted to learn how to handle conflict using these skills. We went so much deeper than that.

"I had trouble digesting everything you said about trauma, the whole brain science thing, and using the restorative process to heal both individual and generational trauma, but intuitively, it made sense. I'm glad you wrote all this down because it's going to take me some time to digest too. I'm not an auditory processor. I need to read something several times before I understand it.

"The conversation I had with my director was very empowering for me. I wouldn't have been able to have that conversation if I didn't get all of your support and guidance. Your support gave me the courage and practical skill to 'speak into' my values and hold what she was doing accountable, but with empathy. To use your words, we both mattered in that discussion. Like everyone else, I'd like our discussion to continue."

"Thanks, Joan. Melissa? What about you?" I asked.

"Like Joan, I came into these discussions to learn how to implement restorative practices into our healthcare facility. I like that we got that, or at least, I did. But you took us way deeper. The message I'll take with me is that there is a lot more at stake than just putting in a few simple restorative practices to resolve conflict. Restoration goes much, much deeper than just sitting in a circle and talking about how a surgeon or physician spoke rudely to a nurse or tech. I'm fascinated by the whole paradigm, worldview, mindset concept.

"I found your experience with EMDR to be not only fascinating and touching, but also invaluable, both on a personal level and on a professional administrative level. I intend to research it more and see how we might facilitate people pursuing that when trauma is an obvious motivation in destructive interaction.

"I generally understood the S.H.A.R.E. process because you came to our facility and did a workshop. But the S.H.I.F.T. technique is something we really need in our facility. I like what you said about 'imagine if everyone in a workplace was not only trauma-informed, but trauma-responsive in their communication habits.' We deal with physical and emotional trauma every hour of every day. But we don't know how to interact with or support each other when we are the ones who are experiencing relationship-based trauma that may have roots in our own personal history," Melissa added.

"Or as a result of empathy burnout," said Barb.

Kris spoke next. "I'd like to piggyback on what Melissa said about worldview. I'm very familiar with trauma, brain science, and EMDR. That's the landscape we traffic in at our center. Your story made sense even though I've never heard such a detailed explanation of the experience of the process. But the bigger, deeper, more ancient philosophy of restoration, to be honest, spoke to a much deeper part of my soul. This is a feminine worldview," she said.

"I agree, but what do you mean by that?" I asked.

"Well, look, Justice Yazzie explained the restorative approach as a horizontal paradigm. You described it as a 'relationship-centric' paradigm. You said restoration is all about relationship. It's about power-sharing rather than power-seeking. It's the antithesis of a paternal-driven hierarchy where 'might makes right,'" she said.

"The restorative approach is a receptive approach. It welcomes. It integrates. It seeks to heal rather than punish. It's wisdom that is emergent. That's female wisdom. It births wisdom. Call it pagan, but it's holistic. It's about flow. It's about interdependency. It's about connection and integration, not exclusion and violence. It's about balance and harmony," she said.

"So, if restoration is a feminine sensibility and wisdom, what role do men play?" I pressed.

"I think you need to ask men what role they see," said Kris.

Brad interjected. "I'd like to respond to that. First, we're taught to accomplish. That's not inherently bad or wrong. But when we're told that accomplishment is what decides if we're worthy or not, if we're 'men' or not, then any means of getting there becomes fair game. So right away, our relationship is with accomplishment rather than relationships themselves. Accomplishment is our primary and primal objective. I saw an interview with a film director, I wish I could remember his name, but he said, 'Winning is the new moral compass.' To win is moral. To lose is shameful.

"Personally, I don't think this is 'new.' Conquering has been around since forever. It served a purpose in hunting and war, but not in terms of suppressing other people and certainly not in understanding the deeper meaning of life or advancing an enlightened society.

"Second, young men have no models to show us the virtue of humility, the value of restoration and peacemaking, and necessity of service to others. Service is where true satisfaction and meaning lies. If young men don't get it at home, it's up to teachers, coaches, and mentors.

"I have a friend for whom I have profound respect. He's a Chief Deputy of Detention at a county correctional facility. He didn't have to do that. He could've comfortably retired from the police force after twenty-plus years. But he chose to work at the facility because he felt a calling to be of service to young men in crisis—and the community, who for the most part have no role models. It was the calling to be of service that pulled him back, and much deeper into the 'bowels' of incarcerated male despair. He's nurtured a successful reentry program. He sees incarceration as an opportunity for healing a wounded male psyche.

"This is a guy who is by any standards, masculine. Why? It's not because he is trained in enforcement and martial arts or guns. It's because of his values. Those values of service to others is what he is modeling not only for the inmates, but his staff as well. That's leadership.

"The problem, the tragedy, is that this archetype is not glorious. It's not vaunted or hallowed. You don't get medals in the media for this. Instead, you get men like our former president who can become artifacts of a power-over sickness. These are not men in the ancient ways of being masculine. They are wounded boys who never learned that our primal role is to facilitate peace and civility. This is one of the main reasons I wanted to participate in these discussions, to teach our clients how to make peace with each other.

"So, when we ask, 'What is the role of men in restoration?' it is to facilitate it. If it's female wisdom, great. Men have been sitting in circles around fires since fire was discovered. But our job, or role, is to be of service to that, to be fire keepers. That's just my opinion," said Brad. "I should add that when I say, 'female wisdom,' I'm referring to relational wisdom and that extends to our LGBTQ+ communities."

"That's beautiful, Brad," said Melissa. "If I can add, the circle is the ultimate symbol of female energy."

"The womb" I said. "The birthplace of peace and certainly life itself. Metaphorically, that's what I've been trying to illustrate. Restoration is emergent. We don't know what restoration is, or will be, until we engage in this discussion. What I've tried to do is provide the communication skills, the process of engagement to facilitate that emergence."

"Aaron, you've been quiet so far. What's the message you received from either this discussion or overall?" I asked.

"So much to unpack here. I'm not sure I can articulate what I'm thinking or feeling. I like what Melissa said about there being a lot more at stake in the restorative process. I felt a pit in my stomach listening to your story and what happened to you both in your family and at school. But then it made me realize the importance of exposing and understanding the passage of trauma through generations.

"I really like the term 're-storying.' Trauma-tracking is retelling a story, or maybe telling the story of what happened for the first time. More importantly, what your story told me was that we can change how we relate to anything that happened to us, like trauma.

"Your experience of restoration on a personal level served as a call to action for me. I can relate to some of your experiences both in your family and certainly at school with bullying. The call to action is a call for me to do my own work of addressing how what happened to me is still happening to me on the inside.

"What resonated with me the most is the spiritual aspect of restoration. I can completely identify with your experience of what you called an 'organic arising' of an awareness of a presence.

"When I was growing up, nature became my 'God.' I spent a lot of my childhood roaming in the woods. The peace and feeling of 'home' that I experienced when I would go stand at the edge of a meadow, watch the sun come up and see the dew glisten on the meadow grass, and then watch the birds wake up and start chatting away, was holy to me. I felt a part of that and connected to 'all that is,' to use your term, that I never felt in church. I belonged in that meadow.

"I was raised on a farm and attended an evangelical church every Sunday. It was too noisy for me. I couldn't wait to get back to something more real and quieter—that meadow. That meadow was my real church. That meadow had a presence that comforted me. That meadow was my surrogate mother. I knew I wanted to be an environmentalist when I was nine years old.

"But I also can identify with your journey through retribution. For a while, I aligned myself with what I would call 'eco-retribution,' punishing the people who were violating the environment. I spiked trees and I even dismantled a road-grader one time when a logging company was building a road to haul trees they had cut down. Then I realized that all I was doing was hurting the people who were just trying to make a living. That's when I enrolled in college to get a degree in environmental sciences. I wanted to be a part of the solution and not just an angry critic.

"I loved your story about John Tucci and his commitment to saving lakes. That story gave me hope and flamed a fire in my belly I've had my entire life," said Aaron.

"That's what I mean by fire keeping," said Brad.

I replied, "If I can add, Tucci's work didn't stop with restoring lakes. He expanded his vision to restore eastern hemlock forests being decimated by an invasive beetle (hemlock woolly adelgid 'HWA'); 90% of the geographic range of eastern hemlock in North America has been affected by HWA as of 2015: [26]

> *Major changes in ecosystem structure and function, including hydrologic processes, are expected with the loss of hemlock. Loss of the eastern and Carolina hemlock from hemlock woolly adelgid infestation will likely result in many ecological shifts in eastern North America. (Wikipedia)*

"John used the same restorative approach he used with lakes to restore forests. With lakes, he recognized that what was missing in the ecosystem was dissolved oxygen. With hemlocks, he recognized that what was missing was a species-specific natural predator of the wooly adelgid."

> The Pennsylvania Department of Conservation and Natural Resources Bureau of Forestry has released hundreds of thousands of adult S. tsugae beetles into affected hemlock forests of the eastern United States to determine its effectiveness at controlling the spread of the adelgid. [27]
>
> From 1995 to 1997, experiments in Connecticut and Virginia found that releasing adult Sasajiscymnus tsugae beetles into infested hemlock stands resulted in a 47 to 88% reduction in adelgid densities within 5 months of introduction. [28] The beetle's lifecycle is in parallel to the lifecycle of the hemlock woolly adelgid.

"John's company, Tree Savers, is the only commercial source of biological control agents for HWA being raised and provided to 'meet the needs of private landowners, non-profit organizations, and even government agencies.'

"Once again, he's working from within the ecosystem, but his efforts on a community and institutional level demonstrate using restoration as an organizing principle. Nobody wants to lose hemlock forests. What John did was not only provide a solution but also create a circle of collaboration between stakeholders to enact that solution. He assembled scientists, policy-makers, and local community-based organizations in a concerted effort," I said.

"Wow," said Aaron.

"Is there anything else you'd like to add?" I asked Aaron.

"Just that like everyone has said, I don't want these conversations to end," he said.

"Maybe what you can do is start a restorative discussion with your colleagues," I suggested.

"I knew you were gonna say that!" said Barb.

"Tune in again next week for another episode of 'As the World of Restoration Turns,'" I quipped.

Epilogue

How do you end a book, a conversation, about restoration? That's really two questions. How do you end a book, and how do you end a conversation about restoration?

I asked a trusted friend and advisor, Ted Klontz, Ph.D., "How do you know when a book is finished?" He said, "You stop writing."

I asked another friend who's written several books the same question. He said the same.

"Stop writing. Finish it. End this particular conversation. Say what you really mean. Make a strong statement. Call people to action. And then send the final draft to your editor and shut the damn computer off. Stop thinking about it. Walk away. Let it go. Save what more you have to say for another day, another book. Go stand in a river, Will."

I took their advice and stopped writing and returned to rivering. But a conversation about restoration never ends, nor should it.

Two Narratives

There are two central narratives being told in America right now. One is a fear-based narrative where diversity ("the other") is interpreted as a threat. The other narrative is one that recognizes the necessity of diversity for our survival as a species. It is a fear-less narrative that celebrates diversity with encouragement, invitation, and engagement.

The fear-based narrative is disintegrative. Its power depends on tearing people apart and casting us as enemies of each other. It is an adversarial narrative. The fear-less narrative is integrative. It is an advocacy narrative. Its power emerges from continuous engagement and recognition of shared humanity.

The fear-based narrative is a protectionist narrative which exalts sameness, gentrification, and uniformity.[1] Immigration, integration, and inclusion are rhetorically weapon-

317

ized by political actors to incite terror, foment racism, separatism, and build barriers. Its ultimate logic is one of violence, retribution, dominance, and control.

It's the illusion that exclusion is the only way. To make and keep America "great" we have to keep "those people" out—even if it means ripping children from the arms of mothers and fathers and putting them in cages.

This is a very dark, dangerous, and world-destroying narrative that can only exist in a morally bankrupt discourse rife with hatred, dehumanization, bigotry, and bitterness. Like all terror narratives, its power depends on exploiting a primal instinct for survival.

It does so with stories that demonize difference. Its power as a narrative relies on the convolution and/or suppression of truth and voice. It's a defensive discourse designed to divide, deceive, dissolve, and destroy democracy. It's a bitter narrative that produces bitter people.

The fearless narrative values and embraces diversity, social ecology, social justice, and the awareness that integration is the process by which diversity feeds a healthy social organism.

Immigration, integration, and inclusion are not expressions of "liberal idealism," but necessary nutrients to a prosperous and vibrant social ecosystem.

Fearless Narrative	Fear-Based Narrative
Diversity is regenerative	Diversity is threatening
Inclusion is necessary for growth	Exclusion is necessary for protection
Equity is an asset that sustains us	Equity is a liability that destabilizes us
The "other" is us	The "other" is the enemy
Power emerges through engagement	Power must be seized
Accountability requires understanding	Accountability demands retaliation
Communication is about interaction	Communication is about transaction

It would be easy to dismiss what I'm saying as a bunch of theoretical indulgence and that any discussion about these two narratives is best suited for a "woke" academic setting. But in fact, these two narratives represent two competing worldviews, two mindsets with fundamental core beliefs about life, the purpose of relationships, and what it means to be human, that impact us all. The fearless narrative invites any and all people to share their perspective.

And where these two narratives become real, tangible, and felt is in our day-to-day lived experience of each other in our families, schools, institutions, and workplaces, communities, and our relationship with the environment. What do we want that experience to be?

Narratives, the stories we tell ourselves about ourselves (consciously or not) have consequences. They direct our thinking, behavior, choices, decisions, and our regard for each other. Narratives impact our physical, mental, emotional, spiritual, and environmental health. Rather than simply being "stories" or myths that describe or represent an imagined reality, narratives create that reality in how they direct human behavior.

Understanding the power of narratives, accepting that they are not just stories but blueprints for how to be in relationship with ourselves, each other, and our world, presents us with a few questions.

First, which narrative would we rather inhabit and move forward? If you're reading this book, there's a good chance you much prefer the fear-less narrative.

Second, where do you see these two narratives playing out? Part of what this book has tried to accomplish is to help you spot the signs of a fear-based narrative and mindset. Those signs are evident just about everywhere we train our eyes. They're observable in how we parent; our leadership and management styles; our behavioral policies in our workplaces and institutions; how we resolve conflict and misconduct; how we achieve justice; how we regard and reconcile history; how we relate to the environment and our environmental policies, school curriculums and classrooms; and how we relate to ourselves.

Third, and what this book has primarily been about, how do we change the narrative? How do we break from a fear-based paradigm and shift to a fear-less paradigm? What's it going to take? It's been my argument and experience that one way is by restorative communication practices.

What happens when we make that shift? What are the outcomes? What are the principles and practices that make that shift possible? What resistance and objections can we expect as we work to shift our approach from a fear-based mentality to a fear-less experience? What will the "betwixt and between" stage look and feel like? What will we become? Who will we choose to be?

Lastly, and most importantly, the question we need to ask ourselves is, "Are we willing to do the necessary personal and collective soul-searching and work to make that shift? Are we willing to embrace our own fears, face them, recognize that we all have them, learn from them, and support each other to move full-heartedly and restoratively forward? Not just with those who agree with us, but those who ardently believe fear and dominance are the only way. Are we willing to 'sit in the middle' of this tension and embark on the restorative way?"

Okay. Enough words. Time to go stand in a laughing river, make the most elegant cast, and watch a big rainbow trout rise and then ignore my fly. I have no doubt that trout have a sense of humor. They're what makes the river laugh.

Notes

Chapter One

1. Rohr, Richard. 2022. "Quest for the Grail: A Heroic Journey." Daily Meditations: September 4, 2022. https://cac.org/daily-meditations/a-heroic-journey-2022-09-04/.

2. French, David. 2023. "Politics Can't Fix What Ails Us." New York Times, May 4, 2023. https://www.nytimes.com/2023/05/04/opinion/politics-civility.html.

3. Bruner, Edward M. 1986. "Experience and Its Expressions." In *The Anthropology of Experience*, edited by Victor W. Turner and Edward M. Bruner, 14. Chicago: University of Illinois Press.

4. Bruner, 14.

5. Bruner, Edward M. 1986. *The Anthropology of Experience*, edited by Victor W. Turner and Edward M. Bruner. Chicago: University of Illinois Press.

6. Nietzsche, F. W. 1968. *The Will to Power*, translated by W. Kaufmann and R. J. Hollingdale. New York: Viking.

7. Gennep, Arnold van. 1960. *The Rites of Passage*, translated by M.B. Vizedom and G. L. Caffee. Chicago: University of Chicago Press. (Original work published 1908)

8. Turner, Victor W. 1986. "Dewey, Dilthey, and Drama." In *The Anthropology of Experience*, edited by Victor W. Turner and Edward M. Bruner, 43. Chicago: University of Illinois Press.

9. Turner, 39.

10. Turner, 42.

Chapter Two

1. Trask, Robert L. 2001. *Mind the Gaffe: The Penguin Guide to Common Errors in English*. India: Penguin Books.

2. Zehr, Howard. 2005. *Changing Lenses: A New Focus for Crime and Justice*, 3rd edition, 86. Harrisonburg, VA: Herald Press.

3. Scarry, Elaine. 1985. *The Body in Pain: The Making and Unmaking of the World*. New York: Oxford Press.

4. Edgar, Andrew and Peter Sedgwick. 2002. *Cultural Theory: Key Thinkers*, 126. London: Routledge.

5. Edgar and Sedgwick, 126.

Chapter Three

1. For a deeper dive into the "retributive paradigm," see Zehr, Howard. 2005. *Changing Lenses: A New Focus for Crime and Justice*, 3rd edition, 86. Harrisonburg, VA: Herald Press.

2. Zehr, 81.

3. Zehr, 81.

4. Yazzie, Robert. 2005. "Life Comes from It." In *Navajo Nation Peacemaking: Living Traditional Justice*, edited by Marianne O. Nielsen and James W. Zion. 42–57. Tucson: University of Arizona Press.

5. Yazzie, 44.

6. Sagan, Eli. 1985. *At the Dawn of Tyranny: The Origins of Individualism, Political Oppression, and the State.* New York: Knopf. (In Yazzie, Robert. 2005. "Life Comes from It." In *Navajo Nation Peacemaking: Living Traditional Justice*, edited by Marianne O. Nielsen and James W. Zion. 46. Tucson: University of Arizona Press.)

7. Van Ness, Daniel W. and Karen Heetderks Strong. 2002. *Restoring Justice,* 2nd edition, 7. Cincinnati: Anderson Publishing.

8. Van Ness and Strong. 2002, 8.

9. Van Ness and Strong. 2002, 8.

10. Van Ness and Strong. 2002, 9.

11. Van Ness and Strong. 2002, 10.

12. Van Ness and Strong. 2002, 10–11.

13. Berman, Harold J. 1983. *Law and Revolution: The Formation of Western Legal Tradition*, 255–256. Cambridge, MA: Harvard University Press. In Van Ness, Daniel W. and Karen Heetderks Strong. 2002. *Restoring Justice*, 2nd edition, 10. Cincinnati: Anderson Publishing.

14. Cuartas, J., D.G. Weissman, M.A. Sheridan, L. Lengua, and K.A. McLaughlin. 2021. "Corporal Punishment and Elevated Neural Response to Threat in Children. Child Dev, 92: 821–832. https://doi.org/10.1111/cdev.13565.

15. TMP–Marian Response to Release of Names of Accused Priests, Brothers. March 28, 2019. https://archive.hayspost.com/2019/03/28/tmp-marian-response-to-release-of-names-of-accused-priests-brothers/.

16. Database of Publicly Accused. Retrieved October 11, 2022. https://www.bishop-accountability.org/accused-by-state-ks/.

17. Heinzl, Toni. 2001. "Suit Claims Molestation by Priest." *Fort Worth Star-Telegram*, May 8, 2001. https://www.bishop-accountability.org/news13/2001_05_08_Heinzl_SuitClaims_Ronald_Gilardi_6.htm.

18. Capuchin Province List of Credibly Accused Friars Has Hays, Victoria Connections. March 28, 2019. https://archive.hayspost.com/2019/03/28/capuchin-province-list-of-credibly-accused-friars-has-hays-victoria-connections/.

19. Fisher W. R. 1987. *Human communication as narrative: Toward a philosophy of reason, value and action.* Columbia: University of South Carolina Press.

20. Sunwolf and L. R. Frey. 2001. "Storytelling: The power of narrative communication and interpretation." In *The new handbook of language and social psychology*, 2nd edition, edited by

P. Robinson and H. Giles, 119–135. New York: John Wiley & Sons.

21. Hauser, G. A. 2002. *Introduction to rhetorical theory*, 192. Prospect Heights, IL: Waveland Press.

22. Burke, Kenneth. 1966. *Language as Symbolic Action*, 16. University of California Press.

23. Abrahams, Roger D. 1986. "Ordinary and Extraordinary Experience." In *The Anthropology of Experience*, edited by Victor W. Turner and Edward M. Bruner, 46. Chicago: University of Illinois Press.

24. Langellier, K. M. 1999. "Personal narrative, performance, performativity: Two or three things I know for sure." In *Text and Performance Quarterly* 19: 125–144. doi:10.1080/10462939909366255.

25. Kay, Elizabeth. 1985. *Chimayo Valley Traditions*, 22. Santa Fe: Ancient City Press.

26. Ibid., p. 21

27. Steele, Thomas J. and Rivera, Rowena A. *Penitente Self-Government Brotherhoods and Councils, 1797–1947*. Santa Fe: Ancient City Press

28. Scarry, Elaine 1985. *The Body in Pain: The Making and Unmaking of the World*. New York: Oxford Press. p. 200

29. Poena. https://en.wikipedia.org/wiki/Poena.

30. Scarry, Elaine. 1985. *The Body in Pain: The Making and Unmaking of the World*. New York: Oxford Press.

31. Scarry, 237.

32. Scarry, 23.

33. Scarry, 173.

34. Scarry, 183.

35. Scarry, 183.

36. Scarry, 191.

37. Scarry, 192.

38. Scarry, 193.

39. Scarry, 199.

40. Scarry, 200.

41. Scarry, 201.

42. Scarry, 201.

43. Scarry, 204.

44. Scarry, 205.

45. Scarry, 205.

Chapter Four

1. Anderson, James N. 2014. "What in the World Is a Worldview?: Part 1." January 22, 2014. https://www.crossway.org/articles/what-in-the-world-is-a-worldview-2/.

2. Kuhn, Thomas. 1962. *The Structure of Scientific Revolutions*. Chicago: University of Chicago Press.

3. Lévinas, E. 1948. *Time and the Other, and Additional Essays*, translated by R. A. Cohen. 1987. Pittsburgh, PA: Duquesne University Press.

4. Rohr, Richard. 2019. *The Face of the Other*, Daily Meditation: January 31, 2019. https://cac.org/daily-meditations/the-face-of-the-other-2019-01-31/.

5. Yazzie, Robert. 2005. "Life Comes from It." In *Navajo Nation Peacemaking: Living Traditional Justice*, edited by Marianne O. Nielsen and James W. Zion, 50–51. Tucson: University of Arizona Press.

6. Zehr, 81.

7. Yazzie, 46.

8. Van Ness, Daniel W. and Karen Strong. 2006. *Restoring Justice*, 3rd edition. Cincinnati: Anderson Publishing.

9. It's darkly ironic that the very people we have historically abused and marginalized by our own western justice methods of punishment and incarceration are who we now ask to teach us about their ways of justice.

10. Yazzie, 45.

11. Yazzie, 47.

12. Ross, Rupert. 1992, 2006. *Dancing with a Ghost: Exploring Aboriginal Reality*. Penguin: New York.

13. Langellier. 1985.

14. Yang, Andrew. 2022. "Opinion: The data are clear: The boys are not all right." Washington Post, February 8, 2022. Opinion | Andrew Yang: The boys are not all right - The Washington Post.

Chapter Five

1. Sullivan, Dennis and Larry Tift. 2006. *Handbook of Restorative Justice*. Edited by Dennis Sullivan and Larry Tift. New York: Routledge.

2. Bailey Maryfield, M.S., Roger Przybylski, M.S., and Mark Myrent, M.A. 2020. "Research on Restorative Justice Practices." *Justice Research and Statistics Association* (Research Brief). December 2020.

3. Sweet, Jacob. 2021. "The Loneliness Pandemic: The psychology and social costs of isolation in everyday life." *Harvard Magazine* (January–February 2021). https://www.harvardmagazine.com/2021/01/feature-the-loneliness-pandemic.

4. Rothenbuhler, Eric W. 1998. *Ritual Communication: From Everyday Conversation to Mediated Ceremony*, 15. Thousand Oaks, CA: Sage.

5. Wood, Julia T. 2013. *Interpersonal Communication: Everyday Encounters*, 95. Boston: Wadsworth.

6. City of Boulder, Colorado. 2006. Code enforcement study session [Memorandum]. February 28, 2006.]

7. Bruner, J. 1987. "Life as narrative." *Social Research* 54, 11–32. Langellier, K. M. 1989. "Voiceless bodies, bodiless voices: The future of personal narrative performance." In S. J. Dailey (Ed.) *The future of performance studies: Visions and revisions*, 207–213. Annandale, VA: National Communication Association.

8. Hochschild, Arlie R. 1979. "Emotion work, feeling rules, and social structure." American Journal of Sociology 85, 551–575.

9. About CASEL: Our History. https://casel.org/about-us/our-history/.

10. Bledsoe, William A. 2016. *The Seven Principles of Conscientious Communication: the 7R's.*]

11. Van der Kolk, Bessel. 2014. *The Body Keeps the Score: Brain, Mind and Body in the Healing of Trauma*. New York: Viking.

Chapter Six

1. Van der Kolk, 210.

2. Smith, Kevin. 2019. "Replication Data for Friends, Sanity, Health PLoS One." https://doi.org/10.7910/DVN/WCPGAU, Harvard Dataverse, V1, UNF:6:4+9XbIMDr4xzU-JE6Yfd0pg==.

3. Smith, 2.

4. Smith, 9.

5. Porges, Stephen W. 2011. *The Polyvagal Theory: Neurophysiological Foundations of Emotions, Attachment, Communication & Self-Regulation*. New York: W.W. Norton & Co.

6. Van der Kolk, 59.

7. Van der Kolk, 78.

8. Porges, Stephen W. 2020. "The COVID-19 Pandemic is a paradoxical challenge to our nervous system: a Polyvagal Perspective." *Clinical Neuropsychiatry* 17(2), 135–138.

9. Porges. 2011, 186.

10. Carter, Rita. 2010. *Mapping the Mind*, 83. Berkeley: University of California Press.

11. Bader, Michael D.M.H. 2018. "Depression as a Social Disease." February 28, 2018. https://www.psychologytoday.com/us/blog/what-is-he-thinking/201802/depression-social-disease.

12. Sweet, 2021.

Chapter Seven

1. Center on Positive Behavioral Interventions & Supports. https://www.pbis.org/.

2. Narvaez, Darcia. 2014. *Neurobiology, and the Development of Human Morality: Evolution, Culture, and Wisdom*, 11. New York: W.W. Norton & Company.

Chapter Eight

1. Narvaez, 245.

2. Narvaez, 245.

3. *In U.S., Decline of Christianity Continues at Rapid Pace: An update on America's changing religious landscape*. Pew Research Center, October 17, 2017. Acquired May 14, 2023, from https://www.pewresearch.org/religion/2019/10/17/in-u-s-decline-of-christianity-continues-at-rapid-pace/

4. McFague, Sallie. 1993. *The Body of God: An Ecological Theology*. Minneapolis: Fortress Press.

Chapter Nine

1. Transgenerational Trauma. https://en.wikipedia.org/wiki/Transgenerational_trauma.

2. Van der Kolk, 210.

3. Felitti VJ, Anda RF, Nordenberg D, Williamson DF, Spitz AM, Edwards V, Koss MP, Marks JS. Relationship of childhood abuse and household dysfunction to many of the leading causes of death in adults. The Adverse Childhood Experiences (ACE) Study. Am J Prev Med. 1998 May;14(4):245-58. doi: 10.1016/s0749-3797(98)00017-8. PMID: 9635069.

4. Harjo, Tim. *Strengthening Families for the Future: Exploring Trauma at Mashantucket Pequot*, White Paper, 7.

5. Van der Kolk, 219.

6. Van der Kolk, 233.

7. Van der Kolk, 232.

8. Van der Kolk, 232.

9. Van der Kolk, 64.

10. Van der Kolk, 39.

11. Van der Kolk, 56.

12. Van der Kolk, 56.

13. Van der Kolk, 56.

14. Van der Kolk, 57.

15. Van der Kolk, 57.

16. Van der Kolk, 59.

17. Van der Kolk, 59.

18. Van der Kolk, 60.

19. Van der Kolk, 61.

20. Van der Kolk, 133.

21. Van der Kolk, 82.

22. Van der Kolk, 115.

23. Van der Kolk, 115.

24. Van der Kolk, 117.

25. Van der Kolk, 176.

26. Van der Kolk, 176.

27. Van der Kolk, 157.

28. Miller, Lisa. 2015. *The Spiritual Child: The New Science on Parenting for Health and Lifelong Thriving*, 52. New York: St. Martin's Press.

29. Miller, 15.

30. Miller, 29.

31. Miller, 25.

32. Miller, 28.

33. Miller, 76.

34.   Miller, 29.

35.   Van der Kolk, 113.

36.   Van der Kolk, 113.

37.   Van der Kolk, 113.

38.   Van der Kolk, 113.

39.   Van der Kolk, 7.

40.   Keating, Thomas. 1999. *The Human Condition: Contemplation and Transformation*, 14. New York: Paulist Press.

41.   Keating. 1999, 14.

42.   Keating. 1999, 15.

43.   Bourgeault, Cynthia. 2004. *Centering Prayer and Inner Awakening*, 94. Lanham, MD: Cowley.

44.   Van der Kolk, 83.

45.   Abdul-Jabbar, Kareem. 2023. Substack: "My take on news, pop culture, sports, and whatever else interests me." May 5, 2023.

46.   Acoma Massacre. https://en.wikipedia.org/wiki/Acoma_Massacre.

47.   Bibo v. Town of Cubero Land Grant. 1958. https://law.justia.com/cases/new-mexico/supreme-court/1958/6453-0.html.

48.   Chilocco Indian Agricultural School. https://en.wikipedia.org/wiki/Chilocco_Indian_Agricultural_School.

49.   Retrieved July 27, 2017, from http://fountainhillcenter.org/articles/male-socialization/chasing-dragonsplastic-swords/

Chapter Ten

1.   Witherspoon, Gary. 1977. *Language and Art in the Navajo Universe*, 191. Ann Arbor, MI: University of Michigan Press.

2.   Hadley, Michael L. 2001. *The Spiritual Roots of Restorative Justice*, edited by Michael L. Hadley. New York: State University of New York Press.

3.   Shapiro, Francine. 2001. *Eye Movement Desensitization and Reprocessing: Basic Principles, Protocols, and Procedures*, 6. New York: Guilford Press.

4.   EMDR Institute, Inc. What Is EMDR? https://www.emdr.com/what-is-emdr/.

5.   Van der Kolk, 255.

6.   Shapiro, 7.

7.   Shapiro, 7.

8.   Van der Kolk, 261.

9.   Van der Kolk, 261.

10.   Shapiro, 41.

11.   Van der Kolk, 261.

12.   Shapiro, 31.

13.   Shapiro, 30.

14. Shapiro, 48.

15. Manifesto-for-a-Post-Materialist-Science (2014) retrieved 12/5/2023 from https://opensciences.org/files/pdfs/Manifesto-for-a-Post-Materialist-Science.pdf

16. Keating, Thomas. 2005. *Manifesting God*, 62. New York: Lantern.

17. Rohr, Richard. 2007. *Scripture as Spirituality*, 27–29. Franciscan Media.

18. Keating. 1999, 15.

19. Rohr, Richard. 2011. *Falling Upward: A Spirituality for the Two Halves of Life*, 85. San Francisco: Jossey-Bass.

20. Rohr. 2011.

21. Lynch, Zach. 2010. *The Neuro Revolution*, 134. New York: St. Martin's Press.

22. Newberg, Andrew and Mark Robert Waldman. 2009. *How God Changes Your Brain: Breakthrough Findings from a Leading Neuroscientist*, 51. New York: Ballantine.

23. Keating, Thomas. 1996. *Intimacy with God*. New York: Continuum Publishing.

24. Newberg, 53.

25. Rohr, Richard. 2016. "Contemplative Seeing." Daily Meditations: December 2, 2022. https://cac.org/daily-meditations/contemplative-seeing-2016-12-02/.

26. Kok, Loke T.; Scott M. Salom, et al. "Biological Control of the Hemlock Woolly Adelgid." Virginia Tech College of Agriculture and Life Sciences, Department of Entomology. https://en.wikipedia.org/wiki/Hemlock_woolly_adelgid.

27. Shelton, Anthony. 2013. "A Guide to Natural Enemies in North America." Ph.D., Professor of Entomology, Cornell University. https://biocontrol.entomology.cornell.edu/index.php.

28. Shelton. 2013.

Epilogue

1. Narvaez. 2014.

Acknowledgments

How does one thank all the people who have made a difference in our lives? In this case, it is the contributions, support, influence and love through the decades that are present in this book.

In the immediate, I owe a tremendous gratitude to Tim Brandhorst, J.D., for his careful and purposeful guidance in publishing this book. His expertise, friendship and counsel facilitated the completion of a book covering twenty-two years of experience in restorative communication practices. In the same breath, I need also to acknowledge the Law Offices of Marc J. Lane and Marc's inspiring mission to promote and support positive and sustainable social and cultural change.

If there is one person who has had the most influence in my understanding of restoration and restorative justice it is Dr. Beverly Title. Beverly was an early pioneer in the field of restorative justice practices. She was a visionary who helped establish restorative justice programming in both the justice system and K–12 schools not only in Colorado but internationally. Though no longer with us, she remains as an inspiration for all of us who knew her, respected her, loved her and continue to follow in her footsteps.

Retired Public Safety Chief Mike Butler was also an early thought leader, advocate, and pioneer who partnered with Beverly to develop, implement, support, and sustain restorative justice programming on a municipal level. Before Mike retired, he and community activist and business leader Dan Benevidez began Sunday pilgrimages to walk the streets, knock on doors, and meet the citizens of their city. That effort led to what became known as *The Belonging Revolution*.

It's equally important to recognize the vision and leadership of former Colorado State Senator Pete Lee. Pete's commitment to reforming Colorado's criminal justice system resulted in legislation establishing comprehensive restorative justice policies and programs statewide. I've often thought about how many lives have been transformed because of Pete's legislative prowess, and his wife Lynn's tireless efforts to legitimize and advance restorative programming.

There are several professors from my doctoral program that recognized the importance of this work in restorative practices and guided my thinking and research.

Dr. Lawrence Frey introduced me to the validity of first-person communication activism research, a way of knowing and contributing to social justice in a community by becoming a part of that community.

Dr. Stanley Deetz, Director of the Center for the Study of Conflict, Collaboration and Creative Governance at C.U. Boulder, gave me the opportunity to see the value of the restorative approach on a global landscape of geopolitical conflict and injustice.

Dr. Bryan Taylor, Director of the Peace and Conflict Studies Program at C.U. Boulder, helped me to see the value of implementing restorative practices in organizations to shift organizational climates toward a more relationship-oriented culture.

Dr. Gerard Hauser helped me to understand the rhetorical power that restorative practices embody such as accountability, atonement, amends-making, and civility.

Dr. Sam Gill introduced me to Indigenous traditions of healing and the work of Elaine Scarry, who recognized the relationship between the body and stories of threat and retribution.

Dr. Brian Daniell served as a role model for the teaching of interpersonal communication. Dr. Daniell and his wife Vicki helped facilitate the return of my family's inherited portion of a Spanish land grant to a Native American tribe.

I would have nothing to say if it weren't for the contribution of the countless clients, students, and participants in restorative dialogues, who were courageously willing to be vulnerable in their search for resolution, healing, and restoration.

At the same time, whatever skill or craft I may have in facilitating restorative dialogues and practices comes from my collaboration with some remarkable practitioners such as Kerri Quinn, Deb Witzel, Annie O'Shaughnessy, and so many others. As a craft, restoration is a "boots on the ground" and "butts in the circle" education. As facilitators, we learn best from each other.

I have had numerous mentors along the restorative way. Mentoring is equal parts wisdom, friendship, and accountability. David Bork heard me speak about the Restorative Way at a gathering of young men in recovery, immediately saw its potential as a way to resolve conflict in a family business environment, and supported me to grow and expand the restorative method into family businesses and shared family enterprises.

Michelle Keeling and Dr. Tim Robison, M.D., have been instrumental in advocating for and implementing Restorative Way communication practices in hospitals.

I owe deep gratitude to Anne White. Anne, along with Frances Lewis, Chris Mullally, Matt Johnson and others, saw the value and importance of the Restorative Way as it relates to schools, families, and communities. Anne oversaw the implementation of Restorative Way programming and practices in an elementary school and realized its implications for growing civility, citizenry, empathy and accountability in a range of other contexts. Anne helped me refine my methods to ensure an institutional sustainability of the Restorative Way for young people and parents. Anne is an advocate, colleague, inspiration, and dear friend.

Matt Walton has been a lifelong mentor and friend, consistently supporting me to grow spiritually in this practice of restoration over the course of thirty years. Matt has been a life-coach, mountain climbing partner, and accountability buddy. Descending after summitting Mt. Whitney one early spring, Matt became snow-blind, and his friend David Hill and I guided him down the Mountaineer's Route. Matt quipped, "It's a good thing I can't see where you're both leading me," as a massive block of ice the size of a car slid yards away from the three of us. Both David and I agreed.

Dr. Ted Klontz continues to mentor me in the art of deep listening and witnessing. Ted helps me and so many others "have conversations" with those quiet but undeniable parts of ourselves that are too often neglected, silenced, and suppressed. Ted is, in a multitude of ways, an elder and carrier of ancient wisdom.

There are three people who have helped me promote restoration on a public level. Dr. William Evans, M.D., gave me the opportunity to explain the Restorative Way on public radio. Molly Rowan Leach continues to assemble a global audience by interviewing world-changing restorative practitioners and thought leaders through her podcast *Restorative Justice on the Rise*. Kathryn Camp, editor and publisher of *The Mountain Pearl* magazine, has helped distribute the Restorative Way to parents to help them guide their children through inevitable social traumas and into a space of safety, security, hope, and courage. A special thanks also goes to Jennifer Byrd for sharing her lifelong journey of restoration, and offering encouragement, wisdom and support for this work.

I need to also thank Mark Jones and Shamila Pilendiram in Australia. Mark shared his heroic story of recovery and restoration from childhood sexual abuse. Shamila saw the world-changing value of Restorative Way practices and helped me build a series of online courses designed to reach parents, schools, businesses, and organizations.

There are brothers of other mothers that have walked beside me on this restorative path. Adam Smalley and I met in an acting class thirty-eight years ago. Over the course of those years, Adam has made my life rich, meaningful, and spiritually invigorating. Adam continuously reminds me that "now is now, not then, and not when." I don't know where I'd be without Adam's depth of humor, wisdom, love and guidance.

Michael Tupy kept me from taking myself too seriously, and continuously offered his love and support of me and this work. An accomplished screenwriter, Michael shared his understanding and experience in storytelling. Michael is truly an imaginative genius.

Bob Heimbigner is my childhood brother of another mother and lifelong climbing partner. Bob and I spent countless days sitting in a tent on the side of some mountain buried in snow, waiting for the tempest to subside both outside and inside talking about the trajectory of our lives, summits we've missed, mistakes we've made, and what we've learned. One mistake was climbing Grand Teton too early in March after a 36-inch snowfall. Sitting on the upper saddle of the route, Bob and I stood transfixed and terrified as an entire slope released and came barreling down toward us and then, at the last minute, separated, sparing us. Bob's two famous quotes on that day were "time waits for no one" and "avalanches have no compassion for our stupidity."

There are numerous other friends who have contributed immensely to my understanding of restorative practices. Walt and Connie Davis caught "the restorative fire" and became both co-facilitators and dear friends.

Ben Emery stepped into this work and onto the restorative way when he was in college and came through the university's restorative justice program. I trained Ben as a facilitator, and he went on to facilitate restorative practices in New Zealand, Brazil, Ireland, and Germany.

Molly Eaton taught me about restorative education for preschoolers. Witnessing how she works with young children to develop them socially and emotionally has convinced me that the future really does have rainbows and joy on the horizon.

John Tucci, fierce environmental restoration advocate and friend, taught me how to look at lakes, forests, and the environment in general through the restorative lens. What can restoring a lake tell us about human restoration?

I give deep thanks and appreciation to my family. My father taught me about peacemaking. My mother taught me about fighting for the dispossessed. My brother Ken set a very high bar for education and athletic performance. His wife Phyllis kept our family together during difficult times. My sister Mary has always been the "north star" of healing, spiritual development, and joy in our family. My daughter Tayler has taught me about the necessity for music, silliness, tenderness, and reaching for the stars. I didn't understand unconditional love until she was born. Her mother Jana continues to teach me about forgiveness, friendship, patience and commitment.

My ancestors have taught me about atrocity, the need for generational inquiry and responsibility, and the necessity of acknowledgment and repair.

Lastly, I pay homage to our Indigenous brothers and sisters, people of color, LGBTQ+ community, and any marginalized others who in spite of continual abuse somehow have the grit to remain true to their identities and wisdom traditions, offering hope and instruction as we search for the heart of our shared humanity.

About Dr. Will Bledsoe and Restorative Way

When people first experience the restorative process, a "restorative light bulb" turns on. This light is bright and far reaching. Conflicted situations, circumstances and interactions that used to frustrate and push us apart now have restorative potential.

Through the restorative lens we see a way that people can come together and discuss difficult, often painful, and sometimes traumatic events in a manner that is open, honest, and purposeful.

The Restorative Way is "empathically pragmatic." It activates the human heart in service of solving problems. It seeks to uncover the underlying feelings, issues, conditions, beliefs and thinking that not only keep us from trusting each other, but treat each other as enemies.

When we come to a shared understanding of what is happening, realize and discuss the impact on a human level, and work together to resolve issues, we are reclaiming civility and restoring human dignity. When accountability and empathy converge, hearts and minds align.

* * *

Will's immersion in the field of restorative practices began twenty-two years ago when he sat in his first circle. After witnessing the convergence of accountability, repair, and mercy in a criminal context, he was convinced (as are so many others in the field) that the restorative process is more than just a method. It is, in fact, a way of looking at the world and human imperfection through the lens of relationship.

Will has spent the last two decades trying to look through that lens to help families, workplaces, and communities address and resolve conflicts and issues with civility.

In addition to his private consultation practice, Dr. Bledsoe is currently an adjunct professor of communication. He has been a restorative justice program builder and director, trainer, and implementation coach.

Learn more about Dr. Bledsoe and Restorative Way at www.RestorativeWay.com.

www.ingramcontent.com/pod-product-compliance
Lightning Source LLC
Chambersburg PA
CBHW080416030426
42335CB00020B/2465